The *Human Factor*

The *Human Factor*

*Evolution, Culture,
and Religion*

Philip Hefner

Foreword by Arthur Peacocke

FORTRESS PRESS
MINNEAPOLIS

THE HUMAN FACTOR
Evolution, Culture, and Religion

Cover design: Keith McCormick. Minnesota Office of Tourism photo.

Library of Congress Cataloging-in-Publication Data
Hefner, Philip J.
    The human factor : evolution, culture, and religion / Philip
Hefner.
        p.   cm. — (Theology and the sciences)
    Includes bibliographical references and index.
    ISBN 0-8006-2579-X
    1. Man (Christian theology) 2. Religion and science—1946-
3. Theology—Methodology.   I. Series.
BT702.H44   1993
233-dc20   93-20032
                                                                            CIP

The paper used in this publication meets the minimum requirements of American National Standard for Information Sciences—Permanence of Paper for Printed Library Materials, ANSI Z329.48–1984.   ∞™

Manufactured in the U.S.A.   1-2579

97   96   95   94   93   1   2   3   4   5   6   7   8   9   10

to mentors
Ralph Wendell Burhoe
Bernard Meland
Jaroslav Pelikan
Joseph Sittler

and to colleagues
The Institute on Religion in an Age of Science
The Chicago Center for Religion and Science
The Lutheran School of Theology at Chicago

Contents

Foreword

No one today can contemplate the state of late twentieth-century humanity on this planet earth without a sense of deep foreboding and of hope deferred. The breakdown of the communist empire of the USSR has but taken off the lid of a Pandora's box of long-repressed ethnic hatreds, many of them fueled by religion, and the planet itself is groaning under the burden of pollution generated by a burgeoning human population that is augmented by religious imperatives and motivations. The catastrophic effects of these and many other evils are, if anything, enhanced by the irresponsible application of the technology that science engenders. Moreover, the international community of nations in their various assemblies seems impotent to decide or to act effectively in the face of these and other critical challenges to the general life of humanity on this planet.

Yet, if the state of the social and international scene is serious, that of many individuals is even more dire, in a "confusion worse confounded"—even for those in the more affluent North who are not totally engrossed in basic survival. The secularization of the Western component in that Northern world proceeds apace, for the revival of fundamentalist religion more often than not simply serves to cut off its adherents from the vital general concerns of humanity and the world through a retreat into private heavens of their own imaginings. Vast numbers of people in that secularized world in which scientifically informed technology dominates the scene are rudderless and, basically, hopeless. They do not know what meaning to give to life—what humanity is *for*.

It is as if a large portion of even well-fed and educated humankind finds itself today in that same dark wood in which Dante places himself at the beginning of *The Divine Comedy,* that entanglement of frustration, despair, and dereliction of his middle years:

> Midway this way of life we're bound upon
> I woke to find myself in a dark wood,
> Where the right way was wholly lost and gone.

In the perplexities and loss of hope of our present times, we know only too well what he means. But in the story Dante is led by the figure of Virgil, the embodiment of Human Wisdom, to the very threshold of Heaven, through which he is guided by Beatrice, the representative of all those agencies that have become for humanity "the God-bearing image, the revelation of the presence of God."[1] She

1. Dorothy Sayers, "The Greater Images" in *The Divine Comedy,* vol. 1 (Harmondsworth: Penguin Books, 1949), 68.

finally leads him to that sublime ultimate vision of the mystery of the divine, the way to which has been the underlying theme of the whole allegory:

> High phantasy lost power and here broke off;
>> Yet, as a wheel moves smoothly, free from jars,
>> My will and my desire were turned by love,
> The Love that moves the sun and the other stars.

For most of us moderns, including postmoderns, this is a vision for which we may well yearn but one we do not expect to be consummated. Moreover, the embodiment of human excellence with respect to knowledge that most would recognize today would be not a poet but a scientist. But, although we certainly obtain knowledge from science, can we acquire wisdom from it? Can it be a source and resource for enabling human beings to understand their place and function in the world and what they are for in its ongoing processes? That is, can science as such reveal the meaning of human existence in a world described by the evolutionary perspectives of the sciences? The prevalence of the dis-ease in the West to which I have drawn attention suggests not, for the scientific perspectives are today widely disseminated but patently do not satisfy the yearning for meaning.

The religions of the world in general, and Christianity in particular, have always claimed to be that source and resource of basic meaning for humankind, as Dante symbolized in the figure of Beatrice. However, today the pressures on the human psyche, not least those generated by the applications of science in technology, have rendered these traditional resources apparently irrelevant to a large proportion of those in the secularized West as they are engulfed and almost overwhelmed by the global issues that are now impinging even on the individual. What is to be the response of Christian thinkers to this situation (and indeed those of other religions, but I write, as does the author of this book, from within a post-Christian society)? What does the classical menu of Christian systematic theology (God, sin, incarnation, grace, redemption, the work of Christ, the last things . . .) actually have to offer to human beings embedded in, pinned down by, these newly apparent global forces? What perspectives can those insights that Christian faith believes to have perennial significance bring to bear on our actual human situation as we now understand ourselves and the world in the light of the sciences?

It is the chief virtue of this work, for which I have the privilege of writing a foreword, that it does not shrink from facing these issues that are potentially so traumatic for Christian identity and continuity but, at the same time, so crucial (*mot juste!*) for human flourishing. Philip Hefner is well equipped by his personal experience to be, if not a Virgil or a Beatrice, at least a theological Dante to us by unveiling, if only putatively, a new vista on our scientifically dominated world whereby human being and becoming can be located *sub specie aeternitate,* that is, in the perspective of the divine purposes for all of creation. He has had the rigorous *Bildung* of an education in Lutheran systematic theology, which has been and still is his principal professional activity. He is one who has been profoundly shaped by the Lutheran church and its tradition, both in the forms of their catholic substance and of their protestant critique, and has deeply imbibed of that tradition.

But Philip Hefner's focus has never been narrowly ecclesiastical or merely "churchy," as anyone who knows him personally can readily testify (a visit with him to the theatre is a feast both of anticipation and of appreciation!). He is convinced that the realm of life is the context for theology and that the transformation of life wrought by God in Christ is the prime datum of Christian theology. As he wrote, early in his career, at the end of his *Faith and the Vitalities of History:*

> Theology stands under a double responsibility—to preserve the Christianness of its statements while at the same time speaking relevantly to the situations in which it finds itself. Theology must, therefore, recapitulate its essential Christian character in every present moment so as to be genuinely alive, Christianly speaking, within the circumstances which its environment sets before it.[2]

That environment to which he refers is preeminently a scientifically dominated one. It was fortunate for him, and so now for us his readers, that in those early years he was brought into close contact in Chicago with others who were deeply concerned with that overall determinative effect of science in our culture, the response to which is so vital for any viable discernment of human meaning, whether religious or otherwise. I refer here, of course, to his mentor, Joseph Sittler, and to the Institute on Religion in an Age of Science and its associated activities and especially to Ralph Burhoe.

Thus, for nearly three decades now, Philip Hefner has been in almost daily dialogue and personal friendship with a wide range of scientists, and especially those concerned with the biological, human, and social sciences. I know of no other systematic theologian who has so assiduously strained to listen to what the sciences are telling us about the world and about human nature and then to consider its implications for the very truth of what the Christian church is, or should be, trying to proclaim.

His book must speak for itself and it is not for a Foreword prematurely to steal its thunder. Suffice it to say that I am convinced that the understanding of human beings as created co-creators[3] with God is one whose time has arrived for

---

2. Philip Hefner, *Faith and the Vitalities of History* (New York: Harper and Row, 1966), 183.

3. A possible near-equivalent description of human beings as "created co-creators" that might have advantages in some contexts is that of "co-creating creatures."

a generation that is witnessing the enormous impact of humanity on the rest of creation and is seeking the meaning of its own existence and function in that context. There have been hints and forerunners of the thesis so fully developed here, going back to the Christian humanists of the Italian Renaissance.[4] But only in this work of Philip Hefner—the fruit, I know, of the gestation of many years of discussion and dialogue with a diversity of scientists, philosophers, theologians, clergy, students, and academics of all kinds—do we at last have a full, systematic, and beautifully organized treatment of this concept developed in a way that is methodologically lucid and genuinely exploratory.

As such it is a testimony to the ongoing vitality of the systematic theological enterprise of the Lutheran tradition, and it constitutes a genuine launching pad for that integrating and creative new Christian perspective that alone can hope to have a trajectory into and in the next century, when the influence of the scientific world view is likely to be even more dominant over thought and action than it is today.

—Arthur Peacocke

---

4. For references see note 127, p. 305, of my *Creation and the World of Science* (Oxford: Clarendon Press, 1979). The context is an earlier brief and undeveloped attempt of mine to urge the relevance of this concept of humanity as co-creator with God the creator.

Preface

This book sets before the reader the fruit of my own effort to make sense of traditional Christian faith in the context of the welter of contemporary knowledge and experience. In the terms of my professional craft, this volume aims at a theological anthropology in the light of the natural sciences. At the end, my hope is that the effort provides some illumination for what I perceive as a dangerous confusion in our times about values and the moral life. The journey that is represented here is full of methodological twists and turns, and in this preface I will comment briefly on how I have chosen to negotiate the difficulties.

When my first published book appeared in 1966, several reviewers complained that I tried to do too many things in one volume, that I mixed different types of thinking (in that case, history and constructive theology) without justifying the mixture or clarifying how the recipe would work. I have no doubt that some readers of the present volume will conclude that age has simply intensified what were once distracting youthful tendencies.

My writing habits may have their roots in the work of Lydia Martha Hof Mittelstadt, my maternal grandmother. She was a sharp-witted woman, possessed of enough self-confidence to let her honest intelligence show in public. A few years ago, I ran across several of her personal recipes, written in her own hand for relatives and friends. I find her style of cooking to be similar to my style of writing, particularly at the level of methodology. Her cherry soup recipe, for example, advises, "Add quite a bit more water than you would for sauce. Thicken if desired. We had some yesterday with bing cherries, only kind we see. Added lemon juice as they are rather flat without cherries' juice." The recipe closes with the words, "My recipe is a joke. Realize that." Perhaps the recipe is a joke, but the soup is a rare treat for anyone.

For borscht, she suggested, "Lima beans fresh are nice, and if you have stock, a few string beans, tomato juice. Beets either cooked or pickled can be diced and used instead of fresh and a little of juice. You may not have whey, so a little cream may do. You can have only beets and tomato juice, but then the two beans make it better." She closed with, "This may work out." Her borscht always worked out.

In the jargon of the philosophy of science, we would say that Lydia Mittelstadt wrote her recipes out of the context of discovery rather than from the context of justification. It takes considerable ego strength to present one's work to the public in that form. Perhaps she wrote that way because her experience demanded it, and she did not have the time or inclination to recast her work in a *Joy of Cooking* format. At many times in the preparation of this book, I have followed the method of "You may not have whey, so a little cream may do," and I have vacillated between the two conclusions: "This is a joke; realize that" and "This may work out." I have read and thought and written a great deal about how one should proceed in doing theology and in relating it to the sciences, but as I worked through the present manuscript, often it seemed to me that too much methodological reflection would either inhibit me from saying what I wanted to say or else simply be an effort to justify what I wanted to do anyway.

James Gustafson has written extensively about the sort of enterprise I am attempting, the conversation between theology and the sciences, specifically the human sciences. In a recent piece, he underscores, as he has in the past, the importance as well as the difficulty of synthesizing insights from theology and the sciences. He is critical of the attempts of several persons who have been influential in my past, including the process theologians, as well as Ralph Burhoe and Pierre Teilhard de Chardin. The flaw of the process thinkers, he says, is that they "opt for general principles of interpretation developed in abstract metaphysics," whereas the latter two simply extrapolate theological claims from specific research (Gustafson 1991, 71).

Like my grandmother, I wander between these two extremes, knowing full well that insights, like cherries, do not come in the abstract. Just as borscht has to emerge from what our ingenuity can put together new each time we go to the fridge—it cannot be made from the succulent leftovers we remember from last month—so, too, our theology takes shape from the interaction of tradition with the present situation. We cannot easily extrapolate some theological conclusions from any single body of scientific research. Gustafson describes the importance of the enterprise in terms that I would gladly take as my guidelines:

> The discussions can become more precise as theologians and moralists locate the long-standing issues in current studies of the nature of the human. At stake is the theological and moral status of the natural. The human sciences provide us with a new prologue to a perennial issue. Engagement with them is important to render moral and theological anthropologies more intelligible. . . . Such engagement is also important in the process of justifying arguments for human accountability that are made by theologians and philosophers. . . . For some of us these sciences have to inform quite deeply a theological and moral perspective that seeks "to create a framework of interpretation which can provide overall orientation for human life" [Kaufman 1985, 26], as well as an orientation to specific occasions of human activity. (Gustafson 1991, 76–77)

My predilection for mixing different ways of thinking—in this case, several of the sciences, theology, philosophy, history, literature, and art—and for methodological opaqueness stems from the context of my work and of my discovery. My primary responsibility is to teach Christian doctrine to candidates for ordained ministry and other full-time church workers, but I spend a large proportion of my time with scientists and other academics, many of whom are skeptical, at best, of the church I belong to and the theology I teach. My home is in one of the great urban and university centers of the world—Hyde Park, Chicago— but I am accountable to every pastor and every one of my church's 11,000 con- gregations across the country, most of them in settings quite different from my neighborhood.

Much of the material in this book was originally written for public lectures in a variety of settings besides my seminary classroom: continuing education for clergy; college undergraduates (Bethany, Texas Lutheran, and Williams Colleges); the peer group of theologians and religious studies scholars in the American Academy of Religion; general and specialized university audiences (Tulane, Michigan Technological, Oklahoma, Virginia Polytechnic, and Yale Universi- ties); adult workshops in congregations (Bethany in Batavia, Illinois; Holy Trinity in Minneapolis; and St. Paul's in Albuquerque); the general education audiences at Chautauqua and Star Island; interdisciplinary groups at the Evangelical Acad- emy at Loccum, Germany, whose director, Hans May, provided the setting and ideas for many hours of fruitful interchange. The Human Genome Initiative proj- ect at the Center for Theology and the Natural Sciences, Berkeley, California, has been the seedbed for ideas that have most recently entered into this work. My participation in the Loccum conferences was funded in part by the Lutheran School of Theology at Chicago and the Vesper Foundation of San Leandro, Cali- fornia; the Genome Project is funded by National Institutes of Health Grant #HG00487.

Having benefited from the hospitality of all of these groups and others not mentioned, and having learned from each of them, I must say that I have pre- sented the same material in much the same style to all of them. Freshman under- graduates may have found me unintelligible at times, while research professors of biology and philosophy found me to be frustratingly simplistic. Likewise, what appears in the pages that follow may be obscure to some readers and at the same time too facile for others. Other readers may be jarred by the mixture of aca- demic jargon and the language of oral presentation, or by the obvious repetitions and lacunae that characterize a work some of whose sections were prepared for different occasions over a period of years. I will settle for the judgment that James Gustafson made after pointing out the flaws in the method of one of my mentors: "The enterprise has the merit of a challenge, however" (1978, 391). As I empha- size in chapter 2, what this book aims at is *to challenge*. I make no other claim, and I ask that it be judged by the criteria pertinent to such an aim.

I have deliberately avoided footnotes. Consequently, I have had to compro- mise by including in the text some material that would ordinarily be in notes, while omitting certain kinds of comments that are inappropriate for the text, particularly observations by and about other authors whose work overlaps mine.

The type of synthetic work that I attempt here is often criticized, as Gustafson once said of Burhoe: "Inferences from scientific data and theories to theological and ethical conclusions are often weakly warranted" (1978, 391). I have dealt with this serious issue in several articles (Hefner 1981, 1984d), particularly focusing upon questions of how to relate *is* and *ought*. I regret that those essays cannot be included here, and I refer the reader to them.

This book was not written in one sitting, nor were the chapters conceived or written in the order they appear in this volume. My advice to the reader is to read around in the book, perhaps taking the chapters in the following order: 1, 2, 3, 6, 9, 13, 14, 15, and then the rest in the printed sequence. The Theory of Created Co-Creator is summarized on pages 264–65. A diagram depicting a major conceptual element of this work is found on page 198.

This book owes its existence in this form to a splendid group of friends and acquaintances, of whom I will mention a few, recognizing that some will inadvertently be omitted. It was Carol Rausch Albright who first saw the coherence of the materials I was working on, even before I was explicitly aware of it, and she edited an early version of the manuscript. Nancey Murphy introduced me to the thought of Imre Lakatos; his philosophy and her interpretations of it have been immensely fruitful for me. Marjorie Hall Davis, Arthur Peacocke and Kevin Sharpe, and Michael West also worked through an entire version. John Albright, Thomas Gilbert, Rodney Holmes, and William Irons went to extra lengths to give me critique and access to sources. The Star Island Forum of the Institute on Religion in an Age of Science deserves special thanks: Marjorie Hall Davis, Solomon Katz, Philip Ode, Arthur Peacocke, Karl Peters, and Loyal Rue. Among others who read the manuscript and gave me advice or other assistance, I want to mention Kris Alexander, Frank Birtel, Elizabeth Bjorkman, David Breed, Richard Busse, Ronald Cole-Turner, Mihaly Csikszentmihalyi, Wim Drees, Lindon Eaves, Michael Hefter, Jürgen Hübner, William Lesher, Wesley Nyborg, Alan Riddiford, Michael Ruse, Karl Schmitz-Moormann, Ingrid Shafer, Franklin Sherman, John MacDonald Smith, Wentzel van Huyssteen, Jeffrey Wicken, and Warren Zemke. Dorothy Dean gave me Lydia Mittelstadt's recipes. Chris Eldredge made possible the computerization of the manuscript. Rebecca Kammerer-Beltz has enhanced the book immeasurably by providing the indexes. My education of recent years has been furthered by more good people than I can remember or count, and my thanks goes to all of them. And Neva, as always, holds a place of preeminence.

Acknowledgments

"The Geese" from *Hybrids of Plants and of Ghosts* by Jorie Graham, copyright © 1980 Princeton University Press, is used by permission of the publisher.

Chapter 4 originally appeared in *Zygon: Journal of Religion and Science* 27, no. 3 (September 1992).

Excerpts from "A Problem from Milton" from *Ceremony and Other Poems,* copyright © 1950 and renewed 1978 by Richard Wilbur, are used by permission of Harcourt Brace & Co. and Faber & Faber, Ltd.

Excerpts from "Sunday Morning" from *Collected Poems* by Wallace Stevens, copyright © 1923 and renewed 1951 by Wallace Stevens, are used by permission of Alfred A. Knopf, Inc., and Faber and Faber, Ltd.

Excerpts from "The Idea of Order at Key West" from *Collected Poems* by Wallace Stevens, 1936 Wallace Stevens and renewed 1964 by Holly Stevens, are used by permission of Alfred A. Knopf, Inc., and Faber and Faber, Ltd.

"The Age of Reason" and "At Luca Signorelli's Resurrection of the Body" from *Erosion* by Jorie Graham, copyright © 1983 Princeton University Press, is used by permission of the publisher.

Chapter 7 originally appeared in *Free Will and Determinism,* ed. Viggo Mortensen and Robert C. Sorensen, copyright © 1987 Aarhus University Press, Denmark, and is used by permission of the publisher.

Excerpts from *The Biological Basis of Human Freedom* by Theodosius Dobzhansky, copyright © 1956 Columbia University Press, are used by permission of the publisher.

Chapter 8 originally appeared in *Zygon* 28, no. 1 (March 1993).

Excerpt from "Variation and Selective Retention in Sociocultural Evolution" by Donald Campbell in *Social Change in Developing Areas,* ed. H.R. Harringer et al. (Cambridge, Mass.: Schenkman, 1965), is used by permission of the publisher.

"Mind" from *Things of This World,* copyright © 1956 and renewed 1984 by Richard Wilbur, is used by permission of Harcourt Brace & Co. and Faber & Faber, Ltd.

Excerpts from *The Creative Explosion: An Inquiry into the Origins of Art and Religion* by John Pfeiffer, copyright © 1982 John E. Pfeiffer, are reprinted by permission of HarperCollins, Publishers, Inc.

Excerpt from *Icanchu's Drum: An Orientation to Meaning in South American Religions* by Lawrence E. Sullivan, copyright © 1988 Macmillan Publishing Co., a division of Macmillan, Inc., is used by permission of the publisher.

Chapter 11 originally appeared in *Zygon* 26, no. 1 (March 1991).

Excerpts from *Explaining Religion: Criticism and Theory from Bodin to Freud* by J. Samuel Preus (New Haven: Yale University Press, 1987) are used by permission of the publisher.

The diagram of biocultural evolution on page 198 is used by permission of Solomon H. Katz.

Part 1

The Theoretical Perspective

1

Scripting the Human Venture

In studying the universe scientifically, you don't find a point. Now what kind of point would you want to find? I would love to find that human beings are part of a drama which is built around us, and that we are the central actors in the cosmic drama—that the whole expansion of the universe and the birth of the sun and the evolution of life on earth was directed for us, that we are the key players, and that when we do something the whole universe is watching. That may be true, but if you believe it, you are not going to find evidence to support it in the discoveries of science. You don't find hints at that in scientific knowledge.

Do human beings play an especially important role? I think in fact they do, but it's one that they make up for themselves, one that they create as they go along. In a way, it's a more noble role. Here we are in this great expanding universe which doesn't pay much attention to us and we're creating a little island of life in which there is beauty, scientific research and loving each other. We do it all ourselves. We make it up as we go along. In a way I find that more beautiful and more noble than if we were just playing a part that had been laid out for us in advance.

So many people need to believe that we have this particular relationship to the universe that we were scripted from the beginning.

Well, we are important. It may be that there is no objective importance that registers in the cosmic equations, but the importance is what we give to things, and I think that's not entirely unsatisfactory.

—Steven Weinberg

In the conversation quoted above, the physicist Steven Weinberg (whose Nobel Prize-winning work in particle theory is relevant to cosmological theories of how the universe came to be and how it develops) touches on a fundamental dilemma that faces us all: How do we relate what we know as empirical facts and the larger or ultimate meaning of those facts? How do we establish a fit between the facts of our experience and larger meanings?

Weinberg's comments are particularly useful because they exhibit so clearly the human dilemma. He wants to base his life on the best hard knowledge that is available. For him (and for most of the rest of us), this means knowledge that has been gained by the winnowing methods of the sciences; hence his view that those who believe human beings are of central importance in the universe will find no supporting evidence in scientific studies (see also Weinberg 1977, 154). However, as human beings, physicists still need to find their work, their lives, and their loved ones important. In other words, beyond the facts, they seek the meaning of those facts, particularly the facts of their own life and work. Where do they find a concept that will convey that meaning? Weinberg's answer lies in his own courageous assertion that human beings bestow upon themselves the sense that they are important. We make up ideas of our own meaning and importance as we go along, and that is enough meaning to base one's life on.

Scientific studies of the universe certainly do not support Weinberg's final position, any more than they support the view he rejects, that we are the central actors in the drama of the universe's emergence and expansion. However, his view seems not so blatantly contradicted by scientific studies as the human-centered view. The universe may indeed appear to take no special notice of us, but we give ourselves that notice, and that's enough for a philosophy of life. Most people would question that our saying it is so really makes us important in the universe.

This book will finally reject Weinberg's conclusions, but he serves as a model for us nevertheless. He insists upon framing a concept of a larger purpose that can give meaning to his life and work, and he wants that concept to square with the most reliable knowledge available to him. We see him rejecting one concept as too out-of-touch with that knowledge, but moving on to another concept that is more credible to him but just as little susceptible to verification as the truth about the meaning of his life and work.

The Questions of Meaning and Purpose

This book grapples with the issues that Weinberg sets before us, of which the central one is: Just who are we human beings and what are we here for? This basic issue lies at the heart of the world's religious traditions, including the Hebrew-Jewish-Christian stream in which I stand. The question of the rationale for human life on planet earth, however, is one that reaches out to touch all persons in all of their activities, not just the overtly religious dimension of human existence.

It is becoming clearer every day that conditions on the planet are moving toward severe crisis precisely because the human sector either does not know properly how to conduct itself or else willfully chooses a path that leads to ever greater distress and breakdown. In such a situation, the questions Who are we? and What are we here for? are not to be confined to the realm of philosophical and religious meditation. They are questions whose answers influence every aspect of our human existence—war and peace, political and economic justice, hunger, poverty, education, child-rearing, career, sexuality, the conception and birth of new life, as well as the conditions of dying and the breadth of medical practice.

Furthermore, it is clear that how we respond to the basic questions of what human life is and how it ought to be conducted must be both universally and particularistically conceived: universal in that answers to the basic questions must enable adequate and wholesome futures for the planet and all of its inhabitants; particular in that they must be life-giving to all regions of the planet, to all sorts and conditions of persons upon the planet, as well as to its nonhuman sector.

Experience and Universals

Many thinkers today in principle rule out the discussion of universals. These thinkers deny the commonality of experience among humans that would make universally valid concepts and mandates relevant or even possible. The commonality is disputed along gender lines, or those of ethnicity, social class, age, or personal history. Universal meaning across boundaries of culture, it is said, is problematic or even unthinkable. In what follows in this book, I will honor particularity—any position that is grounded, like mine, in evolutionary theory could hardly deny particularity and diversity at the very core of life.

I will also, in contrast, rather stolidly insist upon universals. Human beings inhabit one planet, we have emerged from one species history, and we are—whether we like it or not, whether we acknowledge it or not—woven together with the entire human race and with the totality of the planet's dynamic systems in such intimacy that it seems foolhardy to me to entertain the notion that serious thinkers might reject the effort to fashion comprehensive conceptualities and interpretations that can enhance our understanding and behavior.

Obviously, one cannot generalize without careful empirical study. Statements that claim to be universally valid must be tested on a case-by-case basis to see if their claims hold up. A considerable body of sophisticated work in the various sciences that study human beings upholds the existence of universals (D. Brown 1991; Barkow, Cosmides, and Tooby 1992, chap. 1). My controlling conviction is that in and through our diversity we share the common destiny of one planet and the systems that constitute its life. Consequently, we must speak in terms of that common destiny, without violating our particularity.

Frameworks and Religion

I share Steven Weinberg's concern, insofar as I too in these pages attempt to sketch a framework of meaning that can include our human lives as they work their way in the world about us. Like Weinberg, I find myself giving attention, on the one hand, to large frameworks that claim to provide meaning for life by coordinating in a coherent manner a great deal of experience and also, on the other hand, to the smaller, more detailed experiences that provide me with concrete certainty, because the experience they are rooted in seems to me to be indubitable.

When I speak of larger frameworks, I think of religious beliefs, such as Saint Paul's "all things work together for good for those who love God," or the Ten Commandments' "Honor your father and your mother, so that your days may be long in the land that the Lord your God is giving you," or "Blessed are the dead who . . . die in the Lord . . . for their deeds follow them." Our common life is full of such larger meanings, whether it is the injunction that hard work pays off in success, or the converse, that it is not what one knows that gets one ahead so much as who one knows. The problem is that these larger frameworks do not lend themselves to verification by sure knowledge. Those who love God in Saint Paul's way have often ended up as persecuted and martyred. The very existence of two contradictory folk maxims about how to get ahead indicates that our knowledge does not give us a sure formula for attaining success.

Our more specific, falsifiable knowledge, conversely, may be certain, but it is often unsatisfying because it provides so little larger meaning. When that knowledge is scientifically obtained, it carries with it probability factors that are frustrating. For example, we may know that within a certain range of quantity, a given chemical in the air will cause cancer among a certain percentage of the population. This knowledge is relatively unsatisfying when we cannot understand why some persons die of the cancer and others do not, and why inhibiting the industrial emission of that chemical will actually enhance the standard of living of some while it throws others out of work.

Not all of our more certain knowledge is so scientifically specifiable, however. We can be experientially certain, in our social experience, that minority persons are discriminated against and face poorer opportunities in life. We can even be quite certain about what needs to be done to achieve greater justice for minorities. Nevertheless, this knowledge in and of itself does not provide larger meaning for us. For example, it does not tell us whether the quest for justice is of great significance in the world that was formed in the Big Bang and proceeds according to the natural laws that the physicist, chemist, biologist, and social scientist can discern. Nor does it tell us whether it would be better for the minority person to escape the unjust society or to fight against it; and if the latter, whether peaceful or violent struggle is better for a given person at a given time. Nor does this knowledge explain why some groups, like women and Jews, have suffered injustice in so many societies for so many generations that it has seemed to be their destiny to suffer.

Sometimes the scientific knowledge is simply incommensurable with our search for meaning. Big Bang cosmology, for example, may make it more difficult to assert that the human species is central to the universe, but it does not provide any information that would help us understand what human beings are for and why they have tried so diligently over the centuries to construct large systems of meaning that can ground their life and work.

The last 350 years of Western history, which many would call the modern period, has taken an unfortunate course in its tendency to pit the human quest for larger meaning through metaphysics and religion against the knowledge that comes from experience, particularly scientific experience. Whitehead (1933, chap. 7) points to this tendency when he speaks of the "antagonism between science and metaphysics" that made it impossible for the Enlightenment, which was largely scientific in its approach, to appreciate or appropriate the work of the medieval scholastic philosophers, whose philosophies possessed the resources for integrating the discoveries of the emerging science with the quest for larger meaning.

The modern period in fact advanced the *negative* proposal formulated by Auguste Comte in the first half of the nineteenth century: that the theological approach to comprehending reality, as well as the philosophical approach that succeeded it, were superseded by the scientific approach. Consequently, the prime contributions of religion and philosophy—namely, their large frameworks of meaning—were rejected as obscurantist. Religion and philosophy in fact could not dismiss this charge out of hand, because many theologians and philosophers did in fact adopt the stance of dogmatism, rejecting the notion that the emerging science could alter their speculative frameworks.

Today, a substantial number of humanist thinkers exist, some of whom call themselves scientific humanists, who have not totally given up on Comte's program. This group includes some of the most brilliant and serious minds of our time, including some who have informed my own thinking. Although most of them would deny that they are in fact metaphysicians, the efforts of these humanists could be characterized as the attempt to frame a naturalistic, science-based metaphysics. E. O. Wilson, the entomologist celebrated for his work in establishing the field of sociobiology, may be the most important of these thinkers (1975, 1978, 1987).

Despite the efforts of these thinkers and their not inconsiderable impact, the *positive* proposal of the modern period, that science could produce substitutes for the frameworks of meaning that had been produced during the earlier periods of Western history, has not fared well. Millions of men and women today hold fast to their traditional religious and philosophical frameworks of meaning. These adherents of traditional religion often feel themselves at odds with the best and most reasonable knowledge of our time, particularly with contemporary science. Even though not even the naturalistic metaphysical frameworks of the scientific humanists—despite their more rational external forms—are finally validated by scientific knowledge, the traditional religionists feel most sharply the tensions with contemporary science. In our North American culture, the continuing battle between creationists and evolutionists is but one representation of this tension. The depth of this tension is manifest by the fact that almost without exception, the popular news media hold to the view that evolutionary theory and belief in the Bible are incompatible. When we see clearly the conflict in which our age has placed us, we understand that Steven Weinberg is a representative figure for our dilemma.

Nevertheless, a widespread conviction also exists that antagonism between science and metaphysics is no longer bearable or necessary. This conviction is one of the underlying reasons why many thinkers believe that the modern period is coming to a close, that we have crossed the threshold into a postmodern era. Such a conviction does not overlook the built-in tension between frameworks of meaning and concrete experience, particularly as that experience is filtered through the methods of the sciences. It recognizes that concrete experience seems to be intrinsically intractable when we seek to incorporate it into our large schemes of meaning. On one level, the scientist is well acquainted with this tension. Data derived from experiment and observation require conceptual or theoretical frameworks if their significance is to be grasped, just as every theoretical proposal is empty until it is meshed successfully with the data. Nevertheless, postmodern views do not, by and large, agree with Comte that this tension necessarily falsifies metaphysics, myth, and symbol.

Experience as Scientific and Social

This book rests on the conviction that large frameworks of meaning, like those proposed by religion and metaphysics, are unavoidable and required if the human quest for meaning is to be fulfilled. At the same time, those frameworks are useless and empty if they are not brought into conjunction in a credible manner with the concrete data of our scientific and social experience.

When I speak of experience as both scientific and social, I am pointing to the two great sources of the data of our experience, for which we seek larger meaning. These two sources have in fact overwhelmed the consciousness of men and women today, thus creating the crisis of meaning that confronts us. I refer to these two sources with the terms *science* and *liberation* (Hefner, 1987b). This book will exhibit more clearly the impact of science, but at every point I want to acknowledge the importance of liberation in our quest for meaning.

The perennial task of religious faith as well as of theology is to understand the world around us and our place within that world in the light of our religious tradition. Human experience of the world has always been dynamic, constantly changing and being enriched as time goes on. Today, however, we stand at a point in which humans have participated in a 350-year-long explosion of experience and knowledge of the world that has produced in most fields, in just the last generation, more new information and theory than was gathered in all of the previous years of human existence on the planet. Both directly and indirectly, this huge increase of knowledge is the result of the emergence and refinement of what we call modern science. Science is the most massive and successful means of gaining knowledge that humans have ever devised.

When linked to technology, this scientific knowledge becomes a powerful means to accomplish the intentions of those who control the technology. We easily associate scientific knowledge with amazing discoveries of the natural world, such as the basis of medical practice, agriculture, and the space program. Science-based technology also has enabled the population explosion, the emergence of the so-called global village, the repression of populations by dictators, and the overthrow of dictators by protesting citizens.

The explosion of knowledge adds to the interpretive task that faces religious faith. It does this in two ways. In the first place, the increase in knowledge means that there is more new experience of the world to be understood in the light of religious faith. Before the modern period, for example, faith was not called upon to inform our understanding of life in the face of technology that can prolong an individual life beyond the point where it is useful or even desirable. Now that is one of the most common of our challenges.

Beyond the sheer amount of new knowledge, the increase and novelty of that knowledge render more ambiguous and even inadequate or inaccurate some of the religious wisdom that has been handed down to us as inviolable. An item in point is the command in Genesis 1:28–31 to "be fruitful and multiply, and fill the earth and subdue it; and have dominion over the fish of the sea and over the birds of the air and over every living thing that moves upon the earth." Although the usefulness of such a command in the distant past of the human race can be imagined and justified, in our present situation it is precisely multiplying and subduing that have become problematic for human beings. At the very least, such packets of traditional wisdom must be reinterpreted, and in some cases they must be revised or replaced.

It is no wonder, consequently, that science challenges and enriches religious faith. For persons of faith, the encounter with science adds to our understanding of the world and of ourselves; even more, it adds to our understanding of the holy that stands at the center of our faith. For the Western religious faiths, the encounter with science adds to our understanding of God and God's ways and purposes for us. For the person of religious faith, the encounter with science is itself a religious and a theological event.

The course of the modern period, with its tendency to pit scientific knowledge and the large interpretive work of religion and metaphysics against each other, has made it impossible for many persons to recognize the constructive interaction between science and religion. For many religious believers, science is simply a deconstructive force that threatens faith, while for staunch secularists, religious wisdom is a problem that must be shunted aside in order for progress to occur.

For this writer, theology and religious faith are still vital, necessary enterprises. The challenges that face theology in its task of relating all experience to God are, however, monumental, far beyond the capabilities of one solitary thinker to deal with. Having come through the intensity of a modern period that has committed itself to demonstrating the obsolescence of religion, it is understandable that religious communities have put relatively little priority on integrating the knowledge of modern science into their faith and thought. Strangely, however, the circumstances that make the task seem so large and overwhelming also open the way for possibilities.

We live in a three-cornered situation, which also undergirds and encourages the attempt to relate science and religion. First, scientific understandings have snowballed on such a large scale that we are now able to glimpse whole pictures of knowledge that were not available to us until recently. Second, the sociocultural situation on the planet is at a critical point that accentuates the need for new ways of putting our knowledge together so as to guide human actions. Finally, although science and its technology are more clearly a premise of our continued existence than ever before, signs are everywhere that people are dissatisfied with the thesis of secularization, which holds that religion and metaphysics are vestiges of our human infancy that will be supplanted by scientific knowledge. We desire a religion and metaphysics that work for us as we seek meaning in our present situation.

Many, perhaps even a majority of, Western intellectuals, particularly those who are pacesetters in providing conceptual frameworks by which we can understand our contemporary world situation, are much more skeptical of the viability of traditional religion than I am in this book. I will refer to these thinkers, for whom I have great respect, as *humanists* or *serious humanists*. These thinkers are often engaged in the same sort of effort as characterizes these pages. Their efforts, however, hold to a naturalistic premise—that is, they seek to speak of ultimacy, meaning, and human values in ways that do not invoke symbols, myths, and rituals that have traditionally been spoken of in supernaturalistic terms. I include such thinkers as the biologist Edward O. Wilson, and philosophers Hans Jonas, Richard Bernstein, and Michael Ruse in this group.

I look upon such thinkers as workers in the same vineyard, even though persons like myself still find the tradition of classical religion to be a rich resource for dealing with our common questions of what human being is about. We share a common aim and a common obstacle. We all are seeking the larger meaning of this world and our lives in it, and we are all faced by the impossibility of erecting finally conclusive philosophical arguments for that larger meaning.

The naturalistic humanists are often thought to be closer to philosophical conclusiveness than thinkers who employ traditional myths and symbols, but they are not. Naturalistic concepts and terminology may appear to be more plausible, but when it comes to affirming a basic meaningfulness to things that will sustain death-defying action for the common good, both naturalism and traditional religion will have to venture into realms that are philosophically at loose ends. Certainly, however, publicly discussable ways exist for deciding whether ideas and assertions are worth taking seriously and, up to a point, whether one set of ideas and assertions is more worthy than an alternative set—only up to a certain point, however. Every person will finally have to make a choice between alternatives that seem equally worthy. Having made that decision, we are accountable for it and at the end of the day can invoke credibly no other authority for our decision than ourselves and the traditions that have formed us.

Identity and Stories

Weinberg's reflections illustrate an important characteristic of human life today: We form our personal identities by relating to stories that tell us something about ourselves. Through these stories we acquire our self-understanding. For the most part these stories confront us where we live, without any aggressive effort on our part to seek them out. On the most personal and individual level, we learn that we have parents, brothers and sisters, aunts and uncles, grandparents, and in the process we learn that we are identified through a family. This family had a history prior to our birth; the family has come from somewhere, and therein our own roots are revealed to us. Our family story tells us also about our ethnic identity.

As the years go by, we acquire an economic and social class awareness about ourselves, and this is also our story. We learn the history of our nation, and this larger epic confronts our personal and ethnic and social class stories. All ethnic groups in the United States learn, for example, that their identity has something to do with Puritan immigrants, with Native Americans from whom the land was taken, with slavery, and with the Bill of Rights.

The multiple stories that tell us about ourselves pose a challenge, because they must be integrated into a whole, a coherent larger story that reinforces our identity. The task of integrating our stories and attaining coherence is not an easy one. What does my late-twentieth-century identity have to do with the massacres of American Indians more than a century ago, or with the enslaving even before that of the African-Americans? Social protests are often rooted in the insistence by individuals and groups that they do not like the nation's story and want the

next chapter to be different so that their personal stories can fit more authentically.

If we are religious, we learn still another story, that of our religious community, and this, too, must be integrated with the other stories that tell us about
ourselves. How do I relate myself to the people that were liberated from Egyptian
bondage three thousand years ago? How do I relate the successes of my life to
the covenant blessings of the creator God, or my failures to an ancient couple
who ate forbidden fruit in a mythic garden in a primeval time?

Integrating all of these multiple stories into one that each of us can freely and
honestly call "*my* story" is a major challenge, and it does not happen without
effort, critical skepticism, and joy, as well as sadness and great courage. Sometimes
the process entails so much pain and difficulty that we become psychologically
ill or enter into some form of therapy before we can integrate and accept freely
our various stories. We learn that the various stories are of different types, and
that each one may be useful for some kinds of self-understanding and not for
others. Our ethnic story, for example, may tell us about where our family came
from and why it has fared the way it has in certain circumstances, but it does not
necessarily reveal to us what our moral code should be or define for us who our
friends should be or with whom we should fall in love. Some of the stories are
clearly rooted in empirical fact, whereas others are more symbolic, even mythic,
and they must be approached accordingly.

The Stories of Science and Religion

This context of story is the setting in which I introduce my reflections upon
science and the relationship of science to religion. There are those who deny that
science is chiefly a compilation of facts. They insist that science is more significantly a method for learning and establishing knowledge. Others focus upon the
assumptions of science and its underlying foundations, the philosophy of science.
These approaches are surely correct and useful for us. My primary concern, however, is to insist that science has indeed provided us with a vast encyclopedia of
facts about the world and ourselves, and it has also, both implicitly and explicitly,
placed those facts within coherent narratives. Insofar as science does this, it comes
across to us as yet another story that tells us about ourselves. The science-based
story is a powerful one, if only because our schooling and our culture often tell
us that it is the most important story of all, the most universally accepted, the
"truest."

The story that science tells us is also perhaps the most difficult one for us to
integrate with our other stories. The scientific story is so complex, so vast, dealing as it does with the unimaginably large as well as the incomprehensibly small,
that it does not fit easily with stories of family, ethnic group, success and failure,
war and peace. Perhaps most important, as Steven Weinberg's conversation makes

clear, the truth-power of the scientific story does not include any firm knowledge about the empirical validity of our personal, social, national, and religious assumptions about the meaning and purpose of human existence. Consequently, although it may tolerate these other stories, it cannot undergird or reinforce them in the name of scientific certainty. Because the scientific stories are so powerful, we naturally look to them to help us discover the meaning and purposes of our lives, but we find that they provide us no immediately accessible help in our search for meaning.

A few words about my own story can serve as an appropriate entree into the argument of the pages that follow. I am a Christian theologian who can neither understand the tradition out of which theology has taken its origins and identity nor express its further meaning, apart from an understanding of the world in which the enterprise of doing theology takes place. As commonplace as this observation may seem, my last thirty years have been taken up with the attempt to understand just what it means. What follows represents a succession of episodes in my years of searching to understand the world in which Christian faith has occurred and what its message in and for that world is.

For some, this may seem to have been a futile search for relevance, especially so since relevance as such has increasingly come to be viewed as an unworthy goal for the theologian. Such readers may believe that relevance is tantamount to faddism. Relevance in itself is hardly the issue for me, however. This searching is, rather, rooted in a basic conviction about the essential nature of the Christian faith, a deep-down sense of that faith that places the sort of quest I have undertaken intrinsically and necessarily at the center of the theologian's vocation. I believe that the Christian faith, at its foundation, is a message about the nature and destiny of the world. This faith entails the affirmation of God, and it claims to share in the revelation of God's truth. There is no way, however, for this truth from God to reach us and take hold among us except in the form of a message about who we are and what our destiny is.

I expressed the basic position that stands behind this searching in a 1970 essay:

> The reality and nature of God will be unfolded in the course of our probing the nature of the world processes in which we live and move, and as we seek to understand our relationship to those processes. . . . This is so because such probing moves through the array of empirical data to the most fundamental considerations of our nature and destiny, as well as to the reflection upon the ultimate nature of the ambience of world reality in which we find ourselves. The Christian theologian will, of course, bring the heritage of that tradition (and the perception that has been shaped by that tradition) to the probing of these questions, and will interpret what is discovered in its light. But that theologian will also have to become familiar with and sensitive to the structures of reality and thought that are distinctive to these questions, and which may appear strange to inherited theological categories. In coming to terms with these structures the theologian will gain genuinely new knowledge of God and of the significance of Jesus Christ, exceeding what the pre-

vious generations of tradition have known and conveyed, even though in continuity with that legacy. The process of bringing these new structures into relationship with the Christian tradition—a process of reciprocal amplification, critique, and synthesis—will be an exciting and risky theological adventure. (Hefner 1970)

It has taken me more than twenty years to gain a beginning recognition of what these words mean.

The knowledge that humans gain about themselves and their world, including the knowledge that Christians believe they have gained from God and about God, comes as these same human beings make their way through the processes of the world—nature and history—as themselves creatures and products of those processes. Therefore, even though the Christian faith purports to be truth from and about God (and the believer sincerely holds this to be the case), the appearance of that faith is an event within the processes of the world and its unfolding, and the faith presents a truth about that world. When the theological proposal embodied in the Christian faith is properly understood to be within and about the world, then it is possible to understand more fully what significance it has as truth from and about God.

The Task of Understanding

A major task that confronts the theologian, then, is to understand just what the nature of this world and of its processes are, as adequately and at as basic a level as possible. This understanding is not to be perceived simply as a matter of scouting the territory into which theology is to march, for the purpose of subduing it at a later time. Nor is it a sizing up of the vessel into which the theologian's insights are to be poured. Rather, we cannot properly grasp the import of the faith unless we have a knowledge of the world about which that faith is a statement. Understanding the point of the faith or discerning its import is decisively dependent upon adequately comprehending the world that is its referent and linking the statements of faith to that world. Science, therefore, becomes an essential component for doing theology.

As an example, one need only focus upon the question of how human beings have come to be. If humans are a special creation that has been inserted abruptly into the earthly ecosystems, then the traditional Christian doctrine of creation refers primarily to that insertion (at least as far as humans are concerned), with only incidental significance attached to the observable kinship between humans and the rest of creation. Furthermore, within this framework the redemption of humans may well have little or nothing to do with the created order as such, but rather it may be chiefly a statement to reassure us that we will indeed be extricated from the earthly scene as miraculously as we were inserted into it.

If, on the contrary, we proceed from an evolutionary perspective, building on the knowledge from the various sciences that suggests an emergence of humans within and through the very agency of the ecosystems of planet earth, then the insights of the faith take on a different meaning. The kinship between humans and the rest of creation is no longer incidental, but an important testimony to the way in which we were created, testimony that is also relevant to the question of what the purpose of our creation is. We were created in and through a vast process of material elements and dynamics. What it means to be human cannot be separated from reflection upon our role within this vast process and the role of the process in our formation. Redemption, whatever we conceive it to be, then becomes a promise about what this billions-of-years-long process can and might become. Relationships between humans and other aspects of the evolutionary process become significant at many points. At the same time, the nature and the import of faith are clarified, since faith insists upon permitting this promise concerning nature to be determinative for life and thought.

Because the final truth of faith, like the truth of all proposals that speak of ultimacy, may well elude the falsification that is possible with more certain types of knowledge, it is exceedingly critical that the import of any faith proposal be clear so that its significance can be assessed even if it is not easily tested, and also so that ways of testing it might be imagined. Without delving more deeply into the details of this example, it should be clear that our understanding of the world in this instance is decisive for our judgment as to what the faith means to say. Knowledge of the world illumines what the import of the faith is, and at the same time it suggests how the promise contained in Christian faith can be effectively articulated. Joseph Sittler made this point in an analogy: culture relates to the Christian gospel as counterpoint relates to tune—the significance and possibilities of the tune are unelicited except in the contrapuntal context (1961). This may simply be another way of stating the ancient maxim, so essential to faith, that unless everything (in this case, all of nature) has meaning, nothing (in this case human being) can claim meaning.

Consistent with these methodological concerns, the reader will discern a basic negative theme underlying these essays. This theme constitutes the basis for an almost polemical tone at points, just as it reaches proportions that justify my saying that it is a fundamental fear that haunts me: that theology and the Christian faith that underlies it will be content to be obscurantist, to be absent from the marketplace of ideas where human beings today discuss and take seriously the basic proposals about what this world means, and human life within it. There is no doubt in my mind that, in the Western world at least, theology is no longer counted among those disciplines of thought that deal significantly with the world and the truth about it.

Again, Auguste Comte (1798–1857) conceived of human history as moving from the theological mode of understanding through the metaphysical to the positive scientific mode. A form of his analysis is broadly, and with various nuances, a prevailing mind-set among intellectuals today. When combined with some of Freud's assertions, this view appreciates religious faith and theology as essential characteristics of humankind in an earlier phase of history that, compared to our present times, seems largely to have been the phase of its infancy.

Religion is often considered useful for the well-being of society, chiefly because it fosters earnestness about the daily responsibilities of the good citizen, worker, and family member. Comte himself believed this, and E. O. Wilson holds to a version of the same opinion (1987, 82–83). Political leaders recognize that lip service to religion is essential if they are to placate certain segments of their constituencies. However, religious faith and its conceptual theology are virtually never consulted for serious knowledge about the world and our lives in it. Governments, scholarly societies, universities, corporate business, the arts, and the media seldom if ever look at faith and theology as potential resources for gaining knowledge.

An examination of the news media confirms this insight dramatically. Although many of the most fundamental problems of our age, focused in the most troubled spots in the world, clearly possess a religious dimension, we seldom read or hear analysis of what religious perspectives can contribute to our understanding, certainly not at the level of competence regularly encountered in accounts of the political, economic, and social dimensions of these problems. Appalling ignorance of religion regularly appears in the reports of the news media. The same degree of ignorance in economics or foreign affairs would not be tolerated. The argument of the following pages makes no naive claims to presenting scientifically falsifiable knowledge, but it does attempt to formulate a theological statement that makes a difference in our understanding of the world and our action in it.

I recognize that the theologian, who is on the quest that I have spoken of, must cast the net broadly. Even though this volume limits itself primarily to the depths that are charted by the physical and natural sciences, the reader should not conclude that I am oblivious to the social sciences, the arts, and the economic, political, and social realms with which faith also has to do (Hefner 1987b). The contrary is the case. Besides personal predilection and historical accident, however, I have other reasons for pursuing the questions within the materials of the sciences I have focused upon. These sciences have, after all, fashioned what is surely the most significant means that our epoch has discovered for gaining knowledge. For many, if not most, persons alive today, to "know" something means to comprehend it scientifically.

Nevertheless, Christian faith and theology, together with most of the fields we call the humanities, have failed miserably to take the measure of the sciences, to allow the knowledge achieved by them to open up new vistas for understanding human existence in any of its aspects, not to mention the domain of theology,

God and the creation. Theology has far to go if it is to engage the possibilities offered by the sciences for articulating the Christian insights in a way that is intelligible, let alone cogent, within the configurations of mind that have been nurtured in the bosom of the modern sciences.

The sciences describe the context within which human beings have emerged and continue to live, as well as the processes by means of which we continue to live. Although the sectors of human life described by the social sciences, the arts, and the humanities have seemed in the past more existentially compelling than those of the natural sciences, the emergence of high technological civilization shows this perception to be misleading. The truth of Joseph Sittler's comment has been borne out, that the situation today to which all serious proposals must be addressed "includes both the world as nature and the world as history" (1978, 30–35). Although my argument here does not bring nature and history together in the sense that Sittler demands, I do mean to set one sector of the stage for that achievement.

This volume traces specifically the kinds of issues and domains of knowledge and reflection that this theologian has had to deal with in order to pursue the pathway just described. Its value may rest on how adequately it sets an agenda for others who share my concern for thinking through their faith and placing it squarely in the center of the human quest for truth about our world and ourselves in it.

The Task of Constructing Theory

This volume aims to make progress toward the goal that I have been speaking about by attempting genuine theological construction. Construction is its first priority, even if that means (as it surely does) taking shortcuts with analysis and substantiation. I take a cue from the natural scientists: that the first task is to present a proposal for consideration and debate. The proposal must be interesting enough and credible enough on the surface to invite exploration. That the proposal be adequately substantiated is not a priority, since substantiation either comes or fails to come through in the ensuing discussion. Nor is it necessary that the proposal claim to be unassailably true. If it can reasonably lay claim to be true in any sense whatsoever, that claim will also emerge or fail to emerge in the exploration. What is essential is that the proposal appear to be interesting and fruitful for exploration—fruitful above all.

Underlying the process of articulating the proposal is the contention that, in order to make the contribution that I have suggested in the foregoing, genuine *theory* must be offered. In our time it is chiefly through the construction and examination of theory that knowledge is gained, and because theology is otiose if it does not contribute knowledge, theology must seek to construct theory and offer it up for examination. In this spirit, this volume proposes the theological theory of the created co-creator. The argument aims at elaborating the proposed theory only enough to engage an audience for further fruitful discussion and examination.

In proposing itself as a candidate to be considered as theory, the proposal represents itself as a hypothesis to be tested. Why are hypothesis and theory so important? Because they stand as a conceptuality possessing explanatory power; that is, they give us comprehension of a large body of data that otherwise would be raw and uninterpreted, or nothing more than meaningless blips on our screen. The theory is accepted so long as the community for which it is relevant concurs that it is helpful for comprehending what cannot be interpreted more adequately through other means. A theory cannot be demonstrated with finality or validated conclusively, even though it can be falsified. It is considered to be viable or useful so long as the attempts to falsify it (or test it) are productive for our understanding, or at least more productive than tests of alternative theories.

In addition to my interest in furnishing knowledge and comprehension of the data of experience, I seek also to speak theologically in a fashion that is integrated with the various other disciplines that focus upon the human being and its life. Jerome Barkow, Leda Cosmides, and John Tooby speak of the need for "conceptual integration" (1992, 4–6) and for an "integrated causal model" that will connect the various sciences and enable the contribution of each discipline to be recognized within the context of the totality of our knowledge (chap. 1). Timothy Goldsmith has called for a similar model (1991, 141). I hold this to be of the highest importance for scholarly theology today, and integral to the current concern in theological circles for a public theology that can enter into intelligent conversation with all of the disciplines that we employ for gaining knowledge.

Christian faith does not ordinarily speak of its insights and their theological elaboration as theories to be tested or falsified. Rather, these insights come to the religious community as direct discourse, as declarative statements; that is why they are called revelation. To the human community at large, however, as well as to the reflective members of the believing community, even revelation is a theory to be tested, a proposal in the public marketplace of ideas that people of faith make for understanding human life and its meaning.

If the truth be told, revelation functions in this way for the inner, uncritical life of the community of faith as well. The theories of religion pertain to the deepest and broadest reaches of life and reality. They are tested finally only in the attempts of persons to live in accordance with them. How they are recognized as falsified is difficult to determine. Nevertheless, they are theories for understanding, and they challenge us to test them in the rough-and-tumble of our lives. This testing includes, consequently, the full range of human existence, from critical intellectual examination to the testing in personal and moral realms. Saint Paul spoke of this testing as working out our faith in fear and trembling. When we know what it is that a person or a community believes is significant enough to test (or attempt to falsify) with their own lives, we know what the substance of their faith is.

Pertinent to this way of understanding theological constructions (including moral injunctions, doctrines, dogmas, and theological systematization) is the reflection that has related theology to the theories of Noam Chomsky concerning language and its acquisition. Theologians who devote themselves to such reflection focus attention on the concepts of performance and competence (Schreiter 1985). *Performance* refers to the actual lived-out use of a language—usually the language we acquire in our natural childhood upbringing—whereas *competence* is that which makes it possible to generate what seems to be an almost endless range of performances in that language. Grammar attempts to describe the competence, but it cannot do this with real success. Competence as such remains hidden until it expresses itself in performance. Grammar therefore describes performance in such a way that it can approach a normative description of the competence from which performance emerges. As we have said, grammar is necessary, but it never succeeds fully in its task of setting forth competence.

When applied to Christian faith,

> tradition is analogous to the entire language system. Faith is analogous to language competence. Theology and the expressive tradition (liturgy, wider forms of praxis [including moral behavior]) are analogous to language performance. The loci of orthodoxy (however construed: scriptures, creeds, councils, confessions, magisterium) represent a grammar, mediating competence and performance. (Schreiter 1985, 115f.)

Faith cannot be finally described in any fullness; theological constructions are performances that propose themselves as useful elements of normative grammar, and they are continually tested in further performance to determine whether they can indeed serve as elements of grammar. This, I suggest, is another way of describing the process of testing hypotheses, particularly in religion and theology. Theological affirmations function as possible theories that are accepted, modified, or winnowed out entirely according to whether they do in fact help to account for the performance of faith in thought, worship, community life, and behavior.

The Basic Argument

The argument set forth in the following chapters is undergirded by a rather simple structure that can be sketched as follows:

1. *Who are we human beings?* We are, first of all, thoroughly natural creatures. We have emerged from the natural evolutionary processes. These processes have bequeathed to us a constitution that is informed by both genetic and cultural material.

To be genetically informed means that within us lives the legacy of our planet's evolving history of motivating behavior by preprogrammed messages, and that this legacy is of primordial significance for us.

We are also creatures of culture, which means that we must consciously and self-consciously assess the world we live in and construct frames of meaning that interpret and justify the decisions we make concerning our behavior in this world. The history of this process through the millennia constitutes another system of information in whose legacy we also live, and to which we offer our own revisions and additions.

This description of who we are speaks to us about certain basic structures and processes that constitute us. We must observe those structures, and those processes must function adequately, if we are to live. I suggest that these descriptions are the basis for speaking of a natural teleonomy. By that I mean that the observing of the natural structures and the functioning of the natural processes point to a concept of the purpose and meaning of human being. The concept thus derived is a statement of the teleonomy that may apply to humans. The biocultural phenomena by themselves do not tell how the structures are to be observed, nor how the functioning of the processes is to be carried out. The biocultural sciences, *qua* science, do not tell us to what goals the structures and processes should be directed, nor the limits or value of human intervention into the structures and processes. But these sciences do tell us that whatever meaning and purpose human being possesses take the shape of the nature that evolutionary processes have bestowed upon us.

The teleonomy is grounded in the fact that we are biologically formed culture-creators; the context is the nature from which we have come and of which we are concrete instances. It is within this continuum of nature that our purpose, meaning, and significance are defined.

2. *What is our situation today?* Planet earth has reached the point where the success of human beings in actualizing who we are—*self-aware creators of culture*—is critical for the entire planetary ecosystem, including the planet's nonhuman inhabitants. Our present era presents such radical challenges to us that our ability to assess our world and to construct frames of meaning that will engender wholesome behavior is seriously destabilized and confused. This is a challenge to our ability to fashion a viable system of cultural information. It can also be described as a challenge for us to fulfill the teleonomy of our basic human nature.

3. *Myth and ritual emerged in a similar situation somewhere between 100,000 and 20,000 years ago and provided the information that enhanced human life in survival-threatening conditions.* In the Upper Pleistocene era, the circumstances of life changed so radically that it is difficult to imagine the challenge that faced prehistoric humans. In this situation, myth and ritual were indispensable bearers of the information that was necessary to suggest, justify, and motivate the behavior that

would save *Homo sapiens* from destruction. This information was accessible through the cultural system that early humans were able to fashion, and myth and ritual were significant, even central, components of that system. By the term myth, I mean a story that is of ultimate concern. I follow Paul Ricoeur's description: "Myth will here be taken to mean what the history of religions now finds in it: not a false explanation by means of images and fables, but (1) a traditional narration which (2) relates to events that happened at the beginning of time and which has the purpose of (3) providing grounds for the ritual actions of persons of today and, in a general manner, (4) establishing all the forms of action and thought by which we understand ourselves in our world." (1967, 5)

By ritual, I refer to those sets of symbolic actions that portray the behaviors that are called for if we are to live in harmony with the depictions set forth in our myths. The story of Adam, Eve and the serpent is an example of a myth, and its depiction is that all humans are sinful. The liturgy of private or public confession is a ritual in which the behavior appropriate to our sinful condition is acted out.

4. *What is required of us today?* Today, science and myth/ritual must function together to perform the same function for our era—namely, to provide the information that will serve the natural order, and us humans within it, as it struggles under survival-threatening conditions. It is science that sets forth the fundamental descriptions of our human teleonomy, but it is myth and ritual that make the basic proposals concerning the direction, meaning, and purpose of the structures and processes whose fulfillment shapes the form of human being.

The Book's Outline

The progression of chapters in the ensuing pages aims to accomplish the task described in the foregoing. Part One presents an extensive summary of the proposed theory of the created co-creator by stating its three main elements and the auxiliary hypotheses that give the theory its fuller elaboration, unveiling the breadth of what it aims to interpret. The next chapters carry the discussion of the theory further under the rubrics of the three themes that bear its weight of interpretation: nature (Part Two), freedom (Part Three), and culture (Part Four). The theological framework in which I propose to interpret the argument of the book constitutes the final section (Part Five).

2

A Theology of the Created Co-Creator

This book proposes nothing less than a contribution to genuine theory. By *theory* is meant a concept or network of concepts that articulate a clear and simple idea that can be elaborated to provide insight into a wide range of data and issues. I follow the general lines of the analysis (Hefner 1988c) set forth by the philosopher of science Imre Lakatos (1978), particularly as interpreted by Nancey Murphy (1990b). Recognizing that it would be inappropriate to expect a methodology derived from the sciences to be immediately and without transformation applicable to theology, I underscore that I follow Lakatos in principle, but that not all of the details of his philosophical proposal will fit my theological method perfectly.

Falsification and the Testing of Hypotheses

Lakatos elaborated the notion of a research program; that is, that the goal of an intellectual proposal, in whatever discipline it arises, is to provide ideas that will prove to be fruitful if their suggestions are pursued and tested carefully. Fruitfulness is defined as the production of new insights, either into problems that previously defied understanding or into altogether new areas of knowledge. Lakatos designated the simple idea at the heart of the program with the term *hard core*. In his view, this core provides the basic insight of the program and is usually of such a nature that it cannot be falsified or verified as such. For example, one might think of the core of Darwin's program of evolution through variation, survival, and selection, or of Freud's program of understanding the human psyche. Neither evolution nor Freud's concept of the psyche as a tripartite structure consisting of id, ego, and superego can be verified per se or falsified. Nevertheless, the brilliance of these core images, much like Thomas Kuhn's (1970) celebrated paradigms, is what constitutes the epoch-making contribution of Darwin and Freud.

The hard work of cogent argument takes place in the company of auxiliary hypotheses that are drawn from the hard core, and it is these hypotheses that ought to be subject to falsification. The auxiliary hypotheses reveal the range of the program's reach and its significance. Constructively, these hypotheses provide new facts, that is, they enable new insights into perennial questions or even suggest questions that have not been asked before. By itself, in isolation from falsifiable auxiliary hypotheses, the significance of the core idea(s) is not discernible. It is through these hypotheses that the program lights up a stage that had hitherto lain in darkness or in uneven shadows.

I borrow the term *falsification* from the philosophy of science, where it has undergone a process of clarification and refinement during the past half century. Karl Popper gave major currency to the terms *falsifiability* and *falsification,* and even though his use of the terms is now considered by most philosophers to be rather crude, I will cite his intention for these terms as a clue to my own use of them (1976a, chaps. 1, 6; 1972b, chap. 1).

Popper insisted that the person who seeks after truth will want to relate ideas of truth to the world of possible experience, and he defined truth as empirical if it could be related to this world. Because experience can never conclusively verify an idea or theory, the quest for truth is actually served better by the process of seeking to refute a proposed idea by experience; in the process of such refutation, not only will we discover that negations of the idea are true, but we will also be provoked to explore new avenues and to think new thoughts. Popper described a theory as falsifiable if it could do two things: make clear what statements are inconsistent with the theory (these are "potential falsifiers") and also what statements it does not contradict (or which it "permits") (1972a, 86). Both of these functions are relevant to what I have said above concerning auxiliary hypotheses. When one understands what is inconsistent with a proposed idea or theory, as well as what does not contradict it, then the concrete significance of the idea comes to the fore; when this happens, the quest for truth is served.

I do not propose to import Popper's theories—nor even those of his follower and critic, Imre Lakatos—into my theological thinking in any simplistic manner. Rather, I suggest that they be adapted heuristically rather than literally, endorsing the suggestions that theological theories should be referred to the world of possible experience and that it is desirable to discern what a proposed theory negates as well as what it affirms. I will refer to this process of falsifying by several terms in the following chapters. Much of the time I will simply speak of the requirement that theological proposals must be amenable to public discussion, to underscore the heuristic style that I mean to employ. I follow the insights of philosopher Arthur Fine, adapting them to this discussion, that we should approach our theory-formation "without rigid attachments to philosophical schools and ideas, and without intentions for attaching . . . [our efforts] to some ready-made philosophical engine" (1986, 177).

The concern for clarity with respect to what, in the world of possible experience, might or might not contradict an idea or theory should be high on the theologian's agenda. Perhaps no other complaint is made so frequently by contemporary thinkers against theology than that theological ideas are often so fuzzy that their precise import is difficult to discern. In the face of this conceptual blurriness, many thinkers consider the chief question to be not whether one agrees or disagrees with theological ideas, but rather just what those ideas could possibly mean. This is no simple challenge, because no consensus exists, within theology or outside it, as to what constitutes falsification of theological ideas.

In this book I will not enter into sophisticated methodological discussion of this problem, but I do intend to advance the discussion by attempting theological proposals that invite examination that satisfies Popper's two criteria—namely, to clarify what might negate the proposals and what does not contradict them. I am convinced that until this clarity is provided, theology cannot enter effectively into public discussion of its proposals; it is my hope that part of the fruitfulness of my suggestions will be their suitability for such public discussion.

It is the testing (including the attempted refutation or falsifying) of auxiliary hypotheses that accounts for Darwin's monumental significance for biological and medical sciences today, for example, as well as for the long season of psychiatric preoccupation with Freud's work. Darwin continues to be a stimulating presence in biology while Freud is descending in influence, but this does not gainsay the fact that Freud's was for a period a fruitful research program. That his ideas are more and more found wanting means that the epoch of his program may be coming to an end, and therefore the Lakatosian judgment that it is a degenerating program is merited. For five decades, however, much psychiatric research was carried on in the exploration and testing of Freud's hypotheses. Today, most researchers would think that Freud's program has become degenerative, whereas Darwin's program is obviously still progressive. Darwin's original ideas have been criticized and revised, however, and evolutionary thinkers are moving beyond Darwin's positions in several areas, but his work continues to be fruitful (Ruse 1979b, 1986b).

It is clear, therefore, that being right or wrong is not the only value of a research program, or even the chief value. Rather, the value lies in the program's fruitfulness in opening up constructive insights (new knowledge) to those who seriously subject its auxiliary hypotheses to discussion and possible falsification. This capacity to stimulate new insights, or the lack of such capacity, is the chief criterion for judging proposed theories. Lakatos termed these insights "new facts" and "dramatic, stunning, and unexpected" interpretations of the world. The ability of the theory of the created co-creator to generate new facts is given detailed attention in chapter 15.

Such a criterion of fruitfulness may be accepted as a commonplace by many academic disciplines, and it may be a prized attribute for practical human affairs. In theology, however, it may appear a strange criterion, because theologians ordinarily strive to be right rather than fruitful. The tendency has been to subject theologians to the obligation to be "correct" with respect to interpreting the past, rather than to be fruitful with respect to the future.

For many centuries, the church considered innovation from the deposit of traditional faith to be a sign of apostasy; conversely, replication of the past was a mark of faithfulness (Wilken 1971). The Lutheran concern for correct doctrine (*pura doctrina*) embodies this concern, as does the Roman Catholic emphasis upon conformity to the teaching authority of the church (*magisterium*). The emphasis upon fruitfulness should not be viewed as indifference toward the truth or as aversion to tradition and its shaping force. Rather, a Lakatosian approach rests upon the assumption that fruitfulness is the form in which truthfulness or correctness manifests itself in the ambience of our theoretical understandings. Indeed, fruitfulness is the closest our theories can attain to the truth.

Although I shall not discuss this issue at length, both ontological and epistemological claims exist in the argument that fruitfulness stands in a significant relationship to whatever it means to know the truth or to have a correct understanding of the truth. To define the term *truth* is a thorny task, and I will not go into its philosophical intricacies here. However, the reader will understand my intent when I say that packets of information are true to the extent that, if we accept them and follow their lead in our quest for knowledge, they will not disappoint us by proving to be unfruitful or dangerously distorting. True information is information that we can trust to be fruitful. My discussions of the terms *God* and *the way things really are* (see below, pp. 32–35) develop this understanding of truth further.

The Lakatosian concept of a progressive research program represents still another significant move within the current reflection upon truth and how humans know it. Certain suggestions set forth under the rubric of postmodernity and anti-foundationalism challenge the sense in which we consider human understanding and the statements that proceed from it to be in touch with what is real. The several schools of philosophical realism claim in one way or another that our statements refer to something real; referentiality is a deep concern. The Lakatosian approach chooses to circumvent discussions of the real and of referentiality by suggesting that it is not necessary or even fruitful to be caught up in debates about what is true or real in and of themselves (Murphy 1988). Such debates are better carried on around the issue of fruitfulness, which pivots on the discovery of "new facts."

This does not mean that we are not concerned with what is true or real, but rather that what we assert about these two issues should be related to the fruitfulness of our assertions. After all, none of the contesting parties can finally demonstrate its superiority in such a debate. Realists, postmodernists, and anti-foundationalists alike can meet on the common soil of the test for fruitfulness.

Whether or not the existence of God can be proven, for example, theological statements that provide new insights into the nature of the world and human life in it are welcome and constructive proposals, even if their assumptions concerning God and the divine will are yet to be demonstrated to all critics in a cogent manner. The same can be said of postmodern proposals, even if their skepticism and relativizing moves are never finally demonstrable in a way that is persuasive to all. Comparable judgments may be said about the various types of realist suggestions.

Indeed, in an intellectual climate like the one in which we live today, with so many conflicting metaphysical and epistemological perspectives abounding, the Lakatosian appeal to fruitfulness may be considered a welcome proposal for enabling public discussion of important issues, even if only as a provisional measure. I recognize that the Lakatosian scheme is not without its own metaphysical and epistemological assumptions, but they are brought to bear in ways that need not impede discussion as the realist/postmodern/anti-foundationalist styles of discourse seem to.

What I have just said about Lakatos's concept of the progressive research program describes my hopes and intentions for the proposals set forth in this book. The core of my proposal may be stated as follows:

Human beings are God's created co-creators whose purpose is to be the agency, acting in freedom, to birth the future that is most wholesome for the nature that has birthed us—the nature that is not only our own genetic heritage, but also the entire human community and the evolutionary and ecological reality in which and to which we belong. Exercising this agency is said to be God's will for humans.

I will elaborate this core by highlighting three basic elements in its structure, stating each element in the form of a hypothesis. From this elaborated form of the core, I draw out nine auxiliary hypotheses. The reader will note that whereas the core of the theory is an explicitly theological proposal, each of the auxiliary hypotheses is stated in such a manner that theological presuppositions are not necessary for its discussion. These hypotheses can be subjected to scrutiny, energetically probed for their significance and fruitfulness, without necessarily adopting the theological stance of the author. Consequently, to the extent that the auxiliary hypotheses are fruitful and credible, to that same extent the status of the hard core is enhanced.

In the following chapters, each of these auxiliary hypotheses will be the subject of discussion and appropriate testing. In the course of this testing, the world of the created co-creator theory will be lit up like a theatrical stage. On that finally lighted stage, it should become clearer just what the theological core of the theory is attempting to engage and interpret in theological terms.

As with the process of falsification, full consensus is lacking on what the testing of hypotheses involves. Many biologists, some high-energy physicists, and the vast majority of social scientists employ formalized and quantitative procedures in testing their hypotheses, utilizing regression analysis and analysis of variance (Gigerenzer et al 1989). The majority of physical scientists and humanities scholars bring data and hypothesis together in less formal ways, accepting or rejecting the hypothesis according to whether it seems to make sense of what is known.

It will be obvious in what follows that I speak of testing hypotheses in this second mode. Biologists and social scientists will not find my method to be like theirs. I do mean, however, that hypotheses in theology should in some discernible manner meet Popper's two criteria of falsification—that the acceptance or rejection of the hypotheses should be grounded in correlations with or deviations from knowledge drawn from the world of possible experience, and that the discussion of the adequacy or inadequacy of the theological hypothesis should be carried out in publicly available discourse.

The Human Animal

At the outset, I said that the Christian faith is a message about the nature of human being and the destiny of the world. How is that message to be understood?

For the purposes of this discussion, my starting point for understanding the nature and destiny of the world and humans in that world will be the knowledge of human being as the natural sciences have illumined it in recent decades. In a fuller sense, I begin with a theological anthropology that takes seriously a biocultural evolutionary model within the physical ecosystem. I devote relatively little attention to the physicochemical dimensions of evolution, but they are, of course, the presupposition of the biocultural. Solomon Katz has described this model as follows (see also pp. 197ff. and figure 12-1, p. 198):

> Biocultural evolution consists of a series of interactions among: the biological information resident within individuals and populations in the form of the genetic constitution (i.e., the DNA); the cultural information which is the sum of the knowledge and experience which a particular society has accumulated and is available for exchange among its members; and thirdly, a human central nervous system (CNS), which is of course a biologically based system, whose principal evolved function with respect to this model is to facilitate the communication or storage of individually and socially developed knowledge and awareness. (Bowker 1983, 356; Katz 1980)

When taken seriously in a theological framework, this model is fruitful for our thinking about the human animal.

One of the most startling perspectives that this biocultural model gives us is what I shall call the two-natured character of the human. This may indeed be the most interesting and deeply significant insight that these sciences have given us into human being. *Homo sapiens* is itself a nodal point wherein two streams of information come together and coexist. The one stream is inherited genetic information, the other is cultural information. Both of these streams come together in the central nervous system. Since they have coevolved and coadapted together, they are one reality, not two (Goldsmith 1991). To speak of them as two, whether as streams of information or as building blocks or realities, is metaphorical. Even though such language of duality may be unavoidable and even necessary for heuristic purposes, it is as misleading as it is useful. The confluence of these two streams of evolutionary information in the human being has been noted for a long time; this meeting of the two gives rise to the perennial discussion about "nature" and "nurture" as two building blocks of human life.

We are far from understanding adequately how these two dimensions of human life and its evolution are related. We do know that they often appear to be quite different from each other and that they proceed with different sets of dynamics and principles. We also understand that they have been selected to mix sufficiently well to differentiate humanity from other forms of life and that, even though they flow in different channels, these channels merge in the human brain. The relation between them is at times a tense one at best. The cultural reality can easily put the biological to death, just as the latter can apparently withhold its cooperation with the former. It is the cultural agency that makes life interesting; culture lifts human existence to its heights, and it also plunges us into the depths. Nevertheless, for humans the genetic agent has both mandated the necessity and provided the possibility for the cultural reality, just as it holds the final cards in the game of life, and if those cards are played in a fatal manner, culture is obliterated. The cultural and the genetic have coadapted to each other and to their common environments so as to coevolve, in a relationship that may be termed symbiotic (again speaking metaphorically).

The model of biocultural evolution requires this concept of genes and culture as two streams of information that comprise the human being. The information that we call culture does not remain stored in the human central nervous system. It soon is transferred to other forms of storage—the designated "rememberer" or shaman, drawings, writing, eventually libraries and computers. In other words, the data that comprise culture are stored outside the human body, in what is called *extrasomatic information.* Biocultural evolutionary models include this extrasomatic information, both as stimulant to cultural evolution and also as that which does evolve (figure 12-1, p. 198).

How these two dimensions of human being—genes and culture—are related is the subject of intense scientific scrutiny. No theory can claim wide consensus in explaining their interrelationship. Ralph Wendell Burhoe's suggestion, which I have just alluded to, that they constitute two "organisms" that are coadapted in *Homo sapiens* and that they coevolve within the species in a symbiosis, is one of the most interesting of the proposed theories. His theory underscores the idea that the management of this symbiosis, within the larger system of reality in which we live, in an important sense is what human existence is all about (Burhoe 1976a, 1979).

Gerd Theissen has utilized Burhoe's theory (and other related ones) brilliantly to interpret the biblical faith. Theissen's insight is that the faith embodied in the Bible actually constitutes a proposal for cultural evolution to lead the biological creature into a qualitatively new phase of existence. This new phase gives content to the concept of God's will for humanity. As cultural evolution negotiates the passage into this new phase, it transcends certain dimensions of biological inheritance, those which are obstacles to the new phase; at the same time it ushers the biological into a new set of circumstances that qualify as the fulfillment of the genetic heritage. Jesus of Nazareth is the focal embodiment of this cultural evolutionary proposal (Theissen 1985).

The earthly career of this two-natured creature, the human being, is characterized through and through by the marks of being conditioned and also of being free. The conditionedness of the human being is rooted in its evolutionary development. *Homo sapiens* has emerged from a deterministic process that extends back to the origins of the universe. Furthermore, humans are ecologically situated so as to be perched on a delicate balance within a specific planetary ecosystem. Both its emergence from the evolutionary past, with the rich heritage that entails, and also its present ecological placement define the human being within finite limits (Hefner 1992; see also chapters 3 and 4).

Within this deterministic evolutionary process, freedom has emerged, and with it our reflection is provoked in a deeply dialectical mode. That freedom should be produced out of determinism seems startling, until we understand that freedom apparently is in the interest of the deterministic evolutionary system (T. Peters 1991). What we call freedom is rooted in the genetically controlled adaptive plasticity of the human phenotype (Dobzhansky 1956, 68). This plasticity takes a unique form in the human being, constituted by (1) exploration of the environment to consider appropriate behaviors, (2) self-conscious consideration of alternative decisions and behaviors, and (3) a supportive social matrix that both allows for exploration by the individual and at the same time demands that group relationships and the welfare of other individuals as well as of the whole society be respected (see part 3 for a fuller discussion). The last-named element is the biological ground of values and what we term morality.

Freedom in the sense that I have just pictured it is linked with responsibility. The essence of freedom in human affairs is that human beings can take deliberative and exploratory action, while at the same time they and they alone must finally take responsibility for the action. They must take responsibility for the future developments that are entailed in any actions, in the sense that they are the creatures who must live with the consequences and respond adequately to those consequences. If the consequences are undesirable—and if the human actors are not extinguished by their mistakes—they alone have the responsibility and the possibility for compensating for errors. This evolutionarily fashioned context reinforces conditions that are suitable for the emergence of values.

The fact that conditionedness and freedom have emerged together in *Homo sapiens* is of no little significance. In chapter 5, I refer to this phenomenon as an evolutionary preparation for values and morality. This development indicates that the dimensions of "oughtness" and value are built into the evolutionary process and need not be imported from the outside (Wicken 1989). Recent developments in a number of sciences, including Ilya Prigogine's work on the thermodynamics of nonequilibrium processes and Manfred Eigen's work on biochemical processes, have taught us to recognize how determinism and indeterminacy, conditionedness and freedom, are built into the basic structure of all natural processes (Peacocke 1979a, 1979b; Prigogine 1980; Eigen and Winkler 1981).

It appears that as the evolution of the biosphere has continued through the animals that have more complex central nervous systems, oughtness and values are intrinsic to the process. It is a value-driven process (Pugh 1977; Wicken 1989). The genetically controlled adaptive plasticity of the human phenotype is confronted with the intrinsic demand that it make choices between alternatives. Among the alternatives are those that are not presently actual but that can be imagined and made actual. Survival hinges upon these choices. The choices have consequences, and choices must be made as to how those consequences will be dealt with. The chain of choice, feedback, consequence, and response to feedback is endless.

What I have just described is the ambience of values—the emergence of values as a requirement for life and its evolution, the clarification of values, the achieving of consensus about specific values, and the taking of responsibility for actualizing the values.

The Theological Theory

This description of the human being is a summary of certain elements that are derived from empirical study. It presents a challenge to the theologian, because it is this view that must be given theological interpretation and significance. In the process of providing such an interpretation, I shall fulfill my intention of clarifying how the Christian faith is a message about who we are and what our destiny is.

The empirical description becomes, therefore, the occasion for a comprehensive theological theory. This theory will attempt to provide a conceptuality of explanatory power, taking into account the criteria described above, pages 23–25; further, it presents itself as a candidate to be an element of a normative grammar of Christian faith. As such, its raison d'être is to give us a more adequate glimpse into what it is that constitutes the competence of Christian faith, to use Schreiter's phrase from the previous chapter.

The theory consists of three elements, each of which corresponds to essential aspects of the empirical description. First, the theory presents one unified image that can serve as a summarizing concept for all that we know about the human being. Second, the theory includes a specific conceptuality that can interpret the dimension of conditionedness that we have noted in the empirical description of human being. Finally, the theory also includes a specific conceptuality that can interpret the dimension of freedom that is contained in the empirical description. In its most succinct form, the theory can be expressed in the following manner:

1. The human being is created by God to be a co-creator in the creation that God has brought into being and for which God has purposes.

2. The conditioning matrix that has produced the human being—the evolutionary process—is God's process of bringing into being a creature who represents the creation's zone of a new stage of freedom and who therefore is crucial for the emergence of a free creation.

3. The freedom that marks the created co-creator and its culture is an instrumentality of God for enabling the creation (consisting of the evolutionary past of genetic and cultural inheritance as well as the contemporary ecosystem) to participate in the intentional fulfillment of God's purposes.

The Use of the Term God

For reasons that I clarify in chapter 13 (see pages 213–27), I have no intention in this work of developing a philosophically sophisticated concept of God. That is a task that I leave to a subsequent work. As the later discussion underscores, I focus upon the information about God that is carried in myth and ritual, and this information takes a different form from that which is carried by sophisticated philosophical systems of thought. Obviously, it is desirable that the conceptuality employed in talking about God be honed by critical philosophical reflection, but in this book my focus is upon what we derive from the ambience of myth and ritual. When I use the term *God,* I refer to that which is ultimate, somewhat in the manner of Paul Tillich, who spoke of God as the "name for that which concerns us ultimately" (1951, 211f.). That which concerns us ultimately is the focus for theology, and in the exploration of ultimate concern, we come upon both the meaning of God and the dimension of the holy in human existence (Tillich 1951, 1–13, 211–218).

In this book I most frequently speak, not of ultimate concern, but rather of *the way things really are* and *what really is*. *God* is the term men and women use to signify that what they are talking about, what they have come upon in their experience, touches upon the way things really are. In chapter 5, I explore this in a preliminary way in my interpretation of Jesus' experience of the world as set forth in the Sermon on the Mount (see pages 84–88). I also follow Tillich in his insistence that we can speak about God only in symbolic, not literal, language, and this too may account for my preference for myth and ritual as the chief resources for understanding God.

When we use the terms *the way things really are* and *what really is* in reference to God, we thereby indicate that we are concerned with the way things are in the profoundest dimension, that of ultimacy. The concept of the created co-creator, for example, functions in several dimensions, but to relate the concept to God and God's will is to signify the profoundest dimension. Tillich (1951, 11–15) brought the concepts of being and nonbeing into his discussion of the ultimate. Ultimate concern manifests itself in the ambience of concrete, finite life as that which enables us to share in our profoundest being. The ultimate is not abstract, but rather is accessible only in the concreteness of life. To reject it or to trivialize it is to cut ourselves off from what is our most genuine being—that is, to separate us from the way things really are. Our being is always in dialectical relationship to our nonbeing.

Throughout this book, in discussion of the theory of the created co-creator I am asking, implicitly or explicitly, whether the vocation that the theory depicts for the human species is a matter of ultimacy, that is, a matter of being or nonbeing. This questioning pertains to every element of the discussion, particularly, for example, the issues of teleonomy, freedom, and the formation and exercise of culture.

I may clarify my intent by citing an example of the contrast between information about God carried in myth and ritual and that conveyed by a concept of God. Consider the words ascribed to Jesus in John 15:12–13: "This is my commandment, that you love one another as I have loved you. No one has greater love than this, to lay down one's life for one's friends."

As information conveyed by a concept of God, this commandment becomes part of a world view that is constituted essentially by a concept of God in which love for the neighbor is understood as essential to God and our loving is shown to be commensurate with that world view and required by it. It follows that theologians find themselves under the imperative to construct concepts of God that make this love credible, both as a commandment and also as a meaningful behavior in the world.

The same command, when received as information conveyed by myth and ritual, takes on a different character, at least initially. As conveyed by myth and ritual, one's response is that love for the neighbor is a matter of ultimacy. As surely as gravity is part of the way things really are in the natural world, so love for neighbor is also integral to the way things really are. This is tantamount to saying that apart from love for neighbor we are not fully human beings, and this in turn is the question of being and nonbeing. We may not be in possession of a clear concept of God, and yet we will nevertheless believe that love for the neighbor is a matter of ultimacy and that "God wills it," in the pattern of Jesus' own life.

In terms of philosophical points of reference, what I have designated as information from myth and ritual received in terms of behavioral motivation is more in the realm that Kant reflects upon in his *Critique of Practical Reason* and *Critique of Judgment,* or in the tradition of the Existentialists, whereas the conceptual mode is more akin to Whitehead's *Process and Reality.* We may speak of different modes of access to God as ultimacy: through the conceptual and through the motivation of behavior. The optimal condition is to function in both modes, and for them to correlate with each other in a congenial fashion. However, it is quite possible to be devoted to the conceptual while ignoring the behavioral, and the converse is also possible.

In this book, I will use such terms as *God's purposes, God's will,* and *God's grace.* The philosophically acute reader will find traces of a metaphysical concept of God in such usage. However, my overt intention is to assert with such terms that certain information is received as partaking in ultimacy, in the way things really are. In chapters 11, 12, and 14, for example, the reader will find that I consider altruistic behavior to be linked to the self-giving love of Jesus' sacrifice, and I assert that such behavior is God's will. What I mean is that to adopt such behavior is itself to participate in ultimacy, to be in accord with the way things really are, and thus to be in touch with what is fully human.

I will also suggest, in chapters 5 and 14, that we may characterize the way things really are, the realm of the ultimate, with the quality of the personal, and that we may consider that realm to be a resonating ambience to human self-giving that is undertaken in love. Personally, I am not in possession of a sophisticated concept of God that can provide philosophical grounding and coherence for these convictions about self-giving love and the resonating character of reality. But the lack of such a concept does not render that love and that resonating quality any less ultimate for me, any less rooted in the way things really are.

I believe that the contribution of myth and ritual is that they convey this information to us without necessary dependence on a philosophical apparatus (see my reliance on philosopher Arthur Fine in chapters 13 and 14). That contribution is particularly helpful in a time like the present, when the relationship of our concepts to what is real is so much an object of uncertainty and debate, as is evident in the current conversation about postmodernism, epistemological realism, deconstructionism, and the like. I find good reason to incorporate this distinction between information conveyed by concept and information conveyed by mythic and ritual motivations for behavior into a larger research program for further exploration. Furthermore, in doing so I am taking seriously the actual processes of evolution and the human being that has emerged within those processes.

Human beings, through the activity of their central nervous systems, receive information, defined as representations of the environment that motivate behavior (see the fuller discussion in chapter 9, pp. 145–56). This information does not come in the form of concepts. We receive information, for example, that we are hungry or that we are in pain, and even though our survival is at stake, that information conveys no concept of survival as such. Human beings construct larger pictures and concepts that put the concrete information into perspective, thus enabling us to say that hunger should be satisfied, and in such a way as not to put our health in jeopardy. We have solid knowledge that the mind operates in this manner, and I recount its details in chapter 6.

As Whitehead has explained (see page 90 below), these concepts may be so deeply engrained that they appear simultaneous with the experienced information, and indeed they condition how we receive the primal information—at times beneficially and at times detrimentally. Nevertheless, they are the work of the human mind secondary to the reception of information as such. As important as concepts are, for the most part we cannot wait to respond to the behavior-inducing information that we receive until we have fully formed and tested concepts at our disposal. We must act on the basis of information that is underdetermined by the data. As I shall elaborate at length in chapters 9 and 10, deliverances of myth and ritual function in this way. Just as we must eat even though we do not have an adequate concept of survival to guide us fully, so the myth and ritual pertaining to John 15:12–13 urge us to love our neighbor, as a matter of our being or nonbeing, even though we do not have a fully satisfactory concept of God to guide us.

This is in no way intended as a denigration of concepts of God, but rather as a description of how human beings do in fact live. I reiterate that the task of framing an adequate concept of God must be undertaken, and there are many theologians and philosophers at work doing this. In this book, however, conceptualizing God is not the chief agenda. My approach in this respect is consistent with my working definition of truth—that information which, if we trust it, will not prove to be unfruitful or perverse.

Human as Created Co-Creator

Theologically, we take account of the two-natured human animal who is both conditioned and free by asserting, first of all, that *the human being is created by God to be a co-creator in the creation that God has brought into being and for which God has purposes.* We state this briefly in the term *created co-creator.* This term provides the summary concept that gathers together what we know about the human being and also integrates the other two elements, those that refer to human conditionedness and freedom.

Both the noun and the adjective are important. The adjective *created* corresponds to the conditionedness of the human being. First, it recognizes that the human being is placed within an ecosystem, in an intimate interrelationship with an environment that conditions the human in significant ways. *Created* also refers to the genetic component of the two-natured creature, underscoring that neither the individual nor the group has control over the inheritance of our genetic composition, our genotype. Even the prospects of genetic engineering do not gainsay the fact that our genome is bestowed upon us; we do not select it. The genetic component is also characterized, however, by the processes that allow the free human creature to emerge. Cultural conditioning is incorporated into the term *created,* although it must be noted that culture is also the most dramatic locus of the human being's freedom. The genetic and the cultural share in both conditionedness and freedom. The genotype is the source of our being conditioned, but it also provides the resources for freedom to emerge, else we would not be free. Conversely, although freedom reaches its most efficacious form in human culture, that culture is both conditioned by genes and environment and also is a basis for conditioning traditions that shape each new generation.

To be created is to be derived, to be dependent upon antecedent factors (environmental, biological, cultural) as well as contemporary sources (environmental, cultural). The term *created* indicates that the human species did not design its own nature or its role in the world. Consequently, no value judgment is implied in placing the human within the total evolutionary process. Since humans cannot credit themselves for their role in the process and their capabilities, they cannot be said to be morally superior or inferior to any other species or entity in the same ecosystem.

The image becomes genuinely theological when we include the assertion that humans have been created and given their place in the process by God. In its theological dimension, therefore, the first element in this summary concept speaks of the primacy of God and the divine creating activity. Whatever we mean by the term *God* and whatever conceptuality we employ for thinking about God, that God is the ground of this process in which humans have emerged.

For humans to be created means also that they exist within, and for the sake of, the matrix of creation in which they have emerged. *Homo sapiens* did not emerge to be conquistador, dominating and pillaging as the opportunity arose. Rather, as creature, the human serves the process of the creator, and all of the possibilities, activities, and achievements of the creature are to be referred to the created order and the purposes with which it has been endowed. Karl Peters (1989) refers to this dual nature as creating yet conserving, and he links this duality with other dualities in human nature: material/cultural and instinctual-emotional/rational.

The created dimension of the co-creator points to the inadequacy of profoundly dualistic understandings of the human being. My 1976 attempt at worldview building and ontological construction ("The Foundations of Belonging in a Christian Worldview") employed the idea of belonging as a basis for overcoming dualism. The created co-creator theory should be construed within such a hermeneutic or interpretational framework of belonging as I suggested there, when I argued that we can no longer tolerate understandings of human nature that insist upon separating us from our fellow human beings, from the natural ecosystem in which we live, or from the evolutionary processes from which we have emerged. Humans are by nature creatures constituted both by receptivity and belonging. Any concept of *Homo faber,* aggressive technological operator, that overlooks these basic qualities is clearly inadequate and even perverse. I wrote:

> Human beings know, however, that if they belong to each other, to the ecosystem, and to the process out of which that ecosystem was born, they belong *as human beings,* and that means as a species that is self-conscious and consequently able to plan, receive feedback, alter its plans, and act upon the wisdom it has accumulated in the process. [Later (1984a, 326; 1988a, 228), I extended this analysis of human distinctiveness to include the taking of responsibility for our actions.] To be human beings includes the possibility and the responsibility to create and to share in the creation of our own world in a manner and to a degree unknown before in the history of this world. If we are to speak of our sense of belonging, therefore, that must not be construed as a diminishing of human beings as initiating and self-creating. Receptivity and activity are correlative in human existence, and belonging must include them both as polar realities. We underline the correlative importance of human beings as active creatures when we exhort them to remember that they belong, that they are receptive and dependent, and then urge them to *act* upon that recollection! (Hefner 1976, 163)

Paul Tillich utilized the image of polar relationships to good advantage (1951, 198ff.). The image depicts the independence of the poles, even their position as antipodes, while at the same time embracing their fundamental relatedness. In the search for proper ways of conceptualizing the relationships between receptivity and activity, as well as between the character of being created and also co-creator, polarity is one useful resource.

The affirmation of divine purposes is central to this understanding. Those purposes serve both as an indication that gives substance and a basis for hope to the creation, and also as a criterion for determining and assessing the work of the co-creator. The most important and arresting aspect of this basic image is the assertion that the human being was brought into being by God and that God's purposes govern the cosmos, including humans. Furthermore, God's purposes for the human species are to be referred to God's purposes for the creation as such. Apart from this referent that is God, the theory would not be theological.

While this affirmation of God's purposes is the most problematic aspect of the theory because it is the most difficult to make credible, it is this affirmation that lifts the empirical understanding of human being into the realm of higher existential significance. This aspect of the theory suggests the method of teleonomy that forms one of the auxiliary hypotheses of the created co-creator theory (see below, 39ff.). The insistence that the process of the human being's emergence within the evolutionary process of the cosmos is the work of God, as well as the specification of the purpose of that emergence, throw light, furthermore, on the distinguishing thrust of Christian faith.

The noun *co-creator* corresponds to the freedom of the human being. Freedom is defined in this connection neither as liberty (the classical liberal and prevailing American view) nor as the ability to make and shape the world (the prevailing Marxist view). Rather, freedom refers to the condition of existence in which humans unavoidably face the necessity both of making choices and of constructing the stories that contextualize and hence justify those choices. In technological civilization, decision-making is universal and unavoidable; it is the foundation for that civilization. Since technological civilization has altered the circumstances of living so radically, this necessity of decision-making and story construction is intensified. I call this freedom, because finally only humans (whether as individuals or as groups) can make the decisions and only humans can construct the stories that justify them.

Two examples raise issues that will be the subject of fuller discussion in later chapters, are illustrative. First, ancient wisdom (the Ten Commandments) enjoins us to honor fathers and mothers as God's mandate. Technological civilization forces us to decide whether permitting or refusing medical interventions to prolong a parent's life fulfills the command. Humans cannot avoid the freedom to make the choice, and only humans can construct the stories that justify such choices. Second, environmental policies require a myriad of value judgments concerning the comparative values of the earth and of humans and other forms of life. Humans cannot avoid such policy-making and the value judgments inherent to that policy. Further, only humans can construct the stories that provide the justifying arguments for such judgments. Genesis 1:28 ("Be fruitful and multiply, and fill the earth and subdue it; and have dominion") exists to be interpreted, and it has been taken in anthropocentric, anthropo-serving directions, as well as in eco-friendly directions. Humans cannot avoid the interpretations and their justifications.

Despite the unfortunate connotations that several critics have attached to the term *co-creator,* I feel compelled to use it, because it articulates most adequately the character of this situation of freedom in which the evolutionary processes have placed *Homo sapiens*. This concept of freedom is the focus of an auxiliary hypothesis to the created co-creator theory (see below, pp. 45f.). I have been urged by critics to substitute another term, such as *creative creatures,* for created co-creator. However, I find neither this term nor other proposed alternatives to be adequate for conceptualizing the dual nature of the human being—a creature who has been brought into existence by nature's processes, and who has been given by that nature the role of free co-creator within those same processes.

Freedom, as I have described it, speaks of the extraordinary capabilities of the human creature, as well as its unique place within the planetary ecosystem. The freedom that characterizes the cultural component of human nature is included here. Although, clearly, the co-creator has no equality with God the creator, inasmuch as the former is a contingent creature and dependent upon the creator, nevertheless the very use of the word *creator,* even in a derivative sense, establishes a distinctive quality for humans. Furthermore, the word points to the essential character of the human: to be a kind of co-creator.

This first basic statement sets the created co-creator squarely within the context of the creation and its purposes. Co-creatorhood has no meaning apart from this context. That God has purposes for the creation introduces the concept of destiny and links the human being directly to that destiny. Both the creation and the human being have purposes for their existence, and the two are intertwined within the larger notion of God's destiny for the entire creation.

This element of the created co-creator core introduces a number of considerations that are articulated in the form of auxiliary hypotheses.

The first consideration is that of purpose—human purpose and, by inference, the purposes of all of nature. Certainly it is not possible to assert a teleology for nature, except as an item of faith. Alasdair MacIntyre (1984) has reflected in an influential manner upon the loss of teleology following the rise of modernity and the sad consequences of that loss for our efforts to understand the meaning of human life and to construct adequate moral concepts. He suggests that either we fall into the chaos of competing moral claims, wherein personal opinion is elevated to the position of chief criterion, or we regenerate the Aristotelian tradition of virtues that flow from the human desire for excellence and eudaemonia.

The theory of the created co-creator suggests another alternative: that by reflecting carefully upon the empirically understood nature of the world, specifically *Homo sapiens,* we can discern structures and processes that require certain responses if they are to function and if their very existence is to make sense. These required responses suggest certain values that can be said to be consistent with empirically understood structures and processes. The required responses and the imputed values can be said to be *teleonomic;* that is, although they cannot be said to constitute the preordained teleology of human beings and the rest of nature, they can be said to represent a credible correlate to structures and processes that are innate in the human being (Birtel 1990).

We might go so far as to state a teleonomic axiom:

The structure of a thing, the processes by which it functions, the requirements for its functioning, and its relations with and impact upon its ecosystem form the most reasonable basis for hypothesizing what the purpose and meaning of the thing are.

This axiom is also a basis for beginning to reflect upon values. In a theological perspective, the teleonomic axiom is grounded in the creative action of God; if we have been created in the form of certain structures and processes, then God must will those structures and processes to be, in some sense at least, fulfilled. This constitutes a version of natural law theology. How this functioning and fulfillment are carried out, however, is subject to human freedom, which includes the human search for what fulfillment means in each instance (see above, pp. 31).

Such a teleonomic method must be followed with subtlety and caution; it is a work of human construction, its conclusions are subject to interpretation, and it leads to no instantly clear-cut and universal conclusions. However, such reasoning does focus upon empirical descriptions that are amenable to public discussion and consensus, as do the conclusions that may be drawn concerning their implications for understanding purposiveness in human action and by extension for the rest of nature. Consequently, discussion of values and purpose can attain more than individualistic and relativistic status, even if universality and absoluteness are always difficult to discern. We can formulate these considerations as follows:

Hypothesis #1: Integral to *Homo sapiens* and its evolutionary history are certain structures and processes, the requirements for whose functioning may be said to constitute, at least in a tentative way, goals and purposes for human life.

This hypothesis makes itself available for testing and falsification to the extent that any descriptions of the structures and processes of any thing, including human being, are subject to examination as to their accuracy and adequacy. The teleonomic conclusions drawn from such descriptions are also subject to examination.

The first consideration, that of purpose, rests on the assumption that nature is a primary source for gaining knowledge of human life and its raison d'être. In a theological framework, nature is understood as creation, namely, as the work of God. For Jews and Christians, there is no other originating source of the natural world except God. This is the thrust of the doctrine of creation out of nothing (*creatio ex nihilo*). Consequently, a naturalistic as well as a theological perspective would conclude that nature is all we possess as the chief source for understanding what the world is about. Even those religions that speak of a divine revelation must acknowledge that revelation happens within nature, and that it is received, understood, and interpreted through the thoroughly natural structures of a natural animal, *Homo sapiens*. The historian of religions Gerardus van der Leeuw (1957, 346; also cited in Long 1963, 149) suggests that this is the distinctive element in Hebrew and Christian cosmology, that the equation for reality is composed of only these few members—God, the nature that God has created, and the future history that God has in mind for that nature.

A second set of considerations, which also rests upon the acknowledgment of nature's preeminence as source and ambience for knowledge, suggests another auxiliary hypothesis, which I formulate thus:

Hypothesis #2: The meaning and purpose of human beings are conceived in terms of their placement within natural processes and their contribution to those same processes.

The testability of this hypothesis lies in the examination of all proposals that describe, first, the way in which humans are related to nature and its evolutionary history, and second, the wholesome or destructive consequences of human behavior toward the rest of nature. Such matters are indeed open to public scrutiny, and even though scientifically certain consensus may not be possible, not all such proposals are equally valid.

A number of considerations are bundled together with this hypothesis concerning human purpose and the rest of nature. First of all, we are assuming that, due to the placement of human beings within the natural evolutionary processes in which they have emerged, nonhuman nature may provide clues to the character and purpose of human being, even as human being provides understandings that illumine the nonhuman segments of nature. Second, this hypothesis sets the stage for one of the most deeply held assumptions of this book, that the Christian faith is a proposal about the meaning of nature—an assumption whose elaboration runs like a thread throughout the text.

Third, with this hypothesis, we lay the groundwork for a pragmatic criterion of truth and a contextually large and complex framework for its application. If *Homo sapiens* is indeed embedded within a world of nature in which humans have emerged and which forms the theater of their operations, then, I hypothesize, it is reasonable to suggest that the purpose of human existence is to be referred to this web of natural interrelations within which humans exist. On the one hand, the significance of the human species is defined in terms of the evolution of nature in which humans have emerged, while on the other hand, the purposes that humans intend should be construed as proposals that contribute to the life of those natural processes. Later on, I shall argue that Christians would reach this same conclusion from reflection on the life and death of Jesus. These considerations suggest the following:

Hypothesis #3: A concept of "wholesomeness" is both unavoidable and useful as criterion governing the behavior of human beings within their natural ambience, as they consider what their contribution to nature should be.

This is necessarily an uncertain and ambiguous criterion, because any concept of wholesomeness is open to scrutiny, precisely because all behaviors are not equally beneficial for either humans themselves or for the rest of nature. A definition of wholesomeness must be forged through consensus.

The two immediately preceding hypotheses propose that nature is the arena for human purpose and that concern for nature's wholesome state provides a pragmatic criterion for our thinking. Such proposals imply a special status for the natural order, and this status forms the substance of a further hypothesis:

Hypothesis #4: Nature is the medium through which the world, including human beings, receives knowledge, as well as grace. If God is brought into the discussion, then nature is the medium of divine knowledge and grace.

This hypothesis is tested by examination of the specific assertions that are said to be gleaned from nature, whether as statements of knowledge or grace, to determine whether they are plausible within our publicly discussable understandings of human nature.

The Evolutionary Process as Conditioning Matrix

The second basic statement about human being is this: *The conditioning matrix that has produced the human being—the evolutionary process—is God's process of bringing into being a creature who represents a more complex phase of the creation's zone of freedom and who therefore is crucial for the emergence of a free creation.* The theological interpretation of what it means to be created is synonymous with the task of interpreting theologically the process of evolution, including the mechanisms of natural selection, which forms the conditioning matrix for human being. There is no more difficult and important challenge for the theologian, nor for the human mind in general. In substance, this statement amounts to interpreting the evolutionary process as the work of God.

The range of reality that is relevant for this task is enormous. It includes the entire scope of cosmology, the process of the development of physical reality, matter in its various configurations and stages, as well as the biosphere, human history, and culture. The concept of selection is just beginning to be used by scientists in the physical realm, but it has been integral to the biological sciences for over a century. Natural selection resists not only theological, but also all humane interpretation, for two fundamental reasons: (1) to empirical observation, the processes of selection seem to be without overall purpose or meaningfulness, and (2) they appear to be replete with what humans consider to be evil, pain, injustice, and disregard for persons. Theological tradition places such issues under the rubric of theodicy, which refers to efforts to resolve the problem of how evil and suffering are to be related conceptually with the belief in a good and powerful God. For the theologian, nowhere do the problems of theodicy bear down with greater weight and urgency than in the consideration of the processes of natural selection.

Much of theology and many philosophies have simply ignored the relevance of the selection processes. Such a strategy is embarrassing, however, because selection processes are woven into all the processes of life, apparently by the action of the Creator God. Those theologies that have attended to these processes have often resorted to one or another version of supernaturalism—for example, the view that life on earth may be marked by the cruel deaths of natural selection, but in life hereafter, the pain and unfairness of selection will be matched with the divine compensation of eternal blessedness. Such a strategy may take selection seriously, but denies its significance by positing that the destiny of the human being lies elsewhere, in a realm outside the order of creation, in such a way as to devalue the evolutionary realm in which selection occurs. Thereby, the entire created order is devalued in a manner that is in conflict with the central thrust of the Jewish and Christian faiths.

The Christian faith, to the contrary, has traditionally placed the goodness of the created order at the center of its understanding of reality. The creation is dependent on God as its source and none other, and this conviction is enshrined in the doctrine of creation "out of nothing" (*creatio ex nihilo*). Furthermore, this doctrine is extended most emphatically in the affirmation of "continuing creation" (*creatio continua*). These two affirmations form the foundation of an outlook that understands the created order to be reliable and friendly, in the sense that its processes make for the fulfillment of the human being and the rest of nature, rather than their betrayal and degradation. Of all the affirmations of the Christian Scriptures, none ranks above the confession that God is faithful to the creation that has come into being by God's own free intention.

The confluence of the problems intrinsic to our understanding of natural selection and the fundamental confidence that Christian doctrine places in the created order set the stage for the massive issues of theodicy that beset our theological interpretation. The integrity of Christian faith will insist on "saving" the natural order as a realm of value within God's creation, no matter how large the problems of evil loom.

The conditioning matrix that is constituted by evolutionary processes is understood by Christian faith, however, not simply in terms of what it has been and is now, but in terms of what it can become, and what it can become in the light of God's intentions. This conviction is determinative for our interpretation. In their technical vocabulary, theologians call this an *eschatological* perspective; it is constitutive for Christian faith and theology. The purposes of God include that the creation should freely acknowledge its creator and fulfill that creator's will in freedom.

Viewing the selection processes from this perspective, which posits a divine intention for a free creation, has prompted John Hick to set forth a promising train of thought. If indeed it is God's will that there be a free creation, it is necessary not simply that the world be created in a condition of freedom, which God presumably could bring into being by fiat, but that the creation be created so that it *can become free* by its own choosing (Hick 1981). By using the term *choosing to be free,* we point not to a Promethean wrenching of freedom from God by human choices, but rather to the actuality of the process of becoming free as it transpires within the medium of human volition and hence participates in that volition. To speak of freedom as programmed from without is in itself not enough; it is a contradiction of the idea of freedom. To be created instantaneously in the condition of freedom would not be fully consistent with the divine intention, inasmuch as the creation would have had absolutely no part in its own becoming free. God desires not only that the world be free, but that it freely desire that condition.

Hick speculates that the system of natural selection is the sort of characteristic one would look for in a system that can develop the capacity to choose to be free. Such a system requires an epistemic distance between the condition in which the creation finds itself at any given moment and that which it will attain. The evolutionary system based on natural selection is predicated upon such a distance, which is traversed only through the organism's own efforts. The processes of the physical realm, particularly the processes of biological evolution in accordance with the dynamics of natural selection, fit the requirements that Hick believes are essential for becoming free.

As a basis for dealing with theodicy, this suggestion does not simply ratify the course of history in a positivist sense, as if to argue that whatever is, is God's will. Rather, it discerns that what has been may be reinterpreted in the light of what it is to become. The brutality of the biological selection processes may indeed be what has brought us to this or any other given moment. However, those processes are understood and interpreted by what they *can and shall become.*

This emphasis on what the process can become will prove, in my later discussion, to be the basis also for subjecting the process to critique and for attempting to take it in new directions. Indeed this project of taking the process of evolution, the conditioning matrix, in new directions is what is at stake in the emergence of cultural evolution from the biological processes. The raison d'être of the two-natured human animal is inseparable from this modulation of the evolutionary processes. Far from being discontinuous with the previous phases of the conditioning matrix, however, the appearance of the two-natured human creature is itself an integral component of the conditioning matrix.

This interpretation of the conditioning matrix of evolution as the work of God to allow for the emergence of that which is necessary for the fulfillment of God's intentions requires of us a particular view of the natural processes as themselves participants in God's grace and vehicles of that grace. The encounter with God takes place within the processes of nature, and the critique and/or call for new ways of thinking and living is itself an event within the natural order, as a fulfillment of the creation. Furthermore, we recognize in this interpretation that freedom did not emerge abruptly with the human species, but that its necessary and enabling conditions are deeply rooted in all of physical and biological reality, as the theories of quantum physics and chaos, for example, demonstrate.

Like the first element, the second element of the created co-creator core gives rise to auxiliary hypotheses.

Hypothesis #5: Freedom characterizes human existence as the condition in which humans have no choice but to act and to construct the narratives and symbols that contextualize that action. Such contextualization provides justification, explanation, and norms for guiding and assessing the action. This condition is intrinsic to the evolutionary processes at the level of *Homo sapiens.*

The testing of this hypothesis lies chiefly in the assessment whether it is useful for understanding human life in its natural context. This hypothesis should be linked to the later discussion of culture.

This proposal concerning freedom rests upon the scientific theory that is the single most provocative factor for this entire study.

Hypothesis #6: *Homo sapiens* is a two-natured creature, a symbiosis of genes and culture.

This hypothesis is tested by reference to an entire body of relevant scientific literature. It should have been clear from the outset of this chapter that this hypothesis from the evolutionary and psychological sciences has been the trigger for a great deal of what the created co-creator theory seeks to illumine.

Freedom as Key to God's Intention

The third basic statement about human being is this:

The freedom that marks the created co-creator and its culture is an instrumentality of God for enabling the creation (consisting of the evolutionary past of genetic inheritance and culture, as well as the contemporary ecosystem) to participate in the intentional fulfillment of God's purposes.

The formulation of the theological theory culminates in the freedom of the co-creator, from the perspectives of the empirical description to which it responds and also of the theological hypotheses that constitute its raison d'être.

Three concepts in interrelationship form the core of this interpretation: freedom, purpose, and eschatology. Each of these has figured in the preceding discussion, but they merit particular emphasis here. The constellation of these concepts forms the heart of what our theological theory asserts about the human being and God's will for the creation.

God, according to the Christian tradition, has created the world out of a divine intention, and this intention is the ground for the purposes of creation. The creation is not otiose, but rather exists in the context of God's purposes. The will of God is that the creation should fulfill its God-grounded purposes out of its own intentionality. This is an extraordinarily important consideration, too often ignored. In the engagement with the sciences, this view of the creation establishes a link to the scientific concern for the functions of natural phenomena.

Functionalism is a difficult concept for theology (as well as for some of the other perspectives in the fields of the humanities), because it seems to harbor the biggest bogeyman of all—reductionism. Theology is lamed by its aversion to the theological significance of functional interpretations of reality, including natural phenomena. Unless it can explore this significance of functional interpretations, it cannot really come to terms with God's ordaining the creation to be an evolutionary process, comprised of discrete evolutionary processes. Nor can it take the full measure of the implication that the creation, as an evolutionarily constructed system, is a system in movement, and therefore a system that has purposes. In a more technical theological analysis, this means that the creation is fundamentally both eschatological and value-laden or moral. Further, these considerations lead us to conclude that freedom is fundamental to the constitution of the creation. These issues stand at the heart of the created co-creator theory, focusing with particular intensity in the first four auxiliary hypotheses. Freedom, as described in hypothesis #4, is especially critical for this bundle of concerns.

Freedom, as conceptualized in the theory, integrates self-awareness, decision, action, and responsibility, as this was elaborated on pp. 44–45 above and more fully described in chapter 11. As my reference to Hick suggested, this requires not only that the creation be in a condition of freedom, but also that it shall have chosen to become free. The world, therefore, since it is fundamentally a realm of becoming, is defined not so much by what it has been and is now, but rather by what it can become. Although it is true that God had purposes for the creation from its beginning and that those purposes are in some sense programmed into the creation, the purposes of the creation cannot be extrapolated in any simple manner from the beginnings. The continuities of evolution can be read backwards, but they cannot be predicted in advance. Any given phase or epoch in the world process is incapable of foreseeing or predicting what the epoch subsequent to itself will be.

This characteristic, when considered along with the concept of purposes, renders our perspective eschatological. To the extent that the term *teleology* refers to preprogrammed goals that can be extrapolated from the original programming, we cannot think of the creation as teleological. The manner in which we used the term *teleonomy* in the discussion of the first element (pp. 39–40 above) is eschatologically conditioned, in that it speaks not of purposes that can be derived or predicted from natural structures, but rather speaks of them as consistent with these structures. Indeed, the eschatological perspective is integral to the effort to determine just what the teleonomy of the natural structures and processes is. The theological import of the term *eschatological* affirms that God is able to provide new possibilities and new futures without destroying the life-giving continuities with our origins. In what follows, the discussion will suggest that the eschatological dimension is linked closely with human culture and the brains that generate behavior and culture.

The description of the human being as a two-natured creature, constituted by the symbiosis of genes and culture, enables us to locate the eschatologically structured freedom and co-creatorhood most intensely in the domain of culture. This is true even though the phenomenon of culture has emerged from the matrix of a deterministic system.

In a number of ways, we have spoken in these pages of a tension between the biological and the cultural components of human being. This area of tension is critical to understanding the human and God's will for it, but it points to a complex issue that must be approached with subtlety. It is clear that culture is bound inextricably to the genetic substrate from which it has emerged and with which it co-exists. Culture depends upon the biological survival of its human host. Whatever designs culture has, it must constantly look to the survival requirements set by the genes and the ecosystem in which both genes and culture live. At the same time, culture is also always seeking to determine how far it can stretch genes and ecosystem in order to fulfill what seem from the cultural perspective to be desirable and useful novel ends. With the metaphor *stretch,* I refer to the tendency of culture to create continually new conditions in which the genotype must survive and flourish, conditions that are genuinely novel when compared to the conditions of the past, including those in which the genes originated.

When culture has reached the stage of development that we now witness, this stretching activity looms just as important and necessary for adequate living as the activity of watchful protection over the genetic and ecological substrates. Not only is the stretching a matter of survival in a complex technological society, but it is also necessary for culture's fulfillment of what it perceives as its destiny.

Whatever the human being acts out culturally fully implicates the genetic and ecosystem symbionts. It is human culture that builds bridges and dams, but it is iron ore and clay and lumber that supply the material for them, and it is the terrain with its flora and fauna that are affected by these structures. In this sense, the entirety of the ecosystem and of biological evolution is participant directly or indirectly in the freedom of human culture. The goals and practices of culture, consequently, touch not only upon the purposes and destiny of the human actor, but also those of the entire created order (at least with respect to planet earth).

These considerations ground the suggestion that the purposes for which God has intended the freedom and co-creatorhood of the human species pertain not only to the human being itself, but also to the entirety of the process of evolution and the terrestrial ecosystems. The stretching activity of human culture is ultimately a possible instrumentality for the fulfillment of the divine purposes for both humans and the rest of the created order on earth. This stretching through culture is the nub of the human being's co-creatorhood.

Furthermore, since the human species has emerged from within the deterministic process of evolution and exercises a kind of co-creatorhood within the present planetary ecosystem, that evolutionary process and ecosystem can be said to participate in the freedom of the human being. That being the case, the freedom of the human constitutes a zone wherein the entire creation can be said to participate for better or worse in the outcomes of a more highly evolved freedom. The human being is thus the agent for a new level of the creation's freedom, and an agent that God has raised up. In this context, the significance of my insistence upon the pragmatic criterion becomes obvious, if the vocation of the human being is not to become demonic.

The breadth of the created co-creator theory, particularly in light of the issues raised in this elaboration of the theory's third element, becomes clearer when we consider a number of auxiliary hypotheses that flow from this discussion. Three remaining hypotheses emerge, some of which are obvious from the earlier elaboration of the first two elements.

Hypothesis #7: The challenge that culture poses to human being can be stated thus: Culture is a system of information that humans must construct so as to adequately serve the three tasks of interpreting the world in which humans live, guiding human behavior, and interfacing with the physico-biogenetic cultural systems that constitute the environment in which we live.

This hypothesis is tested by reference to the relevant scientific literature.

Although the insight that culture (or nurture) is an essential co-symbiont in human being is hardly new, it is seldom understood how massive a challenge faces human beings in the formation of their culture. Nor is adequate attention generally given to the fact that the challenge to shape an adequate culture has faced humans since their emergence in the evolutionary processes, at least 100,000 years ago. Consideration of this unique challenge posed by *Homo sapiens'* essential nature as a creature of culture stands at the core of what the created co-creator theory seeks to interpret theologically. It bears a great deal of the weight of the entire theory.

Hypothesis #8: We now live in a condition that may be termed technological civilization. This condition is characterized by the fact that human decision has conditioned virtually all of the planetary physico-biogenetic systems, so that human decision is the critical factor in the continued functioning of the planet's systems.

This hypothesis is tested by reference to the relevant scientific literature.

This hypothesis contains within it several interpretations of contemporary human life on the planet that may at first seem startling. First, it places technology firmly within the evolutionary processes of the universe, recognizing it as a phase of cultural evolution. This in turn makes technology a natural and plausible consequence of the basic nature of *Homo sapiens* as a creature constituted both by genes and culture. Such a placement goes directly counter to prevalent views that conceive of technology in a dualistic and alien relationship to nature, or that place humans and technology in a polarity over against nature. My view holds that both humans and technology are parts of nature. I am fully aware of the great manipulation and destruction that technology exercises over the rest of nature, but I address this critical state of affairs within a nondualistic framework.

Second, by linking technology to the elements of freedom and decision, as these factors are described in other elements of the created co-creator theory, this hypothesis sets technology firmly within the realm of the evolutionary process-become-aware itself, and poses the crisis of technology in terms of its challenge to our self-awareness and our efforts to discern human purpose in the most adequate way. It follows, in this framework, that an adequate view of human purpose is inextricably tied to the view of the planet's future.

Hypothesis #9: Myth and ritual are critical components of the cultural system of information and guidance. They are marked in linguistic form by declarative or imperative discourse, and their concepts are vastly underdetermined by the data of evidence. In light of human evolutionary history, these marks were necessary if culture was to serve its evolutionary function.

This hypothesis is highly speculative, but it can be subjected to scientific scrutiny for blatant errors.

This hypothesis shares with hypothesis #7 a great deal of the interpretive weight of the created co-creator theory. Whereas the assertions of the seventh hypothesis can be elaborated rather persuasively from knowledge that is widely accepted, the ninth is not only highly speculative, but has no possibility of being tested in a satisfactory manner. Its cogency rests on its success in clarifying why primordial elements of religion—myth and ritual and a concern for morality that is rooted in them—are seriously destabilized by secularized scientific knowledge, yet humans all over the world stubbornly refuse to allow myth and ritual to be supplanted in their hearts and minds as a resource for guiding their personal and cultural lives.

This hypothesis provides a framework for understanding the basic function of myth and ritual in human evolutionary history. At the same time it clarifies why destabilization, far from being a surprising development, is a challenge that myth and ritual always confront. Indeed, if myth and ritual are performing their functions in a serious manner, destabilization appears as intrinsic to their character. Furthermore, in the context of the entire created co-creator theory, this hypothesis suggests how religion and science may be interrelated more adequately and more wholesomely. The cogency of this hypothesis is dependent on the credibility of these suggestions.

As with the seventh hypothesis, the canon of fruitfulness attaches itself with particular force to the ninth hypothesis. Precisely because so little empirical material exists that would tell us with certainty about the earliest emergence of myth and ritual, this hypothesis presses us to seek those explanations that are most fruitful for understanding myth and ritual today and for relating them meaningfully and wholesomely to contemporary life. This book's later discussion will focus particularly upon the two features of myth and ritual cited here: that their linguistic forms are those of direct, often imperative, discourse; and that they require us to accept them in the face of far too little empirical justification to make us fully comfortable with them (philosophers term this *underdetermination* by the data).

In light of the foregoing hypothesis, I suggest that *Homo sapiens* is a proposal for the future evolution of the planet. This suggestion is the final outcome of the rejection of dualisms to interpret human beings in their relationship to the rest of nature. Since this statement is intended primarily for heuristic purposes, its testability resides in the judgment whether it is useful for understanding what human being is about.

At this point, the discussion has set forth the range of the created co-creator theory and my hopes for it. There is a fine line between hope and arrogance, and I trust the reader recognizes that I have set forth this grand scheme modestly as an instrument for fruitful exploration, and not as an imperialist claim to have understood all that lies along its frontiers. The following chapters consist of probes, sweeps of the searchlight over a poorly lit stage, that in part indicate what sort of substantiation might be invoked for the theory of the created co-creator and in part elaborate what sorts of explorations it calls for. These chapters are not conceived as linear elaborations that enable the argument to move in a direct line toward conclusive demonstration of what has been set forth in this chapter. Rather, this chapter can be considered to be the hub, from which the succeeding chapters are spokes radiating outwards. Whether the whole forms a coherent wheel depends upon whether it stimulates fruitful further thought in ways that will give the structure mobility.

Part 2

Nature

3

Nature as the Matrix of Being Human

There is a feeling the body gives the mind
of having missed something, a bedrock poverty, like
falling

without the sense that you are passing through one
world,
that you could reach another
anytime. Instead the real
is crossing you,

your body an arrival
you know is false but can't outrun. And somewhere
in between
these geese forever entering and
these spiders turning back,

this astonishing delay, the everyday, takes place.
(Graham 1980)

In her poem "The Geese," of which these lines are the conclusion, Jorie Graham describes her experience when one day as she was hanging out the wash she noted that geese were flying overhead and spiders were working in the yard around her spinning their webs. She seems to be making the point that our minds have the capacity to deceive us, to miss something that is important about our own human nature. What the mind misses, the body reminds us of: Our lives are not so much a traveling through nature's space and time, as if we were making progress on a journey or conquering obstacles in our way towards a destination that is important to us, as they are stations on a journey whose traveler is something that transcends us, and for whom still more stations lie beyond us. We are not so much moving through and over nature, as we are natural creatures who represent a discrete station on nature's way. We are not sovereign over nature, but rather an occasion within nature's sovereignty.

Joseph Sittler (1904–1987) made this same point from an explicit theological perspective when he expressed his belief that the challenge of our times comes in the necessity to understand human history within the context of the history of nature. His generation of theologians, as well as my own, was nurtured on the insistence that sacred history (we called it *Heilsgeschichte*) was more real than secular or natural history. Sittler urges us to recognize that natural history is the matrix in which human history, including those narratives that we consider to be sacred, transpires.

Jorie Graham makes the point in her striking image that we are not passing over or through the world and its history, as the Vespuccis and the Pizarros and the Cabots triumphantly crossed the seas in their search for conquest and empire. Reality, rather, is crossing us. We are not riding on Chicago's Jackson Park elevated train, passing station after station on the way to O'Hare International Airport, where we will take wing for a flight into the wild blue yonder. Rather, we are a station through which the tracks run, through which the real passes. Our bodies are an arrival, which may be false, in the sense that it is neither permanent nor the whole, but it nevertheless cannot be outrun. And the mind should know this, since it is pinned firmly to the body by the webs of biochemistry, limbic tissue, and neocortex.

Sittler recognized that these issues were not only the object of scientific and philosophical-theological import, but that they have taken residence in the perceptions and sensibilities of our common life. He tried to convey this sense with his concept of *life-world,* which he defined thus:

> I do not just mean interiority but the multiple contacts with the world outside whereby the interior is enriched and questioned and opened up and refined, the world of literature, social fact, political life, urban life, the rise of science and its child, technology, the quick-food world of McDonald's, the quick-satisfaction world of the entertainment industry, the mechanized processes of the state education, the whole mass culture in which my children have grown up. I mean by "life-world," then, everything that impacts upon the organism as sensation and invitation. (1978, 30)

He saw the life-world of our time impinging upon his children, for example, when he reflected on the differences between his childhood geography book ("which I dearly loved") and his daughter's fifth-grade geography text. His textbook taught him about "how many sheep are raised in Australia and how much wheat was gathered in North Dakota." Hers began with an opening chapter on the galaxies. "She started with a picture of nature which was cosmic in scope; I started with Australia and North Dakota and where that stuff out of which they make Shredded Wheat comes from" (1978, 32).

Sittler phrased his large conclusion from this vignette in this way:

> So the natural world is now a second huge dimension of contemporary reflection. . . . Since 1900, the world as nature has occupied the mind of modernity as much as or more than the world of history. . . . The life-world that characterizes our time and to which an adequate christology must be proposed includes both the world as nature and the world as history. I would suggest that so does the biblical world. The biblical thinker goes from reflection on nature ("when I regard the heavens, the work of thy fingers, the moon and the stars which thou hast ordained") to a historical reflection ("what is man?"). Our time has a scope of reflection that includes both the world of nature and the world of history, but we know much more about nature than the psalmist did. (1978, 31–32)

To speak of the human being's relatedness to the rest of nature is in some respects a platitude, but it has received far less attention than it deserves, particularly in the shaping of our philosophical and religious concepts. We must internalize this insight in the deepest way possible, and when we do, it radically rearranges our understanding of what it means to be human. Nowhere is this rearrangement more dramatic than in the realm of theological understandings. Sittler knew that substantial biblical and theological foundation exists for considering the appearance and continuation of the human species as events of the same process as nature's history. In one sense, the theory of the created co-creator is an elaboration of Sittler's insight.

Nature as Ambience For Understanding Humans

The first four auxiliary hypotheses outlined in chapter 2 focus upon the determinative impact of nature for our attempts to understand who and what we are as humans. These hypotheses are:

#1: Integral to *Homo sapiens* and its evolutionary history are certain structures and processes, the requirements for whose functioning may be said to constitute, at least in a tentative way, goals and purposes for human life.

#2: The meaning and purpose of human beings are conceived in terms of their placement within natural processes and their contribution to those same processes.

#3: A concept of "wholesomeness" is both unavoidable and useful as criterion governing the behavior of human beings within their natural ambience, as they consider what their contribution to nature should be.

#4: Nature is the medium through which the world, including human beings, receives knowledge, as well as grace.

The first hypothesis, the teleonomic axiom, points to the most fundamental claim that the created co-creator theory makes. The theory proposes an image that speaks of the meaning and purpose of human being, correlated to *Homo sapiens'* natural constitution, within its environment on planet earth. Turned on its head, this axiom proposes that humans cannot be properly understood apart from a knowledge of the natural structures and processes in which they have emerged and which constitute their natural character, and that it is possible to hypothesize human meaning and purpose from an understanding of this character.

This hypothesis flies in the face of at least three kinds of conventional objections.

The first is the deep-seated notion that religious concepts of human meaning and purpose derive from otherworldly sources of revelation rather than from within nature itself. To this, I respond that whatever assumes the status of religious revelation must now be conceived as knowledge that emerges from nature and whose content is about nature.

The second objection flows from the conventional interpretation of the so-called naturalistic fallacy, which holds that one cannot move from the *is* to the *ought,* from statements of description to prescription. To this, I respond that the naturalistic fallacy understood in any simple way is no longer tenable (Katz 1980; Hefner 1981). The philosophical, as well as the scientific, discussions of the last twenty years have dramatically recast the is/ought issue. The teleonomic axiom does not involve crass, unreflective moves from is to ought, but rather speaks in tentative and careful ways of both the possibility and the necessity to make such moves.

The third objection comes from those who deny that universal statements concerning human beings are possible. So-called postmodern perspectives, including relativistic or cultural-linguistic hermeneutic approaches to local communities, refuse to engage in discussion of cross-cultural, universal ideas. To this objection, I argue that the denial of universals is itself an example of a careless universal statement. On the contrary, every statement that claims to be more than particular must be tested on a case-by-case basis against solid empirical studies. Of course, many pretenders to universal validity will thereby be disqualified. However, when we carry out such testing, we discover that a great deal of empirical knowledge has been accumulated about human beings that is cross-cultural and cross-epochal in its reach and that meets the standards of rigorous methodological scrutiny.

Human Being—More than Cultural Creature

In a nutshell, the created co-creator theory argues teleonomically as follows: Our thinking about the meaning and purpose of human being proceeds from the observation that the evolutionary processes themselves have given rise to a creature characterized by self-awareness, decision-making, action, and self-assessment based on the reception of complex feedbacks. This emergence is enabled in large part by the evolved central nervous system that characterizes *Homo sapiens*. It is this human creature, thus formed, that is the prime creature of culture on our planet—at least to this point in time.

If we are to correlate our thinking about human purpose to the nature—the dynamics and structures—of the human being, we must focus upon the natural characteristics as those just described. That focus will draw attention to both the culture-creating capacities that distinctively human characteristics make possible and necessary and also to the matrix of natural processes in which humans have emerged. Therefore, however we conceive of human purpose and meaning, our conceptions will, according to the teleonomic axiom, have to pertain in a central fashion to human nature as it comes to expression in the capacities for and the behaviors of culture-creating and culture-enacting.

The premise underlying this train of thought consists of the belief that the emergence of natural structures and processes is not in vain. If there is purpose and meaning to human or any other being, it will be continuous with the natural equipment that has been provided to that being. For the human being, this natural equipment points in the direction of the created co-creator; that is the heart of the theory. The basic assumption that makes the teleonomic axiom possible is the burden borne chiefly by the first auxiliary hypothesis. This assumption itself is scarcely falsifiable, but the matter of whether there is a fit between the concept of the created co-creator and the natural equipment of the human being is definitely subject to testing. If the fit is not clear to many persons, then the concept and the statements of purpose that might be derived from it are rendered dubious.

It is here, in connection with elaboration of the first hypothesis, that the reader gets a glimpse of how the author's belief in God makes its impact upon the created co-creator theory. I hold to no detailed philosophically elaborated concept of God, such as marks certain other theological approaches. Rather I speak of what difference it makes for us to speak of God and to confess faith in God. I prefer to clarify what difference belief in God makes, rather than to pretend that I possess some rigorously formed concept that really applies to God.

As long ago as 1970 I argued that belief in God impinges upon us most strongly by shaping what we believe about nature and how we talk about it (1970, 13–16). The assumption that the emergence of natural structures and processes is not in vain is my way of affirming God and also showing what difference it makes to introduce God into the discussion. It would be impossible to account for the inherent worthfulness of the natural processes apart from the affirmation of ultimacy that is grounded in God or in the equivalent of God (Ogden 1966, 1–71). Furthermore, it would make no sense to speak of meaning and purpose attaching to the natural processes, nor to speak of those purposes teleonomically, apart from the grounding that this belief finds in ultimacy or God.

Culture Entwined with Nature

Particularly in the second and third elements of the theory (auxiliary hypotheses 5–6), where the emphasis is upon self-awareness, decision, action, freedom, and culture, the creative initiatives of human being will be the center of the theory's attention. The nub of the argument in the context of the second hypothesis, however, is this: inasmuch as the information necessary to construct the human being, as well as the actual processes of development and the environment in which humans have arisen, are what we call the realm of nature, whatever humans do in their culture-creating and culture-enacting must be referred to the natural order that is their source and ambience. The purpose of human being, consequently, is directed to the rest of the natural realm.

This conclusion may well be the most far-reaching one in this book in its rearrangement of the images that govern our perceptions both of human purpose and of the relationships between humans and the rest of nature. Those whose images are grounded in religious belief often think of human purposes in terms of obedience to God and God's will, in a manner that directs human efforts away from the natural world in favor of what they perceive as a God-ward direction. To this proposal, I suggest that the circumstances of human creation and development would seem to imply that God's will for us humans transpires within the larger realm of the divine will for the entire natural order, as creation.

Others, including those who ground their beliefs in religion as well as non-theistic humanists, may image human purpose in ways that emphasize the up-building of the human community—love, justice, peace, and the extension of basic human rights. Because much of our thinking rests on a dualism between humans and the rest of nature, this concern for the human community has tended to be either indifferent toward the natural order or downright hostile toward it. Against this point of view, I argue that whatever it means for humans to find fulfillment, which certainly includes love, justice, peace, and the like, that fulfillment must be defined within the larger framework of the natural order.

Whatever our understanding of human being and its culture-creating, culture-enacting character is, the second auxiliary hypothesis insists that that character is intended to benefit the natural order in which human beings emerge and live out their careers. The direction God-ward leads us reflexively to nature.

The Pragmatic Criterion

The preceding commentary on the first two hypotheses raises the question of what criterion is most adequate for guiding our discernment of human purpose, placed as it is within the natural order. This is a large and complex issue, and in this book, admittedly, I do not discuss it in any elaborate fashion. Many other thinkers are engaged in such reflection (Engel and Engel 1990; Kaufman 1985; K. Peters 1992; Rolston 1987). What does seem clear, however, is that the criterion will have to focus, at the formal level, upon what is beneficial to nature. This in turn means that the criterion will have to be a pragmatic one in the sense that it will have to be empirically discernible as in some manner beneficial. Criteria that are clearly indifferent to benefiting nature or actually harmful are thereby falsified. For my purposes here, I speak generally of this criterion under the rubric of *wholesomeness*.

Nature as Ambience of Knowledge and Grace

The fourth auxiliary hypothesis is, from one perspective, simply a truism and an obvious derivation from the preceding hypotheses. For scientists and many others, it is a commonplace that nature provides us with knowledge. It is not so common for us, even for many scientists, to accept that the human mind, the knowing subject, is also an entity of nature (Hefner 1987a, 145–48). The astrophysicists Bernard Lovell and John Wheeler have spoken of the emergence of the human mind as a cosmological event (Rolston 1987, 168–69). Scientists recognize that the natural world is a rich repository of information. Philosophers and other thinkers influenced by Charles Darwin speak of evolutionary epistemology, thereby describing the emergence of the human mind, its processes of knowing, and the significance of its knowledge as part of nature's evolution (K. Peters 1982, 392–97; Richards 1987, 574–93).

These interpretations rule out any dualistic thinking that would separate knowledge and nature. They rather help us to understand that our knowledge is part of nature's process of understanding itself. The physician and popular writer Lewis Thomas has used the vivid image of humans as the eyes and advance guard of the planet. A century before, Gerard Manley Hopkins, Irish Jesuit and poet, wrote in his poem "Ribblesdale":

> And what is Earth's eye, tongue, or heart else, where,
> Else, but in dead and dogged man? (1953, 52)

These lines are the climax of a soliloquy on nature's unrivaled capacity to be ("Thou canst but be, but that thou well dost"), rendered poignant by its inability to speak or to be aware of itself, except in and through *Homo sapiens*.

Religious thought has an especially difficult time recognizing that its knowledge has emerged within the history of nature and represents a form of nature's own coming-to-knowledge. The greater our understanding of how the human central nervous system has emerged and evolved into its human form, however, and how this system interacts with its natural environment at every step of its development, the more we are impressed with the very natural character of the mind and its knowledge. Critical philosophies of the past two centuries, including those of Karl Marx, Ludwig Feuerbach, Sigmund Freud, and the Frankfurt

School of Sociology, make the same point, and they are augmented by our growing recognition of the impact of gender and culture upon our mind and its
knowledge (Jay 1973).

For some, these observations about the natural character of mind and knowledge seem to demean religious knowledge and render knowledge of God impossible. Even though such conclusions are not justified, we must nevertheless recognize that even our cherished revelation is knowledge that is thoroughly
conditioned by nature.

We may have even greater difficulty acknowledging that nature is a medium
of grace. However, we must recognize that the self—its values and preservation—and its community relationships are natural phenomena; they have
emerged within nature's history and within an environing context of nature.
Most of what we commonly conceive of as grace, whether in religious terms or
not, pertains in some way to the correction, regeneration, redirection, or fulfillment of the self and its communities. Furthermore, the criteria for our discernment of what is authentically gracious are inevitably and indissolubly related to
self and community.

To say this is not to overlook that those criteria are also eschatologically conditioned; that is, they must focus on the as-yet-unrealized possibilities of self and
community as much as they concentrate on present conditions. An example of
this relatedness is the set of ideas associated with Christian belief in eternity and
life after death. No matter how strongly we speak of transformation and of our
inability to know about the hereafter, we are thoroughly convinced that redemption and eternal life refer to the selves and to the communities that we know in
our earthly life. These selves and communities—and also the characteristics that
we consider constitutive of their essential properties, such as love, relationships
of intimacy, and the characteristics of the church—are entities that have evolved
within nature and are deeply conditioned by such natural factors as genotype,
social processes, and gender.

Perhaps I can put this point most simply thus: that upon which God bestows
grace and that which God redeems for eternal life is that which God has created
through natural processes. If we take the full measure of these insights, then we
must conclude that knowledge and grace are in no way an escape from nature,
but rather are in themselves natural happenings and critical elements of what
nature is and can become. When we bring our religious faith and our concepts
of God to such reflections, then we must pour whatever significance that faith
and those concepts have into the earthen vessels of our nature. The most important thing we can say about our faith and belief in God is that they require us
to believe that nature is indeed a realm of grace.

4

Nature as God's Great Project

God, human beings, and the rest of nature. . . . This triad has inspired a vast conversation over the centuries, a conversation that has been limited neither to our own epoch nor to our own culture. The chief pivots of concern in this conversation have been: How should humans understand their relation to nature? Are we or are we not a part of that nature? How should our understanding of this relationship influence our behavior in the world? How does God relate to the world? What does God intend the relationship to be between humans and the rest of nature? In the Western religions especially, the question has arisen whether the painful position that humans hold in a natural world that often seems to be uncaring is not itself the most cogent argument against the existence of God.

Richard Wilbur, a former U.S. Poet Laureate, has reflected upon this theme at some length. In one of his shorter poems, "A Problem from Milton," dating from the 1950s, he suggests that whereas in the Garden of Eden the rest of nature goes its course, unthinking and with apparent zest, Adam drives himself to distraction in his effort to understand how he should behave and why.

> In Eden palm and open-handed pine
> Displayed to God and man their flat perfection. . . .
> And yet the streams in mazy error went;
> Powdery flowers a potent odor gave. . . .
> The builded comber like a hurdling horse
> Achieves the rocks. With wild informal roar,
> The spray upholds its freedom and its force. . . .
>
> Poor Adam, deviled by your energy,
> What power egged you on to feed your brains?
> Envy the gorgeous gallops of the sea,
> Whose horses never know their lunar reins.
> (Wilbur 1988, 311)

"Flat perfection" characterizes the natural world apart from humans, because everything in that world goes its way unreflectively, unaware of whatever reins might govern its motions. It is humans who are the "deviled" creatures, and the devilment is connected with their brains. As reflective creatures, they have to ask questions of why, questions of meaning, questions of where the reins really are and what they signify for the ways humans ought to live. The devilment that besets the human race grows out of our tendency to ask these larger questions, to fly to the heaven of ultimate meaning, when that flight to heaven turns out to be hell for us.

In another poem, entitled "Mind," Wilbur likens the mind to a bat that can fly all alone in a cavern.

> It has no need to falter or explore;
> Darkly it knows what obstacles are there,
> And so may weave and flitter, dip and soar
> In perfect courses through the blackest air.

But he realizes that his simile of mind to bat is not as perfect as the bat's sensors in the cave unless he adds something.

> The mind is like a bat. Precisely. Save
> That in the very happiest intellection
> A graceful error may correct the cave.
> (Wilbur 1988, 240)

The bat's perfection, like that of the palm and pine and ocean wave, lies in its unreflective accommodation to what it can do within the confines of its environment. The human mind also seeks accommodation, but with the added dimension that at certain moments of both competence and graceful probing, even when its creativity errs and the mind mistakes what the environment's reins would require, that error may alter the environment in ways that render both the mind's probing and the cavern more perfect. This lucky fit—despite its resulting from a "mistake," or because of it?—Wilbur calls "the very happiest intellection."

The Human Niche

In their present condition, so overnourished are their brains that Adam and Eve face the monumental challenge of discerning the reins that determine human life, where they are and what they require. This is not first of all a question of what will serve the biological perpetuation of the species. Rather it is essentially a question of niche: Where do humans fit? What are the requirements and the possibilities of their niche? Discerning just what can constitute Wilbur's "happiest intellection" has become a question of our being or nonbeing, and thereby the question qualifies as thoroughly theological.

Fully Natural

The sciences provide us with a relentlessly vivid message concerning how humans are related to nature: We are constituted by natural processes that have preceded us, we have emerged within the career of nature's evolving processes, and we bear the indelible marks of those processes. In short, we are indissolubly part of nature, fully natural. At this late date in the twentieth century, the point surely does not require belaboring. In previous decades, it was chiefly the poets and philosophers who spoke of a unitary process of evolution that stretches from the formation of the universe (perhaps in what is termed the Big Bang) through cosmic history to planet earth, the emergence of DNA, the emergence and unfolding of human culture, and on into the future. Before the end of our century, it is likely that the scientists will have put together that picture of evolution.

What are the chief learnings that can be derived from the sciences concerning the relationship of human beings to the rest of nature? First, we recognize that nature has a history, and we owe both the fact and the form of our present existence to that history. The model of kinship is appropriate for representing this intense interrelationship (Ode, 1994). The concept of kinship points not so much to our sibling relationship with the ecosphere, but rather to our primary continuity with nature's processes, and our origin and future within nature.

The pertinent metaphors here are drawn not so much from ecology as from genetic kinship. The elements that comprise the periodic table we all learned in high school, and which also form the building blocks of our own bodies, were produced in previous epochs of the universe's history, many of them in the monster furnaces of the galaxies. The concreteness that defines us bears the marks of life's pilgrimage on our planet. *Bricolage*—constructing new things from the materials at hand—is evident throughout the biosphere. Whether we note the formation of jawbones from antecedent gill slits or the triune structure of the human brain that contains within itself the neurological ancestry of reptiles and ancient mammals, it is stunningly clear that human being is a segment of a process that can be related reasonably, on the basis of empirical observation, to the whole of nature. When we add the testimony of genetics and the results of nucleotide sequence comparisons, including those that deal with mitochondrial DNA, the sense of our kinship within one human community and with the higher primates is rendered intense indeed.

Alongside the image of kinship, we are also aware of the ecological model for representing the intense interrelatedness between humans and the web of the natural ecosystems in which we live. This model describes the structure of how we live with our natural kin. In some ways this is a simpler and more graspable image, particularly since the delicate balance and interweaving of the many factors that make our continued existence possible on the planet becomes more vivid to us every day. Negatively, the dangers of disrupting this balance are also susceptible to vivid representation. Even though we presently still have not taken it with enough seriousness, our current thinking gives more attention to the ecological model. It is often a more palatable image than that of kinship, because it is less intense. It can be understood (though inadequately) as consisting only of external relations between us and the rest of nature, whereas the image of kinship insists upon a decisively internal relatedness.

On the basis of these scientific perspectives, there can be little doubt that *Homo sapiens* is nature's creature. How are we related to the rest of nature? We flourish only within an intimate ecological fabric, and within the relationships of that fabric, we are kin to the other citizens of nature's society. Our interrelatedness is best conceptualized according to the model of genetic relatedness. Nature's processes have produced us, we are constituted by our inheritance from its past, and we live in the ambience of its creative balances today. There is a kind of nonnegotiability to the message that science delivers on this point. Our kinship with nature is not a matter of our preference, nor is it an issue that calls for our acquiescence. It simply is.

Struggling to Find Our Fit

Against the background of what our scientific understandings tell us, it seems strange that the fundamental problem of our time is that we do not know where we fit into nature, nor how our patterns of living can be creative and also harmonious with the rhythms of the rest of nature. In those cases where we do have a glimpse of how the indicative of our kinship with nature is to be translated into imperative, we often resist and choose to go in different directions that seem to offer greater pleasure.

As powerful as the knowledge and the experience of our belonging to nature is, we struggle with that belonging. We are creatures of culture, those learned patterns of behaving and understanding whereby we create the world views and mores that literally put our worlds together and tell us where we fit. Our culture, enabled by our brains, rooted in our consciousness, and adapted to our bodies and their genetic evolution, does not allow us to exist as Richard Wilbur's "gorgeous gallops of the sea, whose horses never know their lunar reins." In the main, we have to discover those reins, clothe them in our own symbols, investigate them, define their bounds and their possibilities, and then decide how we want to relate to them.

Our lack of proper fit with nature rests finally in this essential aspect of our character: We have to discover what our kin in nature know by genetic programming. We distance ourselves from nature's laws through our symbol-making tendencies. We insist that what other citizens of our ecosystem must receive as imperative, we can treat as hypothesis to be tested and manipulated. The bat takes the cavern's walls of stone as absolutes to be observed; the human mind takes those same walls as proposals for negotiation and proceeds to compose a list of demands for presentation. And the process of negotiation is always accompanied by a significant degree of human error and lack of understanding.

What we are experiencing today is that we are poor negotiators; we have not understood what proposals we ought to make. We are largely inept in carrying out "the very happiest intellection" that can allow us freedom and yet gracefully correct the cave to our benefit and that of the rest of nature as well. Consequently we exercise our kinship poorly, whether it be with our fellow human beings or the rest of nature.

The Problem of Culture and Symbols

Some people believe that the symbol systems that offer the most wholesome expression of our relatedness to the rest of nature are primitive or ancient ones, those that derive from Stone Age people and the native American religions of North and South America. Most of these ancient attempts, however—as well as many more recent ones—are seriously flawed. They have not been rendered in forms that are credible and serious options for contemporary living, they are limited in scope, and they are ineffectual in comparison with the less wholesome, prevailing images and symbol systems that speak of our relations with nature. These prevailing symbol systems derive from our Hebrew-Christian traditions, as well as from our secular wisdom. Instead of relatedness and kinship, they speak of our responsibility for nature as its stewards or masters, and of the possibilities nature presents to us for exercising our creative abilities and propensities to re-shape it, to make it conform to us and serve us. In the main, humans have sym-bolized their work upon nature as furthering its development and improving it, thus placing the weight of the good on the side of *doing unto* nature rather than accepting a place *within* it.

The primary instrument by which humans act upon the rest of nature is cul-ture, which is in effect a learned and symbolic system of information and guid-ance for behavior that must supplement the programs of information and guidance that genetic evolution has bequeathed to the human species (Burhoe 1981, chaps. 6, 7). Culture is a rich and manifold system of information that includes many facets; here I can speak only in general terms that will ignore the differentiated aspects of culture and their dynamics.

To speak more specifically, the confusion and out-of-kilteredness between hu-mans and the rest of nature centers in our inability to discover the proper correla-tion between these two systems of information and guidance, the genetic and cultural. The cultural system is the locus of the difference between the human mind and Wilbur's bat. Just as the genetic system can be our undoing when it guides us in maladaptive directions, so the cultural system can work at direct odds with the welfare of humans and the rest of nature. Clearly, our principal challenge is that of interrelating our genetic and cultural systems of information within the configuration of our present bio-sociocultural environment. The relationship of religion and science plays out within this framework of putting the question (Csikszentmihalyi 1987, 1991).

Alienation From Nature as Sin

In the West, both critical secular reason and the Hebrew-Jewish-Christian religious traditions tell us that the lack of fit with nature is wrong, dangerous, and profoundly unnatural.

The voices of critical secular reason are obvious all around. They drive the discussion of the so-called environmental crisis, at the level of science, technology, personal lifestyle, and government planning. Western thinking greatly favors what I called earlier the ecological model for relating humans and the rest of nature. Where we acknowledge this relatedness, we prefer it to be an external quality, thereby rendering it as nonessential to our being as possible. We call nature our home, the house in which we live; we speak of our dependency upon nature, in the sense that it provides what we need for life.

On the basis of these images, we like to think of humans as caretakers, stewards, creative dominators with respect to nature. These images do not carry the weight that kinship does. The kinship image suggests that we are part of nature, not on the basis of external relations, but in the internal sense; we are a segment of nature's own processes, and those processes have inwardly shaped us. The concepts of *bricolage* and the conclusions drawn from nucleotide sequence comparisons, including mitochondrial DNA comparisons, are not adequately imaged by models that emphasize external relations; they require the more emphatic images that arise when we speak of kinship and genetic interrelationship.

The religious traditions are also powerful, if ambiguous, in their insistence that to be misfit within nature is wrong. The story of Adam, Eve, and the serpent speaks of a flaw that cuts right through the fundamental character of the human creature. Adam's apple-eating is often interpreted as original sin in the sense of the first or initial sin that has condemned us all, and many people correctly reject this as an impossible myth. More profoundly, a millennia-long tradition also exists that interprets original sin as that which accompanies our origins, our very emergence as humans. We may term this the fall into personhood, as Paul Tillich (1957a, 29–43) does.

Or we may focus, as Ralph Wendell Burhoe has, upon the inherent conflict within us between the information inherited from our prehuman evolutionary past that governs our genetic constitution and the cultural information that our brains make possible (1981, 65, 201–28). The prehuman programming animates Wilbur's palm and pine that are coiled in flat perfection, and also the built comber whose horses never know their lunar reins, whereas the brain-based cultural programming always asks whether our destiny is not rather to become like God.

Donald T. Campbell's theories pit the selfish, genetically programmed, and competitive individuals against our complex social forms that require altruism and cooperation if they are to work (1975, 1976). Much of our sin may also be charged to the fallibility and vulnerability of our mental equipment—we do crash into the wall of the cave on occasion, with terrible results for ourselves and others, even for succeeding generations.

Whatever other explanations may be at hand, the religious interpretations in the ancient traditions of the book of Genesis express the essential sin in images that often include humanity's being out of kilter with the rest of nature: "cursed is the ground because of you; in toil you shall eat of it all the days of your life." Such images include the pain of child-bearing, the enmity between humans and snakes (Gen. 3:14–19), and in a most startling manner, the action of God in the covenant with Noah to form a pact with nature that will protect the earth against humans, the imagination of whose hearts is evil from their youth (Gen. 8:20–22).

In the teachings of Jesus in the Sermon on the Mount, with its amazing insistence that God metes out justice and love in the natural processes, we encounter a quintessentially religious perspective on nature. Jesus chides his listeners for not being in close enough touch with the natural world to perceive the love enacted in its processes. The birds of the air, the lilies of the field, the grass that flourishes and then dies are examples, not of an impersonal natural law, but rather of how God blesses the entire creation (Matt. 6:25–31). The rain and the sunshine that fall upon the just and unjust alike are models for how we should direct our love toward all persons, friend and enemy (Matt. 5:43–48). Such fragments of our tradition have proven to be so confounding that we scarcely even discuss them as the straightforward maxims they appear to be in the original texts of the New Testament.

Domination

Neither the secular nor the religious traditions, however, give us adequate help in assimilating the nonnegotiable message of the sciences that we are part and parcel of nature.

Our secular understandings by and large inculcate within us the sense that being "natural" or "only nature" is too little for creatures of our capabilities and attainments. The secular spirit prizes human beings for what they can do with nature, how they can manipulate and "develop" it.

The two great social philosophies of the twentieth century—democratic capitalism and communist socialism—both value persons on the basis of what they produce and what they consume, in materialist terms. Production is conceived in terms of what can be done with the natural resources at hand, and consumption is synonymous with how much of the human products can be taken out of nature and put into human possession so as to enable the possessor to live a life as unlike the natural world as possible.

Our rituals of cosmetizing the living and the dead—which have spawned and supported two considerable industries—represent our fear of being only natural creatures. Technology speaks powerfully of a sense that leaving nature in its pre-human state is somehow a betrayal of human genius. With our technology we continually redesign our current artifacts, thereby rendering every previous achievement obsolete. We then proceed to make the current design essential to our lifestyle, leaving the natural state always farther behind.

In contrast to secular traditions, Western religious traditions are more ambivalent about nature (Santmire 1985, esp. chaps. 1 and 10, pp. 216–19). They have most often been interpreted to be harmonious with the secular spirit; for example, the exalted sense of human status as expressed in Psalm 8:

> What are human beings that you
> are mindful of them . . . ?
> Yet you have made them a little
> lower than God,
> and crowned them with glory
> and honor.
> You have given them dominion
> over the works of your hands;
> you have put all things under
> their feet.

This Psalm verse echoes the creature who in the first chapter of Genesis was created in the image of God and given dominion over all things. Islam holds similar traditions, which may be summarized under the phrase, "God is, and man is his caliph" (Cragg 1968, chap. 2). Nature belongs to God, and it exists for humans in their effort to serve God (Rahman 1980, 78–79).

In addition, Western religious traditions include perspectives on life that can be interpreted dualistically, urging upon us the view that our destiny lies not in nature's world of flesh, but in some other world of the spirit. These traditions are represented in substantial numbers of individuals and communities who have graced the pages of history prior to and after the first century of the common era. These communities have in effect questioned whether the natural order and its viability should even be given consideration when our final destiny is to be with God, quite independently of our natural life on planet earth. Better to burn, if that hastens the journey into Abraham's bosom.

In contradistinction to these traditions that discourage us from identifying our career with nature's history, others lay the basis for understandings that God's historical work with humans is articulated within the larger history of nature (Sittler 1978, 30–32). At best, however, these traditions attain only an ambivalence toward humans as kin with the rest of nature. We read, for example, in Psalm 90:

> You turn humankind back to dust,
>   and say, "Turn back, you mortals."
> For a thousand years in your sight
>   are like yesterday when it is past,
>   or like a watch in the night.
> You sweep them away; they are like a dream,
>   like grass that is renewed in the morning;
> in the morning it flourishes and is renewed;
>   in the evening it fades and withers.

In the Psalmist's context, this naturalness of the human is a cause for puzzlement and anxiety. In Jesus' Sermon on the Mount, we are asked to understand that our career, no less than that of the transient grass, is the object of God's concern and love.

Equally venerable traditions speak of our kinship with nature—for example, the Jewish liturgies, particularly the recital of the Kiddush and the sense of the Sabbath as depicting not simply rest and recreation, but the harmony that exists primordially between Yahweh, humans, and the rest of creation. Humans join the rest of nature in being God's possession (Hertz 1975, 108–9).

Some Islamic scholars speak of all of nature as *muslim*, that is, as being within the fundamental structures operating as God created and intended; human free will is to extend this natural *islam* by volition in a way that nature cannot (Cragg, 1968, 34, 38–39; Rahman 1980, 65). Nature and the Qur'an thus bear the same message (Rahman 1980, 71). The notion of human kinship with the rest of nature is suggested in the words of a contemporary Islamic philosopher, Seyyed Hossein Nasr:

> In fact man is the channel of grace for nature; through his active participation in the spiritual world he casts light into the world of nature. He is the mouth through which nature breathes and lives. . . . Man sees in nature what he is himself and penetrates into the inner meaning of nature only on the condition of being able to delve into the inner depths of his own being and to cease to live merely on the periphery of his being. Men who live only on the surface of their being can study nature as something to be manipulated and dominated. But only he who has turned toward the inward dimension of his being can see nature as a symbol, as a transparent reality and come to know and understand it in the real sense. (Nasr 1968, 96)

The second chapter of Genesis pictures the human being in terms of dust that has received the spirit or breath of God. A substantial segment of the Christian tradition has taken this as a model for conceiving of God's work throughout the natural realm. Sacraments have been defined as natural things with the addition of the spirit or promise of God. One may read from this definition in either direction: that human being is the paradigm for conceiving how God is present throughout nature and history, or that humans fit under the sacramental paradigm that applies to all of nature. Christian understandings of the Holy Spirit have often moved in the same direction. The Spirit hovers over the waters at creation, just as it gives life to the desert plants and animals, raises up charismatic leaders, accompanies the birth of the Savior, and is poured out upon entire communities.

Although these traditions still lack precise conceptual expression, they do predispose us to receive the scientific suggestions that *Homo sapiens* is to be understood as part of nature's process, not only ecologically, but in terms of kinship with all that has appeared within the processes of nature's evolution. However, at best, they are balanced with the traditions that speak rather dualistically of human being as a different order from the rest of nature. Our traditions are genuinely ambivalent.

The Islamic sense that nature represents the words or *logoi* of God—that there is a "parallel (or even identity) between the revelation of the Qur'an and the creation of the universe" (Rahman 1980, 71)—may serve to characterize our situation today with respect to understanding how humans are intended to relate to the rest of nature. The sciences bear nature's message that we literally stand in kin-relationship, in terms of our origins, to all living things. Put in nonreligious terms, our deficiency lies in our inability to understand either the fundamental indicative or imperative of that message. We are unable to relate that message to the most basic values of human life. In religious terms, our deficit lies in the fact that we cannot represent to ourselves how the scientific message of our kinship with nature can qualify as the logos, the word, of God.

The challenge to our discernment is clear. To understand our kinship with nature, that we are part of nature's process and that our niche is within that process, and to discern the fundamental significance of that kinship would be to make both a constructive and a prophetic contribution to the soul and mind of our culture that is painfully needed. Such discernment would be constructive, because it would at least set the stage for thinking through some of the greatest dilemmas that face us. It would be healing to a culture whose political confusion and social trauma are exacerbated because it is not certain why its spirit hurts. Such discernment would be prophetic, because it unmasks the ignorance and arrogance that reinforce our unwillingness to see our niche as part of nature's process.

Knowledge that Serves Life

In order to qualify as knowledge that genuinely serves life, our discernment of our niche as part of nature's process will have to give expression to a number of basic considerations.

1. This knowledge will have to teach us how to talk about ourselves as intrinsically part of the processes of nature. We speak uncertainly because we fear that being part of nature's processes will diminish us. We misconceive that the distinctively human will be reduced to the prehuman.

Here Nasr's insights are necessary, that penetrating into the inner meaning of nature and our relation to it requires that we delve into the inner depths of our being at the same time (1968, 96). We are what the processes of nature can and have become. We are to be construed as part of nature's probing to determine just what it can become. This does not diminish the creativity that marks the human creature in its cultural dimensions, but it rather clarifies what the creativity is and what its natural function is. Nature is illumined as much when we scrutinize and gain insight into what it has become in *Homo sapiens* as when, conversely, we seek to understand human being by studying nonhuman nature. Our knowledge of nature, far from diminishing human nature to the laws of biochemistry, illuminates the significance of nature as the progenitor of *Homo sapiens*, who in this context we would want to name as the diviner of ultimate meanings within the natural processes.

2. We must understand that what we are, what we do, and what we aim for as humans is to be referred to the processes of nature and to their future. Our very existence illumines what the processes of nature can become, precisely because we truly are what the processes of nature have become. We must begin to recognize that that is our chief significance as creatures and the most decisive guideline for the motivation and directing of our actions. A great transformation in our conception of values must take place in this connection, because we do not generally consider the enhancement of nature's processes to be an adequate object of our motivations and actions. A decidedly noninstrumental valuation of nature is called for.

Jesus' life and death as the church interprets them serve as a model at this point. His life and death were not instrumental to his gaining any particular value for himself. They constituted his career trajectory, so to speak, and as the temptation stories tell us, his life and death were of intrinsic value. He lived and died for the benefit of those with whom he came in contact; he did what he did for the sake of benefiting the world by witnessing to and obeying what he believed was fundamental truth. In the community where I worship on Sundays, after we present the gifts of bread and wine and money prior to the Holy Communion meal, we often pray: "With these gifts we offer ourselves and dedicate our lives to the care and redemption of all that you have made." In that prayer, we articulate the intention to accept the model of Jesus' life and death as normative for our own.

We must learn that this is what our lives, as part of nature's processes, are reckoned against: how they appear when measured against the ultimate well-being of the natural process from which we have emerged and which has shaped us to become what we are.

3. We must recognize that, in light of our status as a phase of nature's processes, our niche can also be understood as one of preparing for the best possible future for those processes. In their cultural life, humans fully implicate the rest of nature in the human

adventure. At the same time that we define this human project, we are also defining the rest of nature and molding it to the contours of that project. The
shaping of human culture must now take as one of its primary considerations
what is the best possible future not only for humans but for the nature-human
complex.

The model of education or child-rearing may be pertinent here, although it
serves as only a limited analogy. The emphasis is not so much on molding the
children to become what we want them to be, but rather contributing to them
that which will provide the greatest possibility for a wholesome future, so far as
we can make such judgments. Such is the character of our responsibility toward
the rest of nature.

*4. We must learn how to discern the dimension of ultimacy in nature's processes and how
to conceptualize them.* Humans are the discerners and the conceptualizers of ultimacy, and this is both our being and our office in nature's processes, as they have
brought us to this point in time, and also in their future unfolding. We are not
nature-worshipers as some ancient peoples were. We distrust the term *survival* if
it refers simply to the biological perpetuation of life, because we suspect that if
that is what nature is up to, it is not enough for us. We also know that the phases
of the natural process do not last forever. Extinctions are the rule in nature. Species die out, grass flourishes and dies, to be thrown into the oven. But the process
of nature's continual changing or evolving does not.

In the Western religious traditions of Judaism, Islam, and Christianity, the
creation of the natural order is the greatest project toward which the divine creativity and energies have been expended, so far as human knowledge can ascertain. These processes are intricate and marvelous. They are, apparently, what God
wants to do. And redemption of all sorts is, after all, another—perhaps the humanly most significant—large outpouring of divine energy and intentionality
toward the natural order.

If nature is God's great project, then by devoting ourselves to its care and
redemption we are pouring our resources into the same effort that God has
poured the divine resources into. Can we learn to think such thoughts, articulate
them in words, and permit them to guide our actions?

Paraphrasing Nasr, I would propose that the challenge facing us is first of all
to recognize that the study of nature and the discoveries that we achieve from
that study are a form of theological enterprise. Secondly, when that study and
discovery are turned to an examination of human viability, that is, the question
of the human niche, they touch upon questions that literally pertain to our being
or nonbeing, and thus are directly theological. The message or communication
that we receive from nature is parallel to the communication that we receive
from our canonical Sacred Scriptures. This parallelism, of course, is conveyed in
part by the image of the Two Books, an image that is several centuries old in the

West, figuring in an important way, for example, in the founding of the Royal Society of London in 1660.

The significance of this image for our present cultural situation, however, is far from being appreciated in its depth. Briefly put, the challenge to the sciences and the critical reason that builds upon the sciences is to recognize that the knowledge attained by scientific research forms the matrix and the substance for some of humanity's most fundamental values. We would do well to recognize that when devoted to these questions, the sciences are dealing with issues of ultimacy. Such an awareness will have great impact on how we perceive some of the questions now under discussion, of which perhaps the definition and exploration of *survival* is the most central.

For the religious communities and their theologians, the challenge is to recognize that because the natural world is indeed God's greatest project, true and profound knowledge of God involves the attempt to discern what niche or niches are most fitting for *Homo sapiens*. For theology, this entails the conclusion that theology is not on track unless it can interpret the traditions of the religious communities as revelation about the natural order. (Again, we understand the natural order always to include human beings and their culture.) This leads directly to the sense that the spiritual life has not been properly understood nor has God been rightly obeyed, therefore, until the believing community pours the quality of effort into the processes of nature and their future that parallels what God has committed to those processes.

5

God-Talk and Human Experience of the World

In a time not too long ago, to talk about "God in an age of science" would have conjured up images of a bitter controversy. One can almost hear the 1925 Scopes trial—liberal secularists arguing that the supernaturalistic concepts of God simply cannot be entertained in a naturalistically conceived world as described by the sciences, while their evangelical Christian counterparts insist that as contradictory as it may seem to modern science, we are far better off in wagering our lives on the traditional God of Abraham, Isaac, and Jacob than to settle for the cold porridge of naturalism. Although it has been argued in complex ways, the nub of this conflict is not that difficult to discern: In terms of both the science and the religion that were involved, nature was conceived so as to exclude the God who was being invoked, while the God was conceived so as to render the scientific views of nature irrelevant.

Some celebrated scientists still argue as if they were defending Scopes more than half a century ago (think of Richard Dawkins's 1986 book, *The Blind Watchmaker*, whose subtitle proclaims: "why the evidence of evolution reveals a universe without design"), and some Christian preachers both influential and serious still fit the stereotype. In my discussion here, I will employ most of the same "cards" that my stereotypical players of sixty-plus years ago put on the table, but I will play those cards in a different manner, within mental frameworks quite different from theirs.

One card holds that the world views in which we think of God and relate to God must not flaunt the possibilities and the constraints that are suggested by scientific discoveries and methodologies. We might call this the science card. Another card is the sheer givenness of God-talk and the correlative experience that undergirds it, and the sense that even if this experience is poorly understood and articulated, it will not go away. We could call this the God card.

The necessity of the first card is witnessed by the continuing insistence that every child, in every society that I know of, be schooled in at least basic science and mathematics. The presence of the second card is signaled by the research of sociologist Andrew Greeley, showing that in all of the countries in Western Europe and North America, over half of the persons sampled tell interviewers that they pray daily; in three countries, including the United States, the proportion is substantially higher. Furthermore, except for the years of the Vietnam War, when the figure declined, that percentage in the United States has remained constant for over forty years (Greeley 1991).

If I am playing with the same cards that forced a total impasse in the discussion of the God question in an age of science more than sixty years ago, what characterizes the new way I shall be playing those cards today? I will let two twentieth-century American poets set the stage for my portrayal. The first is Wallace Stevens. His poetry dates from half a century ago, but like many poets, he was a generation ahead of most of us in his sensibilities. In his poem "Sunday Morning," he pictures a woman enjoying a lazy, sensuous Sunday morning:

> Complacencies of the peignoir, and late
> Coffee and oranges in a sunny chair,
> And the green freedom of a cockatoo
> Upon a rug mingle to dissipate
> The holy hush of ancient sacrifice.
> (1954, 66–67)

Religion has no appeal or usefulness to her, because it does not intersect the life that is important and everyday for her:

> What is divinity if it can come
> Only in silent shadows and in dreams?
> Shall she not find in comforts of the sun,
> In pungent fruit and bright, green wings, or else
> In any balm or beauty of the earth,
> Things to be cherished like the thought of heaven?
> (67)

She does not live in the "grave of Jesus, where he lay," but rather in a natural world that can be explained naturally by the sciences, so what is Sunday morning to her?

The Sunday morning person cannot live, however, without a sense of meaning and purpose, and Stevens touches on this in "The Idea of Order in Key West," where he looks to another woman, this time a nightclub chanteuse, to make his point. It is essentially the same point that physicist Steven Weinberg has made: that we are obliged to construct our meanings and purposes. The poet's singer

> was the maker of the song she sang.
> The ever-hooded, tragic-gestured sea
> Was merely a place by which she walked to sing. . . .
> She was the single artificer of the world

> In which she sang. And when she sang, the sea,
> Whatever self it had, became the self
> That was her song, for she was maker.
> (1954, 129)

The singer's constructions are not confined to the moment in the bar, for they are one with the "blessed rage for order" that we all feel. Her ordering pertains not just to the sea, because we must also put in order the stories "of ourselves and of our origins."

The contestants of 1925 would be offended by my image of card-playing. It is Stevens who gives expression to the present sense that we cannot extricate ourselves from the game. There may be, we hope, meaning and divinity apart from our cards and their play, but for us, there is no experience of God and meaning except in the play of the cards, as we choose to play them, or hold them, or fold them. The distance from the Sunday morning's coffee and oranges in the sun to the night singing on the water requires a journey from the passive awareness of emptiness to the active shaping and singing of songs.

My second poet is a younger contemporary, Jorie Graham. Writing fifty years after Stevens, she takes his sensibility a step farther along the path to insight. In her poem "The Age of Reason," she focuses upon reason's ceaseless quest to know and to gain the truth.

> How far is true
>   enough?
> How far into the
>   earth
> can vision go and
>   still be
> love? Isn't the
>   honesty
> of things where they
>   resist,
> where only the wind
>   can bend them
> back, the real weather,
>   not our
> desire hissing Tell me
>   your parts
> that I may understand
>   your body,
> your story.
> (1983, 19)

How far is true enough? Human reason doesn't know, because up to now it has never gone all the way. Furthermore, it is incapable of going all the way. Reason does not have the capability of climbing some hill to get an overview of all there is. We do not gain the truth by seeking an overview of the whole of reality, but rather by pressing on into the depths of things until we reach the point where they resist. At that point of resistance, particular things reveal their stories to us, and in and through the particularities, reality itself is known.

In another poem, "At Luca Signorelli's Resurrection of the Body," Graham tells the story of the fifteenth-century painter Luca Signorelli, who in his work sought to reveal the truth of the human body. But as the poet gazes upon his murals in a parish church, she realizes that

> the wall
> of the flesh
>   opens endlessly,
> its vanishing point so deep
>   and receding
> we have yet to find it,
>   to have it
> stop us.
> (1983, 76)

If the world around us opens endlessly, its resistance point is ever receding, so that we cannot reach the grappling point that is the source of knowledge! Luca Signorelli was so frustrated by this endless opening of nature that when his only son died a violent death, he had the corpse placed in his studio,

> on the drawing-table,
>   and stood
> at a certain distance
>   awaiting the best
> possible light, the best depth
>   of day,
> then with beauty and care
>   and technique
> and judgement, cut into
>   shadow, cut
> into bone and sinew and every
>   pocket
> in which the cold light
>   pooled.
> It took him days
>   that deep
> caress, cutting,
>   unfastening,
> until his mind
>   could climb into
> the open flesh and
>   mend itself.
> (76–77)

Reason's probing into the depths never reaches the final resistance point where reality is unveiled enough to satisfy the quest for truth. Not even Ockham's razor is sharp enough to go all the way. But going all the way is not required for the encounter with truth—the probing is itself an encounter with the reality we wish to know, and hence the probing is a truthing process. It is the way our minds climb into the open flesh of nature's reality and mend themselves.

I said that Stevens and Graham would set the stage for my reflections on how we approach God-talk in an age of science. What I have gleaned from them crystallizes into four statements: (1) Truth is not really truth for us unless it fills all the spaces and times in which we really live our lives. (2) We shall not find this truth apart from our own efforts to construct the meanings that work in our lives. (3) This construction, however, takes place only in our ceaseless caressing and grappling with the world around us. It is in the resistance we encounter in that caressing and grappling that we find the truth. (4) Because we can never hope to push our world to the point where it is up against the wall, unable to move no further, we must understand that truth *is* the process of the caressing and grappling. Our goal is not to capture the truth, but rather to participate in the truthing process, to have the courage to climb into the open flesh of the natural world and commit ourselves to pressing reality's flesh.

Our God-talk, then, like all our talk, emerges from and expresses something about our contemporary experience of the world. God-talk is one of the communiques we send out from our forward position, having climbed into the open flesh of the natural world. For most of us our view of that natural world and ourselves in it is, at its deepest levels, thoroughly conditioned by scientific understandings. The eyes through which we perceive its flesh carry out their act of seeing through the constructs provided by the sciences. The chanteuse within us sings songs about the world whose composition betrays a scientific ordering. Consequently, the experience that is rendered through God-talk will carry the marks of that scientific ordering.

God-talk and scientific conceptualizations may mingle in our songs of the world in the manner of melody and counterpoint. The melody may be our personal contribution to meaning, but by itself the significance of a melody remains unclear. It is in tandem with its counterpoint that it delivers its message. Science does not constitute the only element in our songs' counterpoint, but it is our chief concern in the present context.

My first point, then, concerns the status and function of God-talk in an age of science: *God-talk should be viewed as expressing something about our experience of a world that is scientifically understood.*

God-talk and Our Pictures of Nature

In the preceding discussion, I have been skirting a basic motif of Western thought: that the themes of God, nature, and human beings are interrelated. Our cultural tradition of philosophy and theology has found it impossible to reflect upon God without including nature and human beings in the discussion. My use of Stevens and Graham was a contemporary updating of this perennial Western intuition. The maxim that closes the section above is a recasting of the traditional insight.

The second member of this triad, nature, deserves special mention. It can be argued that all of our concepts and images—including those that pertain to ourselves, the human situation, the possibilities and destiny of humans, the nature of community, personal and corporate morality, as well as those that pertain to God and other expressions of ultimacy—are conditioned by our concepts of nature. In a sense our pictures of nature provide basic constraints that govern everything else we think about. These pictures of nature often work deep within our psyches, even monitoring what it is permissible for us to think at pre-articulate levels.

Furthermore, these concepts of nature are largely bequeathed to us by our culture. The picture of nature that is communicated to a child in her early years, in school, and in the culture's media will determine to a large extent how that child grows to conceptualize the possibilities and obligations of her own life, as well as how she pictures her encounter with ultimacy. One could argue, for example, that what makes the question of God in an age of science interesting, and hence discussable, is that our present concepts of God still carry the marks of being conditioned by concepts of nature that neither science nor most persons today accept as valid. One of the great challenges for those who take God-talk seriously is to frame concepts of God that reflect contemporary understandings of nature.

It is critical for our reflection that we gain a clear sense of what is meant by the concept of God. It is equally critical that we gain a clear sense of what we accept as the most adequate concept of nature, because without clarity and credibility in our talk about nature, there will be no force to our talk about God.

R. G. Collingwood, in his classic work, *The Idea of Nature*, explains that in the West we have moved through three epochs in our conceptualizing of nature, each characterized by a governing analogy. The ancient Greek concept was based on the analogy between the world of nature and the individual human being. Nature was viewed as an intelligent organism—nature, the macrocosm; the individual human being, the microcosm (1945, 8). Max Wildiers reminds us that this Greek view became the foundation of the medieval view, which filled in basic details—for example, that nature is a perfectly ordered whole; this order is immutable, holding from creation until the end of time; the order is also hierarchical, the occupants at the top being nobler, better, and more powerful; and finally, the entire order is anthropocentric (1982, 57–58).

The Renaissance view of nature, which really sets in with Copernicus in the early years of the sixteenth century, insisted that nature as studied by science is devoid both of intelligence and life. This view of nature was based on the analogy of the human experience of designing and constructing machines. Nature becomes the lifeless machine, and if there is a God, God is nature's clockmaker or millwright (Collingwood 1945, 8–9). The difference between Aquinas's God the Prime Mover and Joseph Butler's God the Clockmaker may lie not so much in the two images of God, but in the images of nature that Aquinas and Butler held and the constraints those images imposed upon the possibilities for talking about God. The same kinds of constraints would apply to talking about the human mind.

The modern view of nature can be marked, for convenience, with the work of Darwin and with the advent some decades later of the so-called New Physics at the turn of this century. Clearly, this view is relatively new, and even today we can lament that the machine view of nature predominates in many quarters. The modern view conceives of the process of nature in analogy to the processes of human affairs as studied by historians (Collingwood 1945, 9–10). Collingwood's precise statement of the analogy may be faulty, but it is clear that an evolutionary mode is permeating our view of nature, with the consequence that nature is looked upon as a historical process with built-in qualities of change and dynamic. Machine images seem inadequate, function replaces substance, a wholistic dimension presses itself upon us, and teleology enters the discussion in new ways.

I can hardly overemphasize how significant our views of nature are for the possibilities of talking about God. Nor can I overemphasize how virtually all of the God-talk that is current in the plural cultures of the world today is the result of long, meticulous, rigorous effort—centuries in the process—to articulate human experience of the world under the impact of pictures of nature that no longer seem credible or even natural for us. We now view nature through eyes that have been fundamentally conditioned by the sciences, and the scientific study of nature, including human nature, does not corroborate the concepts that set the parameters for earlier centuries of God-talk.

This obsolescence of our talk about nature seriously obstructs our sense of what the experience of God might be. Just as observations that are dependent solely on the unaided vision of human eyes will never perceive gamma rays, so also sensibilities that cannot resonate, for example, to nature imaged as a lifeless machine, will have difficulty appreciating theological concepts whose aim is to articulate a vital sense of how God is related to that machine.

Jesus' Experience of the World as Paradigm

God-talk expresses something about our experience of the world. This means that it is utterly contemporary, it is talk that we construct imaginatively, and it emerges from a process in which we interact with our world—we caress that world and it responds to us. Furthermore, all of our talk about our experience of the world is conditioned in a critical fashion by the prevailing views of nature that shape our vision as we process through the world.

I bring this rather abstract reflection down to earth by considering a concrete instance of God-talk. My example is the God-talk of Jesus of Nazareth, gleaned chiefly from what is called the Sermon on the Mount. I will not go into the critical scholarly questions about whether this is the "real" Jesus or whether the Sermon on the Mount is our best source, but I rely on the opinion that this text was put together in about the year 50 of the Common Era by a group of followers who wanted to present a small collection of sayings that would contain the essence of Jesus' point of view—a sort of Jesus vade mecum (Betz 1985, 1–36).

I choose the Sermon on the Mount for a number of reasons: It is an important instance of God-talk that has had enormous historical impact. It is relatively free of philosophical and dogmatic baggage—it is not talk about Jesus, but rather talk by Jesus. It has an earnest, "if I had but one sermon to preach" urgency about it. Finally, it bears unmistakably the marks of having climbed into the open flesh of worldly existence; it is clearly an urgent communique from one who is committed to life's truthing process.

I will highlight three major themes in Jesus' God-talk, first by elaborating how they express experience of the world, and then by examining the significance of Jesus' presenting them as talk about God. The three themes are: (1) the personal quality of the experience of the world; (2) coherence as a characteristic of that experience; and (3) the belief that persons count for something and what they do with their lives counts.

A Personal Quality

One of the greatest misconceptions of traditional God-talk revolves around the terms *person* and *personal*. I refer to the notion that these terms imply that the world owes its existence and its maintenance to a great big cosmic individual, most often conceived as human and as male and as parent. To this is added the notion that in order to experience God, one must be in concourse with this great big person. I will not enumerate here all of the reasons why this is an unfortunate set of notions. The point is that such misconceptions cloud from our minds the real significance of the element of the personal in our concourse with the world. It is true that most learned theologians dismiss such images of God as puerile and uninformed. Nevertheless, those same theologians have not succeeded, by and large, in portraying alternative concepts that are accessible to rank-and-file persons, religious believers or not, and that are vivid representations of what our experience of the "personal" God conveys to us.

Lindon Eaves goes to the heart of this matter when he writes:

> The use of personal language is forced on us by the character of the reality in which we are embedded, and the character of our engagement with that reality. . . . It makes possible the appropriation of history, it articulates our dependence on nature/history, the ambiguity of our experience of reality, and the connectedness between ourselves and nature which is indispensable for life in an unfinished universe. (1991, 502)

Jesus urged upon his listeners the sense that Eaves describes—the character of the world in which we live and the ways we engage it demand personal language. In the sixth chapter of Matthew's account, Jesus says:

> Therefore I tell you, do not worry about your life, what you will eat or what you will drink, or about your body, what you will wear. Is not life more than food, and the body more than clothing? Look at the birds of the air; they neither sow nor reap nor gather into barns, and yet your heavenly Father feeds them. Are you not of more value than they? And can any of you by worrying add a single hour to your span of life? And why do you worry about clothing? Consider the lilies of the field, how they grow; they neither toil nor spin, yet I tell you, even Solomon in all his glory was not clothed like one of these. But if God so clothes the grass of the field, which is alive today and tomorrow is thrown into the oven, will he not much more clothe you—you of little faith? Therefore do not worry, saying, "What will we eat?" or "What will we drink?" or "What will we wear?" . . . indeed your heavenly Father knows that you need all these things. But strive first for the kingdom of God and God's righteousness, and all these things will be given to you as well. (Matt. 6:25–33)

The experience of the world expressed here is forceful. Indeed, it is its forcefulness that makes this passage so uncomfortable and problematic. Jesus addresses several aspects of his experience of the world, including anxiety about physical well-being, specifically about having proper food to eat and adequate clothing. Affluent North Americans can certainly identify this experience, even if it may be difficult for them to identify *with* it.

In addressing this anxiety, Jesus reflects on the place of his listeners in the context of nature, specifically plants and animals. In effect he argues that the men and women who are his audience ought to identify more closely with the nature around them—not only with its pleasant aspects, the beauty of the birds and the lilies, but also with the less comforting passing away-ness of the grass that is alive today and is thrown into the oven tomorrow. Human beings, who are of much more worth than the birds and the lilies and the grass, ought nevertheless to identify more closely with those lower kin, and moreover recognize that the entire natural process is most adequately understood if we conceptualize and articulate the experience of all the creatures, including humans, in terms of a *personal* process. To use Eaves's terminology, the *character* of the reality in which Jesus and his listeners are embedded requires personal concepts and language.

This language of the personal is found too in another passage, which also reports Jesus' experience of the natural world:

> Ask, and it will be given you; search, and you will find; knock, and the door will be opened for you. . . . Is there anyone among you who, if your child asks for bread, will give a stone? Or if the child asks for a fish, will give a snake? If you then, who are evil, know how to give good gifts to your children, how much more will your Father in heaven give good things to those who ask him! (Matt. 7:7–11)

I suggest that Jesus gives expression to this experience of the world in terms of the good heavenly Father—that is, in terms of God-talk—because there is no other way to make this concrete experience credible. The only way is, like Wallace Stevens's chanteuse, to make the song we sing about this experience include personalness at the deepest ontological level possible—namely, to speak of God. Jesus is calling attention not to a peripheral or occasional element of his experience of the world, but to the core of his experience. Therefore this personalness must be given the most fundamental rooting possible, and God-talk does that. Jesus caressed and pressed things until they began to resist, and at that point, his experience moved him to utter "Abba, Father"—the significance being not that "Father" is masculine, but that "Father" is personal.

We err if we think that the chief question that emerges from this portrayal of human experience is whether there is or can be a personal God. More to the point are the questions: What sort of experience of the world is this? If this is authentic experience that some persons share, how significant is it? What does it mean? How is it to be expressed and interpreted? What does the move into God-talk contribute to our understanding and interpretation of this experience? Is God-talk the most adequate means of expression and interpretation? If such experience is significant in the age of science, what account does science take of it and what light does science throw upon it?

Coherence

The passage that we have come to know as the Beatitudes (Matt. 5:3–12) is a key to Jesus' God-talk. The term that we know in English as "Blessed are . . ." represents perhaps the most urgent wisdom that Jesus wished to convey in his lifetime (or, alternatively, the wisdom that the early-Christian community wanted to project as the heart of Jesus' teaching). Jesus here is presenting a picture of what the wisest, most profoundly adequate human life would look like, the life that is most fully in accord with the fundamental nature of reality. That most adequate human being is the one who is blessed.

I will not take time here to analyze the content of the blessings, but their form is clear:

> Blessed are the poor in spirit, for theirs is the kingdom of heaven. . . .
> Blessed are the meek, for they will inherit the earth.
> Blessed are those who hunger and thirst for righteousness, for they will be filled.
> Blessed are the merciful, for they will receive mercy.
> Blessed are the pure in heart, for they will see God.
> Blessed are the peacemakers, for they will be called children of God.
> Blessed are those who are persecuted for righteousness' sake, for theirs is the kingdom of heaven.
> (Matt. 5:3–9)

The content of the experience of the world being conveyed here is that *reality does possess a fundamental nature, and that human life ought to be in accord with that fundamental nature.* I call this experiencing the world as *coherent*. The experience of coherence is expressed in the recurring phrase, "for they will be." An outcome is hypothecated that is harmonious with the state of life that is encouraged. Meekness is in accord with the fundamental nature of reality, and it will find resonance with the coherence that accords with meekness. Embracing peace is in accord with the fundamental nature of things, and so peacemaking will find the same kind of resonance.

Again, Jesus expresses this experience by casting the resonance that bespeaks the fundamental nature of reality in terms of ultimacy, God-talk: "theirs is the kingdom of heaven," "they will inherit the earth," "they will see God," and "they will be called the children of God." Again, because Jesus considered this coherence to be at the core of his experience of the world, he had to root it as deeply as possible, and he does this by God-talk.

When speaking of the lilies of the field and the grass thrown into the oven, he could have expected someone in the crowd to heckle him with, "That's right, so what's the use of living, anyway?" Here he might have expected comments like, "Be meek and others will trample over you!" or "People take advantage of the merciful, that's what!" Only experience that is most vividly convinced of its deep ontological grounding could counter with the preachment that the grass's life, on the contrary, witnesses to a personal graciousness and that meekness is more in touch with the way things really are than self-seeking.

Individuals Count

> You are the light of the world. A city built on a hill cannot be hid. No one after lighting a lamp puts it under the bushel basket, but on the lampstand, and it gives light to all in the house. In the same way, let your light shine before others, so that they may see your good works and give glory to your Father in heaven. (Matt. 5:14–16)

> You have heard that it was said, "You shall love your neighbor and hate your enemy." But I say to you, Love your enemies and pray for those who persecute you, so that you may be children of your Father in heaven; for he makes his sun rise on the evil and on the good, and sends rain on the righteous and on the unrighteous. . . . Be perfect, therefore, as your heavenly Father is perfect. (Matt. 5:43–48)

The elements of personalness and coherence are exemplified in these passages, but so is the view of the importance of individuals and their actions. Again, it is critical to understand these passages as expressions of Jesus' experience of the world. And again, the reference to the realm of nonhuman nature is stunning and problematic. Sunshine and rain are available to all, regardless of their religious beliefs or their moral state. We all know that, because it is part of our basic experience of the world. The heckler might say, "So, nature cares not a bit for what we do with our lives—our actions are meaningless in the continuum of nature!" Jesus' rejoinder is that the availability of nature's functioning to all persons, regardless of who they are, friend or foe, morally upright or degraded, is a parable whose point is that the benefits of culture and personal interaction should likewise be available to all.

Once again, God-talk secures the grounding of this experience as deeply as possible in the very nature of things. This time, the God-talk ups the ante to its highest point: "Be perfect, therefore, as your heavenly Father is perfect." Showing love to those who appear to be the least deserving recipients of our love is to be fully in harmony with the fundamental principles of nature. This is not an argument for the meaningfulness of human existence and moral earnestness; rather, it is the experience of the world such that meaningfulness and earnestness at the profoundest levels must be hypothecated in order to make sense of that experience.

Paradigmatic Issues

The Experience of the World

I have emphasized the concept of God-talk as expression of the experience of the world in order to draw attention to several points. The first is that for most persons who feel comfortable with God-talk, the God question is not one of an abstract and disinterested concept, but of concrete experience. For these persons, something very significant would be left untouched were all their efforts devoted exclusively to abstract philosophical discussions.

Second, although no reliable knowledge exists of how many persons find God-talk part of their experience, it is clear that this experience of the world expressed through God-talk is still occurring in an age of science; it is occurring in the lives of persons who have been conditioned to understand their world in scientific terms at least since their later elementary school years. This is of some significance. To a large extent, this experience is an actuality in an age of science that we must acknowledge, regardless of whether it fits our personal world views. In these cases, science, theology, and philosophy most appropriately ask, not "*Can* God-talk happen?" or "*Should* it happen?" but rather, "How are we to understand that it happens and what does it mean?"

Third, I hope I have made the point that because God-talk is rooted in experience of the world, it is an actuality to be acknowledged rather than a possibility to be adjudicated. However, the question remains as to what this experience of the world really amounts to and whether God-talk is its most appropriate expression.

Why employ God-talk

In my explication of Jesus' God-talk, I concluded in every instance that God-talk functioned to root the experience in the most fundamental nature of reality. In this respect, I am suggesting that God-talk functions much as Alfred North Whitehead believed metaphysical concepts function. The point is to elucidate immediate experience, but the brute facts of immediate experience make no sense unless they can be assumed to be items in a world of ordered relations (Whitehead 1978, 43–46, 14–15). The facts of immediate experience are given to us, the context of a world that is systematically related to the facts is not. The world context and its relations to our experience are what we, like Stevens's singer at Key West, compose songs about.

When modern liberal thinkers first became impressed with the point that Stevens has poetized, they tended to speak less complexly; they depreciated the constructions of contextual meaning that have come to us from traditional sources, in favor of more up-to-date constructions. Some of these up-to-date constructions were philosophical (as in the case of David Friedrich Strauss and Ludwig Feuerbach), and some of them claimed to be scientific (as in the case of Karl Marx and Sigmund Freud). We learned to employ the concept of projection; the traditional constructions of meaning, especially God-talk, were projections of the egos who did the constructing—projections of economic, social, and political interests, and projections of interior psychic needs. They were, to echo August Comte from the eighteenth century, the kinds of projections that comforted the human race in its periods of infancy, but were outgrown by the race in its maturity.

If the modern mind feels obligated to debunk the large contextualizing concepts that were bequeathed to us by the premodern mind, the postmodern mind is having second thoughts. Postmoderns do not for a moment deny that a projecting or constructing of songs is going on. But, recognizing that no concepts can claim to be immaculately conceived, untouched by the artifices of the chanteuse, we also recognize that the contextualizing concepts have emerged from an authentic experience of the world, and we judge the concepts on the merits of what they propose to us concretely.

Earlier in his "Key West" poem, Stevens had written,

> The sea was not a mask. No more was she.
> The song and water were not medleyed sound,
> Even if what she sang was what she heard,
> Since what she sang was uttered word by word.
> It may be that in all her phrases stirred
> The grinding water and the gasping wind;
> But it was she and not the sea we heard.
> (1954, 128–29)

The poet's point is not just that the singer is the artificer of her song—that is a simple enough observation. The issue is complexified by the fact that just as surely as she devises her song, she is genuinely in touch with the water she sings about—"in all her phrases stirred the grinding water and the gasping wind." This places upon the listener a responsibility:

> Whose spirit is this? we said, because we knew
> It was the spirit that we sought and knew
> That we should ask this often as she sang. (129)

In other words, these concepts are both human constructions and also truly emergent from a world that their artificers have climbed into and pressed to the point of resistance. Wallace Stevens and Jorie Graham have it just right; they represent the postmodern temper.

Whitehead is useful in this context, because he describes metaphysical or speculative concepts in terms both of their being human constructs and also of their being connected with transhuman reality. What I have called contextualizing concepts are synonymous with what he calls metaphysical or speculative concepts. In his famous simile of the airplane taking off and landing, he calls attention to the nature of metaphysics: it begins its flight from terra firma and it returns there, but it leaves the ground in order to make its flight. "It starts from the ground of particular observations; it makes a flight in the thin air of imaginative generalization; and it again lands for renewed observation rendered acute by rational interpretation" (Whitehead 1978, 5).

Without the imaginative construct to provide its context in the order of the world's processes, the particular experience is without meaning. The construct must always be tested by actual experience, however, and if it seems to be out of synch with the actualities, it is inadequate and must be revised. However, the contextualizing construct is not bifurcated from the actual experience; the two happen together, because it is the experience of the external reality that has given rise to the construct. The constructs are, therefore, to use Whitehead's term, ontological; that is, they are rooted in the actuality of experience and stand to be judged by that actuality.

To reiterate, although the term *God* is not always synonymous with Whitehead's metaphysical concept, it functions in a fashion that accords with his description of metaphysics. Therefore, the meaning of the term *God* is at least threefold: objective reality, transforming experience, and internal mental construct. Objective reality, because our actual experience of an objective world has given rise to the concept of God; transforming experience, because the concept adds contextualizing meaning to that experience; internal mental construct, because the concept is indeed constructed through our imaginative thinking. If our constructs have to be revised, it is because we have not adequately received the messages of our own experience—and, of course, we are always understanding our own experience of the world inadequately, so we are always revising our constructs.

God-talk as Hypothetical

Not all songs ring true. Not all contextualizing concepts work. They come to us as proposals to be tested. Despite the fact that the contextualizing concepts of religion are most often cast in the form of the imperative, declarative, or the vocative, we must receive them as if they were hypothetical in form. Do they indeed elucidate our immediate experience? Do they put it in context so as to render it more meaningful, in a way that is true to the actuality of the experience? God-talk is also received as such a proposal, but always in the concrete. The hypothesis is not, "There is a God—try to find him or her." Rather, it comes across concretely; in Jesus' case, "As you live your life, you seem to be embedded in a fundamental coherence—don't you think so?" "As you live your life, you are embedded in a fundamental personalness—don't you think so?" "As you live your life, it seems that individuals do count, and what they do with their lives matters—don't you think so?"

When we recognize the impact of these and comparable proposals, we are in a position to discern what God-talk contributes to our experience: grounding in the fundamental nature of things. Paul Tillich had a distinctive way of saying this. He described two formal criteria of every statement that claimed to be talk about God (1951, 11–15). The first is that statements about God must deal with their experience of the world "insofar as it can become a matter of ultimate concern for us" (12). The second is that such statements must deal with their experience "insofar as it can become a matter of being or not-being for us" (14).

Jesus' presentation in the Sermon on the Mount meets both of these criteria. All three of the assertions that we heard push back to the point where the issues of personalness, coherence, and whether our lives count for something are matters of our being or not being; they become ultimate matters for us. Testing their hypothetical truth is therefore a very serious matter. Whatever we say about the God question in our present age will have to face the test of these same criteria. A concept of God that does not press to the fundamental nature of things, so as to become a matter of our very being or not-being, is not really a concept of God, no matter how it clothes itself rhetorically.

If these hypotheses ring true, to the point where they place us in the situation of ultimacy (being or not being), then we are in the range of God-talk, regardless of what specific language is used. We are in the proper range where the concept of God can serve as a contextualizing concept for our actual experience of the world. If they do not ring true, then we must reassess the status of the experience. The challenges raised by Jesus' God-talk have to do with whether we believe there is a fundamental character to reality, and if we do, whether Jesus' experience of it is worthy of consideration. If we accept that there is a fundamental character to reality, what are the most adequate ways to conceptualize it and express it in language? If not God-talk, what are the alternatives?

Science as Challenging and Challenged

At the outset of this chapter, I said that the world we experience is understood scientifically, and that that scientific discernment is reflected in our God-talk. I have said virtually nothing about science in my exposition, however. This omission is explained largely by my concern that my readers properly understand just what God-talk is. I have presented one perspective on that issue. Further, however, I believe that God-talk emerges from our experience of the world; God-talk does not wait on science as such for its emergence any more than, say, love waits on a proper psychology of love before it happens.

Here I ask directly what difference scientific understandings of the world make for God-talk. I suggest three ways to understand this difference.

1. Science can radically reorder Jesus' experience of the world by providing alternative and more credible contextualizing concepts for it. This, in effect, would render unnecessary and incredible the concept of God, by meeting the kind of criterion that Whitehead proposed—that the speculative concept provide the most cogent rendering of the actual experience. E. O. Wilson has suggested this option in his claim that science will displace religion because it will provide an explanation of religion that will render religion itself anachronistic. The capstone to his argument is his presentation of the evolutionary epic as a new overarching myth that is able to provide meaning for human life more credibly than traditional religious myths (Wilson 1978, chaps. 8, 9).

In his 1986 presentation to the Catholic Bishops' Committee on Human Values, Wilson stated incisively his belief that religion and science "depict the universe in radically different ways. At bedrock, they are incompatible and mutually exclusive" (1987, 82). He would argue that Jesus' experience is better explained by the "materialist metaphysic," and that thereby the "profound impulses" that Jesus describes are better contextualized by the concept of the evolution of the genetic heritage common to our species (83).

Although Wilson rejects religion, he does allow for its possibly being true on the twofold ground that "the materialist position presupposes no final answers," while at the same time "it is an undeniable fact that faith is in our bones, that religious belief is a part of human nature and seemingly vital to social existence" (82). The materialist, however, believes that religion persists in human evolution because it confers adaptive advantage (87). If, however, traditional religious concepts are the better contextualizing factors, the presence of God must be capable of scientific discernment; it cannot remain accessible solely through an existential leap.

2. Science might find Jesus' contextualizing concepts applicable to alternative actual experiences. This option insists that Jesus might indeed have communicated reliable information about God, but, after all, our experience is not his; his first-century access to the world need not and cannot be replicated by us in the late twentieth century.

Ralph Wendell Burhoe has moved in this direction in his argument that God *is* natural selection (1981, chaps. 4, 5). He selects seven elements of the traditional concept of God as affirmed by Jews, Christians, and Muslims, and finds that those elements also can serve as contextualizing concepts for the experience of the world as it is shaped by modes of perception that grow out of the evolutionary sciences. He includes such concepts as God the one ultimate reality who is creator and sustainer, God as immanent and transcendent, and God's ultimate triumph and graciousness (1981, 125–37).

A number of thinkers exemplify this position. Several seem to focus on traditional contextualizing concepts of God, as Burhoe does, but they relate those concepts to nontraditional experience. Frank J. Tipler (1989) focuses upon experiences of the world as accessed through contemporary physical cosmology, computer science, and scientific naturalism. Tipler may in fact be taking up Wilson's challenge to discern scientifically the traces of a divine presence. He is certainly following Whitehead's method. Lindon Eaves and Lora Gross (Eaves 1989; Eaves and Gross 1992) take up the experience of the world that attends to our genetic code unfolding through evolution. For James Ashbrook (1984, 1992), experiences focus upon the nature of the human central nervous system. This option would argue, for example, that it is not first of all in the experience of the world as birds, lilies, and grass that we come to the sense of personalness and coherence, but as the evolving genetic code or the evolution of information.

These strategies insist, each in its own way, that the laws and processes of nature are rooted in the fundamental nature of reality, which, even if it is novel in contrast to earlier epochs, is nevertheless elucidated by some of the same contextualizing concepts that worked in those epochs. In their written works, these thinkers employ strikingly traditional concepts: the Lord's Prayer, ancient lists of attributes, and the like. This option stands at the core of my own argument in this book.

3. Science might undergird God-talk, while providing alternative experiences and also alternative contextualizing concepts. This option agrees that actual experiences of the world take different shapes today than they did in earlier ages. It also insists upon contextualizing concepts that, while not totally unknown in the tradition of the West, possess elements of novelty. But it asserts, just as traditional experience did, that this contemporary experience is rooted in the fundamental nature of things in a way that calls for the use of God-talk.

Three contemporary thinkers move in this direction: Gordon Kaufman, Eric Chaisson, and Arthur Peacocke. Interestingly, they seem to be focusing on the same general type of experience of the world—change and novelty, accompanied by order and directionality. Kaufman (1992, 1993) explicitly questions traditional conceptions of God as creator and governor of the world, in favor of a creator-governor who is identified with an underlying cosmic process of creativity; he terms it "cosmic serendipitous creativity." Chaisson (1979, 1981, 1987) builds on experiences and concepts taken from thermodynamic and information theory. He suggests a science-based metaphysics in which the evolving process of nature is itself the ultimate. Peacocke has provided the most winsome of God-concepts, that of the cosmic composer of fugues who interweaves chance and necessity, novelty and order, simplicity and complexity, who engages in creation and redemption as the Lord of the Dance (1979, 104–111).

In reflecting upon God in this age of science, I suggested that we keep before us the image of playing a religion-and-science game that has been played before in this century. Some of the cards to be used were familiar and some new, to be played in new ways. I placed two sets of texts side by side, one ancient and one contemporary. The ancient texts, from Jesus' Sermon on the Mount, propose a God-centered interpretation of human experience in the world that has deeply influenced several world cultures and at least three of the world's traditional religions, over a period of two millennia. The twentieth-century American poetry texts chart the parameters of the contemporary American spirit; they set forth the conditions and styles of discernment that work within our hearts and minds. My zigzag reflections have attempted to let those different texts interact with each other and with the religion, philosophy, and science that form the focus of this book. I propose that it is in such a style that we might most honestly and most fruitfully integrate all of our experience—religious, scientific, and aesthetic—on the quest for meaning.

Part 3

Freedom

6

Freedom as the Determined Human Condition

The unavoidability of freedom rests in the fact that freedom itself has emerged from a causal process that was impersonal, highly determined as it unfolded, and, previous to human being and its freedom, much less complex and sophisticated than that which emerged from it. The unavoidableness of freedom underscores its essential character for human becoming. We are approaching a tautology at this point: The fact that humanity has emerged as a creature characterized by freedom is the ground for asserting both the essential and the unavoidable nature of freedom. (Hefner 1987, 128)

These ideas appear below, in chapter 7 (114–15). When they were first published, they prompted Ted Peters to comment:

> For some time now I have been uneasy about the problem, understood as the conflict between determinism and freedom. I suspect that our common way of formulating the issue is misleading and that we should begin with a couple of undisputable facts. Causal determinism is an observable and confirmable phenomenon; similarly, human free choice is observable and confirmable; but to try to reduce one to the other seems to be unwarranted. (T. Peters 1991)

The proposal embodied in the second element of the created co-creator theory, particularly in the fifth auxiliary hypothesis, insists that freedom does indeed belong to us human beings as integral to our natural character.

Freedom as a Condition of Existence

Freedom, however, means different things to different persons. My primary definition of freedom here is cast neither in terms of liberty ("Don't tread on me!"—the classical liberal and prevailing American view) nor of the ability to make and shape the world (the prevailing view both for Marxists and those who have fashioned an ideology out of technology), although it incorporates both of these, especially the latter. Rather, I refer to freedom as a *condition of existence,* one in which humans unavoidably face the necessity both of making decisions and of constructing the stories that contextualize and hence justify those decisions.

As I shall discuss in chapter 9, in the phase of human history we call technological civilization, decision-making is universal and unavoidable, an essential component for life in that civilization. Since technological civilization has altered the circumstances of living so radically, this necessity of decision-making and story construction is intensified. I call this freedom, because the element of decision is constitutive of the condition I speak of—making decisions, evaluating and contextualizing them, and taking responsibility for their consequences. It is clear that only humans (whether as individuals or as groups) can make the decisions, only humans can construct the stories that justify them, only humans can establish the criteria for evaluating them, and humans take primary responsibility for the consequences of those decisions.

Two examples, to which I referred in chapter 2, may sharpen my reference to freedom as a condition intrinsic to human existence.

First, ancient wisdom enjoins us to honor fathers and mothers. Under the conditions of technological civilization we must decide whether permitting or refusing medical interventions to prolong a parent's life fulfills the command. Humans cannot avoid the freedom to make the choice, and only humans can construct the stories that justify such choices, just as they must take responsibility for cutting life short or prolonging it.

Second, environmental policies require a myriad of value judgments concerning the comparative values of the earth and of human and other forms of life. Humans cannot avoid such policy-making and the value judgments inherent to that policy. Further, only humans can construct the stories that provide the justifying arguments for such judgments. Genesis 1:28 ("Be fruitful and multiply, and fill the earth and subdue it; and have dominion"), put, once again, as a divine mandate, exists to be interpreted. Despite the fact that in the Hebrew "have dominion" is expressed by the verb meaning "serve," the same root naming the servant of Yahweh in Isaiah's Servant Songs (Fuerst 1992; Jenni and Westermann 1976, 182ff.; Cassuto 1961, 121–23), historically it has been taken in anthropocentric, anthropo-serving directions, as well as in eco-friendly directions, and each option has at one time or another been evaluated positively and also justified by means of contextualizing stories. Humans cannot avoid the interpretations and their justifications.

That this freedom has evolved within the world-system is the burden of chapter 7. On the one hand, the processes of evolution have worked by means of natural selection; on the other hand, freedom exists with purposes that pertain to the conditioning evolutionary processes that have preceded its appearance in *Homo sapiens*. Therefore freedom is to be interpreted as part of nature's way of being nature. This constitutes a response to the insight that Ted Peters has provided. This is specified further in the statement that freedom is nature's way of stretching itself toward newness (Hefner 1988a). "Stretching," of course, is a metaphor. More literally, I mean that freedom is one of nature's ways of creating new conditions under which the genes and their programs must exist. In the process, novelty is elicited from those programs.

In the next chapter, considerable weight is given to the work of the geneticist Theodosius Dobzhansky, in his suggestions concerning how freedom has emerged within what he calls the "genetically controlled adaptive plasticity of the phenotype" (Dobzhansky 1956, 68). Today's more detailed knowledge of the evolutionary history of the human central nervous system and how it works, confirms and deepens the insights of Dobzhansky (Jerrison 1976; Deacon 1990a; Holmes 1991; K. Peters 1992).

Knowledge of the human central nervous system introduces something from a scientific point of view that is also significantly present in much current philosophy, literature, and the social sciences—namely, the constructivist element (Knorr-Cetina 1981, 1983). Karl Peters calls attention to this element in the title of his piece on the subject, "Story Tellers and Scenario Spinners." He cites support from neuroscientist William Calvin (1989, 1991b). In a simpler way, the physicist Steven Weinberg has expressed this same notion (see chapter 1). The point is that one of the keys to the survival and advance of the human species lies in the capacity of its brain to observe and interpret information. Constructing adequate contextualizing frameworks, or narratives, in which to place information and interpret it is an essential ingredient of what has enabled humans to evolve as they have.

This view of human being might be summarized by the suggestion that in *Homo sapiens,* a creature has emerged whose remarkable activity of doing and making requires a high order of discernment. The human being must discern what is present in the world, as well as how what is present relates to what is possible, what is desirable, and what is necessary. Further, humans must discern the most adequate justification and interpretation of what they do. Finally, they must take responsibility for what they have discerned and its consequences. This emergence we call *Homo sapiens* is a phase of nature itself.

Thus three elements are brought together that describe broadly the nature of the human being and the ways in which this nature structures human life within definite design constraints: first, the necessity to make self-aware decisions, act on the decisions, evaluate and take responsibility for their consequences; second, to construct interpretations of those actions that make sense; thirdly, to justify those decisions, actions, and interpretations.

In chapter 5, I referred to contextualizing concepts and correlated them to Whitehead's term, *metaphysical* or *speculative* concepts. My argument is that all three of these facets are integral to *Homo sapiens* conceived as created co-creator—action, contextualizing interpretation, and contextualizing justification. All three facets are caught up both in the *created* and the *co-creating* character of us human beings. We have evolved as creatures who developed the capacities for thought-out action, interpretation, and justification, and these capacities have become necessary for our survival—hence, these facets are a legacy bequeathed to us, not our accomplishment. At the same time, as we exercise these capacities and as we do indeed survive, we are actively engaged in co-creating. To call ourselves created co-creators is an actualization of this created co-creating process. Thus, the theory of the created co-creator is itself an instantiation of the process as the theory discerns, interprets, and justifies it.

The teleonomic axiom discussed in chapter 2 suggests that the nature of *Homo sapiens* as created co-creator is rooted in the givenness of nature. The discussion here speaks of the concept of the created co-creator as a product also of the co-creating of images and knowledge that is central to the survival strategies of the creature who is the created co-creator. The concept by which I have chosen to understand and interpret human being in this book possesses both ontological and epistemological status. If the term *postmodern* means anything at all, it means that this kind of interaction between the nature of things and our way of knowing the nature of things is inevitable, inescapable, and indeed conditions the manner in which life and its possibilities open up for us. This fact of human being—both ironic and richly mysterious in its character—is implicit in what I here call freedom.

There is still more to the significance of this freedom and its place in the human enterprise. Human life is marked by the effort to understand the nature of things—not just our experience of the world, but the very nature of things, those universal and enduring features that characterize all (or nearly all) instances of a thing or a constellation of interrelated things. Our experience is momentary—this apple is yellow, this person is dishonest. We seek knowledge that we can rely on to guide us when we next experience an apple or a person, or a flow of interconnected things and events. I refer to this as the attempt to know *what really is* or *how things really are.*

Such attempts are deeply rooted in Western history; they go back to the origins of Greek philosophy, as well as of the Hebrew religion. In his concept of the Idea or ideal Form, Plato gave classic expression to one way in which we seek to articulate the way things really are, one that has been normative for much of Western thinking ("The Republic," Book VI, Jowett 1937, vol. 2, 744–73). For the Hebrews, the Law or the Torah, the word of the Lord God, played the same role.

Our experience forms the arena in which we encounter the natural world and its manifold elements, but, as Immanuel Kant saw so clearly and G. F. W. Hegel elaborated further, "concepts without percepts are empty, but percepts without concepts are blind" (N. K. Smith 1958, 111–12). Concepts bring the order to experience that enables knowledge. Hegel's elaboration served to underscore that we understand a thing, properly speaking, when we are able to grasp, or conceive, its parts and its history together in a whole, called a *concept* (Hegel 1977, 104ff., et passim). Whitehead points to the same concern with his image of thought as the flight of the airplane, giving rise to speculative or metaphysical concepts.

We prize the richness of experience, but our primordial sense is that we need, in addition to receiving the signals of our immediate experience, to understand that experience. The fate of one single apple does not provide the farmer with enough information to guide the activities of growing apples; nor would we determine our behavior toward a person simply on the basis of one fragmentary experience. Without wishing to espouse any particular metaphysical way of speaking, we may nevertheless say that we strive to base our thinking and our actions on that which lies deeper within our experience, the "way things really are"—whether it pertains to growing apples, relating to persons, or determining the vocations of our lives and societies. The Hebrews, and the Christians and Muslims after them, believe that the way things really are is revealed in their traditions of God's word or law or revelation. The huge significance that science has attained in world culture today is in large part due to the fact it, too, is an attempt to determine how things really are.

In our present epoch, we recognize, as Steven Weinberg exemplifies so clearly, that the truth of how things really are is a concept in which we participate, one that we construct in a significant way. Other ages may have believed that truth about the nature of things is given to us, that our task is to conform to it. Astrology, as well as more respectable modes of thinking, adopt this view. The Middle Ages in Europe is often characterized in this manner (Wildiers 1982, 49–58). We believe today that our relation to the truth of things is more participatory or interactive.

How we conceive of and speak about the way things really are is urgently important, because we innately seek to conform our behavior to the way things are (Berger and Luckmann 1966, 92–104). The indicative or *is* forms the norm for the imperatives or *oughts* of human living. Plato and Moses saw this with equal clarity, and so do their descendants. The poignancy of our current epoch is that we perceive that we are by our very nature (that is, created) in a sense co-creators of the images and concepts of how things really are. This is articulated in the concept of freedom as condition of existence.

This condition of being created or determined as free is at the heart of the fifth hypothesis:

#5: Freedom characterizes human existence as the condition in which humans have no choice but to act and to construct the narratives and symbols that contextualize that action. Such contextualization provides justification, explanation, and norms for guiding and assessing the action. This condition is intrinsic to the evolutionary processes at the level of *Homo sapiens*.

The sixth auxiliary hypothesis backtracks in a sense, but to a very important purpose, that of clarifying how deeply the condition of freedom is rooted in the natural constitution of *Homo sapiens*.

#6: *Homo sapiens* is a two-natured creature, a symbiosis of genes and culture.

Descriptions and clarifications of this two-natured character of the human being run throughout the length of this book, inasmuch as this insight derived from the biological sciences is the driving image of the created co-creator theory. Many researchers have agreed that the genes/culture pair constitutes our human nature as two companion streams of information at the heart of our being. Dwight Boyd and Peter Richerson speak of this as "the dual inheritance model" (1985, chap. 1 et passim). They have developed a form of this model to understand human culture and how humans behave in their cultures.

Prior to their work, Ralph Wendell Burhoe developed a compatible form of the model to understand the fundamental nature of *Homo sapiens* (1976a, 1976b, 1979, 1988). Donald T. Campbell has utilized a similar model to study several aspects of human behavior, including evolutionary epistemology, moral behavior, and cultural symbol systems (1965, 1975, 1976, 1991). Many researchers now work within such models, and they have formed the professional Human Behavior and Evolution Society. The anthropologist William Irons has provided an authoritative description of this approach and a bibliography of its most important research studies (Irons 1991; see also Chagnon and Irons 1979). How the relationship between these two streams is to be conceptualized is still not a matter of consensus. I choose to follow Burhoe's suggestion that the image of *symbiosis* is best suited for interpreting this relationship (Burhoe 1976b).

It is important to emphasize once again that talk about the two-natured character of the human being is in no sense intended to suggest a dualistic understanding. On the contrary, the image of *Homo sapiens* presented in this book is antithetical to dualistic modes of thought. One natural process has given rise to all that exists in the universe, including the human being. The emphasis upon nature in chapter 3 suggests that whether one posits a divine source to nature or not, the instrumentality for the creation of human beings is the one process of nature. Within the evolution of this nature, the human is an emergent.

Our experience and understanding of this natural creature, the human being, however, is of a being whose character is variegated and marked by profound tensions. Western thinkers from Plato through Martin Luther, Hegel, Sören Kierkegaard, Sigmund Freud, and Paul Tillich, have noted these tensions, often using the images of animals to suggest the different facets of human nature, generally animals hostile to one another. For example, they have often spoken of humans as horses being ridden by opposing riders. One can acknowledge the authenticity of these perceptions without necessarily subscribing to Platonic metaphysics, Hegelian or Kierkegaardian dialectic, or Freudian psychology.

The reader should keep this anti-dualistic intention in mind in reading in this section about the nuances of freedom and determinism, as well as the analysis in the next section of the distinctions between genes and cultures and the ways in which those distinctions define the field of what we consider to be the fundamental challenges facing the human species today. The discussion of sin in chapter 8 may appear to rest on a dualism of genes versus culture, nature versus nurture, but such a dualism is more apparent than real. Tension exists, to be sure, between the two streams of evolving information, and this tension is so real that it can result in death to the symbionts. Nevertheless, both streams of information have emerged within the one constellation of natural processes. Both have emerged within the realm of biological evolution. Furthermore, within the human being, the health of both genes and culture is necessary for the survival of the individual as well as of the group.

Finally, no discussion of these matters can avoid the use of metaphor, and we dare not overlook this fact. No matter how vividly we experience the tension, we must remember that the fundamental symbiotic belonging of the two streams is as deeply rooted in the way things really are as is the tension. To apply categories of dualism to explain the breadth and complexities of the human phenomenon is too easy a strategy. Though it is far more difficult to probe how the variegated realm of nature—and human beings within that nature—has emerged from one evolutionary process, at the hand of one God, what we gain from that probing is also far more adequate for understanding what we experience and what we believe.

It is precisely because of the dynamic we associate with freedom, and in particular the distinctive form freedom has taken in the human sector of nature, that it is so difficult to move beyond the experience of variety to an understanding of the way things really are. We must remember, however, that the emergence of freedom, particularly in its human forms, is a key element of the way things really are. Having to engage in the rigorous process of discerning how things really are, rather than having unambiguous, unassailably cogent universal knowledge, is integral to human reality, however we conceive of what is real. No philosopher has seen this more clearly than Hegel, in his *Phenomenology of Spirit,* as well as in his *Science of Logic,* and I am surely indebted to his insights.

Science as Freedom's Spur

None of the ideas that I discuss in this book is more central to the project of the created co-creator theory than the concept of freedom that I have introduced briefly in this chapter. Furthermore, this concept of freedom bears a definite and fundamental relationship to the contribution of the natural sciences to this book's substance and form.

As befits a world view that is thoroughly conditioned by evolutionary theory, the understanding of human being that is set forth by the created co-creator theory is not necessarily timeless, but rather one that has emerged in history and is peculiarly relevant to the present . To be sure, the physico-biogenetic constitution of *Homo sapiens* as I have summarized it in these pages belongs to the perennial nature of the species; it did not emerge in recent history. Similarly, the characteristic of freedom and its biogenetic rootage is intrinsic to the human animal. Nevertheless, the picture of the human being that is presented here belongs in a context, and it is a context that is shaped by the emergence of the sciences and their development, including the rise of science-based technology, in the last three and one-half centuries.

Science and technology have created the world in which we live today, and it is because of them that freedom has assumed both its contemporary urgency and its present shape. Perhaps it would be more accurate to say that it is because evolution on planet earth took the course it has taken—in the emergence of the human being, that creature's being an animal of culture, and the culture's taking the form of science and technology—that we face the challenge of freedom as I outline it in this book. Or, to state the matter still differently, the condition of freedom is a phase of nature's evolution on planet earth, the phase of *Homo sapiens* and its science and technology. Let us consider briefly why this is so.

Freedom, as the condition of having to make decisions, evaluate them, justify them, and take responsibility for them, is an urgent, life-or-death matter today. We inhabitants of planet earth are essentially one interdependent global human community, existing in symbiosis with one finite, planetary ecosystem. The human community is stretching the carrying capacity of the global ecosystem to its very limits. Both of these factors—the interrelated planetary community and the pressure on the planet's ecosystem—have come about because of science and its technology. Without medical science and agricultural science and their related technologies, the population of the planet would not have reached its present density. Similarly, the science and technology that undergird transportation, communications, and armaments have contributed to the scope and intensity of the relationships within earth's human sector. Without the size of the population, its global spread, and the science-based technologies upon which that population depends, the carrying capacity of the ecosystem would not be in jeopardy.

In one sense, these developments are not new. The challenge of relating to other tribes or human groups has been a prime factor in human evolution since at least 30,000 years ago, and the allocation of natural resources, including the food derived from plants and animals, has been part of the challenge posed by the growth of population and the necessary interrelations that go with it (Pfeiffer 1982, chaps. 3, 8, 12; Klein 1989, chap. 8). What is new about the situation of our epoch is that the carrying capacity of the planetary ecosystem is approaching its limits, and that unless the situation is mediated through human decision and its fruits, there is virtually no new access for humans to the earth's resources. There are no new herds to search out, no new wildernesses to develop, no new fields of limitless mineral resources to exploit. Indeed, were the present level of technological overlay to be sizably cut back, the world's population would have to be trimmed by many millions of persons. Clearly, science and technology are inseparable from issues of war and peace, social justice, ethnic diversity and conflict, as well as environmental issues. Perhaps the most novel aspect of the current situation is that we are the first epoch to be aware of the planetary condition and our role in it.

Against this background, science and technology form the context in which human life will find either fulfillment or catastrophe or some tense homeostasis of the two. This context is that of freedom; decisions must be made, and we have to be prepared to live with the consequences of these decisions. Science and technology not only provide the context, but their development is also the spur for motivating humans to face up to the necessity of decisions and their complexity. There is more to it, however. Because science and technology are now essential for human life as we know it, and because it is unlikely that we will decide to lower drastically the size of the human population, the future of the planet is thoroughly conditioned by science and technology. Barring catastrophe, the future is one in which science and technology will, even more, condition the basic circumstances of life on our planet. Science and technology thus also constitute the medium through which we will express the future of life on earth.

We should not adopt the erroneous view that science and technology are only externally related to us humans and our dilemmas, only the stage on which we live out our lives. Science and technology are related to us internally, as well, in deep and complex ways. We shape our self-images from the scientific-technological ambience, just as we follow vocations and their educational requisites by internalizing science and technology and submitting to their possibilities as determinative for our lives. Our accomplishments, our longevity, and the state of our mental health depend on scientific and technological factors and interventions—medical, environmental, economic—most of which we wish to maintain.

This description of our present situation on the planet underscores how the course of events is and will be conditioned by science and technology. At the same time, it emphasizes the phenomenon of freedom. Because we cannot survive without making decisions about every facet of planetary existence—human and otherwise—we find ourselves bathed in the ambience of freedom. And it is precisely the all-permeating reality of scientific knowledge and the technology based upon it that gives rise to that freedom and that constitutes the future world in which the fruits of that freedom must prove viable.

7

Freedom and Determinism in Evolutionary Perspective

The proposed theory of the created co-creator is deeply implicated in the phenomena of freedom and determinism. The impressionistic comments of the last chapter require elaboration in some detail. This chapter will provide that elaboration.

An Evolutionary Setting for Freedom

Adequate understanding of freedom and determinism depends in turn upon a fundamental understanding of the evolutionary history of the universe and planet earth within the cosmos. The beginnings of the cosmos are associated with the singularity that is commonly called the Big Bang. From this explosion of energy some 16 to 20 billion years ago, particles, atoms, molecules, and all subsequent "stuff" emerged. The developments include the formation of galaxies and stars, the manufacture of the materials for planets and for life.

During the first two thousand million years of planet earth, from the "primeval soup" and other sources arose complex chemical systems, including the amino acids with the consequent proteins that made possible the various structures and functions of life. Nucleic acids came into being with the consequent DNA inheritance codes that made possible the memory and hence the replication and continuing special evolution of the structures of life. Life evolved the marvelous characteristics of millions of species in the next two thousand million years or so.

In the most recent epochs, nongenetic information systems called nerve networks and brains arose. These made possible adaptational learning thousands of times faster than genetic learning. Brains came into being that could cope with widespread and rapid changes in environing circumstances. But, because the rapidly learned or acquired adaptive information in brains was not genetic and therefore could not be genetically inherited from one generation to the next, it could not evolve as a cumulative heritage.

The creature *Homo sapiens* emerged from this evolution of life, and each individual in this group is itself an evolution, an ontogeny, from the conjoining of the egg and the sperm to the appearance of the mature individual and beyond. The human segment of evolution has become, however, what biologists Alfred Emerson (1943) and Theodosius Dobzhansky (1956), together with the evolutionary theorist Ralph Wendell Burhoe (1976b, 1979), have called the super-organism (Dobzhansky 1956; Kroeber 1952) or supraorganism (Emerson 1943; with modifications, Burhoe 1976a, 1976b) of culture.

The picture of cosmic evolution contains, therefore, at least four segments: Big Bang cosmology, biological evolution, human ontogeny, and cultural development. Although each of these is distinct from the others in its particular laws of unfolding, more and more observers are recognizing that the several phases can be considered as portions or dimensions of one cosmic evolution (Chaisson 1981, Wicken 1987, Bronowski 1970). Scientists themselves are speaking in these terms. The poets are translating the scientific interpretation into the image of our cosmic journey.

Later I shall refer again to the larger stretches of cosmic evolution and their significance for the theme of this book. More immediately, however, I turn to the second phase of the evolutionary history, the emergence of life. An extended citation from the biologist George Wald will provide the background against which I interpret the relevant features in biological evolution:

> The design of living organisms is an altogether different kind of process from technological design. . . . Technological design proceeds by setting specifications and then attempting to meet them. Knowing what one wants to achieve beforehand, one sets about producing this result as skillfully as one can. This is not the way living organisms are designed. Organic design is achieved by the process that Darwin described a little over one hundred years ago as natural selection. It is just the reverse of the technological process. It works by a continuous outpouring of inherited variations. . . . From that outpouring of variations, the struggle for existence constantly weeds out those things that work less well, permitting those things that work better to go on. In biological design, one is dealing with the works not of a great author, but of a great editor. . . . The disorder in the genetic message is essentially random. It is certainly unpredictable. . . . We have here to face a paradox in a sense, for the genetic disorder that involves the individual organism is coupled with a fantastic conservatism in evolution: the random variation that we encounter in ontogeny, the history of the individual, is coupled with an extraordinary stability in phylogeny, the history of the species. (1965, 26–27)

Within the matrix of the twin dynamics of fantastic variation and equally fantastic conservatism, as Wald describes them, light is shed on several sets of emergences as the evolutionary processes have worked themselves out. In my interpretation of life's journey, I rely on the work of Wald and Theodosius Dobzhansky.

For the purpose of this argument, we enter into the description of the evolution of life at the point where it is clear that, as Dobzhansky puts it, "a living being must, then, be at least tolerably fit not just in one environment but in a certain range of environments" (1956, 68). One way in which biological design meets this challenge is genetic diversification. This option consists of genotypes that are specialized for only a limited range of environments, for which they are indeed well adapted and for which they are finely honed by the continuing pressures of natural selection.

An alternative option of biological design is "genetically controlled adaptive plasticity of the phenotype" (Dobzhansky 1956, 68). This option produces genotypes that are able to react to a wide range of different environments by developing phenotypes that can survive and reproduce in each. Genetic diversification may produce a better specialist for a given environment, but changes in environment bring almost certain extinction. The emergence of phenotypic plasticity enables the living being to survive even radical changes in environment.

Lower organisms can afford to follow the first option, since a single individual is not so important to these species. Furthermore, their central nervous systems cannot contain and control the quantity of information that is required for a vast repertoire of phenotypic behaviors. Higher organisms, including vertebrates and mammals, however, cannot afford to compensate for maladaptiveness by sacrificing huge numbers of individuals. Furthermore, these species developed the more sophisticated central nervous systems that allow learning, along with language and symbol systems. The importance of this development was summarized in chapter 6.

Adaptive plasticity of the phenotype is closely correlated with the development of the brain, learned patterns of behavior, and the appearance of the human being. Learned patterns of behavior extend and fine-tune the genetic programming of the phenotype and thereby allow the creature to handle a much more complex set of inputs in a wider range of environments. This learning takes place in two stages. Before humanity, the individual brain could learn much, but the brain's accumulated learning died with the organism. In humans, important brain learning could be "inherited" through *culture*. To quote Dobzhansky:

> At the human stage of evolution, a vastly more important refinement of adaptation to the environment has occurred. For on the animal level learning is not cumulative. Whatever experience is acquired by an individual or a generation, it is not transmitted to the next generation. The next generation has to start again from the beginning. This is indeed not surprising; there is no biological mechanism that can transmit acquired characters. Among animals, evolutionary improvements, including improvements of behavior, still have to take place by the rigid and slow method of transmission of genes from parent to progeny, immediate or remote, but to nobody else. This method of evolution is simply unable to keep up with the speed and efficiency of action that is required because of the complexity of human environments and their rapid changes. (1956, 79)

The human species is the only biological species that has come free from this limitation of heredity, and it has done so through culture. "The important thing is that the learning acquired may then be passed on to anybody, above and beyond the limitations imposed by the biological mechanism of gene transfer" (Dobzhansky 1956, 50).

Tinbergen defines learning as a "central nervous system process causing more or less lasting changes in the innate behavioral mechanisms under the influence of the outer world" (in Dobzhansky 1956, 96; see also Boyd and Richerson 1985, 33). This learning, which goes along with the emergence of symbol systems, language, and culture, is closely correlated with the genetic substratum; it is not disengaged from the genetic constitution, but rather is enabled by it. This genetic basis of learning and culture includes the development of the brain, the cerebral cortex, the physiological changes that support brain development, and also the lengthening of the individual life span in higher invertebrate animals.

The development of plasticity of phenotypic behavior in *Homo sapiens* gives rise to culture (assuming that cultural processes are highly coadapted to the genes). Culture emerged from the biogenetic matrix, that much is certain. The precise course of emergence is not yet fully clear. Culture seems to be extraordinarily flexible with respect to genes, and at times even reputable scientists have spoken of culture as if it were totally free of genetic foundations (Dawkins 1978, chap. 1; G. C. Williams 1988). Dobzhansky puts the matter more carefully:

> Human genes have accomplished what no other genes succeeded in doing. They formed the biological basis for a superorganic culture, which proved to be the most powerful method of adaptation to the environment ever developed by any species. In accepting Kroeber's (1952) designation of culture as "superorganic," no suggestion is made that culture is a product of a supernatural or an esoteric force (no such implications have been put in this expression by Kroeber either). All that this expression means is that the development of culture shows regularities *sui generis,* not found in biological nature, just as biological phenomena are subject to biological laws which are different from, without being contrary to, the laws of inorganic nature. (1956, 121–22)

Alfred E. Emerson (1943) gave the name *supraorganism* to the constitution of many living collectivities formerly deemed to be a single genetic species but later found to be mutually symbiotic aggregations of quite different species when their mutual exchange of benefits enabled them to occupy a more favorable or more advanced niche. No one of the species could occupy the new niche alone, but their mutual collaboration made possible such developments as those of the complex new niches occupied by termites and their symbiont flagellates. In recent decades with the help of microbiology many multiple-species creatures have been made known.

Ralph Wendell Burhoe, utilizing implications of the Dobzhansky-Kroeber notions, those of Emerson, and a number of others, has helped to explain humanity as a super- or supraorganism consisting of two radically different symbiotic heritages of information that opened up a unique niche, radically different from any prior symbioses or forms of life (Burhoe 1976, 1979). In less than a million years, humanity has developed into its present, dominant, global society.

Burhoe speaks of the human symbiosis as coming from two widely differing species of information—one genetic, the other cultural—which today, like many symbiotic systems, are not viable if separated. Over the last million years they have been selected as an organized, living unity. He ascribes to the religious or sacred sector of culture the function that was used to bring culture and genes into such harmonious relation that the symbiosis to enable human society has become possible. As I shall elaborate in Part Four, religion has played this role in motivating, through its myths and rituals, behaviors that are considered on the one hand to be essential to *human* being, and on the other, to be adaptive for survival. Because it has played this role, Burhoe believes that religion will forever evolve as transmitter of humanity's most sacred cultural heritage. The present weakness and reformations of religion mark a critical period in human history not different in principle from many that have occurred before (Burhoe 1976b, 1979, Burhoe and Katz 1986).

All of this brings us to the issue of free will and determinism. Genetically controlled adaptive plasticity of phenotype, evolved perhaps due to its extraordinary advantages for survival in a wide range of complex environments, takes a particular and probably unique form in the human being and its society (see Jerrison 1976). This particular human form is constituted by (1) an impulse to explore the environment and to consider a variety of phenotypic behaviors that may be desirable in the environment; (2) carrying out this exploration in conscious and self-conscious reflection upon the environment and the various possible desirable behaviors, which include (3) entertaining conscious decisions with respect to this exploration and settling on one or more such decisions as the basis of behavior (the behavior then is called *action*); (4) a social matrix, apart from which the human being cannot live, which entails allowing the individual the license to explore and decide, on the one hand, while (5) insisting that group relationships and the welfare of other individuals and the entire society be taken into account in the exploration and decision and action; in this situation, what we call morality and ethics emerge (Hefner 1984a).

In a preliminary way, freedom emerges at this point as an element associated with exploration, with self-conscious consideration of alternative decisions and behaviors, and with the condition of liberty and autonomy of the individual and subgroup that are necessary for exploration and self-conscious reflection upon alternative behaviors. Determinism arises in this context as an element that transcends both the individual and the group, both as a reinforcement for exploration and decision and also as an obstacle to them.

These preliminary references to free will and determinism are not meant as basic definitions nor as final considerations. They serve as intermediate markers in the discussion. The point of these references is that the issues of free will and determinism have arisen in conjunction with natural developments that have emerged from the natural, material evolutionary process that has brought the stuff of the cosmos from its origin some 16 billion years ago to the present state of the human community on planet earth. Unless we recognize this basic fact, we cannot speak appropriately about freedom and determinism.

A Contextual View of Freedom and Determinism

As corollary to the discussion thus far, whatever is signified by the term *freedom,* and what is often considered to be the antonym *determinism,* are not isolated elements or dimensions, but rather a reality that emerges within a context. Freedom and determinism arise with the evolutionary process itself as creatures make their life-way within that process. Freedom and determinism are real for us within the evolutionary course in which we find ourselves on the journey toward becoming both what is given to us to be (without our discernment and decision) and what we believe we ought to be (which does include our discernment and decision). As we are caught up in becoming what we are to be, freedom and determinism are concerns for us. From the outset, therefore, freedom and determinism must be considered in this context.

The contextual approach is often disregarded or put in a subordinate position in discussions of freedom and determinism. Sometimes the two elements are hypostatized, as if they were abstract entities that enjoy an existence in and of themselves. Such discussions overlook the fact that these terms are human constructions, created and elaborated in order to articulate human experience within the course of our evolving life-way. They have no reality apart from this life-way and our human constructing activity.

Still other discussions handle freedom and determinism as if we were interested in them in and of themselves, apart from their context. In these discussions, determinism is often defined as the attribute appropriate to actions that are fully caused by antecedent factors, whereas freedom is defined as an attribute of actions that are not caused by antecedents, but rather by autonomous choice. Such definitions are unhelpful, largely because they isolate freedom and determinism from the relevant context. Humans really have no interest in either freedom or determinism except as they are relevant, either positively or negatively, to our becoming what we ought to be.

Within this context, freedom becomes important to us, not for its own sake, but because it appears to be essential to humanity and its becoming. We experience freedom as a basic element of (1) the impulse to explore the environment, (2) conscious deliberation and decision, (3) the sense we have that we are responsible, and (4) the liberty and autonomy that are prerequisite to exploration, conscious deliberation and decision, and taking responsibility.

Much of our interpretation of freedom is provoked by the awareness that freedom is not only essential, but also unavoidable. I will include a more detailed analysis of the unavoidable character of freedom later, but here I call attention to the fact that humans find on the one hand that the course of becoming cannot be carried out without the impulse to explore and the related activities of conscious deliberation, decision, and taking responsibility. Existence from which these characteristics were wholly absent would not be considered by us to be human. On the other hand, the biocultural basis of freedom is clear. Conscious deliberation, decision, taking responsibility, and the sense for autonomy are rooted in the capabilities of our central nervous system, as neurobiological and biopsychological studies make evident. The impulse to explore the environment represents the basic design option that our evolution has taken (Jerrison 1976; Deacon 1990a, 1990b).

Freedom has emerged within the evolutionary processes that are marked by the qualities of the impersonal and the determined. The engendering processes were much less sophisticated, but freedom was at least incipient within them (some scientists would say much more than "incipient"). If those processes had proceeded in their determined fashion, humanity would not exist today. It is these considerations that lend freedom its character of being determined and essential. In a profound sense freedom is human destiny.

Determinism becomes important for us likewise not for its own sake, but because it appears in the context of our trajectory of becoming, either as a reinforcing element for becoming what we must, or as counter-element. We experience determinism as the historical and contemporary context of our becoming. As historical context, it takes the form of our cosmic heritage, including our genetic and ethological heritage. As contemporary, it includes our natural environment, our social environment, culture, and interpersonal relationships.

Freedom is thus not in and of itself good, as is often argued, nor is determinism in and of itself bad. We approach both of these elements from the angle of our own attempts within our evolved life-ways to become what we believe we ought to become, and we judge both freedom and determinism to be essential, necessary, good or bad in terms of the role they play in that life-way.

I do not claim to have arrived at adequate precise definitions of basic terms, but I offer these provisional operational definitions: *Freedom* is an element of our becoming that is marked by the ability and the necessity for exploring our environment for the sake of discovering new and more adequate ways of living; this exploring is marked in humans by conscious deliberation, decision, and taking of responsibility, and a certain autonomy. *Determinism* is an element of our becoming that always exists within a context that includes both causal past and causal present; determinism points to the context in which the four basic characteristics of freedom transpire. These preliminary definitions will be deepened as the discussion proceeds in this chapter.

I have spoken of freedom and determinism as elements, and in this I follow Paul Tillich, who in turn represents a substantial tradition of Western philosophical and theological thinking when he speaks of "ontological elements" (1951, 163–65, 166–68, 182–86). These elements are a priori concepts "which constitute the basic structure of being." They are a priori, because they are what enable us to receive experience as a perceivable, experienceable reality. They are *not* a priori in the sense that they are known prior to experience; rather, they are "products of a critical analysis of experience." Nor does a priori mean that they "constitute a static and unchangeable structure." They may change, but if they do, another set of conditions must make it possible to have experience (166). The point is that these concepts are a priori in the sense that they "are presupposed in every actual experience, since they constitute the very structure of experience itself . . . make it possible to have experience" (166).

Freedom and determinism appear much like these ontological elements that Tillich describes. The environment-testing and environment-exploring dynamics that I described at the outset, relying on the work of Wald, Emerson, Burhoe, and Dobzhansky, constitute the very structure of cosmic and biological evolution. Thus, freedom does have a priori character, even though the term as such is not to be used to describe the fundamental dynamics except as they occur at the level of higher organisms and possibly only with respect to *Homo sapiens*. Karl Schmitz-Moormann has masterfully described how an evolutionary mode of interpreting the cosmos and planet earth puts the rudiments of freedom at the center of the world as we understand it (1987, 447–58).

However, freedom is associated intrinsically with our life-way within the course of evolution, seeking to become what we ought to be; therefore freedom itself is always asking what the basic meaning of the evolutionary course is. Further, it asks about the fundamental structure and dynamics of that course. Faced with the *ought* of its evolutionary existence, freedom pursues ceaselessly the foundational *is*. Freedom cannot be in and of itself, because that amounts to contingency, and freedom must be concerned with the *ought* of its becoming, if it is not to be idle randomness.

Determinism is the polar concept of freedom. The *is* of the evolving trajectory is precisely what appears to be determined, whether that be the four basic forces that physicists believe may be the foundation of Big Bang cosmology, the laws of particle physics that evolved later, the principles of biological evolution, or the cultural constraints of society and tradition. The causal relationships that have produced us and that form the structures that enable our experience are what determinism is all about, and the true *oughts* of this determinism are what freedom seeks to actualize in more adequate ways.

Determinism, however, is in turn constituted by the process of environment-exploring that comprises freedom. The context of evolution is always evolving.

There was a time when there were no laws of particle physics, just as there was a time when there were no laws of genetics governing DNA, simply because there were as yet no particles before one millisecond after the Big Bang and no DNA in the eons before it formed on planet earth 3.5 to 4 million years ago. We often associate determinism with the concept of eternal natural law or eternal natural causality. As with Tillich's a priori ontological concepts, natural law and natural causality have indeed always existed, but the concrete content of that law and causality have themselves been the subject of evolutionary change.

Freedom and determinism are not only polar concepts; they are also dialectical, even to the point of the negations of the Hegelian dialectic. Freedom calls forth determinism as the structure of the trajectory that freedom seeks to fulfill through its exploring, deliberation, and decision. This determinism is the apparent negation of freedom, but in assimilating itself to that determinism, freedom becomes what it must be. Determinism has given rise over the billions of years of evolution to the freedom that is its negation, but in the process it is clear that the heart of evolution's determinism is the generation of freedom that enables the causal context to persist in new and different ways. Freedom requires the structure of determinism for its becoming. To quote Schmitz-Moormann, "With evolution as the description of our concrete universe, freedom cannot exist without structure and structure, if it is not to fall back into the past, into death, must support freedom" (1987, 456). Ralph Wendell Burhoe put a similar point thus:

> . . . freedom is a power (of living systems), to maintain their order of life from environmental randomicity, given them by the cosmos. It is the power of self-determinism, and hence this freedom cannot exist or be conceived of except as a part of a deterministic system, a determinism provided by the definite pattern or order which gives life its power to maintain the internalized order against the vagaries of a disorderly environment. (1966, 10)

Required Ancillary Concepts

As the themes of freedom and determinism approach the human level in evolution, certain terms have arisen in this discussion that imply end, purpose, and *ought*. This is as it should be, since at the human level, the impulse to test and explore for new and better ways of being takes place within consciousness, self-consciousness, deliberation, and decision. Humans experience freedom as *for the sake* of something, and that "something" is the best possible actualization of what they *ought* to become. Humans search the *is* of the determined context, in order to discover its *ought;* just as they probe the *ought* in order to discover its *is*. In other words, freedom seeks the end or purpose or fundamental nature of the life process in which it finds itself, in order to be obedient to what fundamental nature can become. This is another facet of the innate human drive to discover the way things really are and to shape human behavior commensurately.

Such reflections put us near to the concept of *destiny*. For humans, that which occurs as determinism at earlier stages of the evolution of the cosmos is better referred to as destiny. Tillich writes: "Destiny is not a strange power which determines what shall happen to me. It is myself as given, formed by nature, history, and myself. My destiny is the basis of my freedom; my freedom participates in shaping my destiny" (1951, 185). We might consider whether destiny ought not always to be included in any reflection upon freedom. It is not clear whether destiny is appropriate to prehuman life, because of the term's teleological nuances, but it is still useful to think about the entire evolutionary process in terms of its destiny or vocation.

In the situation of freedom, human beings are always asking the question whether their determined context shares in a destiny. We cannot avoid this question about destiny without trivializing the consideration of freedom and determinism. The issue of destiny is intrinsically a theological consideration.

It is acceptable in some biological thinking, as well as in the philosophical reflection upon biology, to circumvent the theological issue by speaking instead of "epigenetic rules" that organisms develop during the lifetime of the species. Such rules are coincident within the evolutionary process; they have no basis beyond the coincidences of that process. Ethics and even religious systems are granted respectable status as such epigenetic elements that emerge within evolution and are favored in natural selection for the adaptive advantages they bestow. This thinking clarifies how a deterministic biological system can favor the emergence of freedom that works for the survival of the species. Even though this emergence is "untrue" in the sense that it is not the way things really are, it deceives the individual into behavior that is adaptive for survival. In the context of the present discussion, this view would argue that there is no "real" referent for such concepts as purpose and destiny, but that individuals develop behaviors that proceed "as if" these concepts were real. Evolutionary ethics in this sense is once more understandable and respectable in some quarters (Ruse 1986a, Hefner 1984b).

This epigenetic explanation is to be welcomed, because it helps to overcome the dichotomy between spirit and matter, between ought and is, between ethics and nature, and between freedom and determinism. Nevertheless, this approach leaves a number of important questions untouched. Why is survival built into the evolutionary process? What is the significance of the fact that all phases of cosmic evolution seem to be woven on the loom of survival in the face of natural selection? Are all the epigenetic adaptive strategies of the various species totally self-contained? Does any meaning or purpose persist across species boundaries? What is the significance of the fact that the use of free choice in the service of morality and ethical strategies is adaptive in the human species?

So long as these questions arise, the question of whether determinism is really our destiny will be a vital one. Some thinkers will want to introduce the concept of teleology at this point. My own strategy, as I spoke of it in chapter 2, is to probe these issues under the rubric of teleonomy.

The central point to be made here is that freedom, as it has arisen among human beings within the evolutionary context, seeks to be in harmony with the determinist course of evolution in which humans find themselves. This desire to be in a relationship of consonance rather than dissonance with respect to the fundamental *is* of our becoming shapes human judgments about freedom and determinism. We do not prize freedom except as it is consonant with the course of evolutionary becoming and supportive of it. We do not prize freedom that breaks out in self-destructive behaviors. Determinism is a concern because at points it seems to go counter to our freedom, and it raises the fear that our freedom is in dissonance with our evolutionary course. When determinism reinforces freedom, signifying consonance with our deterministic context, then determinism is welcomed. Humans judge freedom and determinism, consequently, according to their relation to human destiny or destinies. When freedom and determinism both support human destinies, there is no conflict between them.

It would seem that determinist processes that lie below the threshold of human self-awareness must automatically follow the thrust of our destiny. On the contrary, we regularly deem these processes as dissonant with the destiny that inheres in our evolutionary course. For this reason, we change the flow of rivers, employ artificial selection in growing plants and raising livestock, alter our physical bodies through medication, surgery, and the like—all in order to conform more fully to what we consider the "truer" thrust of our evolutionary becoming.

Here we encounter the powerful role played by human intellectual construction. Although selection pressures envelop us, quite apart from our awareness of them or our consent, we find that we respond not only to those pressures, but also (and at times more significantly) to our *perceptions* of those pressures and our interpretations of them. This is nowhere clearer than in the human attempt to exercise conscious deliberation, decision, and the taking of responsibility with respect to the true nature of human becoming. That true nature, as I argued in chapter 6, cannot be approached in freedom apart from human intellectual constructions. One of the most critical aspects of human freedom vis-à-vis determinism arises in that zone where preconscious and nonconscious information collides with the intellectual constructions of human self-awareness. The crisis arises first of all in human efforts to recognize such collisions and then in our efforts to interpret the collisions properly. The issues arising from the Human Genome Initiative and genetic engineering are of this sort.

We confront here the fundamental challenge of human nature. The human being is a two-natured creature, as this discussion has implied: a coalition or symbiosis of genes and culture. Recall Dobzhansky's words: "Human genes have accomplished what no other genes succeeded in doing. They formed the biological basis for a superorganic culture, which proved to be the most powerful method of adaptation to the environment ever developed by a species" (1956, 121). Culture has elaborated the freedom that our genes make possible. Our genetic heritage and the environment that we are evolving with provide us with our determined possibilities and constraints. *Our destiny consists of the future to which these genetic and environmental realities can be brought by our culture so as to actualize the most desirable existence for the whole.* When we understand this nexus of factors, then we have placed the freedom/determinism theme in its proper setting. Ralph Wendell Burhoe has written insightfully to this point:

> This kind of dual character (dual programming) [referring to the genetic and cultural duality of humanity] of the individual human phenotype is one of the most dangerous as well as most marvelous innovations of nature in its evolution on earth. . . . It may produce a divided will at war with itself—a living hell—in those brains when and where culturetype and genotype are not suitably coadapted, that is, where the self's two separate "organisms" may not be suitably fitted to function in single-minded harmony. (1982, 126)

Burhoe's comments on the possible "living hell" within the human being point to the turmoil and possible destruction that the dual-natured human being may well experience. The vision of the future to which culture may bring the genetic-environmental-cultural whole is the challenge of the promise to which the human being is called.

The Appearance of the Co-creator

The theme of freedom and determinism becomes most vivid when we understand its relevance for humankind in its present condition. Let us recall some of the basic insights from the opening sections of this discussion and relate them to the proposal set forth in chapter 2. *Homo sapiens* appeared on the scene as an emergent phenomenon. Our species, like all others, was thoroughly passive with respect to its appearance and distinctiveness; from a materialist perspective, the species was produced by the blind and impersonal process of evolution. Whatever our metaphysics or our theology, we must agree that human beings came into being through the process; the evolutionary system became predisposed, on its own terms, toward the adaptive success of *Homo sapiens*.

Within the process, the thread of evolution has been toward the following characteristics that make up the distinctive configuration of the human species: (1) the development of consciousness; (2) individuality within community; (3)

self-consciousness; (4) the ability to make decisions on the basis of self-conscious deliberation; (5) action on the basis of that decision; (6) the reception and assessment of complex feedbacks; (7) correction; (8) renewed action on the basis of correction; (9) taking responsibility for all the preceding eight items.

When these characteristics, in their human configuration, are considered as emergents, then it can be said that human being is a phase of evolution, a phase of the planet. In the context of such an analysis, Teilhard reflected upon the human population as the "thinking envelope" of the planet and as "evolution become aware of itself" (1964). Eric Chaisson interprets this same phenomenon as signifying the transition into a new epoch of cosmic evolution, the Life Era, following upon the Matter Era, just as that epoch followed upon the Radiation Era (1981, 296–99).

Human being has been defined at its beginning by the evolutionary process; this definition takes the form of the determined context in which *Homo sapiens* has found itself. This creature, however, has been defined as a self-defining species, in that the nine characteristics listed above result in the activity of self-definition (Hefner 1973). Exploration of the environment has become for humans a self-definition to a degree that overshadows that of previous creatures. Humans are able to adapt to many environments in part by significantly rearranging them to suit human living. In the process, humans discover their niche by defining that niche to an extent that no other species does.

In a decisive way, however, the human species defines the rest of the ecosystem of the planet when it defines itself. *Decisive* is the key word here. The human species is decisive in a way that no other species or element of the ecosystem is. Other creatures and elements are just as essential as the human; if they disappear or run amok, the entire ecosystem will be affected. The distinctiveness of the human species, however, is that it self-consciously makes decisions about itself, decisions that bestow a definition on other parts of the system. Nearly every element of the ecosystem is defined, for example, by the *uses* the human sector has assigned to it. The very continuation of the ecosystem is significantly affected by *Homo sapiens* and that creature's definition of itself and of its world.

Definition and self-definition become yet another set of themes for speaking about determinism and freedom. This theme leads us to speak of the human as not only a defined self-definer, but as a *created co-creator*. The term *co-creator,* when linked with *self-definer,* opens up for consideration what I believe is the quintessential form in which we experience freedom and determinism today.

The evolved and defined self-definer has been given the possibility by evolution to act in whatever manner the prior conditions of the evolutionary process permit. However, as co-creator, this self-defining human has reached a stage of technological civilization where on the one hand human life in nearly all parts of the world would be impossible unless it is assisted by technology that humans have created; while on the other hand, the technologization and humanification of the planetary ecosystem have reached the point where the maintenance and direction of this technological civilization have rendered the ecosystem utterly vulnerable to human actions. This technological level is a naturally occurring phase of the evolutionary process. The symbiosis between the human species and its ecosystem has reached an extraordinarily complex stage, one at which the maintenance of the ecosystem as a congenial host for the human symbiont hangs by a slender thread whose strength lies in the quality of human decisions and the absence of serious blunders. These considerations form the substance of the reflections in Part Four.

The co-creator has in effect not only created a civilization for itself, but also defined the world operationally in the process, and the future of the planetary community and its ecosystem depend on the further creating work of the co-creator. We left some time ago the era in which humans and the ecosystem could continue in a way that could support the life that humans prefer simply by letting nonhuman nature take its course.

This is the quintessential situation for the theme of the created co-creator, because it is a situation bathed in freedom. The ecosystem is bathed in freedom in the sense that it is genuinely and fully vulnerable to the decisions and actions initiated by its own cutting edge of development, the self-defining *Homo sapiens*.

The capsule of freedom in which we live may be delineated as follows. The human being must adapt to its world system, as must all forms of life, in the face of pressures of natural selection. However, the preeminent and essential means of human adaptation are now cultural—that is, not genetically preprogrammed behaviors, but learned behaviors. Therefore the human being does not merely respond in an immediate encounter to the world. Human beings are dependent on their images, symbols, and intellectually constructed concepts of the world. Humans in the situation of freedom must discover what the world is like, what their niche in the world is, and what adequate and desirable action is called for in that world. In a very important sense, the human being lives in a world of human construction and interpretation, while at the same time the human is dependent for its very life on the consonance of that humanly constructed interpretation of the world system with the objective requirements of the evolving context in which humans find themselves. To be sure, all living creatures must discover what their world requires of them, but only for humans is the discovery so thoroughly a matter of conscious discernment and constructed symbolic interpretation.

Through its mechanisms of discernment and learning, the human creature must make its own decisions about what the world system requires, what sorts of responses will best meet those requirements, what the norms and limits are that the world imposes. The only authority for the human being's world-constructions and the only sanctions for its actions are the authority and sanctions that the human being has discovered and acknowledged. Further, only the human co-creator can determine what the canons of assessment are by which to judge whether the learned responses are desirable and adequate. Finally, the co-creator and none other must take responsibility for the consequences of action; no divine hand or absolute natural law steps in to forestall those consequences.

Examples abound of this quintessential situation of freedom; it is not necessary to cite them. Essentially, this situation underlies the comments by Steven Weinberg quoted at the beginning of chapter 1. Every day we must make decisions concerning our technology that follow the pattern of freedom just elaborated. How should we defend ourselves in time of war? What power sources should we develop? How should our food be grown and processed? Each of these questions finds a technological answer, and all are answers that require our discernment to foresee the consequences as clearly as possible. If our nuclear technology goes wrong, or if our agricultural technology is misbegotten, the consequences will be our responsibility, and only humans can decide how that responsibility is to be exercised. These are all questions of self-definition for the co-creator. Similarly, we are in the throes of defining ourselves in terms of gender; we are not even certain how to define a man or a woman! We are just now understanding ourselves as one global society of particular societies, and the challenges in this sector to the self-defining co-creator are enormous.

In this situation, we come upon the inescapableness of freedom. We are destined to be free. We are deterministically defined as free. This seems strange at first, but by the term *freedom,* I am referring not primarily to an idea nor to an attribute of human capability, but to a situation. The concept of freedom points to an ambience that has emerged with particular force with the advent of the human species. Freedom refers to the situation of having to act while at the same time having to discern and even to construct the norms, rules, goals, and meaning of that action as we go along. This constitutes my primary definition of freedom.

The Polish novelist Marek Hlasko, in a work entitled *The Eighth Day of the Week,* has the heroine say at the end of a frustrating exercise in discerning the requirements of her life, "And now there is only freedom. That damn, crappy freedom" (1958, 125). Determinism is also fundamental to this situation. Not only are we apparently determined to be free creatures, but our freedom must be finally consonant with the objective course of our evolution. We can say that we are not only determined to be free, but we are free to be determined. The conditions that support our fulfillment within our evolutionary course are those in which both the determined elements of our context and the freedom we exercise within that context are consonant with each other and also harmonious with what it is that we are to become.

Certainly the major conclusion to be drawn from such an analysis is that human beings individually and in their societal existence are inextricably caught up in a venture in freedom, and that the proper understanding of structures of determinism/destiny is essential for this venture to survive. We must not flinch from our freedom, and we must employ all our capabilities of discernment to get a true picture of the determining context to which our freedom must resonate.

8

Biological Perspectives on Original Sin

I now press one step further in my reflection upon freedom, bringing the discussion of the previous two chapters into explicit concourse with the Christian theological tradition. It may seem surprising that this step in the discussion leads into a consideration of sin, but the substance of what follows in this chapter will indicate why and how this particular segment of the tradition is appropriate for bringing new insights to the evolutionary issues raised in the earlier discussions.

A word is in order with respect to the presentation of this chapter. At the outset, I briefly introduce issues of culture, myth, and symbol that will form the substance of Part Four. Although this move risks some confusion, it should also underscore that my method is a wholistic one that does not lend itself easily to rigorous sequencing of its various dimensions. The substance of this chapter is analysis of the human condition I have described as freedom; the analysis, however, presupposes concepts of culture, myth, and ritual that are fully set forth only in the later sections of the discussion.

Symbolic and Mythic Background

Paul Ricoeur's (1967, 3–18) useful methodology for understanding and interpreting symbolic and mythic materials forms the basis for my argument that these materials constitute a legacy of primordial information that originates in the earlier history of *Homo sapiens,* as a reading of the world in which they lived and their relation to it. In Part Four, I continue in more depth my efforts to elaborate a theory that attempts to place the origins, function, and significance of this primordial information within the evolutionary process and its implications for understanding the human phenomenon (Hefner 1991, esp. 122–30; Hefner 1992).

Briefly, the theory rests on the scientific suggestions that *Homo sapiens* is in a sense a two-natured creature, constituted by both genes and culture, as chapters 6 and 7 have described. Because humans are fully dependent on both of these systems of information, genetic and cultural, a cooperative interaction between them has evolved—a *symbiosis*. Both systems of information are essential for the motivation, support, and guidance of human behavior. Symbol and myth may be understood as very early forms in which this system of cultural information took shape (Hefner 1991, 122–27).

When one takes seriously the essential role of culture for the survival and flourishing of the species, then it is clear how significant are the forms in which early humans read their environment and their relation to it. More specifically, one recognizes how important symbol, myth, and ritual are as elements in which the cultural system of information and guidance constitutes itself.

Unfortunately, there is little empirical evidence concerning the emergence of symbol, myth, and ritual. The work in this field of such scholars as Andre Leroi-Gourhan (1967), Ralph Wendell Burhoe (1976a, 1979), Julian Jaynes (1977), Eugene d'Aquili (1978, 1983), and John Pfeiffer (1982) is perhaps the most rigorous I have at my disposal, and I recognize that their theories are as yet underdetermined by empirical evidence. However, it is reasonable and even conservative to speculate that symbol and ritual were in existence 50,000 to 60,000 years ago, as indicated by burial sites that show evidence of ritual performances (Klein 1989, 327; Pfeiffer 1982, 99–101). By the same reckoning, art as a social creation, serving social purposes, goes back at least 33,000 years (Klein 378–85; Pfeiffer 1982, chaps. 1, 8, 12, 13). The number of artifacts dating from 20,000 years ago is enormous. The number of paintings and engravings in western Europe alone is conservatively estimated at 15,000 (Pfeiffer 1982, 1). To this must be added the sculptures that suggest a placement within symbolic networks of meaning.

I sketch this prehistorical background in order to reinforce the suggestion that symbol, myth, and ritual are to be understood as primordial units of the cultural system of information that served the survival and flourishing of the human species and its immediate predecessors. This sets the stage for an analysis of freedom in the context of the information borne by the mythic material associated with the doctrines of original sin and the fall. These doctrines have their origin in the symbols and myths that make up that cultural information system even in its prehistoric period of development. It is not known how early the symbols pertinent to this theme occur, but certainly they are well developed as far back as 5,000 years ago. That they occur in archaic religions would suggest that they were present at the same time as the flourishing of cave art and ritual. In Part Four, I reflect upon these matters in much greater detail.

It is important to probe the origins of myth and ritual, the major components of religion, because understanding the origins gives us a significant perspective on the purpose of religion today. To the extent that we understand when these essential elements of human being emerged, we also get a sense for the functions that they played and what they contributed to human life. To the same degree, we also may get a sense of what those elements mean in our lives today.

It is true that in the dynamic processes of human history, myth and ritual might assume different functions now from those they played at the beginning of the human journey. It is also clear that we cannot fully understand the meaning of human life and its essential elements except in the future, when we get a firmer grasp on what human life can become (theologians understand this as the eschatological dimension of meaning). Nevertheless, the more clearly we understand the purpose and function of religion at its emergence and in its earliest history, the more we will also understand what religion was selected for and how it served life in its early period. This knowledge gives us clues concerning the present significance of religion and its function today and in the future.

The highly developed interpretations of sin and evil in myth, philosophy, and theology/doctrine are not properly understood unless we view them as interpretations and elaborations of the more primordial sensing that occurred early on in the history of *Homo sapiens*. The origin of the myths, philosophy, and theology of sin and evil, lies in the primordial human reading of the world and our place in it. Their importance lies in their being part of viable information systems that not only served human understanding, but also human survival.

As with other forms of primordial information, we cherish these symbolic systems in order to learn from them for our own understanding and survival. Such a learning process is not a simple one. Ricoeur, from a position of modern critical reason, spoke of it as crossing the threshhold from the first naiveté to the second (1967, 19–24, 347–57). Those who look at the learning challenge from the hermeneutical stance of postmodernism are just as aware that the premodern information and the modern critique must somehow be brought together for contemporary understanding (Shweder 1991, chap. 1; 35–39; 353–58).

The Doctrines of the Fall and Original Sin

For the purposes of this presentation, I am leaping over the testimonies of the most primitive human experience of sin and evil, as that testimony is conveyed in symbol and myth, to focus on a relatively late rendition of that testimony as it is interpreted in doctrine. Consequently, I am not attending to biblical exegesis nor to the kind of interpretation of myths that Ricoeur's work represents. As I have said above, however, my reflection upon the doctrines rests on an awareness of the more primordial and less discursive symbolic and mythic materials and on the understanding that the doctrines are interpretations of those prior materials.

I recognize, furthermore, that these doctrines and their mythic precursor texts have been interpreted in a variety of ways, especially in the first five centuries of Christianity (Pagels 1988, xxv–xxviii, chaps. 5, 6). This variety may be interpreted in terms of the Western church, represented by Augustine (354–430 C.E.), in contrast to the Eastern church, represented by Gregory of Nyssa (330–395

C.E.); or in terms of the first three centuries of Christian tradition contrasted to the fundamental changes wrought by Augustine in the fourth century and accepted by large segments of the church, especially in the West, in the fifth century. Even the term *original* sin bespeaks a Western treatment when contrasted to Nyssa's rejection of the term, as well as the term *natural sin,* an alternative offered by some theologians in his time, in favor of a view that roots sin in human freedom. The contrast is just as great when we consider the identification in the first three centuries of freedom with the impact of the gospel (Pelikan 1971, 278–82; Pagels 1988, chaps. 1–4). If we take this variety into account, we are struck by the Western Augustinian cast of most theological discussions of sin and evil (R. Williams 1982, 194; Gregorios 1988, chap. 7).

Augustine and His Influence in the West

In his argumentation with Pelagius and his disciple, Julian of Eclanum, Augustine devoted more than a decade of his life to articulating what we call the theology of the fall and original sin (Pelikan 1971, 289–92; Pagels 1988, chaps. 5–6). In a decisive manner, he elaborated the concepts of Adam's fall, the transmission of Adam's sin and its consequences through conception (specifically, sin is carried by the man's semen), guilt, and the necessity of grace. Physical death as well as corruptibility and vulnerability to disease and pain are the consequences of Adam's fall.

Augustine's powerful theological elaborations interweave in a complex manner his own personal experience of uncontrollable sexual desire, his polemics against the Pelagians, his interpretation of the virgin birth (following Ambrose, that it proves that ordinary conception is the source of sin) and of infant baptism (it is practiced because infants are born in sin and thus need forgiveness), and the church-political and cultural contexts in which he lived (Pelikan 1971, 279–331; Pagels 1988, chaps. 5–6). No interpretation of what Augustine or his predecessors and contemporaries taught concerning the fall and original sin is adequate if it does not take into account this total complex of issues: personal experience, biblical accounts, liturgical practice, and political-social contexts.

One classic Western rendering of the doctrines of the fall and original sin, fully in harmony with the Augustinian heritage, is found in the Lutheran Confessions, the *Augsburg Confession,* article two:

> Our churches also teach that since the fall of Adam all humans who are propagated according to nature are born in sin. That is to say, they are without fear of God, are without trust in God, and are concupiscent. And this disease or vice of origin (*vitium originis*) is truly sin, which even now damns and brings eternal death on those who are not born again through Baptism and the Holy Spirit. (Tappert 1959, 29; Latin version)

The Epitome of the *Formula of Concord,* article one, dating from 1580, elaborates on the fall:

> We believe, teach, and confess that there is a distinction between human nature and original sin, not only in the beginning when God created humans pure and holy and without sin, but also as we now have our nature after the Fall. Even after the fall our nature is and remains a creature of God. The distinction between our nature and original sin is as great as the difference between God's work and the devil's work.(Tappert 1959, 466)

This Lutheran version of the doctrines is distinctive in certain ways, yet, even allowing for the various misunderstandings between Catholics and Protestants on these points of teaching, it presents in substance what much of the Western tradition held (R. Williams 1982, 198–205). The basic substance of the Western view holds to (1) an original righteousness stemming from the goodness of God's creation, (2) a deviation that is rooted in human rebellion against God, which is passed on to all succeeding human beings by virtue of their conception in sexual intercourse (which entails concupiscence), (3) the guiltiness that applies to all persons on account of this sin, so that (4) divine grace is required to overcome the sin. Original sin has been interpreted to refer both to the *initial* sin of Adam and Eve and to the fact that the sin applies to all individuals by virtue of their birth, that is, *the sin of their origin as individuals.* This set of categories is important, as my later comments about this duality will show.

The Catholics, represented by Thomas Aquinas, using different philosophical categories involving the formal and material aspects of the sin, refer respectively to the loss of the original righteousness and to the presence of concupiscence (R. Williams 1982, 204).

The mainstream of the tradition wishes to avoid two extremes in thinking about this sin: on the one hand, a cool view of sin as defect, overlooking the ferocity of sinful intention; on the other hand, a view of sin as total depravity that demolishes the God-given original goodness that pertains to humans. I cite the Lutheran versions of the doctrine because they seem, when taken as a whole, to represent the main tradition without the extremes—the *Augsburg Confession* articulating the inherent ferocity of the sin, the *Formula of Concord* insisting upon human created goodness.

Biblical interpretation and theology have reflected upon whether the doctrines of the fall and original sin and their biblical textual correlates are to be taken as history. If so, then the Genesis 2–3 account means to provide an *etiology* of human sinfulness; the initial misdeed of Adam and Eve provides a causal explanation for the present human sinful condition. In terms of doctrine, the question is whether the concept of original righteousness refers to an actual historical period when humans were sinless and from which they have "fallen." Others suggest that the

Genesis account is not an etiology, but rather a *description* of the present state of humans. The Old Testament scholar Claus Westermann represents this position when he writes: "The [Genesis] narrative is not really answering the question of the origin of man, but the question of man experienced as ambivalent" (1974, 109; see 88–112).

Paul Tillich has also dealt with these issues in a representative theological fashion with his insistence that

> theology must clearly and unambiguously represent "the Fall" as a symbol for the human situation universally, not as the story of an event that happened "once upon a time" (1957a, 29; see also 29–44). . . . Original or hereditary sin is neither original nor hereditary; it is the universal destiny of estrangement which concerns every man (56).

Tillich also translates the assertion of original sin in his statement: "Before sin is an act, it is a state" (1948, 155).

The issue of sin being transmitted biologically at birth has also been translated into cultural terms, representatively by Friedrich Schleiermacher in the early nineteenth century. In this perspective, it is culture that transmits to each new human being the tragic web of sinfulness, rather than the biology of sexual intercourse, conception, and birth (Schleiermacher 1928, 279–81, 287–91). Augustine had directly linked the passion of sexual intercourse to sin, passion being the *fomes* or tinder for sin. Hence, every human being was conceived in sin.

Eastern Perspectives

Contemporary with Augustine, Eastern traditions took quite a different turn in interpreting the doctrines of the fall and original sin (Pelikan 1971, 285–86). The Pelagians themselves represented a version of the Eastern traditions (Pelikan 1971, 316). Dating at least from the first quarter of the fourth century of the common era, with Aphrahat (who flourished in the 330s and 340s C.E.), and continuing through Theodore of Mopsuestia (who died in 428 C.E.), we find positions like that described by Arthur Vööbus with respect to Theodore:

> First, Adam was created as mortal. . . . Second, concupiscence already lived in Adam as in a mortal being, causing the fall; therefore, it cannot be a punishment. Third, death is not a punishment for Adam's trespass, but something natural. Fourth, sin has nothing to do with nature. . . . Finally, however powerful are the effects of the trespass of the progenitor, the free will and the moral ability to make decisions between evil and good are not impaired. (1964, 113–14)

Gregory of Nyssa stands in traditions that are consistent with those described by Vööbus (Gregorios 1988, 165–68). His views also hold that concupiscence antedates sin, but is the occasion for it. It is the constant changeableness of human nature that is the locus for sin; in the dynamic continuum of their nature, humans make wrong choices in favor of evil. Sin is thus rooted firmly in human freedom, and its amelioration lies in the redirecting of the free will (Gregorios 1988, 156–80). Human nature is fundamentally good because it originates in God's creation of humans in the image of God.

For Gregory, as for Theodore of Mopsuestia, Western theology, epitomized for them by Augustine, denigrated this goodness of human nature and also misunderstood the significance of freedom. It seemed to impose a new fatalism that denied the goodness of creation. This echoed a position of the Pelagians (P. Brown 1969, 387–88). Gregorios summarizes Gregory's position: "Gregory follows essentially the Semitic tradition, to which the Augustinian notion of 'original sin' is inimical. The Semitic tradition puts the stress on human freedom and responsibility, and it is this line that Gregory also adopts" (1988, 168).

Sin is the result of Adam's free choice, and what we inherit from Adam is not sin but rather its consequences, mortality and corruptibility. Gregory agreed with his contemporary, Severus of Antioch, that "sin is a disease of the will, and the disease is not natural" (Gregorios 1988, 161). Sin is located in freedom, which is part of our basic created human nature. However, this is not to say that our basic nature is evil or sinful; rather, sin emerges in the course of our inadequate and wrongful use of the possibilities inherent in our nature.

If the Western view of original sin is interpreted as sin of origin (rather than first sin), it may be taken to refer to the sin that arises in the activity generated by those gifts with which we were endowed at our creation. This interpretation would support a view that is rooted in both West and East, even though the latter rejects the term *original sin* as they understand it to be held in the West.

The Theological Essentials

For the purposes of this discussion, I will focus upon five elements that seem essential to the Western Christian doctrines of the fall and original sin. I will relate them also to some of the Eastern Christian reflections on sin. (1) Sin is an inherent factor of human self-awareness. (2) We participate in sin as a condition pertaining to our very origin as persons. (3) Sin seems to be inherited in some fashion. (4) Sin is associated with our freedom. (5) Sin is marked by a sense of guilt and estrangement, thus requiring the gift of grace.

Excursus on the Theological Materials

As we reflect upon the theological traditions concerning the fall and original sin, we must keep in mind that these materials cannot simply be lifted out of their context for analysis. In their context they were vehicles for thinking not only about their stated themes, but also about other issues. Two of these sets of other issues deserve brief commentary.

The discussion of the fall and original sin were means by which the thinkers of the first five centuries of the common era expressed their understanding of the moral dimension of human existence, including social and religious values. Consequently, the biblical myths and the related teachings of Jesus provided the ambience in which thinkers in this period explored such questions as the nature of sexuality, the status of marriage as opposed to celibacy, polygamy, divorce, abortion, the necessity of pain, suffering, and death, and the possibility of personal discipline (Pagels 1988, xix–xx; 9–16). My discussion will not attempt to probe these issues, but it should not be overlooked that the issues that I will be focusing upon are heavily loaded with implications for values and moral behavior.

The themes that I am discussing are also a chief locus for thinking about the "nature of nature." Jaroslav Pelikan points out that for major thinkers in this period, "despite all this strong language about sin, the fundamental problem of man was not his sin, but his corruptibility" (1971, 285). Elaine Pagels comments on Augustine's arguments against Julian of Eclanum:

> Augustine's enormous error, Julian believed, was to regard the present state of nature as punishment. . . . Augustine thus denies the existence of nature *per se*—of nature as natural scientists have taught us to perceive it—for he cannot think of the natural world except as a reflection of human desire and will. Where there is suffering, there must have been evil and guilt, for, Augustine insists, God would not allow suffering where there was no prior fault. (1988, 132, 134–35)

Julian's position, in contrast, holds "that we suffer and die shows only that we are, by nature (and indeed, Julian would add, by divine intent), mortal beings, simply one living species among others" (Pagels 1988, 144). Julian insisted that free will is essential to nature, at least to human nature, and, like his contemporaries in the East, he charged that Augustine's proposals deny that freedom. Julian did not deny that sin emerges in the course of our employment of our freedom, but he rejected the notion that our freedom is by its very nature sinful.

That our nature becomes evil through its own free activity does not mean that it was created evil, but rather that it was created with the capacity to become what it has in fact become. Pagels goes on to suggest that despite the intellectual problems in Augustine's position, it nevertheless attempts to make sense—in a way that the more "contemporary" view does not—of the fact that, then and now, human beings manifest "a peculiar preference for guilt" (1988, 147).

The following discussion will have deep implications for how we perceive the "nature of nature." Even though I will not probe the matter in depth, I will argue that the scientific understandings throw light on the "peculiar preference for guilt."

Awareness Grounded in a Symbiosis

The first set of ideas provided by biology to which I shall turn for insights on the Christian assertions of human sinfulness emerges from the understanding of *Homo sapiens* as a creature that is dependent upon and formed by two kinds of informa-tion—genetic and cultural.

Dissonance between Genes and Culture

This dissonance within the individual is a ground for our awareness that sin is associated with our origins in prehistory, represented as the fall, and thus also a ground for the sense of guilt. The two streams of information, genetic and cul-tural, have evolved to their present state through processes of coadaptation that are centered in the human central nervous system. The genetic component has come to possess the characteristics of plasticity that allow not only for the emer-gence of culture but also for it to operate according to its own dynamic processes in ways that account for its success in the face of selective forces. At the same time, culture has had to adapt to the constraints of genetic evolution, since the death of the genetic host spells the end of the culture-bearing creature. Together this symbiosis has formed what geneticist Alfred Emerson (1943) and Ralph Burhoe (1981, 18–20, 173–79) have called a supraorganism, which flourishes because the two strands of information have coadapted to each other and to the environments in which the supraorganism exists. I explored this interpretation in detail in chapter 7.

When we properly understand the emergence of the human central nervous system and the concept of coadaptation of genes and culture within that central nervous system, we recognize that when we speak of dissonance between the two systems of information, we are in no way positing a fundamental dualism between them. On the contrary, the various dimensions of our biocult-ural nature constitute a wholeness. Talk of dissonance and tension is a heuristic device that aids us (so long as we remember that it is a heuristic) in the attempt to understand the richness of our natural character—in this case the sense of sin and guilt.

Paul MacLean's (1973) celebrated concept of the triune character of the hu-man central nervous system—reptilian, paleo-mammalian, and neocortex—pro-vides an additional perspective on the symbiotic character of *Homo sapiens*. Because it is the neocortex that is primary for the formation of culture, MacLean's theories can be included in the discussion of the genes-culture phenomenon. His work, as well as Emerson's and Burhoe's, underscores the importance of the harmonious or coadaptive interaction within each person of the various strands of evolutionary history that comprise human beings. To speak figuratively, a serious conversation and mutual instruction has to take place within each human being between the reptilian, paleo-mammalian, and neocortex dimensions of the brain. In a sense, the neocortex has to teach the other two dimensions how to function in a human way, while the neocortex has to accommodate itself to the constraints of the earlier dimensions.

The prehuman components are active within us, and as Anthony Stevens has explained, they are still engaged in the ongoing process of accommodation to the neurobiological ambience in which they must interact and function in ways that are appropriate to their human context. The evolutionary selection processes are operative in this realm also (A. Stevens 1983, 267–71). MacLean's suggestions are to be understood primarily for their heuristic usefulness (Deacon 1990b, 660–65), but they do give us a sense of the dynamic that accompanies the genes-culture symbiosis and its emergence and development in evolutionary history.

The coexistence between the varied evolutionary strands that comprise human being is not fully harmonious, however. The creatures who precede *Homo sapiens,* and who live almost entirely on the basis of preprogrammed genetic information, relate to the basic rhythms and requirements of their nature with an immediacy that we humans, being the decisively cultural animals that we are, cannot match. Since the evolutionary past is integral to our central nervous system, we can, in a way, remember the times of immediacy, and this in turn gives rise to a sense of discrepancy. To a considerable extent, an element of reflection and enculturation is required in order for humans to bring our prehuman information systems to bear within our existence as creatures of culture. A significant range of behaviors exists, of course, in which such an element is most often not required—the body's autonomic system is one such instance. (Although, for example, the application of medication to this system constitutes a cultural intervention.)

Where the supplementations of culture are necessary, it is often because the deliverances of the evolutionary past are deemed unacceptable, or because human agents sense their finitude and recognize that they need to augment the prehuman information inputs. We may recognize the unacceptableness of the prehuman inputs, for example, in our sense of territoriality, in our predisposition to reinforce the kin group, in certain eating patterns, or in interactions between male and female. We become clearly aware of our finitude and lack of capability when we respond to motivators for achievement, only to realize that we lack the basic capacity, experience, or education necessary to satisfy those motivators in a way that meets our human expectations.

George Pugh reinforces this understanding of the basic sense of discrepancy in his analysis of human values. For example, the desire to excel and the desire to contribute to the group are values bequeathed to us from our evolutionary history—specifically, from the higher primates. However, such excelling or contributing cannot take place until culturally suitable supplements come into play that enable them to be brought to bear in a satisfactory manner (1977, 284–88).

My conclusion from the foregoing is that concepts of the fall and original sin may well be considered to be mythic renditions of this biologically grounded sense of discrepancy. We are aware of the discrepancy as something deeply rooted in our being, primordial to our self-consciousness. This primordial character is what the term *original* conveys—not in the sense of there being a "first" or causative sin, but in the sense that the discrepancy is as primordial as our very origination. This conclusion is clearly related to the traditional concept of the sin of origin as I elaborated it earlier.

Obviously, this interpretation favors the Eastern theological traditions over the Western as the more satisfactory thematization of our biologically conditioned experience. The fall articulates symbolically our awareness that our human identity is constructed significantly on foundations bequeathed to us from a prehuman evolutionary history where immediacy governed as both necessity and possibility. We cannot retreat to our prehuman past; even to desire that is a pathology, because it is a rejection of our human selfhood (Tillich 1957a; Burhoe 1972). Nevertheless, we can and do yearn for a state in which our culture would respond as immediately to the requirements of the way things really are, or God's evolution, as the prehuman motivators (whose messages now flood our central nervous system) did when they drove their host organisms in prehuman environments.

This discrepancy may also be the biogenetic ground of our sense of guilt. The motivators that derive from our prehuman past operate in part on the pleasure principle. To have to deny those motivators is unpleasant to us. The overriding of those motivators with others that derive from the neocortex sets up a dissonance that may cause us to feel unpleasantness or even pain. Vis-à-vis the more primitive motivators, we may thus feel lacking and guilty. In the light of these factors, we may gain insights into Augustine's insistence that a peculiar preference for guilt comes with the human territory. Contrary to his explanations, however, guilt does not flow as a consequence of an initial sin, but rather is grounded in the evolutionary history and nature of *Homo sapiens*.

Culture against Selfish Human Nature

Donald T. Campbell has related the religious symbol of original sin to the experiential and behavioral consequences of the fact that not only has sociocultural evolution emerged as a concomitant to biological evolution, but it is the basis for contemporary urban civilization. He stated his thesis in two celebrated maxims:

1. Human urban social complexity has been made possible by social evolution rather than biological evolution.
2. This social evolution has had to counter individual selfish tendencies which biological evolution has continued to select as a result of the genetic competition among the cooperators. (1976, 189)

Campbell's argument recognizes the necessity of sociocultural evolution for human life as we now know it, but it also calls attention to the fact that, unlike the social insects, who also possess a highly complex social life, the cultured cooperators in the human community are genetically competitors. This results in the state of affairs that Campbell characterizes as "human culture contra selfish human nature" (1976, 187). In an earlier work, Campbell wrote:

> Not only must complex human social interdependence be a product of social evolution; the evolved socially induced dispositions must have directly opposed the selfish dispositional tendencies continually selected for by the concurrent biological evolution. It is this opposition between the dispositional products of biological and social evolution that explains Freud's observations on human ambivalence toward social roles and his contrast with the unambivalent insects. But Freud was wrong in believing that length of time in evolutionary history is the problem; it is, rather, the more fundamental fact of the evolutionary route toward social complexity. (1975, 242–43)

This argument is rooted in Campbell's reading of developments during the last quarter century in the genetics of altruism. He associates himself with the position of George C. Williams, who holds that altruistic tendencies that put the individual at risk will be selected for less frequently in a population's evolution than those that make for selfish gain (D. Campbell 1975, 239). Campbell favors this strict view of the limits of genetic evolution, precisely because it sets up the tension with sociocultural evolution that runs through the center of human social existence. This tension in turn

> makes evolutionary sense out of the otherwise anomalous or incomprehensible preoccupation with sin and temptation in the folk morality that our religious traditions provide. The commandments, the proverbs, the religious "law" represent social-evolutionary products directed at inculcating tendencies that are in direct opposition to the "temptations" which for the most part represent dispositional tendencies produced by biological evolution. For every commandment we may reasonably hypothesize a biological tendency running counter to some social-systematic optimum. (D. Campbell 1975, 243)

In relation to my previous argument, the significance of Campbell's reflections lies in (1) their underscoring that the interface that is characterized by discrepancy is itself the ground of the most distinctive feature of human life—its complex social form; (2) their specifying the nature of this discrepancy as the pressure from cultural evolution for genetically predisposed competitors to function as cooperators; and (3) their introducing the tension between social and individual systems into the discussion of the genes/culture-based discrepancy. Campbell recognizes that genetic competition gives rise to selfishness, greed, and "skin-surface hedonism," where cooperation suggests "counter-hedonic" self-discipline, denial, and altruism. He explicitly correlates the state of affairs along this interface with the classical notions of original sin.

In terms of my previous argument, we could say that original sin and the fall are mythic renditions of the circumstances that Campbell clarifies in his complex genetic/sociocultural analysis. His proposals bear strong witness to the fact that the themes discussed here carry implications for values and moral behavior. They also throw light on the possible matrix out of which the human feeling of guilt arises.

Two questions may be raised concerning Campbell's analysis: (1) Does his rhetoric of cooperators and competitors bespeak a fundamental dualism? (2) Is such rhetoric too much the product of importing metaphors from other sectors of our culture—perhaps from the ideology of free-market capitalism—under the subliminal pressure to enthrone that ideology at the most fundamental levels with the authority that derives from being clothed with "scientific fact"?

Campbell is fully aware that the locus of his cooperators and competitors is the evolutionary process in which intense coadaptation is the norm; therefore the charge of dualism is misguided. Tension and contradiction may indeed occur as behavioral manifestations, but in the context in which Campbell works, that cannot imply an ontological dualism.

As to the second question, metaphors may indeed be transferred, particularly among North American thinkers, from the competitive rhetoric of capitalism to the realm of the scientists. However, Campbell and his peers also speak of co-operation, coadaptation, and coevolution, which certainly counterbalance the competitive images. In the final analysis, the rhetoric must be judged by what actual empirical investigation within a broad community of researchers favors.

Fact Grounded in Imperfection and Finitude

The preceding section dealt with the ground of the feeling among humans that they have somehow "fallen" into sin. The mythic symbol of the fall was corre-lated to the awareness of the discrepancies and tensions that attend the interaction of two systems of information that are basic to the human individual and group—the genetic and the cultural. The discussion turns in this section to the perception that sinfulness is intrinsic to the human condition—as Tillich articulated in his statement, "Before sin is an act, it is a state" (1948, 155), and as the Christian tradition speaks of a defect or disease of our origin (*vitium* or *morbus originis*) (e.g., Tappert 1959, 29).

This aspect of sin is illumined by the understanding of human culture with which this chapter began and which the following chapters explore in detail. Culture is a system of information, guidance, and support that is symbiotic with our genetic information systems and that supplements the genotype and its elabo-ration in the phenotype. Neither the genotypic nor the cultural systems are per-fect in their ability to guide and sustain human behavior. Ralph Wendell Burhoe has described this imperfection:

> Living systems simply are not fully preadapted to all future contingencies. It would seem that we can epitomize the program of life as the unending search for the right

code without our ever fully reaching it. . . . If the failures and inadequacies of the codes of right behavior of any time and place are always with us, to that extent we are always wrong, bad, and evil. And since in evolutionary pictures of life this is the case, we may say that humans in this sense are inherently wrong, bad, and evil. One finds this parallel to religious doctrines of original sin. (1981, 65)

The cultural system of information intensifies this propensity to imperfection, however. Not only does it rely for its development on what Burhoe calls "this unending program of trial and error" that constitutes the process of natural selection, but it also includes within that unending program the elements of human self-awareness, decision, and the accompanying self-aware feedback mechanisms. Moreover, all of these elements in the system of cultural evolution proceed in their work much more rapidly than the mechanisms of genetic evolution. Finally, the cultural system (like all other systems) is finite.

The human cultural information and guidance system must respond not only to the environment in which it is set, but also to its conscious perceptions of that setting. It must determine by its own decision which of alternative perceptions is to be given greatest weight, just as it must determine and authenticate in itself that which is to be authoritative for its processes of selection and action. At every moment, the system is aware that it knows too little, that its projections are based on inadequate data, that its stamina is less than it desires and needs. This awareness is inherent in the central nervous system processes (see chapter 6). Jerrison (1976) and Calvin (1991b) describe the neurophysiological correlates to this probing character of *Homo sapiens*.

For some, this emphasis on fallibility and finitude may seem too bland to describe sin as the Western religious traditions understand it. However, the aspects of human nature described here as fallible are not at all bland; they are the underlying ground of sin in its most virulent expressions.

The foregoing illuminates the biogenetic context in which human freedom emerges, and thereby augments the discussion in chapter 6. Freedom is here defined as the capacity to launch into, and to persist in, the trial-and-error program that evolution sets for us, the probing that Jerrison, Deacon, and Calvin insist is intrinsic to the human central nervous system.

Against this background we recall the emphasis upon free will that much of the theological tradition has associated with the human condition and the source both of sin and of its overcoming. Contrary to Julian of Eclanum, however, this free will appears to emerge within the context of the discrepancy that we focused upon earlier. The sense of discrepancy (and guilt?) does not militate against freedom, but rather may be its concomitant. Although the Western, Augustinian concepts of original sin may be unpersuasive, this set of probes, dealing with finitude and fallibility, gives weight to Pagels's judgment that Augustine deals more seriously with certain aspects of the human condition—namely, the interrelatedness of freedom with a sense of inadequacy and guilt.

Fallibility and the awareness of fallibility are thus built into the human system in a way that is not the case with systems that are not cultural and highly self-aware. All of these factors that I have described are intrinsic to the human creature and its self-awareness, and furthermore they are the occasion for regret and painful or evil consequences; therefore they truly appear as *defect* or *"disease" of origin*.

These factors of trial and error and fallibility stand also as the very source of life and goodness. In Burhoe's words:

> However, it should be noted that this same process in another perspective is good. If life is the supreme value, it is clear that in this universe it can be obtained only by this unending program of trial and error, which continues to build up higher and higher systems of order or life. In this wider perspective evil becomes the agent of the good, wrong or error the means to the right, and death the source of greater life. (1981, 65)

Consequently, the poignancy is heightened. Just as Campbell noted that the tension that produces the awareness of original sinfulness is central for making possible that social form of existence that is distinctive to humans, so Burhoe reminds us that the fallibility that engenders error and evil is not only intrinsic to human being, but is basic to the processes that originate life and allow it to develop in enriching ways. This intrinsic poignancy and complexity, deep down in the character of human nature, grounds the Christian insistence, both West and East, that in its created origins, human being is not bad but good, even though the traditions also insist upon the inescapability of grave sin. Defect of origin and goodness are not contradictory, but rather constitutive of human being in its primordial nature.

This way of speaking is reminiscent of Paul Tillich's description of the demonic:

> The demonic contains destruction of form, which does not come from without, does not depend on deficiency or powerlessness, but originates from the basis of the form itself, the vital as well as the intellectual. To understand this connection is to grasp what is meant by the concept demonic, in its truth and inevitability, that is, in its metaphysical essence. . . . the depth of things, their basis of existence, is at the same time their abyss; or in other words, . . . the depth of things is inexhaustible. . . . The impulse for formation inherent in everything and filling it and the horror of decay of form is founded on the form-quality of existence. To come into being means to come to form. To lose form means to lose existence. At the same time, however, there dwells in everything the inner inexhaustibility of being, the will to realize in itself as an individual the active infinity of being, the impulse toward breaking through its own, limited form. . . . Demonry is the form-destroying eruption of the creative basis of things. (1936, 82–85)

Nicholas Berdyaev's interpretation of chaos and freedom reinforces Tillich's imagery (Hefner 1984c).

In this case, as with the other two sets of data surveyed earlier, the conclusion can be drawn that the symbols pertaining to the doctrine of original sin render the primal experience of being intrinsically inadequate, while that inadequacy is key to the process that makes life possible and enriches it—the *vitium originis*.

Biology and Theology as Mutually Enriching

Commensurability of Symbols and Analysis

Earlier, I suggested that five elements from the historical traditions are essential to the doctrines of the fall and original sin: (1) Sin is an inherent factor of our self-awareness. (2) We participate in sin as a condition pertaining to our very origin as persons. (3) Sin seems to be inherited in some fashion. (4) Sin is associated with our freedom. (5) Sin is marked by a sense of guilt and estrangement. These elements will figure in my discussion of the biological materials.

This discussion of the biological materials leads to the first conclusion that these five elements are borne out by the biological theories. Following Ricoeur, this means that the symbols that underlie the doctrines can be understood as ways of reading the human condition, conceptualized biologically. The first two elements, sin as inherent in our self-awareness and as pertaining to our very origin as persons, have been reiterated several times. The third element, the inheritance of sin, is clear; it is the evolutionary process itself that bequeaths to each individual and each generation the constitutive elements of life that bear the conditions of what we have called sin of origin.

This self-awareness does not, however, gainsay the conviction that humans are created good. The poignancy and complexity that underly the simultaneous acknowledgment of goodness and sinfulness are intrinsic to being human. With respect to the concept of created co-creator, this complexity underscores both the possibilities and excitement of being human and also the sober awareness of our finitude and vulnerability to the defects that ground the most demonic expressions of evil.

The fourth element, freedom, figures centrally in all three sets of biological data surveyed here, inasmuch as those sets of data focused upon the evolutionary emergence and the functioning of culture. The emergence of culture is dependent upon precultural evolutionary processes that are capable of sustaining the presence of culture, in something like a relationship of symbiosis. The functioning of culture is dependent upon the activities of freedom that make possible such phenomena as cultural selection, discernment, and decision. The element of tension between genes and culture that figured in the first two sets of data, as well as the factor of fallibility in discernment and decision expressed in the third set, is rooted in the activity of freedom as it interacts with the biological symbiont of human being and also with the physical environment in which humans live.

The fifth element, estrangement and guilt, also correlates with the biological discussions of the three sets of data. The tensions between genes and culture,

human fallibility, and the reflection of fallibility in human self-awareness are leading causes of the sense of alienation at fundamental levels of human consciousness.

Biological Interpretation as Deepening

The symbolic message of sin as inherent in human nature, the defect of origin,
is deepened by the biological understandings, in that they complexify our sense
of how this defect comes to be inherent. What we have called sin is inherent in
human being because it is a constituent of the processes that make life possible
in the first place and that contribute to life's development. Thus, even though we
are aware of sin and feel its pain (guilt), sin is not present because of some prior
evil action or evil nature. The guilt is better understood as a response to our
inherent inability to satisfy all of the messages that are delivered to our central
nervous system, rather than as a response to an evil act committed in the primordial past of the race. Two of Schleiermacher's theses concerning sin are strikingly
contemporary for this discussion:

> #69. We are conscious of sin partly as having its source in ourselves, partly as having
> its source outside our own being. . . . #72. While the idea that we have thus devel-
> oped cannot be applied in precisely the same way to the first human pair, we have
> no reason for explaining universal sinfulness as due to an alteration in human nature
> brought about in their person by the first sin. . . . In fact, Adam must have been
> sundered from God before his first sin; for, when Eve handed him the fruit he ate
> it without even recalling the divine interdict; and this presupposes a like corruption
> of his nature. . . . If, however, human nature in the first pair was the same before
> the first sin as it appears subsequently alike in them and in their posterity, we cannot
> say that human nature was changed as a result of the first sin. (1928, 279, 291,
> 296–97)

Leaving aside the fact that Schleiermacher's "first pair" belief is impossible for
us to accept other than as a symbolic rendering, it should be noted that he believed he was forced to depart from the Lutheran and Calvinist Confessions to
which his church held fast. In light of my earlier analysis, he embodies the critique of the East against the West. The Eastern traditions rejected the term *original*
sin because they thought of it as the *first* sin. However, following my interpretation as set forth in this chapter, one can recognize the validity and depth of the
term *original* as Schleiermacher and the Reformation traditions understood it, as
"sin of, or pertaining to our origin." Indeed, Augustine, in part, and the subsequent traditions of the West understood the term *original* in this deeper sense.
The inadequate notion of *first* sin constitutes only a part of their understanding.
One has only to think of Book Two of Augustine's *Confessions* (1955, 50–61) in
contrast to chapter 13 of his *Enchiridion* (1955, 365–68), where the "first" sin
hypothesis is accepted.

The Eastern view that human nature is created good, but falls into sin through freedom, is credible when viewed through the biological understandings, but neither that view nor that of the West during the early centuries does justice to the intricate interweaving of goodness, freedom, and the basis of sin and evil in that interweaving.

Modern discussions often scorn the prevailing Western view of the genetic transmission of sin through sexual intercourse and conception. Suggestions that sin's transmission is through cultural instruments find greater acceptance. The biological understandings, with their focus on the genes-culture symbiosis, support the insistence that both genetic and cultural means leave a legacy of sin in each generation, for reasons that should be obvious from the discussion above of each of the three sets of data. Passion or concupiscence is not the key to this transmission, however, as much of the tradition insists; it is not the "bad" or uncontrollable dimension of human sexuality and culture that conveys sin, but rather the human constitution as such, including those elements that make for human distinctiveness and goodness.

These reflections suggest that the interpretation of the fall and original sin as universally applicable myth is more commensurate with the biological understandings than the etiological interpretation that views earlier sins as causative of later sin. However, the causative view is not ruled out. The sins of the parents can be conveyed biologically to the children; one has only to think of "crack babies," fetal alcohol syndrome, and other defects caused by improper prenatal care. All of the attributes of finitude are conveyed genetically, at conception. Similarly, events of culture may also be causative in force.

The introduction of biological understandings into the discussion of sin favors neither a so-called male analysis nor a feminist view, but rather could include both. Judith Plaskow associates feminist views with the protest against "male" views that sin is pride and arrogance, as if passivity and absence of aggressive self-development were more virtuous. Such interpretations tend to be of disadvantage to women—so the argument goes (Plaskow 1980).

A historical survey suggests that the feminist proposals are particularly relevant as critique of the Augustinian position; the Eastern understandings, with their distinctive ways of putting emphasis upon free will, would tend to support the position that Plaskow urges. The interpretations that have been advanced in this discussion can affirm Plaskow's argument. Certainly the inherited biocultural constitution of the human being is equally applicable to both her "male" and "female" experience of sin. The tension between genes and culture, between the social system and the individual system, and also the intrinsic fallibility of humans may take different forms when applied to the stereotypical male or female experience, but the biologically informed interpretations throw light on the experience of sin in both men and women.

Reflections on the Undertaking

First, juxtaposing the biological interpretations to the religious-theological materials illumines several important dimensions of the traditional reflection upon sin. The discussion in this chapter has indicated how biology enriches our understanding of the inherent character of sin, its interrelationship with what makes life possible and with what is good for life. Biological concepts deepen the significance of freedom in our thinking about sin and also the character and causes of sin, guilt, and estrangement.

Second, particular traditional understandings are seriously challenged. It may be necessary to reject some historically popular insights. Notions of the "first pair," concepts of the fall that insist upon some primordial act of early humans that altered subsequent human nature, and certain forms of etiological interpretation are among the elements that must be looked upon with great skepticism.

Third, some ambiguities call for further reflection. The clash of ideas that is exemplified by Augustine's insistence upon guilt as a primordial condition due to a primordial sin, versus Julian of Eclanum's equally insistent argument that freedom is essential to human nature, calls for deeper reflection. The primordial nature of guilt, as a reading of the discrepancy that is intrinsic to *Homo sapiens,* seems to be a reasonable and discussable notion, even though the suggestion that guilt is proof of an original sin seems untenable. At the same time, the essential place of freedom in the human equation seems equally viable as a proposal for discussion, alongside the presence of guilt and its underlying grounds. The guilt/free will complex of concepts begs for more adequate conceptual treatment.

I make these comments not simply on the assumption that science determines what may or may not be believed religiously. Rather, the point is that of Ricoeur: the symbols of the religious tradition are primordial readings of human experience and the human position within the natural and social world. Whether a traditional element is enhanced or rendered obsolete when juxtaposed to science is here dependent upon whether that symbol seems to render adequately what counts as significant human experience, inclusive of science.

Some perennial questions about sin remain, however. Among them are these: Why is human life so intricately and intrinsically implicated with the factors that make for sin and evil? Is Burhoe's explanation (which in one form underlies John Hick's reflections upon theodicy [Hick 1981]) persuasive—that the very aspects of the process of life that make human culture possible are intrinsically the bearers of the possibility for sin and evil? This amounts to the recognition that theodicy is rendered neither more nor less a problem by the interpretations of biology.

This discussion throws new light on the issues of free will versus determinism and guilt, but by no means pretends to resolve these thorny questions. Their discussion is modulated into a new key, but does not disappear.

If sin is what a biologically informed discussion indicates, what does this imply for grace and redemption? Whether viewed in Christian terms or not, does redemption alter the reality of nature so that sin can be overcome? This would imply a rigorous atonement-centered Christology, one that describes how the Messiah has actually effected a change in the created order. Or does redemption model for us how sinful human nature can make for life and its enrichment, fulfilling the human destiny? This would seem to imply a Christology of exemplification, one that portrays the Messiah's work as that of setting forth and accomplishing the purposes that are intrinsic to the created order from its beginning.

The rudimentary probes that have formed the substance of this chapter have not touched in any depth on the constructive work that awaits the theologian and philosopher in fulfilling the task that Ricoeur set before us—to transport the traditional symbols, where they are important vessels of information for us, into the realm of contemporary, second-naiveté experience, and enable them to coalesce with our experience to provide genuine knowledge of reality, for the sake of our wholesome living. That task remains and is intensified by such considerations as we surveyed.

In this chapter, I have omitted any discussion of grace and redemption. These themes will be addressed in Part Four.

Part 4

Culture

9

Culture as Constructed Systems
of Information

My elaboration of the created co-creator now turns to the third and decisive element of the theological theory. The first element focused primarily on *Homo sapiens* as a creature of nature, whose origins lie in the natural processes in which we have emerged and whose purpose for living is referred back to the nature that is our ambience. The second element gave attention to the fact that the human being is a two-natured creature, constituted by streams of genetically and culturally evolved information. Formed by the symbiosis of these two bodies of information, we human beings are intrinsically free, in the sense that we have the capability, grounded physiologically in our central nervous system, to process large amounts of information by means of constructing patterns that organize and interpret that information. Furthermore, our survival has depended upon our using this capability in an adequate manner. In describing human being in this fashion, I am relying on the emerging model of biocultural evolution as the hermeneutic key for understanding ourselves.

Information *as a Technical Term*

At this point, it is important that the term *information* be understood as I am using it in this book, particularly in relationship to human nature, culture, myth, ritual, and religion. I am following what I understand to be the current use of the term in the physical and biological sciences, and I refer the reader to the lucid discussions by Robert Wright, in his book *Three Scientists and Their Gods: Looking for Meaning in an Age of Information* (1988, especially 83–110), and Douglas R. Hofstadter, in *Gödel, Escher, and Bach: An Eternal Golden Braid* (1980, especially chap. 6).

In popular parlance, information is often considered to be trivial, commonplace, part of the "how-to" process, with no profound meaning. We read the printed information on a packet of vegetable seeds simply to learn what particular care we must take in planting the seeds. Instruction manuals of all sorts give us information on how to put Christmas toys together or how to hook up a VCR.

145

We make a telephone call to get recorded information as to what time it is or whether it will rain this afternoon.

Against this background, it is not surprising that we find it jarring to hear the term *information* applied to great literature, culture, music, and to religious traditions that we consider to be profoundly meaningful, perhaps even inspired by divine revelation. We might find it bewildering, if not repugnant, to have culture defined as "information capable of affecting individuals' phenotypes which they acquire from other conspecifics by teaching or imitation" (Boyd and Richerson, 1985, 33), or to read that religions are "bounded systems of information process, in which human beings are offered fundamental resources for the construction of their lives" (Bowker 1976, 363).

Even if they sound strange to our ears, however, careful attention to these quotations, the first from behavioral scientists and the second from a scholar of world religions, tells us that the word *information* is being used in a sense that is far from trivial or one-dimensional. These scholars are referring to information as that which bears messages that have consequences; that is, messages that result in the creation of something that makes a difference for behavior, whether that behavior is the biological processes that make our eyes blue or brown, or the attempt by human beings to live a morally good life. Robert Wright summarizes the scientific concept of information in these terms: "Meaningful information is that which has form, can help create or maintain form, and does so by representing states of the environment and inducing behaviors appropriate to them" (1988, 108).

The weather report is information in that it represents to us a message about our world that may result in our remaining at home rather than going to a baseball game, or our carrying an umbrella with us on an errand. Wright speaks of three kinds of information—reports, instructions, and programs. DNA can also be spoken of as informational in this context:

> the DNA in the cells that are us processes information that represents *their* immediate environments. That is the only way that bone cells, hair cells, and skin cells— all of which are born with same general-purpose DNA, after all—"know" which identity to adopt; their DNA receives reports about what sort of neighborhood they are in, and it then instructs them to act accordingly. . . . Perhaps the best way to characterize the relationship between DNA and meaning is to say that DNA is the *source* of meaning. It takes information about the environment and turns it into behavior—thus realizing meaning in the pragmatic sense of the word. DNA is the place where the two sides of meaning meet, the place where reports become instructions. DNA is thus what first gave meaning to life. (Wright 1988, 109–10)

Against this background, I speak of the human being as the confluence of two streams of information, genetic and cultural. I will also speak in this section of religion, particularly its myth and ritual, as packets of information. The concept of *what really is* or *the way things really are,* as I reflected upon it in chapter 6 and also later in this chapter, comes into play here. At one level, when DNA processes information that represents to our cells their own immediate environments, that DNA is proposing a representation of the way things really are that reaches back into evolutionary history and also extends into the present and the future, and this representation makes a difference for cell behavior. The research that I cited in chapters 6 and 7 suggests that the selective advantage of the human central nervous system lies precisely in this set of factors, that it excels at representing to itself the way things really are with respect to its environment—at least at one level.

At still another level, scientific cosmology and evolutionary theory propose to tell us the way things really are. It is not so clear what impact these representations make on human behavior, even though these theories are in fact formulated in response to observations of the behavior of certain physical and biological objects and processes. Indeed, this book is an attempt to deal with this lack of clarity. Culture, as many anthropologists tell us, is the way in which we humans "put our worlds together"—a definite portrayal of the way things really are, with concrete impact on human behavior (Shweder and LeVine 1984; Shweder 1991).

Religion, as a component of culture, proposes the biggest pictures of the way things really are, and is intensely serious about what sorts of behavior follow from those pictures. In what follows, I employ a concept of religion that may be defined, as Karl Peters (1982) defines it: an evolving system of beliefs, practices, and experiences in which individuals or societies relate to what is thought to be ultimate. The structure of religion includes myths, doctrinal beliefs, rituals, moral behaviors, scriptures, organization, and experiences. My primary interest is in myth, ritual, and moral behavior or praxis. This train of thought is preparatory to the myth-ritual-praxis concept with which I end this chapter.

I use the term *culture* to refer to the form that human freedom has assumed in the evolutionary history of the species. My definition of culture is an eclectic one that echoes the many definitions that have been suggested in this century (Kroeber and Kluckhohn 1952; La Barre 1954; Geertz 1973, chap. 1; Boyd and Richerson 1985, 2, chap. 3; Goldsmith 1991, 125): Culture is a system of learned patterns of behavior and the symbol systems that contextualize and interpret those behaviors. With the nuances of this definition in mind, the reader can better accept Boyd and Richerson's definition quoted a few pages above. It would also be consistent with the argument to say, as Weston La Barre has, that culture is the adaptation of human beings to their humanity (1954, 213).

My view of culture differs from the celebrated definition provided by Clifford Geertz: "an historically transmitted pattern of meanings embodied in symbols, a system of inherited conceptions expressed in symbolic forms by means of which men communicate, perpetuate, and develop their knowledge about and attitudes toward life" (1973, 89). The difference lies not in the emphasis on culture as including symbol systems, but rather in the omission of any reference to learned patterns of behavior or to the biogenetic evolutionary context of culture and its transmission. I would move closer to Lindon Eaves's critique of Geertz for the indifference to the biological ground of human behavior that his definitions imply (1991, 498–99).

The Origins of Culture in Human History

The discussion of culture leads to the third element of the created co-creator theory, the decisive element, because culture focuses the life-and-death issues with which humans must deal in our epoch. At this stage, my proposal deals with the origins of culture in human evolutionary history and its function, including the origin and function of myth and ritual (and therefore, of religion). The theory takes its most speculative turn at this point. Its value rests totally on the wager that its speculation is fruitful for further exploration of the issues it raises, whether its suggestions are finally corroborated or falsified. At the present time, it is doubtful whether enough knowledge exists to support either corroboration or falsification. Why, then, engage in this speculation? For one reason: *Understanding the evolutionary origins and function of culture, and religion in culture, is necessary if we are properly to interpret human life and the crises it faces today.*

The seventh auxiliary hypothesis contains the foundations for thinking about culture within the framework of human evolutionary history.

#7: The challenge that culture poses to human being can be stated thus: Culture is a system of information that humans must construct so as to adequately serve the three tasks of interpreting the world in which humans live, guiding human behavior, and interfacing with the physico-biogenetic-cultural systems that constitute the environment in which we live.

If culture is a system of information that must interpret the world, guide behavior, and interface with the rest of the natural world (including human societies), we can imagine culture's evolutionary origins. Even though culture itself is evolving—growing and changing—by the time they reached the stage of *Homo sapiens,* humans did not have to learn to be creatures of culture; they had emerged as such creatures. The circumstances under which humans had to survive almost from the beginning made demands upon them that required elements of culture that would appear impressive in comparison with the culture even of other higher primates. Because human survival has depended upon culture, much can be learned by reflections on what might have been the circumstances of the origins of culture and religion and their function.

At its kernel, my suggestion in this section is that culture served to let humans imagine, motivate, and later to justify behavior that was a significant extension beyond the behavior borne by biogenetic motivators alone. I speculate that myth and ritual are the chief carriers of the information that motivates and interprets the behavior beyond the biogenetic. This behavior is of a wide range of types—pertaining to cuisine, medicaments, interactions between persons, the raising of children, the hunt, and much more.

Such behavior stands in a complex relation to prehuman behavior. The behavior of *Homo sapiens,* with its added cultural motivations, at times seems to extend the legacy of behavior in the same trajectory as that of the prehuman, as in the case of maternal nurturing of infants (Harlow and Harlow 1969). In other cases, humans turned the inherited patterns in quite different directions; as, for example, behaviors between the genders or altruistic behaviors toward alien tribes (Alexander 1987; Dawkins 1978). In still other cases, novel behaviors arise that have no counterpart in the prehuman legacy, as in the preparation of food (Katz and Schall 1979).

There is much to be gained in another direction by speculating about the evolutionary origins and function of culture in general, and specifically about myth and ritual. My approach is related to, but also differs from, two other approaches—that of the history and phenomenology of religions and that of the so-called ideology critique. In the following chapters I attempt to take seriously the work of the phenomenologists and historians of religion on myth and ritual—van der Leeuw, Eliade, Ricoeur, Berger and Luckmann—while at the same time overcoming the latent inadequacies in that approach.

The work of the phenomenologists is rich in insights concerning the structure and meaning of myths, beginning with so-called primitive religions. However, in its classic insistence that phenomenology is its own justification, in its resistance to functional and reductionist interpretations, this approach tends to give second rank to the evolutionary context of myth and ritual, as well as the context in which survival is at stake (van der Leeuw 1963, vol. 1, 269; vol. 2, 671–89; Bolle 1967, 101–18; Long 1967, 83–87; Eliade 1967; Sullivan 1988, 17–18, 698–99). When this resistance leads to a minimizing of the evolutionary and survival context, it constitutes a defect in method, because it deprives us of important insights into the deepest significance of culture, myth, and ritual—namely, that they convey information or knowledge for the living that takes place within the continuum of nature and its evolutionary history.

It is impossible fully to interpret or appreciate the knowledge conveyed by cultural forms unless we understand how they emerged and what they contributed to human survival and well-being. Here the pragmatic criterion discussed in chapter 2 comes into play. At the same time we must recognize that the historians of religion, while not denying the contextual factors, treat them as they do because of what they consider to be the intrinsic requirements of their subject matter—the study of religion (Sullivan 1988, 18).

Other approaches include what is sometimes called ideology critique or the hermeneutic of suspicion, which I prefer to describe simply as critical thinking, in the style of the Frankfurt School (Jay 1973). This method is essentially in accord with recent proposals advanced by feminist thinkers and Latin American and African American liberation theologians. Langdon Gilkey has applied a similar method with effect to analyzing the place of science in society (1981, 73–120; 1985, chap. 7).

These approaches sometimes view culture, including myth, ritual, and religion, purely as instruments of self-interest and survival. Often, myth and ritual are interpreted as base or negative instruments that need to be criticized so that persons can be liberated to substitute more rational instruments. In viewing myth and ritual as dishonest masks for base interests, these approaches have liberating consequences when they call attention to the "bad faith" that accompanies such presentations of myth and ritual. This same approach, however, is defective when it loses sight of the fact that myth and ritual carry important information for living. We cannot jettison myth and ritual in favor of more desirable information without giving due regard to their status as bearers of information that is often essential for well-being. Even where the survival interests of previous generations must be pruned away, the knowledge-bearing function remains as critical for human living.

Jürgen Habermas, from within the Frankfurt School, has provided some of the most useful suggestions for taking account of the interests or ideologies that are inextricably bound up with our most hallowed ideas, including our basic myths and rituals, without denying the integrity of those ideas (Habermas 1971). Rosemary Radford Ruether (1983), Elisabeth Schüssler-Fiorenza (1983), Sandra Harding (1987), Elaine Pagels (1988), and other feminist thinkers have made comparable contributions. James Cone (1972, 1975, chap. 3), working out of African American sources, provides similar suggestions, as does the literary scholar Henry Louis Gates, Jr. (1988).

Without question, our culture is a chief instrument for our survival, and it bears the marks of our own individual and epochal survival struggle. At the same time it conveys information that originated prior to the human's emergence and struggle, as well as information contributed in that struggle whose significance for later generations transcends our own situation. It is uniquely the human task to discern what is pertinent only to the struggle of past generations and what holds possibilities for the present and future.

The approach to culture, myth, and ritual, that is set forth in this and the following chapters builds upon three current methodologies: (1) history or phenomenology of religion, (2) evolutionary interpretations of human behavior (sometimes called sociobiology and often condemned simply because of that name), and (3) critical thinking.

The phenomenology of religions grounds the deep appreciation for myth and ritual that is here set forth. It builds on the thought, in particular of Paul Ricoeur and Mircea Eliade, that myth and ritual are intrinsically meaningful and bearers of the constitutive meaning that humans attach to their worlds. Lawrence Sullivan gives a recent rendition of this insistence:

> The study of religion must be carried on in a way appropriate to its subject matter. This is not a cry against reductionism, for any interpretation of symbolic life must reduce meaning to its scale and purposes. Rather, it is a reminder that social values and functions, which are never absent from or irrelevant to symbolic action and belief, are themselves symbolic of the religious need to encounter what is sacred and to know what is true in order to ground every aspect of life on what *really is*. (1988, 18)

Evolutionary interpretations of human emergence and behavior form the second cornerstone of my approach. They are essential, because "what really is," or "the way things really are," as culture and religion perceive and portray it, occurs in the context of the evolution of nature, specifically on planet earth and in the realm of human being. I subscribe to Robert Trivers's view that "Natural selection has built us, and it is natural selection we must understand if we are to comprehend our own identities" (Dawkins 1978, vii).

To understand ourselves most adequately requires that we also understand our origins. I hold fast to the position set forth in Part Two that the processes and structures of nature that constitute us are a primary referent of the information that culture, myth, and ritual carry. Nature is what religion's encounter with the holy interprets. This is in no sense a reduction of the holy to the natural, but rather an insistence that the encounter with the holy includes inescapably within it a message about what this natural order is, as well as who we natural human beings are. The encounter with the holy carries a message—not about God alone, nor about the world of nature alone, but about the relation between the two, and the form of such a message is the only means by which we learn the deepest truth about God or about nature. If we do not, therefore, understand our natural constitution, we will be unable to discern the deepest significance of the information about the holy that is conveyed by myth and ritual.

Critical thinking comes into play in my use of both the scientific and the theological apparatuses. Critical thinking compels me to recognize that all human knowledge is in some significant sense constructed by us; critical thinking plays a role in my rejecting both scientism and theological traditionalism. Donald T. Campbell has reinforced the insights of the Frankfurt School in his judgment that the "well-winnowed wisdom" of the past, cultural, religious, and biological, "is wisdom about past worlds," not necessarily about present and future worlds

(1991, 95–96). I would add that the wisdom of the past is also in the service of the interests of past persons and past worlds, which may or may not be life-giving to us and to the future.

I would argue—knowing that this is a vulnerable assertion—that we are compelled to integrate these three methodologies in the interests of more adequate understanding of the truth about *what really is.* Our cultural forms do contain authentic information about what really is; the natural world that science focuses upon is the arena in which we participate in what really is; and because *what really is,* is more than any culture and its forms (even its mythic and ritual forms) and more than the interests that serve any individual's or any group's survival, we must be critical. Of course, even the methodological apparatus, as I have just described it, is limited and vulnerable. Like a twig caught in the raging current of a storm-roiled river, the fruits of the method are more in the realm of hope than of certainty. Nowhere is that more the case than in the highly speculative probes in the fourth part of this book.

The Awesome Challenge of Culture

The second part of the seventh hypothesis proposes that the function of culture is to interpret the world in which we live, to guide our behavior, and to interface with the physico-biogenetic-cultural systems that constitute the environment in which we live. The eighth auxiliary hypothesis should be considered as an elaboration of the seventh:

> #8: We now live in a condition that may be termed technological civilization. This condition is characterized by the fact that human decision has conditioned virtually all of the planetary physico-biogenetic systems, so that human decision is the critical factor in the continued functioning of the planet's systems.

At this point the theory crosses the threshold into the arena where human existence is negotiated in its quintessential form. Earlier I said that human being is spelled out, basically, in the interaction between genes and cultures. Now I restate that insight and elaborate its awesomeness and urgency.

The first awesome consideration becomes clear when we recognize the magnitude of the task that culture faces. Its function is comparable to that of physico-biogenetic systems of information that surround us—namely, to guide behavior. The magnitude of this task dawns upon us when we consider how thoroughly the behavior of the other members of the biosphere—plants and animals—is guided by their physico-biogenetic inputs. Furthermore, as I shall discuss in detail, those other inputs, lacking cultural supplements, are inadequate for humans. My definition of culture underscores this function of guiding behavior: a system of learned patterns of behavior and the symbol systems that contextualize and interpret those actions. Culture's functioning is not yet complete when it provides symbol systems that put one's world together; those symbol systems must also motivate and guide behavior.

Culture's scope becomes clear when we recognize that the cultural systems of information interface directly or indirectly with virtually all of the planetary physico-biogenetic systems. Beginning with our own bodies and extending to the entire ecosphere of the planet and to the other human cultures that we live with, the range of that with which culture must interface is almost beyond comprehension. Here the urgent struggle that is inherent with the quest for human identity comes into full view. The formation of culture is not just of private concern, either to the individual or to the local community that comprises the culture. That formation must synchronize with the ecosystem and with other human cultures. In our present epoch, the crises that threaten our lives grow out of our failure to synchronize as we must with these other systems of information. Human survival can be defined for us today as the process of understanding and seeking congruence with these other systems.

The intellectual and spiritual dimension of culture's challenge is the hermeneutical or interpretive task that culture must perform. In this book, my aim is to make a contribution in this sector of the human struggle. How are we to understand the purpose of being human and the significance of our human venture within our segment of the evolutionary history of nature?

At the core of the eighth hypothesis lies the interpretation of our own era as the time when a human cultural overlay has been imposed upon virtually all of the natural systems that comprise planet earth. Perhaps a more apt image would be that human culture has permeated all of earth's natural systems, with the consequence that all of those natural systems, including human beings and their societies, are substantially—even life-threateningly—dependent upon human decisions and the ability of humans to conceive and execute those decisions adequately.

In our era it is impossible to retreat to a time or place where natural processes still operate on their own, apart from or untouched by human decisions. There is little or no possibility for us to take up residence in locales where we can live purely off nonhuman natural processes. No wilderness remains that is really untouched by human decisions, no foods that are "natural" in a prehuman sense, very little water or atmosphere that is in such a nonhumanified state. It is possible to fantasize to the contrary, but such fantasies are misleading and even dangerous.

This state of affairs is what Teilhard de Chardin and a previous generation of thinkers called the condition of *hominization*—humanification of nature and its evolution. The hybridized navel orange, the automobile, the asphalt parking lot, the computer—these are nature. We call them *techno-nature,* recognizing that techno-nature is, in a real sense, the only nature that now exists on our planet.

Such terminology may be repugnant to many persons. I suggest that the offense grows out of our alienation from nature, from our own nature, and from the distinguishing feature of human nature in our time—culture and the techno-logical form it has taken. Unless this alienation is overcome, humans will not be capable of assuming their authority over their own nature and directing it into genuinely humane channels. There is essentially no difference between the phenomenon of the bee producing honey and the human being fashioning a fast-food burger. The technological overlay that characterizes the production of the burger is as much a part of nature as is the bee, performing in a manner appropriate to the evolutionary context of human culture. That we may attach differing value judgments to the work of the bee and the work of technologically advanced food processing should not cloud our sense of the fundamental sameness of the two activities.

The term for designating this historical situation is *technological civilization.* Technology has been interpreted from a number of perspectives. My hermeneutic for interpreting it emerges from the evolutionary appearance of human culture and the challenges it faces if it is to fulfill its function in the evolutionary process. Technology participates in the same challenges as culture, because technology is part of culture—perhaps the most luminous facet of culture in our time, since it impinges so significantly upon the future of *Homo sapiens* and the planet (Csikszentmihalyi 1987). Technology must be interpreted; it is a behavior to be guided; and it must interface in a wholesome or well-synchronized manner with the full range of earth's physico-biogenetic information systems.

My approach for interpreting technology, drawn from evolutionary history, is nondualistic: technology is a form or segment of nature, and its emergence is grounded in the same neurobiological matrix as human beings and their culture. I speak of technology, furthermore, as I did of *Homo sapiens* and culture, that its purpose is to be referred to the natural order whence it emerged. This angle of vision on technology gives a different interpretation of its significance than some others, especially those that set technology off dualistically from nature and from the supposedly more authentic character of human being (Heidegger 1977).

My interpretation does not, however, weaken my sense of urgency at the crisis that faces humans and their planet in their exercise of technology. Furthermore, I use the term *technological civilization* to suggest that we are confronted not—like the Sorcerer's Apprentice—simply with tools that have gotten out of control, but rather with a fundamental, all-permeating condition of existence that threatens to turn against itself and the rest of nature. Later on in the discussion, I shall underscore that this phenomenon of the good turning against itself is one description of the demonic element of life (Tillich 1936).

My vantage point also throws a different light on the nature of the crisis, its potential disastrous consequences, and on the appropriate response to the crisis. The nature of the crisis is identical to the crisis that attends human culture, as such: Technology must be interpreted (the theory presented in this book provides one such interpretation), and it must interface with the rest of nature's systems so as, on the one hand, to meet the pragmatic criterion of wholesomeness, and, on the other hand, to function within the larger purposes of nature.

A reorganization of consciousness is called for. Humans do use technology; we *are* technology, in the same sense that we not only use our hands and eyes, but we are our eyes and hands. Eyes and hands are not good or evil in and of themselves, but they are good or evil depending on the agency we exercise through them. Our technology can gain control over us, almost demonically, just as our physical bodies can gain control over us if we devote most of our time and resources to body-building strategies or to sexual prowess or to comfortable lifestyles. In comparable ways, any part of us can go berserk, so to speak, and take us over—our intellectual dimensions, our sexuality, or our gregariousness. At this point, we recall the discussion of original sin in chapter 8. Everything that was said about sin in that discussion is to be referred to the concept of technological civilization.

The appropriate response to technological civilization is to recognize that it is human culture, that it is an emergent from human freedom, and that it is constituted by our self-consciousness, our constructions, and our decisions, for which we take responsibility. An appropriate response must be the response of creatures who are themselves natural creatures, and who understand that they are responding to the natural world in the form that it has taken commensurate with their particular epoch in evolutionary history. The agent in technological civilization is the created co-creator.

Living in Technological Civilization

The crisis of our epoch is that our culture is out of touch with the rest of its natural ambience, and this situation is quintessentially imaged in the state of our technology. Furthermore, this culture/technology is the fruit of our self-awareness, decisions, and taking of responsibility—we are dealing with behavior to be guided. It is here that we introduce the ninth auxiliary hypothesis:

#9: Myth and ritual are critical components of the cultural system of information and guidance. They are marked in linguistic form by declarative or imperative discourse, and their concepts are vastly underdetermined by the data of evidence. In light of human evolutionary history, these marks were necessary if culture was to serve its evolutionary function.

This hypothesis proposes that myth and ritual—the heart of what we call religion—are critical components of the cultural system of information and guidance, precisely because they carry the information for living that, if properly interpreted, may speak to us in our current situation. Myth does this by portraying *what really is,* while ritual is the action that is called for if we are to be in harmony with what really is—action expressed symbolically. Ronald Grimes speaks of ritual as "subjunctive, as-if responses" that serve as "an interlude before we enter the arena of the social world where ethical decision making and character formation count" (1990, 164).

We might speak of a complex in which myth portrays reality, ritual presents symbolically the action that reality requires, while praxis translates the ritual into ordinary, everyday living. This way of relating the three elements of the complex is suggested by the work of Mircea Eliade (1959; 1963, sect. 164) and Paul Ricoeur (1967, 5), and it is in accord with current reflection upon ritual (Grimes 1990; Bell 1992).

In speaking of the myth-ritual-praxis complex, I acknowledge that ritual is as widely misunderstood as is myth. Catherine Bell reminds us that we must leave behind "the notion of ritual as an ideologizing mechanism for transforming ideas into sentiments and sentiments into significance" (1992, 182)—a view that is held by most educated persons. Nor are myths, symbols, and rituals to be categorized as functioning chiefly to promote sociocultural solidarity (184). The myth-ritual-praxis construct that I propose requires much more detailed reflection. At this point in its development, I employ it as a way of understanding myth and ritual as critical dimensions of the perennial human effort to scan the world, interpret it, and conduct the business of living in ways that respond adequately to that world, however it is conceived.

10

The Emergence of Myth and
Ritual within Culture

In chapter 4, I referred to two poems by Richard Wilbur, "A Problem from Milton" and "Mind," in which the poet reflects upon the complexity and ambiguity that attend our human attempt to understand our niche in the natural world. Those poems are instructive, also, for their lucid sense that in our condition of puzzlement, we have no alternative but to develop our curiosity and, through long and deep thinking, live our lives on the basis of the best understandings possible.

> The builded comber like a hurdling horse
> Achieves the rocks. With wild informal roar
> The spray upholds its freedom and its force,
>
> Poor Adam, deviled by your energy,
> What power egged you on to feed your brains?
> Envy the gorgeous gallops of the sea,
> Whose horses never know their lunar reins.
> (Wilbur 1988, 311)

Adam notes that everywhere nature is doing its thing, and doing it with no apparent inhibitions. He cannot just *be,* however, following impulse and capacity unreflectively and unrestrainedly; he must discover the reins that would govern his behavior. Adam guesses that there are constraints and configurations that govern his life, but he never knows exactly where they are or what they are about; he never knows exactly when he is trying to reach too high or when he is too complacent.

In "Mind," Wilbur explores another nuance of the same condition.

> Mind in its purest play is like some bat
> That beats about in caverns all alone,
> Contriving by a kind of senseless wit
> Not to conclude against a wall of stone.
>
> It has no need to falter or explore;
> Darkly it knows what obstacles are there,

And so may weave and flitter, dip and soar
In perfect courses through the blackest air.

And has this simile a like perfection?
The mind is like a bat. Precisely. Save
That in the very happiest intellection
A graceful error may correct the cave.
(1988, 240)

The bat need not worry, its sensing systems operate automatically so that it can weave and flitter, dip and soar through its cave. If it misses, it concludes against a wall of stone. The human mind differs from the bat's sensors, and the poet realizes that he has to change his simile. The mind is like a bat, except the mind does not know exactly where the walls of the cave are. And if the mind makes an error in exploring its environment, it does not necessarily conclude against a wall; it may well engage in that "happiest intellection" in which by mistaking where the limits are, mistaking where nature's walls are, it actually improves both on the walls of nature and on itself.

In the "very happiest intellection, a graceful error may correct the cave." Does this occur despite the error—that is, an inadvertent misstep by fortunate coincidence brings no painful consequences—or because of the error? Does the "error" make possible a redefinition of the constraints, thereby creating a novel and more satisfactory set of conditions, both for the human being and for the rest of its environment?

In these two poems, Wilbur is observing an important dimension of human existence in its world. He is exploring the condition of what I termed freedom in chapter 7. He goes well beyond Steven Weinberg, who spoke of humans making up the stories of their own lives and their significance as they go along. Wilbur is suggesting that we construct not just the interpretations that bestow meanings upon the human venture, but also those that give meaning to the world around us. Wilbur would not exempt Weinberg's physics from the impact of human construction.

Our Lack of Knowledge and Its Importance

The point is that human beings, by virtue of the very condition of their existence, seek meaning both for the sake of understanding and for guiding their behavior. This quest for meaning that can guide behavior is equivalent to the definitions of culture on which earlier portions of my argument, especially in chapter 9, are based. Culture is defined as the behaviors we choose, together with the interpretations by which we give meaning and justification to those behaviors—precisely what humans need to supplement their genetically based information system.

In this chapter, these insights will be brought to bear in an effort to understand religion, and in particular, myth and ritual. The discussion here is the most speculative portion of this book, because we have little or no conclusive knowledge about the origins and earliest evolutionary history of myth, ritual, and other aspects of religion. We are not certain when and under what circumstances they emerged on the evolutionary scene, nor do we know the function they played. Much has been written about the content of extant myths and the appropriate methodologies for interpreting them. The scholars who devote themselves to the history and phenomenology of religion, specifically Paul Ricoeur and Mircea Eliade, do not speak of the origins and functions of symbols, myths, and rituals, so much as they catalog and interpret the materials, some of which are very ancient.

This lack of knowledge represents a serious lacuna. To the extent that we do not know the circumstances of origin and the original functions of religion, we do not understand our symbols, myths, and rituals. Much of the human quest for understanding, including self-understanding, is an attempt to learn about origins—the sources of who we are, where we have come from, and what we have been about. In our own century, particularly in the United States, we have witnessed many attempts to gain self-understanding through knowledge of our origins. Women, African Americans, Native Americans, and Hispanics are among the groups that have sought knowledge of their origins and have derived from that quest a considerable portion of their contemporary self-understanding.

A model of this quest for past and present understanding is historian Gerda Lerner's study, *The Creation of Patriarchy* (1986). In one of her most useful reflections, she reminds us that to understand the origins, function, and history of cultural artifacts is to gain an appreciation of those artifacts and also the ability to relate to them in productive ways (1988, chaps. 1, 2). Such understanding increases our capacity both to discern the importance of these artifacts and also to criticize them and reappropriate them in ways that are more meaningful for us today.

Our lack of knowledge concerning the origins and earliest functions of myth and ritual has rendered us blind to their real significance for us. Two extremes have dominated. Religious believers have often insisted that myths and rituals be accepted uncritically, in terms of an eternally present meaning and authority. For large numbers of persons who find certain myths and rituals simply untrue or unuseful, this has led to a loss of credibility for religion. In contrast, the educated elite has, almost since the first ethnographers in the nineteenth century, insisted that myth and ritual are, as Auguste Comte (1798–1857) and E. B. Tylor (1832–1917) argued, figments of a naive, primitive, superstitious era of human history (Preus 1987, chaps. 6, 7).

These interpretations encouraged a wholesale rejection of myth and ritual by those modern persons who obviously believed that they had progressed beyond naiveté, primitiveness, and superstition. The one group can tolerate no historicization or relativization; the other cannot entertain the notion that myth and ritual possess sound information for living. In both cases, we are cut off from a serious understanding of what myth and ritual—two of the most deeply grounded elements in human life for many millennia—have meant for the human venture and what they might mean today.

Culture's Function

I have already set forth the issues of what I call the two-natured character of *Homo sapiens,* genes and culture; in chapters 13 and 14 the issues will be elaborated even more. In this context, I need only remind the reader of the distinction and put special emphasis on the fact that human being requires cultural information as a supplement to genetic information. Culture is essential for the stage of life we call human. Furthermore, religion, including myth and ritual, finds its locus within this cultural stream of information. Culture, and myth and ritual within it, is composed of packets of information that enable human life to persevere.

Culture also functions as a system of information that must motivate and guide behavior—again, in supplementation of biogenetic information and motivators. It is important to keep this function of culture in mind, because it provides the context in which myth and ritual function.

For some, this sort of analysis will seem to be a compromising application of reductionism and functionalism. The traditional abhorrence of these two "isms" among theologians should be held in abeyance, at least provisionally. To separate thought, art, myth, and ritual from function is perhaps peculiar to modernity. Such separation is part of the tendency to remove considerations of value from these dimensions of human living—a genuine secularization. The prehistoric "art" that hangs in many a museum today is profoundly out of place, because it was produced in a context that had little concept of art (Pfeiffer 1982, 17–18; Klein 1989, 380). The same could be said of rituals that are now regularly considered to be entertainment or folk art by the large population that is alienated from the rituals and the cultural contexts in which they emerged. Furthermore, we recall Lawrence Sullivan's comments,

> any interpretation of symbolic life must reduce meaning to its scale and purposes. . . . [However,] social values and functions, which are never absent from or irrelevant to symbolic action and belief, are themselves symbolic of the religious need to encounter what is sacred and to know what is true in order to ground every aspect of life on what *really is.* (1988, 18)

I interpret Sullivan to be saying that the functions of myth and ritual are themselves taken up into the purposes of the religious perspective. If we say that myth and ritual contain information for the guidance and motivation of behavior, we are also asserting that such behavior is a part of the encounter with what is sacred, so that the functional character of the myth and ritual is instrumental to what myth and ritual depict as the way things really are. Myth and ritual are not thereby reduced to means for inducing correct behavior, but rather correct behavior is incorporated into the religious understanding of the way things really are. Conversely, to strip away the functionalism is also to accept that the behavior, as well as its guidance and motivation, is to be alienated from the way things really are. I return to these issues at the end of this chapter.

When we view culture, and myth and ritual, from the perspective just set forth, we gain a renewed appreciation for the massiveness and the complexity of the challenge that the formation of culture posed in earliest times and still poses to humans today. If we can put ourselves in the position of the earlier humans—at the point, say, where *Homo sapiens sapiens* emerged, or even earlier, with Neanderthal, or one million years ago in the first great migration from Africa, or 40,000 years ago when anatomically modern humans emerged—we can begin to imagine how great is the accomplishment of culture and how vulnerable we humans are as we go about the forming of culture. We can also better understand ourselves, the heirs of more than 40,000 years of culture, in our efforts both to preserve that legacy and also to revise and add to the process.

The questions that attend the earliest stages of culture's formation are rooted in mystery. Where did we first learn that corn must be prepared with lime in order to supply a fully nutritious meal? How did we learn to distinguish wholesome from poisonous mushrooms? Or that plants come from seeds? Or that sexual intercourse between close kin is to be forbidden? Where and how did ritual emerge as the symbolic acting out of actual praxis, the everyday behavior, that is necessary if we are to be in accord with what really is?

Imagining the Circumstances of Origin

Whenever and however the creatures we now call human beings came upon the scene, they bore within them biogenetically programmed information that served to drive behavior in other animals, such as the nonhuman higher primates. In its human context, much of this behavior would be maladaptive. Cultural supplements to this preprogrammed information would have been essential, at least at some level, from the first emergence of *Homo sapiens*. Certain behaviors, such as that between men and women, the care of infants, hunting and gathering food, and making tools, were immediate necessities. Behaviors, like hunting, that required great physical strength or speed or unusually well developed senses of seeing or hearing or smelling, had to be modified if humans were to succeed.

In certain cases, the biogenetic motivators required supplementation or even significant redirection. This must have been the case particularly in relations between the genders, between adults and children, and between different families and tribes. Violence toward the "other" is deeply rooted in our evolutionary past. Rather soon, complex cultural overlays were developed and integrated with the biogenetic information systems.

Of course, the motivational power of the countervailing or supplementary cultural packets of information had to match the force of the preprogrammed biogenetic information packets. We see this in our contemporary societies. Most addictions (for example, alcohol, hallucinogenics, salt, food) involve experiences and substances that throughout most of human history were rare or difficult to obtain but are today readily available commodities. Because for most of our history they were rare, the motivators to obtain and utilize them are very strong. Today, these substances and experiences can be harmful and even dangerous, but the motivators predisposing us toward them are still strong. We are in the position of having to supplement or override those motivators with equally strong cultural inputs, and we are aware how difficult and problematic that enterprise can be. The terrible ethnic conflict and violence that besets us today, as well as alcoholism and drug addiction, are examples of our failure to overcome with culture some of the behaviors that are motivated by powerful ancient, even prehuman, information systems (Burhoe and Katz 1986).

If we are able to imagine the condition of the earliest humans, even recognizing similarities to our own situation, we can begin to understand the possible place and function of myth and ritual. Certainly, as in the case of Richard Wilbur's Adam, pictures of the world had to be put together that would provide viable knowledge of the environment in which humans lived. Those pictures had to play the role of contextualizing and justifying certain ways of interpreting the world and consequent modes of behavior. From its emergence, humanity required certain kinds of information that could not be gained by the slow methods of experiential trial and error. One does not start from absolute point zero and develop a picture of the world, even of the local setting, by experience. There are too many facets to the picture that cannot be readily experienced, and furthermore, some behaviors cannot wait upon the results of long-term, or even short-term, trial and error. Governing relations with outgroups, as well as nurturing infants and hunting animals for food, are examples of such behaviors.

In terms of contemporary philosophy of science, we would say that humans required (and still require today) concepts and pictures of the world that are intrinsically underdetermined by the data (Popper 1959, chap. 1; Knorr-Cetina and Mulkay 1983, 3–5, 11–14, 244–47). That is to say, the character of the human being (particularly its distinctive central nervous system), and the exigencies of its living and of its surviving, demand that certain world-pictures, concepts, and theories be accepted as operational absolutes, even though they cannot strictly sustain such claims to absolute status by empirical verification.

Furthermore, these pictures of the world and their behavioral implicates had to make a forceful impact if they were to be integrated with the biogenetic preprogramming that humans bear within themselves as they respond to the demands they face from their environment. In other words, the packets of cultural information had to take the form of direct discourse and imperative. The programmed motivators for rapacious behavior toward women, for example, do not come across as hypotheses to be tested, but rather as commands to be obeyed. The same is true of certain predispositions that humans brought to the hunting of ferocious animals, whether to fight or flee. The cultural supplements, if they were to be effective, had to take the same direct form. Hence the popular aphorism that Moses did not bring down with him from Sinai a list of Ten Suggestions or Ten Hypotheses to Be Tested, but rather Ten Commandments.

Julian Jaynes has proposed a somewhat eccentric interpretation of these characteristics of myth, underdetermination and direct discourse. He posits the separation of the two hemispheres of the brain in the bicameral mind. In this bicamerality (which he believes came to an end in the second millennium B.C.E.) the information for organizing and governing life contained in the right hemisphere of the brain "spoke" its wisdom and commands to the left hemisphere. This "speaking" was heard by humans as the voice of the gods (1977, 1–142, esp. chaps. 5, 6).

Interestingly, Jaynes's theory accords with the interpretation presented here, that such commands were necessary for the development of the culture that *Homo sapiens* required. Even though Jaynes's particular theory of the history of the bicameral brain functioning is highly speculative and no more to be taken as reliable description than my own theories, one need not subscribe to his theory in order to learn from his speculations. Jaynes is one of the few researchers who have exhibited concern for the types of questions that I am exploring here.

Myth and ritual thus are cast in forms that meet the requirements just surveyed—concepts underdetermined by the data and taking the form of direct and imperative discourse. The pictures and concepts set forth the way things really are, and the behaviors are enjoined in the form of commandments. The pictures are the myths, and they are acted out in the rituals; the behaviors are implicates of the myths and rituals. While the myths tell the stories of circumstances *in illo tempore* (in time of yore), the rituals place our action symbolically in that same time; myth and ritual together ground our everyday life or praxis (Eliade 1959; 1963, sect. 164). Julian Jaynes has got it right when he writes: "Rituals are behavioral metaphors, belief acted" (1977, 439).

Evidence from the neurosciences supports the notion that our biogenetic equipment as human beings is built to sustain the formation of culture, in symbiosis with it. We are not simply apes who have a heavy cultural overlay. Rather, a definite symbiosis exists between our biogenetic capacities and the culture we need to learn. One of the most vivid examples of this fact is to be seen in the human birth process. Human females possess a birth canal of a certain size, allowing the newborn baby a head no larger than the capacity of that canal. The baby, however, arrives prematurely in comparison with infants of other species.

After birth the skull can grow; the central nervous system grows to the capacity to which it can be programmed culturally. If it were necessary for the baby to be born with the full equipment that is required for learning what it needs to know in order to be an adult human being, it could never emerge from the mother's womb. Our genetically programmed physiology is such that it can develop the means necessary for the emergence and elaboration of culture.

A Look at European Cave Art

One of the few sources of data that are relevant to the question of when myth and ritual emerged and how they functioned is prehistoric art. Even with these sets of data, however, we must engage in great conjectural leaps in order to interpret what the art means, how it functioned, and what it tells us about human life. For my purposes here, I will refer primarily to the cave art of France and Spain.

The reader should keep in mind a few basic considerations and dates.

> Prior to the emergence of modern people, the human form and human behavior evolved together slowly, hand in hand. Afterward, fundamental evolutionary change in body form ceased, while behavioral (cultural) evolution accelerated dramatically. The implication is that the modern human form—or, more precisely, the modern human brain—permitted the full development of culture in the modern sense and that culture then became the primary means by which people responded to natural selective pressures. (Klein 1989, 344)

One million years ago, it is conjectured, *Homo erectus,* a relatively close ancestor of modern humans, migrated from Africa to Europe and Asia. Neanderthals inhabited Europe between 130,000 and 35,000 years ago. Anatomically modern humans evolved between 200,000 and 50,000 years ago, probably in Africa (Klein 1989, 344). Evidences of human culture abound throughout prehistory: remains pertaining to housing, tool-making, hunting, food preparation and eating, and the like. Intentional burials go back to Neanderthals, and there is evidence of caring for the elderly and disabled at least 22,000 years ago among Cro-Magnon. Art appears at least 38,000 years ago in Africa (eggshell beads; Klein 1989, 381). Human figurines in Europe are perhaps 27,000 years old, and the cave paintings in France and Spain are variously dated from 30,000 to 11,000 years ago. The "Cola de Caballo" in the great cave at Altamira was decorated, according to best estimates, about 16,000 years ago (Freeman, de Quiros, and Ogden 1987, 61–63).

John Pfeiffer underscores the significance of this art:

> The notion of art for art's sake, of paintings and engravings executed by individuals concerned solely with expressing themselves, does not apply to the works found deep in prehistoric caves. Signs of intensive planning indicate the existence of collaboration among many individuals, the pre-dominance of social purpose. . . . Whatever roles art may have played before the Upper Paleolithic [30,000 years

ago]—and for these the evidence simply does not exist—it became several orders of magnitude more important during that period. Art in the broadest sense evolved rapidly, and changed rapidly, in response to changes in the structure of society. Ultimately it became an essential aspect of prehistoric living, as essential as subsistence and reproduction for the survival of the human species. (1982, 17–18)

When we understand the dramatic changes that occurred during the Upper Paleolithic era, we also get a better sense for how the emerging art, myth, and ritual may have functioned for the early humans and their communities. First, these millennia were marked by increase of population, which meant that hitherto rather isolated bands were forced to coexist with others. Neanderthals may have been "a fragmented breed, in the sense that individual bands and groups of bands managed to get along fairly well on their own most of the time" (Pfeiffer 1982, 122), but this changed with the appearance of modern humans. Studies have suggested that if we presently lived as Upper Paleolithic hunter-gatherers did, the United States could provide enough food to support a population of only 600,000 persons; the entire planet could support only 10 million (Pfeiffer 1982, 193–95).

Second, increased population meant that resources had to be understood more precisely and used more efficiently (Klein 1989, 364–69). Mass hunting and mass kills had to become the rule. Near Denver, Colorado, the remains have been found of a bison stampede that occurred 10,000 years ago in which 190 bison were slaughtered. In Europe, sites have been uncovered with the bones of 200 mammoths (on the Russian plain), 1,000 mammoths (Czechoslovakia), and more than 10,000 horses (Solutre, France). This evidence suggests either that many small kills took place or a few organized stampedes and ambushes designed to slaughter a great many animals quickly (Jelinek 1988, 208; Pfeiffer 1982, 59–61). Impressive developments in culture were necessary to enable such kills.

In some respects, these events mark a major emergence of a new mentality among humans and a new phase in their relationship to the rest of nature (Martin 1992, chaps. 2, 3).

> *Homo sapiens* had come a long way in his game drives. He was no longer killing like a normal predator, but like a natural catastrophe. People coming together for mass hunts do not go their separate ways in a hurry. Everyone has a share in the enterprise. There are rules for dividing the spoils, meat to be distributed and stored, dried, smoked, or put into deep-freeze permafrost "lockers." As pre-historic hunter-gatherers tended to assemble for longer periods, subsistence patterns changed. . . . What all this amounted to was more efficient living, more efficient use of natural resources; and that had an interesting double effect as far as group mobility was concerned. People had to know more about the land, about a greater variety of plants and ripening times, about the ways of herd and solitary animals so that they could predict where and when the hunting would be best. . . . Local exploitation certainly encouraged the settling-in, settling-down process, and yet at

the same time it meant that members of the band had to range more widely than ever from their home bases. (Pfeiffer 1982, 61)

The demand for exotic minerals to be used in tools and ornamentation also developed in this era. Trade developed. There is evidence that Cro-Magnon peoples (anatomically modern humans, about 30,000 years ago) transported minerals and ornamental shells, for example, over distances of more than 400 miles, from the Black Sea to France, and from central Poland to sites in Russia, Germany, and Czechoslovakia (Pfeiffer 1982, 64–66). Anyone who has visited the great Museum of Mining in Bochum, Germany, has marveled at the cultural sophistication of prehistoric humans who engaged in significant mining and trading.

Third, because of the great migrations and population increases of this era, groups of humans came into extensive contact with other groups for the first time. Ways of cooperating between bands and groups of bands had to be devised. Twenty thousand years ago, it is estimated, between 2,000 and 3,000 persons lived in France, with 6,000–10,000 in all of the rest of Europe. Ten thousand years later those numbers had tripled. The importance of these figures, which seem almost insignificant by current standards, is that the earliest humans had virtually no experience of living closely together, and few or none of the cultural behaviors and interpretations that make such coexistence possible. It is no surprise that prehistoric row-housing appeared, for example, along the Dordogne River downstream from Les Eyzies; four or five rock shelters housed 400 to 600 occupants (Pfeiffer 1982, 59).

What is the relationship of art, and myth and ritual, to this dynamic life situation in prehistoric Europe and elsewhere? Richard Klein (1989, 380–81) lists six possible functions of wall art, based on his survey of current studies:

1. to enhance hunting success
2. to ensure the bounty of nature
3. to illustrate sacred beliefs (perhaps on ritual occasions)
4. to mark the territorial boundaries of an identity-conscious group
5. to symbolize or encode the social structure or world view of its makers
6. to record the experience of shamans in the trance state

He suggests that portable and personal art served as gaming pieces, counting or recording devices, lunar calendars, totemic symbols of kinship groups, and representations of deities, spirits, or fertility symbols (earth-mother goddesses) (381–82).

Klein's suggestions are consistent with the views of Pfeiffer, Freeman, and other scholars, that what is at stake in the art, with its traces of myth and ritual, has to do with the processing of the tremendously increasing amount of information that was necessary for living in the Upper Pleistocene period. The formation and elaboration of culture depended upon this processing, so that life-ways could be better organized at a higher level of complexity to meet the new conditions of existence that were breaking in upon these prehistoric humans at (for them) breathtaking rates. Although culture certainly antedated the Upper Pleistocene and *Homo sapiens sapiens,* this era in Europe represented a primordial period in the formation and elaboration of the system of information that we call culture, whose function is to guide behavior in accordance with the way things really are.

Once again, we remind ourselves that this functional-reductionist approach to myth and ritual must be construed according to the axiom that we derived from Lawrence Sullivan—namely, that myth and ritual are not thereby reduced to their social function, but rather the social and personal functions are taken up into the portrayal of the way things really are that constitutes the substance of myth and ritual (see page 160 above).

We must also remember the conjectural character of the argument at this point. The art exists in undeniable artifacts, whether in cave paintings or portable, personal art, and the caves show traces of ceremonial activity. What must be supplied are the interpretations that will put all of these artifacts together into a coherent system. We cannot say with certainty that these prehistoric humans had myths and rituals in their cultural repertoire.

Julian Jaynes suggests an elaborate (also highly conjectural) theory of brain evolution as the key to understanding such phenomena. His theory posits a time when the hemispheres of the human brain functioned more independently than they do now; myth represented the "voices" from one of the hemispheres to the other. Jaynes's work is brilliantly provocative, even though it is generally considered to be eccentric. Eugene d'Aquili and his colleagues propose a theory that also rests upon current neuroscientific knowledge of the human central nervous system's structure and functioning, combined with insights from psychiatry and anthropology.

I am relying more on an anthropological, cultural interpretation, one that seeks to integrate d'Aquili's approach, with no particular commitment to Jaynes's interpretation of the history of the brain. My major assumption is that cave wall art and some prehistoric portable art are linked to emerging myth/ritual/praxis complexes. Although the interpretations that I make in this chapter are not finally demonstrable on the basis of present knowledge, they are informed by, not far removed from, current research opinions.

Developments in Cave Art Research

Prehistoric art was first discovered around 1834 in a cave at Le Chaffaud, in the region of Vienne, France (Leroi-Gourhan 1967, 25ff.). This art began to be recognized as a significant legacy of prehistoric human communities during the last third of the nineteenth century, although as recently as 1879 the same scientists who acknowledged the prehistoric provenance of incised bones ridiculed the suggestions that cave art was ancient (26). Abbe Henri Breuil is the acknowledged pioneer in the earliest research pertaining to cave art, and his work of documenting and publishing the majority of cave finds dominated the field during the first half of the twentieth century.

It was not until 1940, with the discovery of the cave at Lascaux, that significant prehistoric cave art was readily accessible for photographing. Andre Leroi-Gourhan, who was director of the Musée de l'Homme in Paris, is widely considered the most important researcher following Breuil. His 1967 work, *Treasures of Prehistoric Art,* is still the most comprehensive presentation and interpretation of this art.

The work of the pioneering generations has been subjected to rigorous critique within the last twenty years. Significant efforts are under way to carry out new observations and analyses of the original materials, as well as of new finds, in ways that are more systematic and sophisticated than was possible in the first half of this century. Consequently, as one would expect, the work of the pioneers is confirmed in some respects and shown to be unreliable in others. The trend appears to be toward more caution in endorsing monolithic interpretations of the caves, in favor of interpretations that acknowledge diversity of motives and purposes for the art (Lewin 1989, 120–24). The paintings, even those on the same wall, sometimes date from different periods, making the comparison of individual figures difficult. Leroi-Gourhan himself participated in the first stages of this new work of redoing the pre-1950 descriptions and cataloging (Leroi-Gourhan 1982, 1984).

At first, in the last two decades of the nineteenth century, scholars approached the cave art from the same aesthetic perspectives they applied to the rest of art history. The inadequacy of such an approach has prompted Margaret Conkey to say (in Lewin 1989, 124), "Perhaps we have closed off certain lines of inquiry, simply by using the label 'art'." Furthermore, scholars assumed that the art was produced by creatures who had barely left their ape ancestry behind, and who thus possessed neither religion nor moral insight but were totally mired in superstition.

Today, researchers employ a number of methodologies for studying cave art. L. G. Freeman (1987, 19–23) describes four of these: (1) psychology, focusing upon the consciousness of the artists; (2) history and sociology, attending to the society in which the art occurred and its cultural configurations; (3) attention to the subject matter itself, noting what it reveals about the artist's surroundings; (4) study of the pertinent materials, tools, and techniques for information about locale, dating, and networks of relationship to other locales.

The new wave of cave art research confirms that the Paleolithic artists differed from us in degree, not in kind. "It is clear to us that by 15,000 years ago, humans had developed essentially modern symbol systems . . . [i.e.,] complex symbolic behavior" (Freeman and Echegaray 1987, 244). The art is rooted deeply in the psychic and spiritual dimensions of how these earlier humans encountered their world and related to it and to the challenges it presented. Freeman writes, "The production or viewing of Paleolithic art would have served an important educational function, as it helped prepare individuals for action in their real environment" (1987, 54).

What we would call the religious dimension is pertinent for understanding this art. This conviction marked the approach of Leroi-Gourhan, and it is carried on, in more critical fashion, by current researchers. Leroi-Gourhan (1967) and Annette Laming-Emperaire (1962) concluded independently of each other that the caves are ancient sanctuaries; they suggest that each cave is to be considered a coherent whole, both in terms of its natural structure and its decorations (Leroi-Gourhan 1967, 109ff., 164–89). These two pioneering interpreters of cave art considered myth, ritual, and religion to be at the center of the attempt to understand the meaning and significance of these sanctuaries.

More recent research challenges the work of Leroi-Gourhan and Laming-Emperaire on the grounds that it is too sweeping, highly impressionistic at points, and to a certain extent based on poorly gathered data. At the same time, the basic concerns of these two researchers continue in the new studies, in an even more critical and sophisticated manner. New research confirms that some of the caves are sanctuaries, and their numinous character is certainly an important element in efforts to interpret them (Freeman 1987, 52–57). These sanctuaries may well represent the efforts of paleolithic people to structure their world within the ambience of what struck them as the disorganized spaces of the caves as they came upon them. They gave "sense" to the caves and thereby

> transformed the chaotic natural environment into symbolically structured space—a cultural environment or "symbol-milieu" that to a much more comfortable degree domesticated and humanized the cave interior. The principles or organization of the new cultural environment would have reflected the ideology of the group, its beliefs about its place in the natural and supernatural worlds, and the conscious and unconscious concerns of its members. In places that served as sanctuaries, the symbolic load would have been even more concentrated and better differentiated than in mere domestic space. (Freeman 1987, 57)

In their thesis, Leroi-Gourhan and Laming-Emperaire insisted that the depictions in the cave sanctuaries "reflect organized relationships that depend on preconceived structural principles shared by the prehistoric artists and their communities" (Freeman and Echegaray 1987, 130). Leroi-Gourhan proposed a "theoretical similarity between the Paleolithic sanctuary and the Christian church stemming from the fact that each must reflect in its own way the fundamental ideological principles that should be manifest in the nature, location, and relationships of its structural elements and decorations" (131).

Freeman and Echegaray are exploring this basic thesis in a painstaking critical study of the decorations in northern Spanish Romanesque sanctuaries in the Altamira region. Their intention is to refine analytic techniques and also to frame hypotheses for discerning the coherences in the "symbol-milieu" of these Christian churches. The research plan involves the application of these techniques and hypotheses to the Paleolithic caves and their art, to determine whether new insights will emerge thereby.

The Myth-Ritual-Praxis Complex

In order to appreciate how myth and ritual fit into the studies of cave wall art, we must acquaint ourselves with the actual physical structures of the caves and how the art was placed within them. More than 150 of these caves in the so-called Franco-Cantabrian region are known (Klein 1989, 378–79). Many of them are deep caves, not easily accessible, and the tortuous pathways to the places where the art is located seem to have been intentionally used to enhance whatever experience was associated with the art. Here is John Pfeiffer's description of the Nerja cave, "a vast multilevel system of underground galleries" on the southern coast of Spain, near Malaga:

> So many things are going on in such spots, so many impressions and the combined impact of all the impressions. The art is itself only part of the experience, often a rather small part at that. . . . The setting is a major factor in the effect of the figures, and the process of getting there, a series of successive narrowings, from the outside world into the cave mouth, and on into the galleries, side chambers, and niches in or beyond the chambers. A kind of extended zooming or closing in enhances the [painted] figures. . . .
>
> Paintings at least 15,000 years old have been found in the chamber: a fish in black outline, a number of abstract forms, and what may be a hand imprint in red. At the far end, blocking direct access to deeper places, is a huge stalagmitic column, and the only way to get around it is by a careful straddling maneuver—by hugging tight, stretching a foot over a sheer drop to a ledge on the other side, and pulling yourself across. That brings you into a recess where you stoop and crawl, then turn over on your back to see more abstract forms, a long-necked engraved hind, a red ibex, and a fish. . . .
>
> It is an unforgettable experience to come all of a sudden upon something as human as a drawn figure in the depths of such rock-dominated settings. . . .
>
> The artist or artists had a field day covering selected surfaces of the room with a variety of paintings, all in black outline. One panel to the left, as you enter from the ante-chamber includes six beautifully clear bison, drawn on a slanting section

of ceiling, a galloping horse with tail flying below the bison, and below the horse another bison strangely elongated and distorted as if seen in a trick mirror. The room contains more than thirty recognizable figures, mainly bison, some painted in vertical positions and one upside down. . . .

At the other extreme are midget caves, like two in the Les Eyzies region. One, located on a hillside along the road to Lascaux, has an opening smaller than a man-hole cover and must be entered backward, a feet-first slide through a narrow hole down into a pit which has just enough room for crouching. Then a twist around for another slide through a chatiere [hole] to a place where it is possible to stand up and see a group of figures including an ibex and, off by itself, an eight-inch engraving of a reindeer. The other site also involves a slide into a pit and a squeeze through a chatiere with two sharp bends to a dead end where you roll over on your back. From that position you see close to your face a red and black horse, the only figure in the cave.

Chambers with room for only one or at most two persons may have been re-served for ordeals, long and lone vigils in the dark. But one wonders if it made any difference that the confined space was part of a larger cave system or the entire cave. Again, the basic problem concerns the use of spaces and patterns of spaces by people who made elaborate plans and had many caves to choose from. In all the caves we have presented so far however, they chose secrecy and darkness.

Note the apparent paradox of using secrecy and darkness to impart information. If the objective was teaching, doing it out in the open where all could attend and share would seem to make more sense. But that would not have served the group's purpose, to achieve imprinted, verbatim memory. Upper Paleolithic teaching was not a matter of lessons to be learned more or less casually, with only relatively mild penalties for second-rate performances or failures. It was life or death, all or noth-ing. Everything had to be remembered by rote and forever, indoctrinated so deeply that people would act without thinking, obeying automatically and unquestion-ingly and absolutely. For that kind of teaching, to achieve that kind of behavior in those days and those regions, secrecy and darkness were essential. (1982, 128–31)

Much more detail from cave art archaeology could be cited to give a fuller sense of what is conveyed by these traces of the first modern humans and their immediate predecessors in Europe. Traces have been found of ritual ceremonies performed by small numbers of people and by large groups. The evidence in-cludes possible traces of musical instruments.

Were myths involved, myths that satisfy the criteria that phenomenologists and historians of religion like Ricoeur and Eliade have given us? We cannot be certain. A figure of a sorcerer, painted high on the wall of the sanctuary of the cave at Trois Freres in the Pyrenees, is said to represent a figure that is prominent in other societies, the Master of the Hunt or Keeper of the Animals, "an exalted being who provides game, establishes rules for the chase and punishments if the rules are broken, and who must be obeyed and appeased when angry" (Pfeiffer 1982, 119). Eliade is reported to have said that the Master of the Hunt is "the most divine figure in all prehistory, the prototype of all subsequent gods" (Pfeiffer 1982, 119).

It is my conjecture that myth is reflected in these early phenomena, and that even at this time, the myth-ritual-praxis complex is present. Myth provided information that represented the immediate environment to those who were exposed to it; it represented what really is. At this stage, perhaps the range of the environment so represented was limited, reaching back not to the primordial origins as did later creation myths, but disclosing the world that was relevant to the Upper Paleolithic humans. Rituals were present, to be sure, as Jaynes has said—behavioral metaphors, belief acted. This apparently applied both to the message of the myth and to the medium of acquiring its information. The myth portrayed the truth about the world of Europe in the twenty millennia B.C.E.; as Freeman says, it prepared individuals "for action in their real environment" (1987, 54).

Not only was that truth to be acted out, however; it was also held as the profoundest, most sacred truth—hence the striking character of the rituals involved even in approaching the cave pictures and ceremonial sites. Rituals of other types and in other places seem to have been present also; for example, the possible female rituals pertaining to the Venus figurines and fertility and childbirth (Pfeiffer 1982, 204).

Praxis is the arena where myth and ritual take hold, interpreting the world in which humans must act, where they must live or die, the world of praxis that must be transformed by the interpretations provided in myth and ritual. Here, too, we see in concrete actualization the evolutionary historical context in which myth and ritual assumed the characteristics of underdetermination by the data and the linguistic form of direct and imperative discourse.

Pfeiffer presents a cogent theory to interpret the cave art and its accompanying myth, ritual, and music:

> The effort put into organizing, as well as the relatively sudden appearance of art in the human record, bears directly on questions of motivation. Summarizing my argument, it implies ceremony and an accelerating need for ceremony, and that is where the nature of the times assumes a special significance. Life had never before changed as rapidly as it was changing then. Survival demanded new ways of transmitting, from generation to generation and before writing had been invented, the contents of an expanding tribal encyclopedia, a body of new rules and traditions about how to do things and how to relate to others. Viewed in this context, ceremony is to be regarded as communication. The mystery and the created illusions, all the thought that went into the selection of the caves, locations within the caves, and the placement of the figures, served to imprint information. (1982, 227–28)

This way of interpreting myth and ritual finds resonance among many interpreters of ancient mythic materials—too many to justify a long discussion here. Myths and rituals have, for example, been discovered to have played a role in conveying information in many cultures of the world: with respect to cuisine in

Latin American Indian societies (Katz and Schal 1979; Katz 1992); to care of the land among the Mayans; to countering the "seven deadly sins" and for reinforcing the "cardinal virtues" in medieval Europe (Csikszentmihalyi 1993).

Some readers may find this way of interpreting myth and ritual to be quite thin description. The literature abounds with condemnations of attempts to explain myth with only one set of interpretive categories or to insist that myth is really "only one thing." William Doty has not only cataloged these warnings, but he has also described the richer, alternative ways of understanding myth (1986, esp. chaps. 1, 2).

I will reiterate and elaborate my earlier comments, in which I expressed agreement with those who worry about reductionistic and functionalistic approaches to religion and culture in general and to myth and ritual in particular. Certainly culture, including myth and ritual, is too rich to be exhaustively interpreted by any single set of categories. Just as surely, one cannot explain all of culture, even as one cannot explain all of biological evolution, in adaptationist terms. Many phenomena in the realm of life are simply expressive, with no particular function, and they possess no intention to respond to an environmental challenge (Gould and Lewontin 1979; Mayr 1988, chap. 9). Pfeiffer himself agrees to this; he does not mean to be giving an exhaustive interpretation of all prehistoric art, not even of all cave art, even though he does believe that his interpretation deals with what is of central importance to the phenomena (1982, 121–24).

At the same time, functionalism is not necessarily the thin, monodimensional exercise that is often depicted by critics. Time and again, when we ask about the function of things, we are stimulated to probe new avenues that produce unexpected riches of insight and knowledge. This is why many critical researchers continue to work within functionalist models, despite the critics (Barkow, Cosmides, and Tooby 1992, 75ff.).

In chapter 9, I spoke of an effort to bring together the approaches of the phenomenologists and historians of religion, on the one hand, and the evolutionary biocultural theorists, on the other. The former are celebrated for their opposition to reductionist, functionalist, and even contextualizing interpretations of symbol, myth, and ritual. Their great contribution is their mining of the rich veins of form and meaning that are borne by myth and ritual, and their insistence that myth and ritual must be appreciated for what they are, apart from any instrumental value. Sullivan quotes Gary Urton approvingly, with reference to ritual dancers, "they do not 'symbolize' anything; rather they *are* that thing" (1988, 18, 699).

The insights deriving from biocultural evolution pertain, not to trivial or arrogant attempts to perform a reductionism upon culture, but rather to significant and undeniable pathways that life itself has taken since it first appeared on our planet. To say that myth and ritual played a function within this pathway is not, as I have already pointed out, simply to say that they are reducible to mere instruments to meet the needs of life's survival; it is also to insist that they speak the truth about life and its survival.

In a later chapter, I will note that myth and ritual can be *wrong;* they can speak less than the full truth about life, or they can speak truth that was once viable but today is virtual untruth. (One wonders about the "truth" of killing 200 mammoths at one time. Was this truly the will of the Keeper of the Animals?) Here I simply underscore that the relation of myth to function can be a double-edged sword. The holy may indeed become integral to a function, but at the same time, the function becomes integral to the holy. If this is not the case, morality is thoroughly and completely secularized—something that the world view of myth and ritual will not allow. In fact, it is secularized intelligence that thinks the holy exists only to perform functions, and it is the continual task of the religious intelligence to insist upon, and to be persuasive about, the fact that the functions which humans consider to be significant exist within the larger ambience of God and the divine intentions.

Lawrence Sullivan deepens our understanding of this latter edge of the double-edged sword in his comments on myth. He uses creation myths as his examples.

> Creation myths of transformation provide an occasion for a general observation about the nature of myth. Creation myths are more than rational explanations of first causes of physical processes or justifications of existing social conditions. It is of course undeniable that myths can be blunt rationalizations of prevailing cosmic, sociopolitical, or existential orders. However, such an appraisal of myth is overdetermined insofar as it focuses on only one of myth's functions, and it therefore cannot give a complete account of the nature of myth. Nor does it put a finger on myth's specific difference from any number of ideological expressions. Law, science, theology, canons of artistic form, political process, military exercise, revolutionary rhetoric, and historiography can all buttress existing forms of thought, action, and explanation because they all function as parts of a given worldview. The self-evident world of society and cosmos needs no mythic demonstration to justify or make clear its existence.
>
> What myth must make evident is the *meaning* of the world appearance, that is, the meaning of the very fact that the world has *appeared*. For reasons provided in myth, that kind of meaning is no longer self-evident or fully apparent. It must be made perceptible through myth in order to clothe fully apparent and mundane affairs in some measure of reality. Here is where myth finds its proper place, subtly related to an explanation of everyday events: myth explains that whatever is . . . has meaning. Concerning itself with the tiniest details of natural and economic history, myth offers an explanation for the fact that every aspect of the world is epiphanic and that the everyday appearance of things is actually significant of reality. Myth is an integral part of reality not because it describes the world which is self-evident but because it characterizes and even directly participates in the imaginal world of

beginnings, a world no longer apparent as such, the real world where the meanings of all apparent signifiers must now reside. Although significance is intimately bound up with forms of appearance, meaning can no be longer be fully self-evident in this world except in a mythic way. (1988, 33–34)

Consequently, even though myth and ritual cannot be reduced to function, if they are not fully implicated in the most important functions of human life, then the *real* meaning of those functions will never be addressed, never articulated, and never known by the people. Sullivan's comments fit the Upper Pleistocene situation very well—it was not self-evident that the dramatic changes and new factors of life had meaning and that they were "actually significant of reality." The medium of the cave art message, the awesome journey through the cave to the art and the rituals, made it clear that the journey, the art, and the ritual had to do with nothing less than *what really is.*

The theory of the created co-creator definitely places itself within the mythic framework, with the intention of contributing what Sullivan describes as the peculiar function of myth.

The reader may have caught an insinuation, between the lines so to speak, that this discussion of myth and ritual in the Upper Pleistocene in Europe, as well as Sullivan's observations concerning the action of myth in making self-evident that which is obscure, may possess a relevance for our present time. But the time for that discussion comes later.

The next two chapters will elaborate the basic proposals of this chapter and chapter 9, in the context of concrete considerations of altruism and the New Testament love command. Relations and behaviors among persons, between groups, including behavior toward those who are strangers or aliens, have figured prominently in this chapter's discussion, even though I have not called special attention to those elements. Chapters 11 and 12 will assume the importance of such behaviors as their starting point and probe it in detail.

11

Myth, Ritual, Morality, and the
Love Command

This chapter will provide another perspective on the created co-creator proposal by looking at the functioning of culture in the realm of myth, values, and morality. The preceding chapter discussed myth at some length, as well as the basic function of culture. This chapter builds on those discussions. By the term *value,* I mean that which is or is thought to be worthwhile, desirable, or good; by *morality,* I refer to a system that contains beliefs about the nature of human beings in their world, beliefs about what is good or desirable, and rules laying down what ought to be done or what ought not to be done (Nowell-Smith 1967).

It should be easy enough to draw a connection between the various aspects of Ricoeur's analysis of myth, as it was explored in chapter 10, to indicate that myth depicts the most basic character of the world, and that *it has the direct intention of grounding thereby the forms of action that we call morality.* This connection between myth and morality is central to my argument, and I will elucidate and elaborate it.

The argument is divided into five parts. Parts one and two seek to clarify why it is appropriate to bring myth into a discussion of values and morality. The third part discusses the dynamics by which the relationship between myth, values, and morality functions. These sections will rely heavily upon the connection between myth and morality. The fourth part focuses upon one particular moral injunction, the command to love, as interpreted by Christian tradition. The final section surveys some of the scientific reflection on altruism and relates it to the love command. In elaborating upon this specific moral command, I hope to show how the more abstract issues that I discuss in the first two parts actually work themselves out in concrete existence.

Evolutionary Preparation for Values and Morality

Michael Levin, a philosopher at City College of New York, has commented on morality in a way that opens up one facet of an important discussion, even if his own discussion is scarcely adequate. Speaking about the academic courses in ethics offered in high schools, colleges, and professional schools, he insists that

> these ethics courses are an utterly pointless exercise. The idea behind them is that anyone can be taught to distinguish right from wrong in much the way medical students are taught to distinguish the pancreas from the liver. . . . But this whole exercise rests on a mistake about what makes people good. Moral behavior is the product of training, not reflection. . . . Indeed, abstract knowledge of right and wrong no more contributes to character than knowledge of physics contributes to bicycling. The idea in both cases is to build the proper responses into nerve and sinew: Bicyclists don't have to think about which way to lean and honest men don't have to think how to answer under oath.
>
> Psychologists have laboriously rediscovered the common sense observation that children first conceive morality as rules for pleasing their parents—only with the fullness of time comes a grasp of the idea of conscientious choice. (1989, 15)

Regardless of whether Levin's critique of present-day ethics courses is correct, his comment that morality runs in deep currents that are built into nerve and sinew before they are the object of academic reflection is both correct and essential.

If we survey our present understanding of values and morality, we shall see that their roots do indeed go deep, even into the prehistory of nerve and sinew. The grounds for this view, in the preliving natural processes, was suggested in chapter 2. The scientific discussions of morality today are disturbing precisely because they dig so deeply into our evolutionary past. We sometimes like to think that only human beings—for that matter, only highly civilized humans—could give rise to genuine moral thinking and behavior. A good deal of effort has gone into the depiction of higher primates and early humans as brutes who mainly aimed at staying alive and satisfying their basest needs. We commonly speak of immorality as "animal," just as we speak of persons who engage in outrageous immoral actions as "animals."

The origin of values and morality cannot be separated, however, from our primordial past. It would be a natural move to subscribe to the belief that values and moral action are conditioned primarily or even solely by the current situation in which we live, the complex dilemma of global interrelatedness, freedom, and ecological crisis, all occurring in the context of a high-tech ambience that is as pervasive as the air we breathe. Obviously, this current situation is the milieu in which we must act out our humanness, the context that provides the substance in which we must fashion our action. However, if we consider this current milieu to be the only component in the moral transactions that challenge us today, we shall be more ill-prepared than we can afford to be to undertake what is necessary for responsible action.

We must understand that although humans are in a unique position with respect both to the moral challenges that face them and their capacity for moral judgment, those challenges and those capacities for judgment are part and parcel of the evolutionary continuum in which they have emerged. Evolution proceeds, we might say, by the process of what the French call *bricolage*. It does not create new materials and parts as it adapts to new environments and produces new and more complex forms, but rather, like the sculptor who works with junk, it presses into service what lies at hand. The human brain and central nervous system are built on the base of components that emerged in the reptilian and neo-mammalian phases of life's evolution on our planet. These prehuman compo-nents are active within us, and as Anthony Stevens has told us, are still engaged in the ongoing struggle to learn how to function in a way that is appropriate to their human context (1983, 267–71).

It is also true that the physical environment in which we live bears the marks of its past. We cannot, for example, teach the ozone layer new tricks; it insists upon functioning in the ways it has learned millions of years ago. The same may be said of social environments, even though the time span of their history is significantly smaller. Ethnic groups do not cast aside behaviors generated millen-nia in the past and begin to practice love toward one another simply because the global community requires it; religious fundamentalists do not allow their beliefs and practices instantaneously to be relativized by modern politics and technology and views of human rights, even when the tempting prize is a higher standard of living.

The potential for the relevance of values and morality emerged in the evolu-tionary process long before humans (Wicken 1989). As noted in chapter 3, the deterministic process itself proceeded to the point where, strangely enough, free-dom emerged. By freedom, I mean the reflective judgment to choose between alternatives that make a difference for our lives and/or the lives of those around us. Some read the potential for freedom all the way back to the Big Bang, locating it in the ongoing indeterminacy of physical processes.

Equating freedom with indeterminacy is a controversial move on whose cor-rectness I will not comment here; the emergence of freedom is clearer when we get to *Homo sapiens*. Chapter 8 examined the idea that the human species is marked by what Theodosius Dobzhansky calls "genetically controlled adaptive plasticity," which gives us great ability to scan our environment and choose be-haviors appropriate to it. Such a scanning process includes the self-conscious con-sideration of alternative decisions and behaviors, and it also requires a supportive social matrix that allows for free exploration by the individual and at the same time demands respect for group relationships and the welfare of other individuals.

The self-conscious consideration of alternatives and behaviors within a social context requires making judgments; these judgments in turn ground the reality of what we call values and morality. The genetically controlled adaptive plasticity of humans is confronted continually with the demand that it make choices be-tween alternatives. Among the alternatives are those that are not presently actual.

Survival hinges upon these choices. Moreover, the choices will have consequences, necessitating further judgments as to how those consequences will be dealt with. The chain of choice, feedback, consequences, and response is endless.

What I have just described is the evolutionary emergence of the ambience of values—moral and nonmoral in character. Values emerged as a requirement for life and its evolution, with the complementary requirements of clarifying values, achieving consensus about specific values, and taking responsibility for actualizing them. The ambience of values is at the same time the ambience of morality, defined as Nowell-Smith did, including beliefs about the nature of humans in their world, beliefs about what is good or desirable, and rules for what ought and ought not to be done.

Some Current Scientific Viewpoints

A great deal of scientific thinking has addressed the issues mentioned above. George Edgin Pugh, a physicist who has moved into artificial intelligence studies and research into values and decision-making processes, provides extensive analysis in his 1977 book, *The Biological Origin of Human Values*. He defines *value* as that which drives a judgment, and he understands the human brain and central nervous system as a value-driven decision system that makes judgments. He follows in the train of the Nobel laureate in brain studies, Roger Sperry, who speaks of values as the most powerful thing in the world, because they drive decision. Thus, the values of peace and war are more powerful than all of the nuclear arsenals, because it is these values that determine whether or not the arsenals will be used. (1983)

Pugh classifies values into two categories, primary and secondary. Primary values are those that are placed into the system prior to the creation of the system, over whose presence the system itself has no control. Secondary values arise within the lifetime of the system, by the system's own design, usually to assist in solving problems. Our evolutionary past has given rise to the primary values, over whose presence we have no say. Secondary values are created by us, through our culture; they are learned values. In the long run, Pugh argues, we must somehow reconcile them with the primary values. The urge to scratch an itch is primary, for example; we cannot eradicate it. The judgment that it is better to stop scratching and apply an ointment, so that we will not develop infected sores by scratching, is based on secondary values that are culturally enabled and motivated.

We share some of our primary values with nonhuman primates. A keen sense of competition between males for status, acceptance, or dominance is one example. However, secondary values of cultural elaboration determine whether that competition or its redirection is encouraged, and whether women are discriminated against when the rewards for competition are passed out. The explicit desire to contribute to the group seems also to be a distinct deeply rooted primary value, inherited from nonhuman primates. Cultural elaboration determines whether that contribution is to a destructive gang of peers, or to a Girl Scout troop, a football team, or a cooking class.

Pugh's analysis sets the stage for a distinction that becomes a sharp tension: that between values that we have inherited from our prehuman past and those that have emerged within our journey as human beings through our own history. That part of the scientific community that deals with our prehuman legacy is attempting to bring this distinction and tension to the attention of the wider population today. In shorthand this might be called the tension between our genes and our cultures. It is the newest expression of the older "nature versus nurture" discussion. The majority of scientists working in this field focus upon this distinction as fundamental to understanding who we are as humans and the dynamics of our moral concerns. In chapter 9, I questioned the dualism that seems to mark some of the scientific approaches because they are inherently contradictory of the evolutionary context and history in which genes and culture have emerged.

No one has put this message more eloquently than Richard Dawkins, in his book *The Selfish Gene* (1978). This book proceeds according to the maxim set forth by Robert Trivers in his "Foreword," that "Natural selection has built us, and it is natural selection we must understand if we are to comprehend our own identities" (vii). Trivers goes on to deliver this punch line:

> Be warned that if you wish, as I do, to build a society in which individuals cooperate generously and unselfishly towards a common good, you can expect little help from biological nature. Let us try to *teach* generosity and altruism, because we are born selfish. Let us understand what our own selfish genes are up to, because we may then at least have the chance to upset their designs, something which no other species has ever aspired to. (Dawkins 1976, 3)

Dawkins stands within the group of scientists who state the genes/cultures conflict in the most bellicose manner (Ghiselin 1974; Trivers 1971). Some of these are represented in the December 1988 issue of *Zygon: Journal of Religion and Science,* particularly in the articles by biologist George C. Williams and the primatologist Sarah Blaffer Hrdy.

William Irons has commented at length upon one of the most sophisticated of the recent scientific works on this question, Richard D. Alexander's *The Biology of Moral Systems* (1987). Alexander, as Irons explicates him, does not set up the tension as simply genes versus culture. Rather, the primary "hostile force of nature" for humans has been other humans, but the reason for conflict between humans rests on the conflicts of individual self-interest, which in turn are rooted in the genetic diversity of individuals, which prevents an identity of reproductive interests (Irons 1991; Alexander 1987, 37–42). This individual diversity affects the life of groups.

Alexander notes that "to say that we are *evolved* to serve the interests of our genes in no way suggests that we are *obliged* to serve them" (1987, 40). Culture can enable us to redirect our obligations, and Alexander believes that forming contracts by means of which we negotiate our self-interests across both individual and group lines is the most important means for dealing with the dire consequences that may come in the wake of the selfish gene. Irons both supports and criticizes this emphasis on contract-forming; he raises the worrisome question of whether such contracts must always favor the stronger and the more powerful in a society (1991, 71–73).

Donald T. Campbell, one of the most influential researchers in this area, has produced several significant sets of reflections on the genes/culture interface. These were surveyed at some length in chapter 8, including those contained in his celebrated 1975 Presidential Address to the American Psychological Association. I reiterate here two of the major theses he proposed there:

1. Human urban social complexity has been made possible by social evolution rather than biological evolution.

2. This social evolution has had to counter individual selfish tendencies which biological evolution has continued to select as a result of the genetic competition among the cooperators. (D. Campbell 1975)

This is not to say that Campbell underestimates the significance of biological evolution in the shaping of the human, but rather that he devotes his chief attention to the interface between genes and culture and to the role of culture on that interface.

Ralph Wendell Burhoe goes further than Campbell's statement that human urban social complexity has been enabled more by cultural evolution than biological. It is cultural evolution that enabled the human to emerge at all. In his preface to the publication of Campbell's address in *Zygon*, Burhoe writes as follows:

> Thus one of the most exciting intellectual problems of our time has become how to explain the mystery of the emergence from a beastly ape into a civilized human. How could culture and cooperative behavioral values or motivations (beyond those within one's family) be grafted onto a beast whose genetic programming is known to be selected for the perpetuation of its own line? How could a beast whose brain's genetic programming could not tolerate a full awareness of the implications of its own demise evolve to cope with an increase of such awareness, even to the point of an occasional self-motivated sacrifice of his body for nonkinfolk? This fascinating problem for science is at the same time an urgent problem for the health of humanity, at a time when eating too much of the fast-growing tree of scientific knowledge in the center of the garden of Eden is causing such an indigestion in moral and

religious knowledge that civilizations and individual psyches increasingly are showing signs of approaching breakdowns, disintegration, and death. (1976a, 159)

Burhoe had suggested answers to this question, even in the title of the article
that he had published in the June 1976 issue of *Zygon,* in which he had responded
to Campbell: "The Source of Civilization in the Natural Selection of Coadapted
Information in Genes and Culture." He proposes the striking hypothesis that
"humanity is not a single species but a new kind of symbiotic community"
(1976b, 282). The significant symbiosis that he is talking about is between the
biological creature *Homo* and "a new creature such as the earth had never seen
before, a creature that is only partly biological, only partly programmed by genetic information" (282). Biological humans (Burhoe calls them *Homo,* without
the *sapiens sapiens*) and sociocultural systems are living in symbiosis and undergoing the process of natural selection as a coevolving and coadapting supraorganism.

In one sense, Burhoe is underscoring the tension between genes and culture
in his idea that they represent two different organisms in a relationship. His basic
understanding is of their cooperation and reciprocity, however, in the image of
symbiosis. A successful symbiosis is necessary for the survival of both the human
genes and culture. Later he suggests that religion plays a special role in culture's
contribution to this symbiosis, in an article entitled "Religion's Role in Human
Evolution: The Missing Link between Ape-Man's Selfish Genes and Civilized
Altruism" (1979). I will refer to this article at greater length later.

This discussion, it should be noted, is another facet of analysis that not only
suggests the credibility of the theory of the created co-creator, but actually intensifies the analysis of how the co-creator has emerged within the process of nature.

Myth's Entrance

This quick survey of scientific materials sets the stage for two fundamental conclusions: (1) Paraphrasing Trivers, we may say that prehuman biological evolution
has built us, and we must understand this evolution if we are to comprehend our
own concern for values and morality and their possibilities. (2) If the human
community was to emerge and continue, cultural supplements had to manipulate
the genetic heritage from the very beginning of the emergence of *Homo sapiens*
so that it could survive under the new conditions imposed upon it by human
existence, without destroying the new human being, but on the contrary en-
hancing the new creature's survival.

Michael Levin sees things correctly when he points to values and morality
residing deep within nerve and sinew—deeper, perhaps, than even he realizes.
This primordial rootage provides energy for the pursuit of values; indeed, we
may say that it is the engine that drives morality. What Levin apparently does not
see so clearly is that this primordial rootage is also a major obstacle to the moral

life, whether that rootage lies in our prehuman past or in our earlier human history. The rootage is an obstacle because, although the information that evolution bequeaths to us at any given point through the process of selection (whether natural or cultural) is genuine truth, it is the truth about past worlds and the life of those creatures in the past through whom the information was conveyed to us (D. T. Campbell 1976, 169; J. Campbell and Moyers 1988, 13). To the extent that neither those creatures nor those worlds are appropriate for us today in our world, that information is obsolete, even detrimental to us. It is for this reason, for example, that the reptilian aspects of our central nervous system have to be taught what is appropriate for human living today. Even as we emphasize this obsolescence, we remember that the reptile in us has to be taught, not eradicated. If it were eradicated, we would die, because it is essential to us and to our life.

These considerations may help us to recognize how large a challenge confronted early human beings as their humanity wrestled at a primordial stage of history with the task of directing and redirecting the prehuman past out of which they were emerging. When I speak of early human beings, unless I indicate otherwise, I am speaking of Neanderthals, dating from 100,000 years ago (Pfeiffer 1982, chap. 6). The emergence of agriculture and civilization is usually dated at 10,000 years ago. Of course, we cannot depict the emergence of the human, or the new conditions of human living, as breaking into view suddenly—as if a hypothetical observer would detect no human beings at all one day, whereas the next day (or year or century) that same observer would suddenly see thousands of humans. Nevertheless, over a longer period of time, the observer would note a new species on the scene.

I will speak of the challenges facing early humans as twofold, keeping in mind the hypothesis concerning culture framed in the seventh auxiliary hypothesis.

First, *Homo sapiens* had to develop a way of adapting their prehuman legacy in order to behave appropriately under the new conditions of human existence. I termed this the development of human cultural supplements to the genetic and cultural legacy. These supplements would not be suitable for their task unless they possessed power to match the engines of the genetic heritage.

Second, in developing these cultural supplements, humans began an enterprise that has attained particular urgency in our time—that of fashioning a system of information, support, and guidance that is comparable to and integrated with the physico-biogenetic systems that preceded it in the evolutionary process and that continued to coexist with *Homo sapiens*.

Of course, humans were not aware of these challenges as such, just as most humans today do not seem to be aware of them. They were simply responding to perceived environments as their genetic and cultural motivators directed them, under the increasing presence of rational thinking. However, the point is that certain of their cultural supplements survived through the processes of natural selection. Donald Campbell (1991) has presented important information on how the selection processes may work, incorporating the Boyd-Richerson work (1985). Mihaly Csikszentmihalyi and Fausto Massimini (1985) have also contributed a number of concepts as to how selection works at the level of sociocultural evolution.

In the context of these considerations, we consider again the hypothesis explored in more depth in chapter 10:

Since the Neanderthal era, 100,000 years ago, religious myth and its accompanying ritual formed one of the most significant cultural inputs by which the prehuman creature was taught to live under the conditions of being human.

For its survival, therefore, *Homo sapiens* could not exist only on the physical and genetic information that serves the welfare of all other forms of life. Humans were fashioned such that they require more information, and this information must be as compelling as the physical and genetic. When we recognize these facts, then we can understand more fully the appearance of myth and its functioning. Three factors are particularly important.

First, myth emerged very close to the primordial ground at which human life was grappling with the vulnerable workings of its complex scanning systems that required judgment and that had to supplement and at times redirect the genetic motivators humans had inherited. Furthermore, myth had to function in a way that was relevant to the dimensions of human existence at which the genetic motivators were relevant. In our skepticism about myth, we are predisposed to overlook the function of this primordiality, especially when our critique is based on assessments that are primarily intellectual and academic. These matters were considered in chapter 10, which dealt primarily with evolutionary history on the basis of archaeological evidences.

Some recent researchers underscore the primordiality of myth and ritual by arguing that the structure and the processes of the human central nervous system not only are capable of receiving myth, but require it (d'Aquili and Laughlin 1975, 1978, 1983; Laughlin, McManus, and d'Aquili 1990; Turner 1983). E. O. Wilson speaks directly of the "mythopoeic requirements" of the human central nervous system, which inevitably result in the brain's ordering the information at its disposal finally into "some form of morality, religion, and mythology" (Wilson 1978, 200; also A. Stevens 1983, chaps. 13, 14). William Doty says of d'Aquili's work, it "has established a new fundamental position in the study of myths and rituals . . . an important synthesis and perspective that promises a more inclusive understanding of myths and rituals than we have ever known" (1986, 212).

Second, myth presents itself as a statement of *what is,* of *how things really are.* This *is* stands as the ground for the learning that the behaviors inherited from the evolutionary past must undergo, as well for the moral imperatives that follow from the myth. Humans must supplement physical and genetic information systems with cultural systems, which in turn are substantially reflective and self-aware. These cultural systems are powerful in large measure because they deliver necessary information, even though they themselves are not verifiable or falsifiable in the way that our self-consciousness might otherwise demand. Cultural information in the form of myth concerns that about which we cannot speak with certainty. It offers surplus conceptualization that deals with the ultimate ground of and nature of reality, with statements about what the whole of reality is like. Such information is necessary (that is what E. O. Wilson means by the "mythopoeic requirements" of the human central nervous system), and myth supplies it.

Metaphysical philosophy also provides this information, but not at the primordial level, and this accounts for this philosophy's lower level of existential relevance for most people. It also accounts for its not infrequent alliance with myth, as occurs in some schools of Platonism, Hegelianism, and Marxism, for example, thereby rendering those philosophies far more cogent to more persons than would otherwise be the case.

Humans regularly find themselves working hard and committing themselves to projects; they need to know whether the nature of reality is such that this hard work and commitment really make sense. Demonstrating love beyond the kinship group is costly and often not pleasurable; humans therefore need to know whether such love is really justified on the grounds that it is more fully commensurate with the fundamental character of reality. Myth claims to provide information about the most fundamental character of our lives and all reality. Leszek Kolakowski speaks of this aspect of myth as the function by which it "refers the conditioned empirical realities to an unconditioned universe" (1989, 41).

Third, myth always expresses itself in direct discourse and in declarative sentences. This is the form in which information about *how things really are* comes to us. Again, this was necessary if myth was to be relevant at the level where the vulnerabilities of life were being lived out. The cultural information of the *is,* which was essential to the flourishing of the distinctly human, could be no more conditional than the genetic programs that direct the biological components of the human animal.

The linguistic form of the declarative poses a great problem for modern persons. We know that the myth is a myth. We entertain the mythic information as if it were a hypothesis to be tested. Under some conditions this is required if we are to be faithful to our rational humanity, even those of us who are devout believers of a religious tradition. Human beings by their nature turn all information into hypothetical discourse. Declaration and command become hypothesis to us, because we are creatures who take part in the ongoing processes of nature by self-conscious participation in and co-construction of those processes. Thus, what is inviolable natural law to other entities is for the human a hypothesis that may or may not be adequate. This is true whether the issue is how babies are to be nurtured, how genetic constitution is to be altered, or how rivers flow and subatomic particles react.

Today, we may recognize the wisdom in the myths, but we cannot believe them naively. We are critical; we can entertain the myths only as proposals, as hypotheses. We can believe only through what Ricoeur terms the second naiveté, which requires critical philosophical analysis and interpretation (1967, 3–24, 347–57). This dynamic underlies the movement away from myth as etiological and explanatory to myth as detector of reality.

These observations suggest a rough periodization of history in the West: The epochs prior to the Enlightenment or modernity are marked by naive realism with respect to belief in myth. The modern epoch, ca. 1650–1950, debunked myth through its critical reason, tending to reject it or reduce it to rational philosophy. The postmodern period, in which we now live, is a deconstructionist epoch; while it affirms the achievement of the critical Enlightenment period, it recognizes the integrity, necessity, and unavoidability of myth. Consequently, we not only wish to believe myth, we actually *do* believe it, but at the same time we keep in mind what our critical Enlightenment past has taught us about myth, and so we believe in myth under the conditions of *irony*. This periodization conforms to Ricoeur's analysis of the two naivetés. It is not far removed from a Kierkegaardian stance.

We test the hypothesis presented by myth in the commitment of our lives. The only persuasive ground for this commitment is the possibility that the hypothesis is a true, declarative picture of the nature of things. While Ricoeur emphasizes the critical philosophical level of this testing of myth, Sören Kierkegaard focuses his intense beam on its existential dimension. When we are hanging in faith over the 70,000 fathoms of water that he spoke of, we are willing to take the leap, willing to be suspended over nothing more solid than the water, because the object of our dialectical faith has to do with *the way things really are*. Otherwise we would not be able to summon the energy, courage, and strength to live by faith in images of and in the ever-present reality of that which is always underdetermined by the facts of our total experience.

The Dynamics of Myth and Morality

We must consider more fully the working of myth to provide a picture of *the way things really are,* because it is central to understanding the way myth and morality are related to each other. Ricoeur stated that "myth provides grounds for our ritual actions and all forms of action and thought by which we understand ourselves in our world" (1967, 5). Mircea Eliade makes the point even more force-fully when he says that "every ritual and every meaningful act that humans per-form repeats a mythical archetype" (1963, sect. 164). There is no other final ground for the power of the ritual and moral action.

All values finally receive their validity from their being rooted in and being in harmony with the way things really are. Although we may not derive our *oughts* from our experience of the *is,* the *ought* would have no real substance if it were not rooted in the *is.* We want to know that our actions are in harmony with the fundamental character of reality. Ultimately that is what grounds both the mandates and the prohibitions of our moralities.

It has often been observed, as Peter Berger and Thomas Luckmann do, that myth first of all projects a

> symbolic universe [that] is conceived of as the matrix of *all* socially objectivated and subjectively real meanings; the entire historic society and the entire biography of the individual are seen as events taking place *within* this universe. What is particu-larly important, the marginal situations of the life of the individual (marginal, that is, in not being included in the reality of everyday existence in society) are also encompassed by the symbolic universe. (1966, 96)

Having projected this symbolic universe, myth provides imperatives for hu-man action. The all-encompassing character of the symbolic universe it describes is what gives myth its moral power. Obviously, humans should act so as to be in harmony with this universe. Laughlin, McManus, and d'Aquili explore this cre-ation of the symbolic universe in their book *Brain, Symbol & Experience,* in which they include cross-cultural perspectives (1990, chaps. 6–8).

This conceptual insight may be particularized in the Ten Commandments. That "I am the Lord your God, who brought you out of the land of Egypt, out of the house of slavery" (Exod. 20:2) is the most important thing we need to know about "how things really are," and therefore we will obey God's command-ments. An accurate historical, psychological, and sociological account of the ap-pearance of Hebrews in the Sinai peninsula would have provided little compel-ling ground for the moral injunctions that followed. Statements condemning thievery because it would weaken the urgently needed social contract, or prohib-iting certain kinds of foods and food preparation because they would cause physi-cal illness, would have been just as unpersuasive, because of course no direct causal line could be drawn at the time of Moses between the behaviors and the consequences.

Lest we consider our present life to be vastly superior to and more sophisti-cated than that of the so-called primitives in Sinai, we must remember the many years it took for Americans to be convinced that they should take seriously the causal links between smoking and alcohol consumption and poor health. The Seventh-Day Adventists have had much more success by simply reminding their members that smoking and drinking violate the will of God. Drug and alcohol therapy do not focus chiefly on the deleterious effects of substance abuse; rather, they work to rehabilitate the user's sense of the world as an encompassing symbolic universe in which human life is worthwhile. The therapy thus acknowledges, at least implicitly, that it is not first of all ethics that will renew the user, so much as conviction about the meaningfulness of the symbolic universe—an unverifiable conviction, one about which we gain our information primarily in mythic form.

The abusive urge of a man to rape a woman does not address the man as a hypothesis to be considered or as a set of causal explanations, nor does the injunction against it. Consequently, the picture of the *is* that grounds the moral injunction does not present itself as a tentative proposal. To take a cue from popular culture, the Ten Commandments would have taken the form of the Ten Suggestions, if the presence of the Hebrews at Sinai had been explained as "quite possibly" due to the favor and action of a power that "upon further reflection one might arguably consider to be" the God of Abraham, Isaac, and Jacob.

The Love Command according to Christians

The essential Christian myth consists of the narrative that includes at least the following events: (1) God made the world, including humans in the image of the maker. (2) Human beings were created in the garden, in unity with their maker and with one another, but they came to be alienated from both, and the alienation manifests itself in their actions. (3) The man Jesus of Nazareth conveyed in word and deed the grace of God and its moral consequence, unqualified love for what God created; thus he embodies both the revelation of God's will and also the redeeming action of God. (4) Jesus broke the boundary of death in his resurrection; we shall be raised also, in the context of God's bringing to perfection and consummation the entire created order.

The elements of the myth correspond to the classical Christian doctrines of creation, fall, and original sin, the incarnation of God in Jesus of Nazareth, who is the ground of revelation and redemption; and the resurrection and consummation. The myth sets before us a truly all-encompassing symbolic universe, in which God encompasses both the origin and final perfection of the universe and also is committed to the welfare of "even the littlest ones" in our world by illuminating and renewing activity throughout the process of history.

What is the most appropriate response that is prompted by this particular casting of the symbolic universe, its primary imperative for action? The most basic value and moral thrust of this myth is set forth in the Great Commandment: "You shall love the Lord your God with all your heart, and with all your soul, and with all your mind . . . and . . . you shall love your neighbor as yourself. On these two commandments hang all the law and the prophets" (Matt. 22:37–40).

Love for God translates into awe and regard for the central reality (to use Gerd Theissen's term) that is the ground of all finite existence that we observe, and also into the accountability by which we hold ourselves to the unreserved effort to adapt ourselves to the central reality that is God. It is the call to believe that our life in the nature that surrounds us is an awesome transaction caught up in the fabric of mystery that is grounded finally in a coherent reality. Further, it urges us to conceive of our lives under the mandate to adapt ourselves to this coherent reality by taking regard for its ways. To love this reality with all one's heart and soul and mind suggests an all-encompassing regard for it and also living in commitment and accountability to it.

Love for neighbor translates into unreserved action in behalf of our fellow human beings. It enjoins the conviction that each of us exists in solidarity with the entire human community—the neighbor is explicitly defined in terms that are not limited by genetic similarities, or racial, national, or cultural ties—and that the purpose of our lives is to live for the well-being of the human community in a self-giving style. Today one would want to speak, as Mihaly Csikszentmihalyi does, of solidarity with all created beings. When this command for love of neighbor is put in the mouth of Jesus, it cannot be disassociated from his own love, acted out in his earthly life, culminating in the last supper and upon the cross.

It is the particular historic vocation of the Christian tradition in which I stand, and in which most Protestants are rooted, to call attention to the fact that this command presupposes the prior love of God for us, just as the Ten Commandments, as they appear in the Hebrew Scriptures in the twentieth chapter of the book of Exodus, are prefaced with God's declaration of intent to be the God of those people and a rehearsal of the major action of beneficence that God had shown to the people. This presupposition is suggested both by the context of Jesus' enjoining this commandment and that of the Hebrew background where the command is also at home, as well as by the style of Jesus' presentation of it.

We may interpret this message as the proposition that the reality system of nature in which we live is itself basically an ambience in which we truly belong, an ambience that has brought us into being and that enables us to fulfill the purposes for which we were brought into being. The central reality that undergirds all of concrete experience and to which we continually seek to adapt is disposed toward us in a way that we can interpret as graciousness and beneficent support. I cite Gerd Theissen's discussion of this love that is directed to us. He relates it to the traditional Lutheran doctrine of justification by grace:

> The New Testament begins from this insight: in their lives all human beings have the "pre-programmed" task of living in harmony with God, i.e., adapting themselves to the central reality, but none of them achieves this aim. Harmony with God is achieved in quite another way: God takes the questionable attempts of human beings to adapt as successful. God affirms them independently of their success

or failure. That is the content of the doctrine of justification. . . . The justification of the godless offers everyone that harmony with the ultimate reality which is the inner goal of evolution—regardless of how near to this goal they may be—or how far from it. (1985, 172–73)

This background conviction is powerful affirmation that our moral action of love for God and neighbor is our way of living in harmony with the way things really are. The total complex—the love of God for us and our love for God and for the neighbor—puts in place the all-encompassing symbolic universe that drives the Christian tradition. It establishes that the fullness of the Christian proposal functions unmistakably as myth is supposed to function.

Scientific Assessment of the Love Command

Today we see an intense concern on the part of several of the sciences for the substance of the love command. E. O. Wilson announced the importance of this concern—one might say, with fanfare—in his celebrated 1975 book, *Sociobiology: The New Synthesis.* He states on the first page: "This brings us to the central theoretical problem of sociobiology: how can altruism, which by definition reduces personal fitness, possibly evolve by natural selection?" (1975, 3).

An avalanche of papers, lectures, and books in the last two decades have focused on Wilson's question, a question that he was not the first to put. The finest minds in anthropology, genetics, and psychology, particularly those who are linked to the emerging field of human behavior and evolution, have reflected on this issue. Many theologians, ethicists, and philosophers argue that what the sociobiologists term *altruism* ought not to be confused with what the religious tradition means by love for neighbor. I respect these arguments, but from the first moment that I read Wilson, I felt that a religious tradition that centers on a man dying on a cross for the benefit of the whole world could not responsibly ignore a scientific discussion about the emergence within the evolutionary process of the possibility of living viably so as to put the welfare of others so high on the agenda that one creature would put its own welfare in jeopardy for the sake of others.

The scientists had no difficulty in establishing the genetic rules by which close relatives could be altruistic toward one another. The problem arises when altruism is practiced toward persons and creatures that are not genetic kin. Why does such a behavior not die out with the death of the foolish individual who practices it? How can it be transmitted and actually flourish? What is its significance?

Donald Campbell has devoted a considerable portion of his published work to the thesis that it was such altruistic behavior that enabled the human community to develop a highly complex urban life. In another jargon, altruism is both a cause and a requirement for the emergence of the global village. Campbell does not speak so much of altruism as love, nor does he restrict his discussion to the

Jewish or Christian faiths. He speaks rather of "counter-hedonic traditions" that allow persons to serve values other than those that provide immediate "skin-surface" satisfaction.

Campbell's 1975 Presidential Address to the American Psychological Association created a storm of discussion because he suggested that the counter-hedonic recipes of the traditional religions were on the whole more reliable guides for human living than the pro-hedonic doctrines of psychotherapeutic practice. His position, therefore, not only asserts the epoch-making significance of altruistic behavior in human history, but it also insists on its contemporary importance.

Further, he advances the notion, in league with several other scientists, that altruism beyond kin is transmitted culturally, not genetically, and that religious traditions are the chief carriers of this value. These religious traditions bear the "well-winnowed wisdom" of altruism that has met the challenges of selection and survived as a significant and essential adaptive option for human behavior. We might also add that he considers altruism too important to be left to the exclusive custodianship of the religious communities. They too often fail to recognize this treasure within their all-too-earthen vessels.

Ralph Wendell Burhoe has also devoted the major portion of his research and writing to the issues raised by E. O. Wilson. He has coined the term *trans-kin altruism*. His hypotheses argue that this altruism is the distinguishing characteristic of humanity; it is what allowed the civilized human being to rise above the "beastly ape-man." He, too, considers religion and the wisdom of religious traditions to be the chief carriers of this altruism, and consequently, he considers religion to be an essential dimension of human being.

Burhoe and Solomon Katz have developed together the thesis that global peace and global morality are likewise dependent upon the religions effectively representing this trans-kin altruism (Burhoe and Katz 1986; Katz 1989, 1991). Religion today is fully as responsible for conflict and war as it is an agency for peace. How can this paradox be accounted for? Burhoe and Katz point the finger at the religions of the world for not carrying their love command far enough. The great advance in human history came when religion enabled altruism to be extended beyond family, tribe, and nation to all members of the religious community. In a global village, where the particular religious communities cross national and cultural borders and where they rub elbows daily with each other and with nonreligious secularists, altruism practiced only toward the brothers and sisters of the faith is not only deficient, it is dangerous—as events in Northern Ireland, India, Lebanon, Palestine, and in other places have demonstrated in our own time.

The Christian would add to the Burhoe/Katz critique of religion that Christians have yet to actualize what the historical Jesus of Nazareth urged and practiced in his own limited lifetime and geographical setting. He seemed to have made it a point to affirm his self-sacrificial solidarity across religious lines, across boundaries of national identity, as well as those of economic and social class and gender.

Assessment

There may well be a convergence of the science and the myth that I have been discussing. The focus has been on the mythic core of one particular religious tradition, but this does not mean that other mythic cores, from other religious traditions, might not also show marks of this convergence. All of the scientists referred to here would insist that the mythic contribution of these other religions must be given full attention.

Other caveats may be raised. Neither Christianity nor any other religion has been faithful enough to its mythic emphasis on the love command. We must return as well to Campbell's reminder that no matter how successfully the well-winnowed religious wisdom has stood the test of history and selection, it comes to every generation in concrete forms that can only claim to be the truth about past worlds and not necessarily about the present and the future. They must carry the label that applies to the world of investment bankers and mutual funds: past success is no guarantee of future performance. Furthermore, some argue religious communities are the greatest obstacle to belief in the love command. They point to the millions of persons in our society and around the world who find the fundamental tenets of religious faith appealing, but find the representation of those tenets in official religious institutions to be offensive. The confessional statement that follows should be heard against the background of my clear acknowledgment of these caveats.

Both the scientific studies that I have surveyed and the religious myths that I have interpreted converge in their judgment that the love command is of special significance for human living. Religious believers need not be troubled that this convergence might constitute a perversion of the religious truth or a reductionism to functionalist processes that are the object of scientific study. Rather, on the one hand the scientific statements are prophetic, reminding the religious communities of the deeper significance of their heritage. On the other hand, the mythic stance in general and the Christian myth in particular would predict that the scientists would come to their conclusions. In general, the mythic view believes that it speaks of the way things really are, and if the love command is central to the myth, it will appear central to scientific study of finite phenomena.

Further, the Christian myth asserts that what we find in Jesus is the rationale of all reality, what the Greeks call *logos,* which is often translated as *Word.* In Colossians, our Scriptures assert that in Jesus "all things hold together" (Col. 1:17). Following Kolakowski (1989), if the myth refers the empirical realm to an unconditioned universe, then it would be rendered useless if scientific studies did not converge, at least to the extent that the myth could account for them. Paul Tillich makes the same point about religious myth and the unconditional, emphasizing strongly that the unconditional stands beyond conceptualization (1958, 4–5, passim).

The myth and the Scriptures do not say that the concrete organizational church or even the dynamics of religious practice hold all things together. More important, the mythic injunction does not prescribe any particular form of love as normative. In the Christian religion, even the cross of Jesus is interpreted figuratively as a norm for his followers; Christians are not urged to undergo literal crucifixions. Rather, the myth and its Scriptures say that in this man Jesus we encounter the *logos* of all reality. I would not be surprised to find the same message carried in the myths of other religions—indeed, I would be surprised if it did not occur in other religions, since they have stood the same test of history and selection that Christianity has; some of them have stood the test much longer than Christianity.

The Christian Myth's Central Contribution

One consideration raised by the Christian mythic material that I have expounded stands out from all the rest: that all morality presupposes and is a response to the prior love of God for us, a love that seeks our well-being and the fulfillment of that for which we have been created. In the jargon of religion, the striking character of this assertion is muted, but in nonreligious terms, it is stunning. Such a nonreligious rendition was suggested above, on page 190: *The reality system of nature in which we live is itself basically an ambience in which we truly belong, an ambience that has brought us into being and that enables us to fulfill the purposes for which we were brought into being. The central reality that undergirds all of concrete experience and to which we continually seek to adapt is disposed toward us in a way that we can interpret as graciousness and beneficent support.*

12

Altruism and Christian Love

Important conceptual issues are raised by the juxtaposition of the biocultural evolutionary sciences, as I describe them in the first section of this chapter, and the role of myth and ritual in human evolution, as I present it in the second section, followed by a discussion of the theological concepts.

The issues emerge, first of all, when we consider that even though the genetic programs that drive human behavior seem insufficient to account for trans-kin altruism, that altruism has nevertheless become a distinguishing characteristic of the human species over the millennia. This leads us further to reflect that, despite their blatant underdetermination by the data and the difficulties of submitting them to reasonable processes of falsification, ancient myth and ritual that carry the cultural programs for trans-kin altruism have proven themselves to possess reliable information for understanding reality and for the guidance of human behavior. Even when, as with some of the cosmological myths, they appear to stand falsified when compared to the findings of contemporary science, they have served the survival and flourishing of concrete human communities. Finally, it appears that even in secularized societies that are heavily influenced by science and technology, the presence and usefulness of myth and ritual—ancient as well as modern substitutes—are far from being eliminated.

It is not at all clear what conclusions are to be drawn from this state of affairs. It is evident, however, that further reflection on these issues is required. Whatever the merits or drawbacks inherent in the literal shape of their stories, myths and rituals carry information that has served human survival, and presented it in modes suited to the history of the species' evolution as a biocultural creature.

A further issue concerns the purpose of bringing the sciences and the myth/ritual into contact with each other. I reject two extreme suggestions that have appeared in the past few centuries: on the one hand that the sciences aim simply at reinforcing the ancient myths and rituals with contemporary forms of argument; and on the other hand that scientific theories can serve as substitutes for the ancient information systems.

It seems more adequate to envision a kind of reciprocal impact, which consists both of mutual critique and possible reinforcement. Clearly, the ancient systems of information require testing. That a packet of information has proven useful and viable in a previous situation is no guarantee that it will serve survival in a subsequent era. Furthermore, some mythic packets are obviously rendered obsolete or in need of revising, such as the injunction "Be fruitful and multiply" or certain myths and rituals that promote unwholesome forms of sexism and ethnocentrism. Ralph Wendell Burhoe has provided an example of how revision is called for in his suggestion that trans-kin altruism as enjoined by religious myth has stopped short at the boundaries of the religious community itself and requires extension (Burhoe and Katz 1986).

At the same time, the religious packets of information will not easily relinquish their overall sense of *the way things really are*. For example, the information that the realm of nature is caught up within a larger purpose, and that this makes a difference for human behavior, will not be jettisoned quickly. Nor will the message that beneficence is a fundamental characteristic of reality and therefore a ground for our own beneficent behavior and self-understanding. The impact of such religious thought will be to urge the sciences to take these views seriously as issues for research. Indeed, it is from this perspective that I interpret the enormous effort of the biocultural evolutionary sciences to understand the phenomenon of trans-kin altruism. Such altruism is a great puzzle to these sciences, as E. O. Wilson asserts, "the central theoretical problem of sociobiology: how can altruism, which by definition reduces personal fitness, possibly evolve by natural selection?" (1975, 3–4).

The very fact that such researchers as Donald Campbell, Richard Dawkins, Sarah Blaffer Hrdy, and George Williams plead strongly for cultural overriding of the genetic programs indicates that they are not ready to abandon the cultural programs that are carried by the myths and rituals, even though, for them, those specific packets of cultural information defy evolutionary explanation (see pages 199–200, below). Their ambivalence at this point is in itself an occasion for reflecting upon the issues involved. This chapter aims to contribute to that reflection by suggesting that three modes of reflection are particularly appropriate to the study of altruism: the biocultural evolutionary sciences, the study of myth and ritual in human evolutionary history, and theology. I attempt in this chapter to conceptualize the contribution that each mode makes. My hope is that further reflection will be stimulated thereby.

Further study might focus upon the complex involvement in these issues of two sets of time frames. One set, to which I have referred, consists of the temporal distance between the originating circumstances and continuation of the ancient myths and rituals on the one hand, and the contemporary biocultural evolutionary sciences on the other. The second set of time frames consists of the distance between the classic Western philosophical and theological discussions of self-interest and altruism and the watershed marked by Thomas Hobbes (1588–

1679), whose individualistic philosophy and psychology form the modern framework for discussing questions of altruism and egoism.

As Alisdair MacIntyre (1967, 462) points out, the Greek sources of thought do not recognize altruistic benevolence as a virtue, and the medieval sources posit the love of God as the ground for human self-fulfillment. Therefore, for neither the Greeks nor the medieval thinkers would it make sense to pit self-interest and altruism against each other. Hobbes, in contrast, sets forth the selfishness/altruism discussion in terms that could be adopted almost intact by the current generation of sociobiologists. Since the religious traditions owe more to the Greek and the medieval thinkers, my discussion actually encompasses the metaphysical tensions between three major epochs of Western thinking, in addition to the differences between prehistoric myth-ritual and contemporary scientific reasoning.

The argument of this chapter is structured by a major thesis, three subtheses, and a number of elaborating statements. *The major thesis:*

1. The concepts of altruism as articulated by the evolutionary biocultural sciences and the love command of the Hebrew-Christian tradition focus upon the same phenomenon: beneficent human behavior toward others, even those who are not genetic kin.

2. The evolutionary biocultural sciences approach this beneficent behavior from the perspective of its placement in the natural history of life.

3. The study of myth and ritual approaches the same phenomenon from the perspective of the functioning of human culture.

4. Christian theology interprets this behavior as expression of basic cosmological and ontological principles.
   Subthesis #1: The concept and theories of altruism as developed by the biocultural evolutionary sciences illumine the distinctiveness of the challenge to human cooperative behavior in terms of its natural history.
   Subthesis #2: A consideration of the evolutionary history of the human species illumines the essential role that myths and rituals—including the myths and rituals of love—have played in the formation and survival of the human species.
   Subthesis #3: The significance of the theological concepts of altruistic love, elaborated from the myths and rituals and also by the scientific understandings, is this: Theology suggests that theories of epigenetic rules or strategies of self-interest are not enough to complete our understanding of altruistic love; we require also ways of discussing the hypothesis that altruism is an intrinsic value, rooted in the fundamental character of reality.

Altruism and the Evolutionary Challenge to Humans

The fruits of research done by the evolutionary biocultural sciences help us to understand concretely that human beings are creatures of nature. These sciences clarify how *Homo sapiens* has been crafted through the processes of evolution and just what the dynamics of those processes have been. One of the most useful depictions of how these sciences understand the human being as a creature of evolutionary emergence is exemplified in the diagram in figure 12-1. This diagram highlights two of the streams of information, both evolutionary in character, that conjoin to make a human being—genetic and cultural.

Humans face a distinctive evolutionary challenge, which they have in large part already successfully negotiated. This challenge is constituted by the high degree of social complexity in which humans live, requiring of them cooperation, coordination, and division of labor (Richerson 1992). Humans must live cooperatively in large communities of persons who are not kin relatives—that is, who are genetic competitors.

The distinctive social setting in which humans live and the pressures it exerts are well recognized by researchers in this field. I have already cited the work by Donald T. Campbell, which has been foundational for this research, and which Richerson carries forward. Campbell's argument recognizes the necessity of sociocultural evolution for human life as we now know it, but calls attention also to the fact that, unlike the social insects, who also possess a highly complex social life, the cultured cooperators in the human community are genetic competitors. This results in the state of affairs that Campbell characterizes as "human culture contra selfish human nature" (1976, 187).

To succeed in their particular environment, with its intense level of social complexity, humans must develop behaviors that no other species we know of

Figure 12-1: Human Beings Viewed through Biocultural Evolution

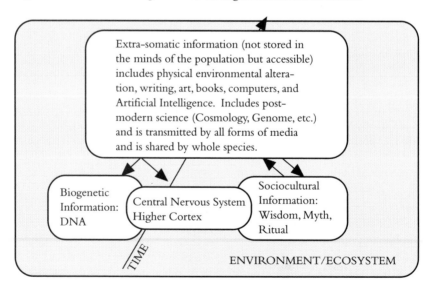

Extra-somatic information (not stored in the minds of the population but accessible) includes physical environmental alteration, writing, art, books, computers, and Artificial Intelligence. Includes post-modern science (Cosmology, Genome, etc.) and is transmitted by all forms of media and is shared by whole species.

Biogenetic Information: DNA

Central Nervous System Higher Cortex

Sociocultural Information: Wisdom, Myth, Ritual

TIME

ENVIRONMENT/ECOSYSTEM

— Solomon H. Katz 1993

has developed: behavior that targets the welfare of conspecifics (and even of other species), even when such behavior threatens to diminish their own fitness and even though those conspecifics are genetic competitors. This behavior is often termed altruism, specifically trans-kin altruism (Burhoe 1981, chap. 7).

We may accept E. O. Wilson's formulation as the prevailing definition of altruism in the biocultural evolutionary sciences: "When a person (or animal) increases the fitness of another at the expense of his own fitness, he can be said to have performed an act of *altruism*" (1975, 117). Paul Allison summarizes Robert Trivers's definition, which is essentially the same: "altruism . . . [is] behavior which reduces the reproductive fitness of the donor while increasing the reproductive fitness of the recipient, where reproductive fitness is the expected number of offspring that survive to adulthood" (Allison 1991, 3; Alexander 1987, 33–41).

As I understand it, the general opinion among scientists who work in this area is that such trans-kin altruism cannot be accounted for on grounds of genetic evolution alone. Campbell's argumentation is rooted in his reading of developments during the last quarter-century in the genetics of altruism. He associates himself with the position of George C. Williams, who holds that altruistic tendencies that put the individual at risk will be selected for less frequently in a population's evolution than those that make for selfish gain (D. Campbell 1975, 239; G. Williams 1988, 393–403). We could just as well cite this opinion from the works of Dawkins (1978), E. O. Wilson (1975), or Irons (1991).

In order to account for altruism within this framework, scientists have employed a number of auxiliary concepts, such as inclusive fitness, reciprocal altruism, and direct and indirect reciprocity. We should guard against a false dualism between genetic and nongenetic evolutionary causes of behavior. Certainly, it is not correct to assert specific genetic coding for action that correlates with specific religious-moral injunctions. At the same time, it is equally inadequate to hold that behaviors as deeply rooted in human life as belief in myths and rituals and respect for moral commands, as well as respect for the specific behavior of self-giving love, would exist today if they were not reinforced by the human genotypes (Irons 1992a, 1992b).

Such considerations as the foregoing set up the fundamental conceptual difficulty: Humans exist in the poignant situation where the demands of their socially complex environment require behaviors that (1) cannot be attained on the basis of human genetic make-up, and (2) stand in tension with, if not outright contradiction to, the genetic programs of information that have enabled humans' emergence within the processes of evolution.

This tension between trans-kin altruism and certain basic programs that constitute the human being was recognized by August Comte when he coined the term *altruism*. He contrasted altruism with egoism, placing the welfare of others ahead of welfare for the self.

Culture is the stream of information that enables trans-kin altruism, the behavior that allows *Homo sapiens* to negotiate its peculiar evolutionary challenge. There have been a number of careful and important discussions of how culture and genes coexist and interact to shape human behavior. Some researchers see genetic and cultural evolution in sharp antagonism to each other (Dawkins 1978; G. Williams 1966, 1988), while others see a relationship of continuity or symbiosis (Alexander 1987; D. Campbell 1991; Burhoe 1981). Among those who give detailed discussions of how the two streams of information interact, Alexander's concept of the contractual character of morality (1987) should be noted, as well as the Boyd-Richerson model of intragroup homogeneity-intergroup variability (1985), with which Campbell aligns himself (1991). E. O. Wilson, elaborated by Michael Ruse, has suggested that culture functions as a set of epigenetic rules that comprise a sort of game in which humans form cultural strategies that override the biological information of selfishness (Ruse 1986a, 1988, 416).

Elsewhere in this study, I have stated my agreement with Ralph Wendell Burhoe's effort to conceptualize the relation of genes and culture as a form of symbiosis. A great deal of human existence can be understood as dealing with the management of this symbiosis. As with any instance of symbiosis, each component must coevolve with the other, coadapting to each other and to the common environment, so as to be selected for survival. Burhoe thus considers the limited kin-altruism that is enabled by the genetic programs to be the essential foundation upon which culture acts to extend altruism beyond kin, but in such a way as not to threaten the existence of culture's host, the biogenetic symbiont. It is incorrect, in Burhoe's view, to speak of the human being unless both symbionts are present. Thus, he considers religion (including myth, ritual, and moral codes) to be the agent for transforming the prehuman ape-man of the selfish gene into a genuine human being who is capable of trans-kin altruism. Burhoe's theory has received significant support among scientists working in this area (Irons 1992a; Richerson 1992).

Thus we arrive at our first subthesis:

The concept and theories of altruism as developed by the biocultural evolutionary sciences illumine the distinctiveness of the challenge to human cooperative behavior in terms of its natural history.

Religious Myth and Ritual in Human Evolution

The cultural stream of information that is essential to the survival of *Homo sapiens* must have operated with appropriate effectiveness as a guidance for behavior from the very beginning of the emergence of the species, and it had to meet certain pressing challenges. If it is true, as I believe it is, that the human species could not survive on its physico-biogenetic evolutionary information systems alone, then it follows that the cultural supplements to the biogenetic information had to possess at least a minimal effectiveness from the beginning, and that their effectiveness had to increase thereafter.

Several challenges faced this emerging system of cultural information. First, the cultural supplements to the biogenetic systems had to operate with motivational power comparable to the genetic motivators. At no point is this challenge more pressing than with respect to altruism. Precisely because human behavior toward non-kin conspecifics must be and has been distinctive, and because this distinctiveness is not generated by genetic programs, the cultural programs need to be forceful. Concerning his own position, Donald Campbell writes that he joins Boyd and Richerson (1985) in "positing that cultural evolution can override biological evolution and lead individuals to do things that are biologically stupid in terms of *individual* inclusive fitness" (1991, 96). Dawkins, Williams, Hrdy, and Alexander seem to agree.

One can imagine how such overriding might pertain to intergroup relations in the growing density of European populations in the period after 40,000 years ago, as well as in relations within kin groups, in child-rearing, and in relations between the genders. The nongenetic motivators for such overriding behavior would have to be strong and free from ambiguity. However, there is a basic contradiction in those scientific suggestions that genes and cultures are at war with each other (Dawkins 1978, chap. 11); as Burhoe points out, they must coevolve, coadapt, and be coselected (1981, chap. 6).

The second challenge facing the cultural information and guidance system for *Homo sapiens* was that it had to be comparable to and interface with the physico-biogenetic systems that preceded it in the evolutionary process and that continued to exist as components of the environment. The needs of the body, the choice of which plants and animals to use for food, learning the habits and migration patterns of animals, developing methods of agriculture, food preparation, and preservation—such challenges require that the cultural systems of information be in fine balance with the noncultural systems that form the environment in which the culture-bearing animal, *Homo sapiens,* must flourish.

Since Neanderthal times, 100,000 years ago, religious myth and its accompanying ritual formed significant components of the cultural information system by which the genetically crafted *Homo* was enabled to live under conditions we call human. This is one of the most speculative parts of the theory I am setting forth. The theory assumes the work of those whose research centers on the nature and function of myth and ritual (Berger and Luckmann 1966; Doty 1986; Eliade 1963; Ricoeur 1967). From this body of thought we may derive a basic structure for understanding how myth and ritual may have functioned in early periods of human emergence.

The suggestion that myth works to provide a picture of *the way things really are* is central to understanding the way in which myth and morality are related to each other. Recall Paul Ricoeur's statement that "myth provides grounds for our ritual actions and all forms of action and thought by which we understand ourselves in our world" (1967, 5), and also Mircea Eliade's that "every ritual and every meaningful act that humans perform repeats a mythical archetype" (1963, sect. 164). There is no other final ground for the power of ritual and moral action.

I have already argued that all values finally receive their validity from being rooted in and in harmony with *the way things really are.* Our *oughts* would have no real substance if they were not rooted in the *is.* Humans want to know that their actions are in harmony with the fundamental character of reality. Ultimately that is what grounds both the mandates and the prohibitions of their moralities (Hefner 1981, 1984d). We might use the terms *indicative* and *imperative,* rather than *is* and *ought.* The myth–ritual complex portrays first of all an indicative, from which the imperative flows.

We refer again to Berger and Luckmann, that myth first of all projects a "symbolic universe [that is] conceived of as the matrix of all socially objectivated and subjectively real meanings" (1966, 96). Within this symbolic universe, myth provides imperatives for human action. The all-encompassing character of the symbolic universe it describes is what gives the myth its moral power. Obviously, human behavior should be in harmony with this universe.

From such considerations as these, we can understand how myth leads to behavior, and how behavior is motivated on the grounds that it is essential for harmony with the way things really are. One might add that ritual constitutes a translation from the myth into symbolic action, which in turn is to be expressed in the praxis of ordinary life. The ritual serves as a means of approaching the central realities of the world and also as a resource and norm for daily behavior. Such an interpretive scheme illumines ancient phenomena, such as the European cave paintings, and so-called primitive religions, as well as contemporary behaviors.

The interpretive framework that I have just described helps us to understand two characteristics of myth and ritual that are often repugnant to modern persons: the casting of myth/ritual in direct (rather than hypothetical) discourse, and the fact that myth and ritual are vastly underdetermined by the data. When viewed in the context of *Homo sapiens'* evolutionary history, these two characteristics are clearly functional and even necessary. Furthermore, these characteristics may be more vital even today than we often grant.

We tend to overlook the probable circumstances in which myth emerged within human history. It emerged within the development of the complex and fragile capacities of the central nervous system. These new capacities served to process information from the environment and supply frameworks for interpreting it in ways that previously had been unavailable to life. Myth survived the selection processes precisely because it functioned at the same level as the genetically driven motivators and transmuted them in ways that were relevant to the survival of the human species. Interpreted in this framework, the primordial character of myth assumes a significance even more profound than those provided by methodologies that fail to take the biocultural dimensions into account.

Some recent researchers underscore the primordiality of myth by arguing that the structure and the processes of the human central nervous system not only are capable of receiving myth, but require it (d'Aquili 1975, 1978, 1983; Turner 1983). E. O. Wilson speaks directly of the "mythopoeic requirements" of the human central nervous system, which inevitably result in the brain's ordering the information at its disposal finally into "some form of morality, religion, and mythology" (Wilson 1978, 200; also A. Stevens 1983, chap. 13).

Linguistically and conceptually, if the cultural information was to play the role I have suggested for guiding behavior in survival situations, it would take the form of direct or imperative discourse. The cultural information of the *is,* which was essential to the flourishing of the distinctly human, could be no more conditional than the genetic programs that direct the biological components of the human animal. As I have already suggested, the abusive urge of a man to rape a woman could not (and cannot, even today) address the man as a hypothesis to be considered or as a set of causal explanations. Similarly, the injunctions against such behaviors must present themselves to human awareness as more than hypothetical possibilities. Comparable examples would pertain to child-rearing, as well as hunting and gathering.

In the previous chapter (pp. 188–89), I described in some detail how one common characteristic of myth—its declarative or imperative linguistic mode—can be understood to be essential to its evolutionary adaptiveness in its originating circumstances. This fact does not gainsay the innate human tendency to turn all declaratives into hypotheticals. Such considerations raise a host of intriguing contemporary hermeneutic issues that are not my agenda in this presentation.

In the previous chapter, I noted briefly that myth and ritual are underdetermined by the data (Popper 1972a, chap. 1; Knorr-Cetina and Mulkay 1983, 3–5, 11–14, 244–47). In the present context, I wish to underscore what I said then, with even more emphasis. Myth and ritual represent essential information that was necessary for *Homo sapiens'* successful living. Human beings, by their very nature (i.e., the nature of their central nervous system and the distinctive form and process of self-consciousness and reflection that it enables) cannot exist without operative understandings of the reality that surrounds them. Such understandings require symbolic frameworks that conceptualize beyond the actual data of their experience. In the terms of philosophy of science, in order to understand the world, humans require concepts that are *underdetermined* by the data.

This is true today, but it was even more so in the early period of the emergence of humans, because their experience was relatively recent. This "surplus" of conceptualization lies in the need to know *how things are* in a conscious way that is comparable to the physical and genetic programs of information that tell other forms of life (and indeed much of the human body) about *the way things are*. For example, even today the physical and biological scientists need to know that the data they observe are part of some causal network that reiterates itself from instance to instance. The concept of such a causal system is not fully demonstrable; yet the concept is utterly necessary, even though it is underdetermined by the data. Myth and ritual play a function similar to that of the causal network, but their information concerns a different region of human life, its most basic meaning and how we ought to live in the light of that meaning.

Today, this characteristic of underdetermination is often cited as grounds for dismissing myth and ritual and for expecting they will be supplanted by more rational constructs. Such commentary overlooks the fact that in their early history, humans faced the necessity of acting on the basis of cultural information in circumstances that hardly allowed for hypothesis-formation and testing. It was a virtue of myth that it provided precisely the kind of information that was required—concepts of ultimate reality that could be (indeed, had to be) acted upon immediately, even though the cumulative experience that might verify or falsify the information was lacking.

Humans still require this kind of information about the nature of things, and they must act upon it even before they can gather data for demonstrating or falsifying it. Further, despite all of the Comtean strictures, humans do continually discover or construct such information packets—myths. In any case, the critique of myth on the grounds that it is underdetermined by data may rest in a deep failure to appreciate the true function of myth in human evolutionary history.

The foregoing considerations raise a host of important questions concerning myth and ritual in human life. I will summarize them here but not probe them at great depth. One set of questions has to do with the credibility of myth. Myth and ritual, or their equivalent, appear to be essential to human life, precisely because we require the kind of information they provide. This has been recognized even by the cultured despisers of religion for at least two centuries. August Comte's version of this insight, at the beginning of the nineteenth century, is discussed at length in chapter 13; E. O. Wilson has argued the same point with elegance in recent years (1987).

At the same time, as many thinkers have observed, we find it difficult, if not impossible, to believe the myths in the way persons in earlier epochs did. Paul Ricoeur uses this situation as the basis for his celebrated discussion of the need for a second naiveté among contemporary men and women that can appropriate myth and ritual as the first naiveté did millennia ago. Are new, more credible myths to be constructed, as E. O. Wilson and Loyal Rue suggest (see chapter 13)? Or are the old myths to be appropriated through critical analysis and reinterpretation, as Ricoeur and others propose?

Another set of questions pertains to the character of myths and their functioning. Myth and ritual function to motivate behavior in accordance with the view of reality that they set forth. Myths that do not meet critical scientific tests for truth, as in the case of many cosmological myths, may nevertheless motivate wholesome behavior. When this occurs, as it frequently does, a conflict exists between two criteria for truth—empirical knowledge versus engendering wholesome behavior. This raises the difficult issues of (1) how to do justice to the behavioral criterion in the face of what appears to be inadequate truth content from the perspective of scientific reason, as well as (2) how to bring the two sets of criteria into harmony with each other, which is one of my chief goals in this book.

In the context of this chapter, we need to recognize that our dilemma is intensified in that we cannot hold the behavioral consequences of myth and ritual in abeyance until such time as we have them recast in more credible intellectual form. Humans require the motivational dimensions as urgently as they need conceptual adequacy.

Things are further complexified when we consider that conceptually adequate world views may be quite inadequate for motivating behavior. This is clearly the case with respect to contemporary scientific cosmology. In April 1992, when the Cosmic Background Explorer satellite (COBE) provided reinforcement for the Big Bang theory of cosmology, scientists who spoke loosely about these data as relevant to belief in God were severely rebuked by their scientific peers. One astronomer criticized efforts to relate this cosmology to God in these words: "Our Big Bang picture is [unsatisfying] to human beings. It doesn't serve our emotional needs in terms of a creation myth" (Flam 1992, 29). He is quite correct. This is little comfort to us, however, because we require such myths and rituals to guide our lives. If we cannot derive them from the most adequate scientific concepts of cosmology, where will we find them?

These questions call for intense consideration in the face of the obvious breakdown of our cultural motivators in the present time. The significance of the so-called religion-and-science field that has developed in this century lies in its recognition of these issues and its efforts to deal with them (Barbour 1990).

Although the Hebrew-Christian concepts of love and the love command are relatively late arrivals in human history, they are to be understood within this myth-ritual-praxis complex of ideas, and their nature and function may thereby be illumined. The theological concepts of love are to be considered as elaboration of the myth and ritual complex. The Hebrew-Christian concepts of love are considered here to be *agape* and *caritas*. The love command is formulated in three ways:

> "'You shall love the Lord your God with all your heart, and with all your soul, and with all your mind.' This is the great and first commandment. And a second is like it: 'You shall love your neighbor as yourself.' On these two commandments hang all the law and the prophets." (Matt. 22:37–40)
>
> "You have heard that it was said, 'You shall love your neighbor and hate your enemy.' But I say to you, Love your enemies and pray for those who persecute you, so that you may be children of your Father in heaven; for he makes his sun rise on the evil and on the good, and sends rain on the righteous and on the unrighteous. For if you love those who love you, what reward have you? Do not even the tax collectors do the same? And if you greet only your brothers and sisters, what more are you doing than others? Do not even the Gentiles do the same? Be perfect, therefore, as your heavenly Father is perfect." (Matt. 5:43–48)
>
> "I give you a new commandment, that you love one another. Just as I have loved you, you also should love one another." (John 13:34)

These concepts of love will illumine the evolutionary history of *Homo sapiens,* even as they are enriched by that history.

The foregoing statements support the second subthesis:

A consideration of the evolutionary history of the human species illumines the essential role that myths and rituals—including the myths and rituals of love—have played in the formation and survival of the human species.

The Christian Idea of Love

The primary term for love in the Christian tradition is the Greek *agape,* translated in the Latin by *caritas* (verb form, *diligo*). Exegetical and historical scholars have elaborated these concepts in great detail. Here I will focus upon how the concept functions and the significance of its claims.

The New Testament injunction to love follows the structure of myth/morality, is/ought, that was discussed earlier. The command to love is placed within the context of a symbolic universe, a picture of the way things really are, and it flows therefrom. The so-called Great Commandment from Matthew 22 is rooted in Deuteronomy 6 and Leviticus 19, where the commands to love God and neighbor are grounded in the being of God itself. We are to love because the very ground of being, God, who has created all things and who is the source of being and history for Israel, has commanded such love. No other ground is cited for this love.

Jesus' "new commandment" in John 13:34 is placed in the setting of the last supper and Jesus' preparation for his own sacrifice. The redeemer tells his followers how things really are and prepares to enact that story in his own life, and then gives them a command that will translate God's will and his own action in their lives: "Love one another as I have loved you." Again, no other ground is given for this love except the will of God and God's preeminent servant, the Son.

The command in Matthew 5, the Sermon on the Mount, is perhaps the most interesting of the three versions of the love command in this regard, for its more intense grounding of love in the way things are. The being and will of God are invoked, as well as the realm of nonhuman nature. The cultural resources, namely love for enemy, are to follow the same nonmoral pattern as the sun and the rain. The evenhandedness of the sun and the rain are in turn grounded in God, because God sends them. God as ground of love is articulated here with the greatest possible force: We are not to follow human examples for love, the tax collectors or the Gentiles, but rather we must be perfect as God is perfect. Note that emulating God's perfection is invoked, not as the ground for morality in general, but for love; specifically, love for the enemies. Gerd Theissen (1985, 160f.) throws light on Jesus' command for love of enemy by suggesting that Jesus presents himself as an option for cultural evolution, a kind of mutation—a strikingly different option for life that can, in Jesus' opinion, survive.

The grounding of love in God should be noted in contrast to a grounding in family or other human relations. It is not mother-love or father-love that is held up as the model (even though God is called "father," no father-qualities are referred to), not kin-love in any respect. God, as creator, as controller of nature, as lord of the nation (Israel), and as redeemer is the referent, the model, the ground of love. Furthermore, the concept of perfection is introduced in connection with the most radical form of love, that which is directed toward enemies.

Saint Paul, in Galatians 5:12–24, speaks of love in contrast to *sarx,* or flesh. This emphasis is consistent with that of Jesus, if we follow those scholars who remind us that flesh is not primarily descriptive of the material world, but rather refers to life that is lived precisely on the assumption that God is not its ground and source. Obviously, then, to live on such an assumption would militate against love as Jesus commanded it. Paul's famous "hymn to love," 1 Corinthians 13, illustrates how this God-grounded love elaborates itself in a community setting.

By grounding love, which I describe as beneficent behavior for the other, in God, that is, in the way things really are, the Christian theological concept of love makes the assertion that this love is an intrinsic value. This represents a great contrast with the Hobbesian interpretation of human affairs that forms the metaphysical framework for the work of contemporary biocultural evolutionary science.

Anders Nygren's classic statement, "Neighborly love loses its specifically Christian character if it is taken out of context of fellowship with God" (Nygren 1953, 95) is to be read in this context. I take it as a reinforcement for the idea that beneficent behavior for the other is an intrinsic value. If a person views it as extrinsic to the gaining of some other value, that person has misunderstood the nature of altruism. Altruism is written into the fundamental nature of human reality; it does not exist solely for the sake of some other value—at least that is the Christian mythic understanding. So we might say, in a poor analogy perhaps, that we breathe because we were made that way, and not primarily to stay alive. Obviously, we do breathe in order to stay alive, but there is an ontic character to breathing, as well, that cannot be overlooked. Altruism may well also serve survival needs, and the Christian believes it does, but the myth and the theology focus more directly upon the intrinsic, ontic character of altruism.

In this respect, Reinhold Niebuhr is correct when he writes that the Christian concept of love may serve not only to fulfill basic human expectations of altruism, but also to clarify obscurities and correct inadequate views (1949, II, 81–90). This need not be interpreted as an assertion that the Christian idea of love is superior to all others, but rather as a simple following out of the consequences. If altruism is considered to be solely instrumental to the attaining of some other end, then confusions arise (after all, self-giving love often is unrewarded) and fallacies enter in (arrogant pretensions, self-righteousness, and so on).

The philosopher of religion John Hick (1981) has correctly, in my view, emphasized that genuine personhood occurs in those situations in which persons choose a course of behavior, so convinced of its intrinsic value that they require no reward except the value of the behavior itself, and thus will not be defeated if the behavior and its value are unsuccessful or unrewarded. Hick's line of reasoning brings the Christian theological claims for altruism into relationship with what constitutes human personhood.

Freedom is also a factor in this equation; the person is constituted to a significant degree (not wholly) by the freedom to give herself/himself on the basis of intrinsic value. Coerced self-giving is not really giving, just as one could argue that altruism that is coerced, including the coercion that comes from the expectation of reward, is not true altruism. It is at this point that the theological and the biocultural scientific views appear to be contradictory. I hope that my conclusions will convince the reader that this contradiction is more apparent than real.

The theological reader will note that I am joining the critics of Nygren who back away from his insistence that agape has nothing to do with the concept of altruism. Similarly, I join those who criticize his interpretation of agape as distinguished from natural love in that it is "spontaneous and unmotivated" (1953, 97). The theological elaboration of agape should not shy away from identifying it with altruism, but rather should distinguish sharply the tendency to make of altruism a self-seeking strategy for attaining other goods.

The mythic-ritual complex, in its theological elaboration, asserts at its deepest level that altruistic love holds the status of a cosmological and ontological principle. Consequently, the Christian love command can be identified with the behavior associated with the biocultural evolutionary concept of altruism, but the meaning and status of altruism are not exhausted by those scientific concepts.

Without question, it is at this point that the mythic packets of cultural information make their most striking claims and where their character as underdetermined by the evidence raises the greatest difficulties. This is also the point at which it becomes clear that, for the Christian at least, the most pressing question that arises in conversation with the sciences is not, Is there evidence for a God? but rather Can we entertain the hypothesis that altruistic love is rooted in the fundamental nature of reality, including the reality we call nature? This pressing question concerns both our knowledge and our behavior.

At the same time, this assertion concerning the cosmological and ontological status of altruistic love makes clear the significance of the strategy of grounding altruistic love in God. The conceptual significance of referring altruism to God, and the relevance for the interdisciplinary conversation we are presently engaged in, is simply this: The reference to God conveys the seriousness with which the Christian tradition grounds altruism in the fundamental nature of reality and consequently considers altruistic behavior to be the paramount quality of any behavior that aims to be in accord with the way things really are.

To affirm altruism as grounded in the fundamental character of reality, recalling the arguments of Hick, is tantamount to asserting that there is in some sense a personal character to fundamental reality and that reality also exhibits a fundamental coherence with altruistic love, personhood, and freedom. These assertions are equally central to the Christian point of view, and they articulate what is at stake in the basic myth-ritual complex of the Christian religion. These basic affirmations should not be trivialized or shunted aside in some abstract discussion of whether there is a God. Rather, the discussion of these basic assertions about altruistic love, personhood, and freedom in themselves constitute a discussion about God.

The foregoing statements support the third subthesis:

The significance of the theological concepts of altruistic love, elaborated from the myths and rituals and also by the scientific understandings, is this: Theology suggests that theories of epigenetic rules or strategies of self-interest are not enough to complete our understanding of altruistic love; we require also ways of discussing the hypothesis that altruism is an intrinsic value, rooted in the fundamental character of reality.

Conclusion

The foregoing statements and subtheses form the foundation of a major thesis, which I stated at the beginning of this chapter.

If even the most widely held scientific theories are underdetermined by the data, basic religious affirmations are even more so. Among the most underdetermined is the assertion that the central reality of this natural world loves the human race and works for the fulfillment of our created destiny. It is so far from being validated for the entire human community by evidence from data that it would not be at all compelling unless it carried the status and power of myth.

Clearly, the sciences cannot come to the conclusion of this mythic utterance—it is far too underdetermined by the data for that. Can the sciences even talk about this assertion of the beneficent power of the reality system in which we live, or respect such an assertion? These questions deserve much more serious discussion. In Christian theological terminology, this assertion is a *skandalon,* that is, a position that is actually repugnant to nonmythic thinking, as well as to mythic views that cannot affirm it. In order to press this serious discussion further, we would have to consider the advantages of affirming the assertion that the central reality loves us preveniently. I cannot pursue this subject here, but I might summarize a long argument with the sheer assertion that it is difficult to justify the morality and counter-hedonic behavior that the scientists endorse if the reality in which we live is not in some way a friendly ambience. Here we come upon a specific instance of Lawrence Sullivan's insight that certain meanings are not evident, except in myth (see pp. 174–75). Only in myth is the reality of altruism evident as a characteristic of *the way things really are.*

At any rate, this affirmation of nature and culture as an ambience of belonging and consonance is at the heart of the created co-creator theory, and it forms the core of the faith assertion of those who would credit the theory as a worthy ground for action in this world.

Part 5

Theological Connections

13

On the Way to Theology

My primary effort in this book so far has been devoted to setting forth the nature of the human being, the teleonomy that nature has provided us. At the outset, I asserted that whereas science describes the structures and processes that form our teleonomy, it is myth and ritual that propose the concrete purpose and meaning with which our teleonomy is spelled out. What remains in this undertaking is to suggest a contemporary proposal for the mythic component of the process of cultural formation that challenges us.

I am not suggesting, as some have, that science deals with questions of *what?* or description, while religion deals with *why?* or meaning. That suggestion is not entirely wrong, but it is far too simplistic. I shall not spill much ink on projecting how religion and science are related; that is a second-order activity that I would have to undertake in hindsight by scrutinizing how they actually are related in this book. However, I do assert that science sets forth the description of the teleonomic structures and processes of nature, including human nature, while religion, through myth and ritual, speaks of the way in which those structures and processes are to be interpreted and the specific directions they are to take within the parameters of what they are capable of.

I will not cut the substance of religion and science into paper-thin slices with a sharp knife. Science may supply images for a hermeneutic, as well as religion, and religion may contain wisdom concerning the facts of teleonomy. I leave it to the reader to discern whether and where I have been inconsistent or even contradictory in the ways I have related science and religion, and I will benefit from such discernment. It is not my first priority, however, to formulate a priori categories of their relationship and then to observe those categories impeccably. This is the Lydia Mittelstadt within me—it may work out.

It is within the realm of possibility that a consensus of thinking persons could be obtained to support the interpretations of the book up to this point. I have no illusions that there can be consensus on the mythic proposals that will be sketched in the subsequent pages. For one thing, I am proceeding from a Western Christian matrix. Thinkers who are in agreement with me on the general contours of the challenge to human being today are more apt to take the position espoused by E. O. Wilson (1978) and Loyal Rue (1989), that some rendition of *evolution* itself must be the raw material for new mythic proposals. My major difference from Wilson and Rue is that I believe we will meet the challenge to our culture-formation from the bottom up, rather than the top down. By that I mean we are more likely to move through and with our existing myth-ritual traditions into new and more adequate myth-ritual formations than to proceed from science-based concepts into new channels. I term the latter a top-down approach, since it tends to abandon the traditions of the last 40,000 years.

Both Wilson and Rue place prime responsibility upon the artists among us for new mythic proposals. I agree on the importance of the artists—poets, novelists, painters, sculptors, and dramatists—but I believe that the primary substance of myth-ritual formation will emerge from the people, the grass roots of popular culture (including the various forms of video media), the reflections of preachers, teachers, politicians (think of FDR's New Deal, JFK's New Frontier, and LBJ's Great Society), and business/technology entrepreneurs (think of technology's impact on the myth of "Progress"; Henry Adams's "Virgin and the Dynamo"). High culture will play a role, but it will not dictate the time and place of new myth-ritual emergences. The new proposals will come more like Our Lady of Guadalupe, from the soil and the sweat of the people—with the midwifery of the artist alongside, to be sure (Shafer 1989, 1991; Greeley, 1988, 1989).

I speak of new myth-ritual proposals much in the spirit of Paul Tillich (1957a, 41–54; 1959, 53–67). Symbols, myths, and rituals are not subject to our autonomous creation and destruction, although our efforts can be influential in determining the course of particular symbols, myths, and rituals. When one of these dies or passes out of coinage, it cannot be reinstated simply by our willing it, nor can new myths or rituals come into being by a snap of our fingers. Out of the intercourse of human life with the environing reality, myths and rituals emerge, flourish, and live out their careers. Without our efforts, myth and ritual will not emerge or be salutary for us, but at best our efforts prepare the soil for the emergents. We work hard to prepare that soil, as this book attempts to, but then we must wait. We will critically reject some candidates that present themselves, but our chief task is to wait for the new shapes of meaning to appear. In the following pages, my effort is to pose the possibility that the Christian tradition is still fruitful as one nurturing matrix from which life-meanings can be mined.

Methodological Notes

In the Preface to this work, I indicated that I would not give intense focus to methodological issues. Obviously, such considerations cannot be avoided, and they have cropped up at several points in this text, particularly in regard to such issues as reductionism and functionalism. In this section, I will turn attention to certain issues of methodology that seem unavoidable.

Concepts of God—Messages of Myth and Ritual

Many, if not most, of the theological thinkers who take seriously the conversation with the sciences do so in the context of formulating conceptualities of God. Examples include Ralph Wendell Burhoe (1981), John Cobb (1965; Tracy and Cobb 1983), Gordon Kaufman (1985, 1992, 1993), Sallie McFague (1985, 1987), Schubert Ogden (1966), Wolfhart Pannenberg (1976), Arthur Peacocke (1979, 1990), John Polkinghorne (1988, 1989), Richard Swinburne (1977), and Henry Nelson Wieman (1946). The reader will note that little or no effort is expended in this volume to fashioning or commenting upon a concept of God, certainly not in the degree of sophistication and philosophical precision that marks most of the thinkers I have just noted.

The approach that is set forth here focuses first of all on the information conveyed by myth and ritual. In no sense do I wage a polemic against reflection upon adequate concepts of God, nor do I believe that one can for very long avoid such reflection, but I confess that that is not my starting point. Chapter 5 represents the approach that I find more congenial. There the first concern is with our experience of the world and of our human neighbors, not with the question: Is there a God? or What conceptualization of God would allow such experience of the world? The issue is more, Can there be love for the neighbor? or Is it possible to trust the processes of nature? rather than, What concept of God would allow us to believe that the hairs of our heads are numbered or that it is in our self-interest to love our enemies as ourselves?

I am attracted to the suggestions made by the philosopher of science Arthur Fine, who argues that the most adequate approach to science is the natural ontological attitude (NOA). By this, he means that a sophisticated philosophical apparatus may be an obstacle to understanding science and testing its claims. The NOA is characterized by trust; it trusts the "overall good sense of science and it trusts our overall good sense as well. In particular, NOA encourages us to take seriously the idea that what the scientific enterprise has to offer is actually sufficient to satisfy our philosophical needs" (Fine 1986, 177; discussed by Rouse 1991). Fine is wary of the philosophical apparatus that claims to have interpreted science correctly and in a unified sense and thereby is blind to its own distortions of science and also to much of the particularity of science. Joseph Rouse joins Fine in preferring "an historically sensitive and open-minded particularism" in approaching science (1991, 625).

Although I respect the sophisticated philosophical concepts of God that have emerged in the two millennia of Christian thought and have no intention of ignoring them or underestimating their worth, I believe that an approach comparable to that of Fine and Rouse ought to be explored in our attempts to appropriate the information conveyed by myth and ritual, including our attempts to talk about God. Despite my high regard for philosophical concepts, they cannot sustain a claim to be a preferred means of understanding myth and ritual, nor of speaking about God. Some form of Fine's natural ontological attitude, which trusts both in the good sense of myth and ritual, on their own terms, and also in our good sense to appropriate or reject them critically, is worthy of exploration by theologians.

Gordon Kaufman's theological program is, in his own words, the attempt to "create a framework of interpretation which can provide overall orientation for human life," and it does so by reconstructing the image or concept of God (1985, 26). Again, I am not critical of such attempts, and I find no fault with the train of reasoning that leads Kaufman to his enterprise. In fact, his concerns overlap mine to a considerable extent (Kaufman 1991, 1993). I, too, would aim at creating a framework of interpretation that provides overall orientation for human life. However, I do not first of all look to a concept of God to supply that framework. Rather, I look to the information provided by myth and ritual, specifically the myth and ritual of my own religious community, but extending into conversation and interrelationships with the broader culture.

When one proceeds from a concept of God, coherence and plausibility are at the forefront. In contrast, the coherence and plausibility of myth and ritual must be sought after, because they are largely latent rather than manifest. Proceeding from the God concept, one argues, since there is a kind of meaningfulness observable in natural processes (Kaufman terms it "serendipitous creativity"), that it makes sense to love one's neighbor and even one's enemy. When, in contrast, we proceed from myth and ritual (in this case the Christian myth of the love command and the kiss of peace of the Eucharist), the argument unfolds in this manner: If you wish to be in harmony with the way things really are, you will love your neighbor and your enemy.

Here the work of Eugene d'Aquili comes into play (d'Aquili and Laughlin 1975; d'Aquili 1983)—myth sets up the questions (Can I really love my neighbor and enemy?), and ritual resolves them (I will act out such love symbolically in the kiss of peace). Myth and ritual do not *explain* the rationality of such love, but rather insist that it is as much a part of basic reality as particle flows and gravity. Concepts of God *do* aim at explanation. Myth and ritual place worship, meditation, and behavior at the forefront, leaving larger explanation as an unfinished task, whereas conceptualizations of God put explanation up front and leave worship and behavior to be dealt with elsewhere.

Without arguing the comparative merits or demerits of these two approaches, I would suggest that they are equally essential and complementary. Either without the other is incomplete. Both approaches work for critical assessment and credibility. Conceptualizing God begins with the tools of critical thinking. My treatment of sin in chapter 8 applies the canons of critical thinking and credibility to the messages derived from myth and ritual.

Each of these approaches has certain obvious advantages and drawbacks. Concepts have the merit of clarity, precision, and rationality, while they are accessible generally only to the philosophically oriented elite and may be somewhat removed from behavior—indeed, discussion of behavior may not even be admitted as legitimate (although Kaufman and Gustafson both see the reinforcement of moral behavior as a function of concepts). Myth and ritual are concrete, highly motivating, residents where "people really live." However, most of the myths and rituals are archaic in appearance and are therefore off-putting to many or seem to be items of distant concern, even though they are intended as means by which we can put our world together meaningfully.

As we leave this issue, we remind ourselves that neither lucid concepts nor impressive myths and rituals can claim finally to be empirically demonstrable as true. Although they operate at different levels of human sensibilities—concepts at the intellectual level, while myths and rituals exist more at the affective level— both concepts and myths/rituals communicate to contemporary persons as hypotheses to be taken seriously and tested.

Is Theology Dead as Explanation of the World?

J. Samuel Preus has produced an extraordinarily provocative and useful work, *Explaining Religion: Criticism and Theory from Bodin to Freud* (1987). Halfway through his analysis of five hundred years of attempts to understand religion, he deals with August Comte. He calls attention to

> what I regard as Comte's two most important ideas: his evolutionary theory and his notion that society must have religion or its functional equivalent; put another way, that the word *religion* may be used to denote certain social functions that occur in any society. (1987, 128)

Comte's evolutionary theory, to which I referred in chapter 1, periodized history into three epochs, the theological (correlated to military social structures), the metaphysical (correlated to feudal structures), and the positive (correlated to industrial social structures). In this interpretation, Comte joined other scholars of the past 250 years (such as E. B. Tylor, J. G. Fraser, and Sigmund Freud) who considered religion to be a phenomenon appropriate to the period of humanity's infantile state of development. As such, religion will pass away or linger on simply as a surviving, obsolete holdover from a bygone era.

In Comte's functional theory, however,

> "religion" denotes a set of functions peculiar to humanity, meeting psychological, intellectual, or social needs. In that sense, it can be regarded as what Parsons has called an evolutionary universal; as such, it can look like practically anything so

long as it meets those essential needs, performs those necessary functions. (Preus 1987, 129)

Paul Tillich has dealt with this understanding of religion in depth in his concept of "ultimate concern"—wherever it manifests itself, there is a de facto religion (vol. 3, 1963, 138–282).

What Comte's analysis means is that the essential ideas of a religion are what evolves away. What remains is its function to serve society. Preus concludes his discussion of Comte:

> All our subsequent writers will agree that religion *as explanation* can no longer endure as it did in earlier epochs. But religion *as function,* Comte suggests, must endure. Indeed, it must be cultivated, promoted and if necessary reinvented. (1987, 130)

In my own experience, I have found that Comte's two ideas about religion have taken a strong hold upon the intellectual classes of North America and Western Europe. Today, the notion that theology, the conceptual dimension of religion, is obsolete as a way of explaining the world poses an undeniable challenge. Among those thinkers who take the conversation between religion and the sciences seriously, E. O. Wilson (1987), Loyal Rue (1989), Ursula Goodenough (U. Goodenough and Rue 1992), and Ward Goodenough (1988) are representative examples of the position that Preus ascribes to Comte.

Ralph Wendell Burhoe also accepted this as a starting point for his work; it led him to the effort to rehabilitate theology as explanation through his program of "scientific theology," by which he means a theological effort to "translate" (his term) the concepts of traditional theology into terms that are credible to scientists. Underlying Burhoe's effort is the conviction that the wisdom of primordial religion, specifically its myths, rituals, and moral codes, is both fundamental to human being and sound. The translation he speaks of would, in his view, purify traditional religious concepts of their archaic inadequacies, while conveying the heart of religious wisdom in a credible manner to a scientifically conditioned class of intellectual pacesetters in our society.

Additional nuances within Preus's argument deserve attention. First, he raises the question of whether the interpretation of religion from the outside—that is, the explanation of religion as the 500-year-long tradition of religious studies that he surveys has attempted it—is reconcilable with the interpretation from the inside, as the believing religious community attempts it. This is the question whether a naturalistic or a religious explanation of religion is more adequate or even more true (Preus 1987, passim; Segal 1990). Robert Segal extends the argument (figuratively speaking, since his work antedates Preus's), by distinguishing between the truth of religion and its origins (1990, 272–76). To explain religion by naturalistic categories, as Comte did, is not necessarily to deny its truth or necessity (which Comte did not, in his second understanding of religion), but it is to deny that it is best explained by the categories of *the holy* or *transcendence*. Naturalism is the issue.

Second, Preus points to the fact that the intellectual community (that is, universities) are more inclined to understand religion naturalistically, as the social sciences (and, I would add, the biocultural sciences) do, whereas the religious communities and the theological enterprise that takes its cues from these communities insist upon religious explanations of religion that depend upon categories like *the holy* or *transcendence*. Consequently, the question is raised whether theology can even entertain the challenge that comes from the scientific study of religion, except for apologetic purposes.

This cleavage between religious communities and those who do research about religion is unfortunate, because the two groups share common concerns that could benefit from dialogue between them. Preus mentions three such concerns: the relation between religion and morality, the question of the anthropological roots of religion (does it require a body-soul dualism?), and the question of the relationship between explanation and interpretation (hermeneutics) (1987, 209–10). Preus concludes:

> Theology, whether in its confessional or generic modes, fails as a unifying paradigm because its peculiar insistence that religions are "manifestations of the sacred" isolates it from the presuppositions that are otherwise operative in the humanities and human sciences. The claim that religions can be studied and understood *only* from a religious perspective excludes fruitful intellectual interaction with people in other disciplines by staking out its own privileged universe of discourse and, so far, failing to show how that universe intersects with the one constituted by the rough consensus of the academy at large. The issue is not whether "transcendence" refers to something extramentally real, but whether the study of religion wishes to enter as a full partner in the study of culture. . . .
>
> The naturalistic approach . . . takes theological interpretation seriously as part of the religious data but not of their explanation. . . . The naturalistic approach is at once more modest and more ambitious than the religious one: more modest because it is content to investigate the causes, motivations, meanings, and impact of religious phenomena without pronouncing on their cosmic significance for human destiny; ambitious, in that the study of religion strives to explain religion and to integrate its understanding into the other elements of culture to which it is related. (1987, 210–11)

Obviously, the issues that Preus and Segal raise are relevant to the project of this book, and just as obviously, I am trying to have my cake and eat it, as well, with respect to these issues. I list the issues once again: Is theology as explanation dead? Can the naturalistic explanations of religion coexist with the religious explanations? Can theology and the believing religious community relate constructively to the community that pursues the scientific study of religion?

The program represented in this book accepts that theology as explanation is dead unless it learns to integrate within itself elements of scientific understandings that undergird explanation for our time in history. Only if it is so integrated will the contribution of theology to the general understanding of human life be available for the general society and acknowledged by that society. My effort to build upon the thought of Imre Lakatos (chapter 2) and to present the concept of the created co-creator as theory are attempts to deal with this issue. My insistence that the theological concept, as well as the myths and rituals themselves, are hypotheses to be explored is part of this acknowledgment that theology as explanation is problematic. On both of these points, integrating scientific understandings and proposing theological concepts as hypotheses, Burhoe has it right, in my opinion. I also draw resources from Paul Ricoeur and much of contemporary biblical scholarship in their insistence that myth is not primarily etiological in function—it does not explain natural phenomena, but rather is a detector or signal of reality.

Theology-as-explanation generally proceeds from a concept of God, on the basis of which the world can be explained. Inasmuch as no concept of God can, according to the canons of rational thinking and empirical study, win more than probable status, it seems unwise to make too great a claim for theology-as-explanation. This is the weakness of the process theologians' approach and also of Gordon Kaufman's.

Some thinkers at this point invoke the option of so-called critical realism, which claims referentiality for religious language on a par with—though not identical to—scientific language (Barbour 1974; Peacocke 1984). I may *believe* that mythic language meets the criteria of critical realism, but I do not agree that the philosophical elaborations of this option have made their case with the rigor that philosophical assertions require. Critical realism, in my view, is more a hope than a conclusive argument (and, indeed, it is the hope of this writer) (Hefner 1985).

Nevertheless, to adopt a point of view that speaks of theology and religion as interpretation, hermeneutics, and nothing more is not adequate. Consequently I object to many of the so-called postmodern and postliberal theological proposals. It is simply inconsistent both with scientific fact and with the instincts of faith to consign religious communities, their myth and their ritual, to the status of nontranslatable "cultural-linguistic systems" (Lindbeck 1984; Placher 1989). Such approaches take no account of the larger function that religion has played within the created order.

Nancey Murphy has proposed a way through this thicket of modernity/postmodernity and realism/antirealism, via what she terms conceptual pragmatism. Her position, still in the formative stage, recognizes that "while concepts are human creation, adopted because of their utility, utility itself is conditioned both by human goals and purposes and by the way the world 'really' is" (1993). She also roots this conceptual pragmatism in a philosophical stance that shifts (1) in epistemology from foundationalism to holism, (2) in its view of language from referentiality to use as the criterion of meaning, and (3) in metaphysics from "atomism and reductionism to a non-reductive view of the relations of parts to wholes" (1993). Such a stance is, in her terms, postmodern, even though she regrets having to use the label because of its ambiguity in contemporary intellectual discussions. Although the stance I have adopted in this book is too eclectic to meet Murphy's rigorous standards, I mean to work from the same sort of pragmatism that motivates her, and also with an understanding similar to hers concerning utility and the way things really are (Murphy 1990b, 1993).

In dealing with these issues, my own program starts, as I have already said, from the actuality of myth and ritual as components of the cultural system of information that is essential to human being. Myth and ritual are rooted in the biological history of planet earth and also in the neurobiological equipment of *Homo sapiens*. They also have a record as adaptive behavior in human history. The question of whether religion is to be explained on grounds that are either naturalistic or transcendent is really not important. The central questions are whether, in some credible and effective manner, the information conveyed in myth and ritual is consonant with the way things really are and capable of motivating and engendering behavior (praxis) that shares in that consonance. God-talk, in the Western traditions, is a way in which we have responded "yes" to these questions. At the present time, the most cogent criterion for judging that consonance is the fact that myth and ritual have perdured, in the face of biological and cultural processes of selection, up to the present day, and that, with revisions, they are viable today.

My arguments may appear a strange blend of faith and naturalism. That blend is intentional, and it represents my attempt (feeble as it may be) to go beyond the current conceptual impasse. Again, I refer to the statements of Lawrence Sullivan that were cited frequently in chapter 10.

> . . . social values and functions, which are never absent from or irrelevant to symbolic action and belief, are themselves symbolic of the religious need to encounter what is sacred and to know what is true in order to ground every aspect of life on what *really is*. (1988, 18)

This statement does not go against Preus's insistence that categories of the sacred and transcendence may not be invoked arbitrarily as explanations of religion. The testimony of myth, from this perspective, is not so much an insistence that it has a transcendent origin, as it is a message about that which is not self-evident to us because we cannot know it except in images and concepts that are intrinsically underdetermined by the evidences. Sullivan writes, "Myth does not simply denote a species of narrative; literary or oral genres are only symptoms of myth. Myth is not a form of lore but a quality of imaginal existence" (1988, 22).

This "quality of imaginal existence" is correlative to the concept of underdetermination, and it occurs in the naturalistically described realm. It is part of the data, as Preus says, but it makes a statement about *what really is,* and as such it requires consideration not only from the perspectives that abide by the canons of the social sciences, but also from those perspectives whose canons are appropriate to reflection upon and assessment of representations of *what really is*. It does not matter, in one sense, how we assess the origins of the representation. To speak theologically, it is one thing to assert that a representation is *from* God and another to assert that it is *about* God or consonant with God's being. (Here I use the term *God* to refer to the realm of ultimacy, the ground of the way things really are.) Sullivan goes on, in terms that appear to me to be consistent with what I have just said:

> Myth is the imagination beholding its own reality and plumbing the sources of its own creativity as it relates to creativity in every form (plant and planetary life, animal fertility, intelligence, art). Myth reveals the sacred foundations and religious character of the imagination. Mythic symbols signify the possibility, variety, and meaning of cultural imagery. Myths are paradigmatic expressions of human culture; as significations that reveal the nature of significance, they make effective metastatements about imaginal existence. (1988, 22)

This statement is congruent with that of Leszek Kolakowski, quoted earlier, that myth "refers the conditioned empirical realities to an unconditioned universe" (1989, 41).

I close this section with a summary statement that flows from the methodological considerations set forth in these pages, and also expresses my intention for the constructive theological proposals of the next chapter. My summary of my intentions takes the form of a passage from biologist Timothy Goldsmith, who speaks sensibly about the kinds of issues I have been considering here. In his book *The Biological Roots of Human Nature,* after urging upon his readers the usefulness of biology, he writes:

> By this I do not mean that anthropology, human psychology, and sociology will "reduce to biology," any more than biology has reduced to chemistry. Each level of organization is presented with properties that derive from the fact of organization and that have to be studied on their own terms. But those terms must relate to the rest of science or the exercise will be of no lasting value. . . . A larger problem facing the social sciences is to generate a theoretical architecture that neither clashes with biology nor consists of such exclusive structures that it is ultimately rendered irrelevant. "Biological reductionism" can be used to trivialize evolutionary biology in an effort to keep it at arm's length, but this is an unworthy goal. The social sciences [and, I would add, the humanities and theology] will have matured only when they are firmly grounded in, and consistent with, the rest of our understanding of nature. In this enterprise, biology and the social sciences [together with the humanities and theology, I would add] should work together, for the discovery of principles that unite hierarchies and cut across species will enrich our knowledge and our lives. To date, only evolutionary biology offers that framework. (1991, 141)

To Goldsmith's text, in every place where he speaks of the interaction of biology and the social sciences, I would add religion and theology. In expressing these views, Goldsmith is in essential agreement with Arthur Peacocke, the theologian and biochemist (Peacocke 1971, 102–8; 1976; 1979, 112–46, 367–71).

Resources from Christian Theology

The next chapter will be but a sketch of what is required if we are to accomplish what Wolfhart Pannenberg sets as the task of theology, namely, to "lay theological claim" to the phenomena described by the sciences, in order to show that the data themselves "contain a further and theologically relevant dimension" (1985, 19–20). In substance, Pannenberg's program is consistent with that which Gold-smith lays down, as modified above—working together with the other disciplines, especially, but not exclusively, with the biocultural sciences, "for the discovery of principles that unite hierarchies and cut across species," to the end that knowledge and life be enriched (Goldsmith 1991, 141). Pannenberg adds the reminder that in this cooperative effort, theology cannot finally avoid the task of arguing cogently its claim to be a representation of the way things really are.

The sketch that follows will not accomplish what Pannenberg calls for, even though I acknowledge the necessity for doing so. However, to the extent that I succeed in setting forth the role of myth and ritual in interpreting the world and thematizing human experience, leading to wholesome behavior, I shall have taken a step toward satisfying the pragmatic criterion and thus suggesting that the information of myth and ritual is indeed consonant with the way things really are.

As entree to our theological construction, we must be clear on three matters: the basis on which we build our theological structure, the purpose to be accomplished, and the challenge to which our theological effort is responding.

The Basis for the Theological Structure

The sources or bases for the theological construction are, first of all, the most fundamental myth and ritual of the Christian tradition. This level of material is the starting point against which all the theological statements are to be measured, even though some of this material will be criticized and even rejected, for reasons that I will clarify in each instance.

The next level of material, as in chapter 8, is the tradition of symbols and theological doctrines that have emerged as second-order reflection upon myth and ritual. Here, the reader will note that those doctrines that are accorded the status of ecumenical dogma, specifically the Trinity and the Two Natures of Christ, will be normative over other doctrines, on the grounds that they are closer to the status of myth and more ensconced within the ritual of the church. I am adopting, in other words, a traditional approach that takes the creed to be the hermeneutical framework interpreting the various traditions of the Christian community (including the biblical and liturgical traditions).

At the same time, my hermeneutical strategy approaches these doctrines and dogmas with the intent to relate them to the matrix of myth and ritual from which they have emerged. I assume a framework of interpretation in which theology emerges from the rich complex of myth and ritual as a constellation of reflective opinion that serves the community as it seeks to relate the mythic and ritual substance to the vicissitudes of ordinary life. Doctrine, as a provisional ratification of certain opinions by the community or certain of its subgroups, is a next step in the process. Dogma represents a further public decision by the community that certain articulations have moved beyond the stages of opinion and provisional ratification to be recognized as elements that are so central to the community's self-understanding and identity that when they are questioned or rejected, the burden of proof rests upon those who raise the criticism. I have dealt with this framework at length elsewhere (Hefner 1975).

This interpretive method is also an attempt to distinguish between the enduring import of the information conveyed by the Christian tradition, on the one hand, and the conditioned forms in which that information has been expressed. This interpretive problem is a perennial one, but it is intensified by my heightened sense of the necessity for critical thinking that goes beyond the interests that this conditioning represents (see p. 150, above). In this respect, my attempt is also informed by the work of Max Wildiers (1982), particularly his demonstration of the possibility of distinguishing between the message of the tradition and the philosophical-scientific forms in which it is expressed, and also by Arthur Fine's proposal for a "natural ontological attitude" (see pp. 215–16 above).

Where do I locate this material? In the Bible, in the liturgies and sacraments of the tradition, chiefly in the Eucharist and in baptism, and in other traditions. As I have occasion to make judgments about these traditional sources and materials, I will only seldom explain my methods and criteria. The informed reader can make his or her own assessment of my handling of the materials. This is much the way I proceeded on the themes of original sin in chapter 8 and the love command in chapters 11 and 12. It is most important at this point for the reader to observe *what* I am doing. Whether this *ought* to be done, or whether I am doing it *well,* are serious questions that I trust will be elicited by the demonstrations in this chapter and the previous ones.

The Governing Purpose

The overarching purpose of this theological construction is to provide resources from the Christian tradition for revitalizing the myth-ritual-praxis constellation that I have described several times in previous chapters. Revitalizing is essential if the contemporary human and planetary condition is to be interpreted, or thematized, adequately, so as to foster the praxis that is adequate and wholesome for our situation. The challenge of our situation has been sketched several times, but I will summarize it in detail in the next section.

When I say that the purpose is to provide resources for the vivifying of the myth–ritual–praxis complex, I keep in mind my comments in the previous chapter, that the actual process of renewal takes place at the popular level as well as in the high culture, and that it is a febrile, vulnerable, unpredictable process. We have no assurance that the resources we provide will figure in the process of revitalization in any central way, nor any indication how they might be rendered if they are taken up in the revitalization. Nevertheless, it is important that we prepare the soil of the process by demonstrating actual instances of new interpretations and by showing that the process is viable. Indeed, the most cogent assessment of what is happening in theology today recognizes that thousands of theological workers, across the globe, are doing just this—presenting the resources from their own work of reinterpreting the tradition, offering them up as potential contributions for the overwhelming task of cultural revitalization that faces us.

This effort to provide resources for revitalization follows generally a three-stage process: retrieval, testing, and restatement. I followed this process in chapter 8 in my discussion of original sin. First, that discussion retrieved various facets of the traditional messages concerning original sin, the fall, and guilt. Then it tested these traditions, chiefly in the light of the biological sciences, but also in light of feminist and critical-historical perspectives. Finally, a preliminary restatement of the myth was made, rejecting the traditions that speak of a "first" or initial sin, in favor of the traditions that speak of intrinsic fallibility and weakness in the very constitution of *Homo sapiens.*

Retrieval requires the greatest competence in historical understandings and scholarship. For example, it was noted in chapter 8 that most discussions of original sin in our culture omit altogether non-Augustinian traditions—a certain sign of less than adequate historical understanding. Testing is guided by many factors. Here I speak primarily of testing in the light of the biocultural sciences and against the requirements of our contextual challenge. This is a facet of applying the pragmatic criterion to theology. Restatement proceeds under the impact of the attempts at retrieval and testing. This final phase is, even more than the first two stages, an exercise requiring imaginativeness and sound instincts both for the tradition and for the context.

The Contextual Challenge

I have spoken many times in this book about the challenge that faces human being today, and it is unnecessary to reiterate what I have said in detail. Evolution in our epoch has brought us to the point where a planet-girdling human community, bound together by technological media of contact and communication, discovers in its self-awareness that the future of the planet and life on it are critically dependent upon the viability of the cultural system of information. Humans require this cultural system for their life; through technological civilization, they have brought it to bear upon nearly all of the planet's natural systems. The challenge, which at the least threatens the survival of the human species and many other species, and at the most seriously qualifies the conditions under which the planet will continue its next three and a half billion years of existence as planet earth (until our star burns it to a cinder), is one that I characterized with the term *crisis of culture formation*. From another perspective, it is a challenge of interpreting, or thematizing, the current human and planetary condition under the rubrics of the myth-ritual-praxis complex of factors.

The crisis of culture-formation that confronts us is of the same dimensions as that which faced our Upper Paleolithic ancestors, except that the scope of our crisis is planetary in character, whereas theirs was more local. Nevertheless, the two situations are similar, in that new elements call for thematization that we have not previously been able (or cared) to create, and so we are under pressure to rearrange our symbol worlds, or, as Mihaly Csikszentmihalyi puts it, to reorganize our consciousness (1991). This rearrangement impinges upon all three factors in the myth-ritual-praxis complex. The humans of the cave-painting era had not thematized working relationships with alien groups, nor efficient slaughter of animals for food, nor the situations of stress caused by relative crowding. Their cultural systems of information were not viable for the new conditions of life without dramatic alterations and new inputs.

Our situation is comparable. Pluralism, or multiculturality, is still with us as an inadequately thematized element of life. Never has this been more clear, on a global basis, than it is today. Justice, defined in terms of equal distribution of life chances and of the fruits of the earth, is just as lamentably thematized in our cultural information systems. War and peace are far from adequately symbolized in the cultures of the world. Equally defective is our thematizing of our placement within the nonhuman systems of nature, within the global ecosystem. Knowing that human welfare, justice, and relations with the rest of nature are all bound together in our planetary life-way simply intensifies the sense that our cultural systems of information do not interface adequately with the companion systems that are also essential for human life and the life of the planet.

We face the same task as our ancient forebears, only more intensely. Our consciousness must be reorganized. Our myths must be recast, our rituals redesigned, our praxis reformed. And all of this by human beings who are free, free in the sense that we must assess the situation, we must discover the proper interpretations and thematizations and policies for action, and we must authorize and justify them all and ascertain where and how they ought to be revised when their defects become apparent. Like our Stone Age ancestors, we are called not only to meet the challenges, but to do so in freedom and responsibility.

To some, the challenge will appear to be simply another call to turn religion and theology to the effort to promote survival. At one level, that is the case. However, to paraphrase Timothy Goldsmith, survival can be used to trivialize the issues in an effort to keep them at arm's length, and this is an unworthy goal. What is survival? It all depends on who is defining the term, and from what perspective (Hefner 1980c).

Theologically, survival must be defined in terms of God, and that means that it has to do with the perduring of the will of God. Survival is not simply a question of a human being's self-interest in maintaining heart-and-lung action indefinitely, nor even in maintaining some socially acceptable quality of life, nor in maintaining jobs for workers who are threatened by one or another dislocation in technological civilization. Survival has to do with the life that God has created, its dynamic, its creativity, its direction, and its quality, *as consequences of the divine will that brought it into being.* It is contradictory to assert, on the one hand, as Christians must, that God created all that is, out of nothing, and on the other hand to approach "survival" as if it were a demeaning consideration to the God who is said to be concerned for loftier matters. We recall the gist of chapters 2 and 3, and the first four auxiliary hypotheses of the theory of the created co-creator.

For myth, ritual, praxis, and theology to give attention to the survival issues of our present context is to face head-on the questions of what God intends for life. The struggle to survive is not a figment of human imagination; it is written into the way things are—whether one's philosophy considers it to be God-given or nature-bestowed, or both. To be concerned with survival of life and the planet at this point in history is to ask after the shape of the teleonomy in which we were made. To probe theologically what survival means is to recognize that we encounter the holy in every aspect of our lives, including those that are life-threatening. Survival will be brought into our myths and rituals, because (following Sullivan), the meaning of survival is not self-evident, and it will remain so until it is properly rendered mythically and ritually. Or as suggested above, page 91, we can accept Paul Tillich's perspective that the contextual challenge we face qualifies as an encounter with God, inasmuch as it touches both upon what is of ultimate concern for us humans and also upon issues of our being and nonbeing (Tillich 1951, 11–15).

14

Rendering the Theological Tradition

The double double entendre (and in at least two languages!) of this chapter's title—"Rendering the Theological Tradition"—is intentional. That both its first word and its last can mean either to convey a treasure with integrity or to betray it in ignominy stands as reminder to all of us who would revitalize myth and ritual, or renew theology, that we stand on a slippery slope. Only history can consign us to ignominy or acknowledge our integrity. The constructive theological sketch in this chapter will focus upon four major themes: nature and grace, human beings as created co-creators, human purpose as self-giving love, and Christ.

Nature–Grace, Grace–Nature

No concept has been reshaped in the Western experience more dramatically in the last two hundred years than the concept of nature. In chapters 3 and 4, represented in the first four auxiliary hypotheses of the created co-creator theory, I drew attention to this radical reshaping. No aspect of our Western consciousness has been unaffected by the new understandings of nature. Indeed, if we follow Collingwood (1960) in his insistence that every concept we hold is conditioned by what we think about nature, then the scope of the change in sensibilities is not surprising. It has challenged the arts, medicine, ecology, psychology, and the list goes on.

The realm of theology has felt the tremors as strongly as any other. Joseph Sittler (1962, 1972, 1978) spoke incisively to this issue, including parts of his 1961 address to the Third Assembly of the World Council of Churches in New Delhi:

> We must not fail to see the nature and the size of the issue that Paul confronts [in Col. 1:15–20] and encloses in this vast Christology. In propositional form it is simply this: a doctrine of redemption is meaningful only when it swings within the larger orbit of a doctrine of creation. For God's creation of earth cannot be redeemed in any intelligible sense of the word apart from a doctrine of the cosmos

which is his home, his definite place, the theater of his selfhood under God, in corporation with his neighbor, and in caring-relationship with nature, his sister. . . . Unless the reference and the power of the redemptive act includes the whole of human experience and environment, straight out to its farthest horizon, then the redemption is incomplete. There is and will always remain something of evil to be overcome. And more. Men and women in their existence will be tempted to reduce human redemption to what purgation, transformation, forgiveness, and blessedness is available by an "angelic" escape from the cosmos of natural and historical fact. (1962, 6–7)

If we live and move and have our being in God, as Saint Paul told the Athenians (Acts 17:28), and if we are creatures who owe their existence fully to God's creating work, as the myth of creation out of nothing tells us, then we must take a new and serious look at the significance of the scientific message that we are fully creatures of nature's evolution (see pages 63–77, above). We come hard upon the conclusion that nature is a medium of grace, as stated in the fourth auxiliary hypothesis (see pages 41–42, above), and also that grace functions through nature. The argument of this book has accentuated intensely the thoroughly natural character of human being. It has also laid the groundwork for speaking of God's purpose for humans in terms of the natural processes and structures whose requirements bespeak a teleonomy for the human. The very intensity of this argument would be a counsel of despair unless this natural realm were also a realm of grace.

The coinherence of nature and grace will no doubt be a neuralgic point for much of traditional Christianity in the West, and perhaps elsewhere as well. Christians have at least three nonnegotiable beliefs that may seem to be threatened by a blurring of the line between nature and grace. (1) They will not wish to lose the spiritual dimension of human being, which seems to be at the heart of what makes us what we are. (2) Nor will they relinquish easily their sense that humans are special creatures in the world. (3) They will, furthermore, wish to speak of the presence of God in the world generally and particularly indwelling human persons.

All three of these fundamental beliefs may seem threatened by the concept of nature and grace as interpenetrating powers. At no point is Collingwood's insight more persuasive than here. The reason these three nonnegotiables seem threatened stems from our traditional Western denigration of the natural. Particularly since the Renaissance, we have viewed nature in analogy to our experience with machines, rendering nature a lifeless entity (see pp. 82–83, above). If grace seems incompatible with nature or with a relationship with nature conceptualized in terms of an intimate interpenetration, it is because we have defined nature thus, not because of the essential symbols, myths, and rituals of Christian tradition.

Creation Out of Nothing

Much of the current theological discussion of the theme of creation out of nothing (*creatio ex nihilo*) in the religion-and-science sector (as well as among process theologians) focuses upon questions of whether it is compatible with Big Bang cosmology, whether it implies a beginning of time, whether it is an accurate representation of the biblical texts, or whether it is an outmoded polemic against certain Greek modes of thought. Although these questions are interesting and very important, they tend to miss the point of the doctrine as second-order reflection upon more basic myth and ritual. I have discussed these matters at length elsewhere (Hefner 1984a, 1984b).

The point is that this world is dependent upon God and none other for its being (Pelikan 1960). This is an assertion that the world in its entirety is, at its most primordial level, grounded in what really is. The term *God* refers to what really is. Although Christian myth (as well as Hebrew, Jewish, and Muslim myth) is insistent that a qualitative distinction be drawn between God and world, creator and created, this distinction is not a distancing force, except where the primordial mythic vision has been lost or syncretistically confused with alien views.

Process theologians to the contrary notwithstanding, there is a great difference in mythic logic between the Hebrew-Jewish-Christian image and Plato's myth of the Demiurge (Cobb 1965; Cobb and Griffin 1977; Griffin 1976; see Hefner 1979). The creation out of nothing puts the reality of goodness, in conjunction with the way things really are and the intimate relationship between these and the created order, at the very origins of nature. Dissonance and deviation from what really is come later, but they are not present at the origins (van der Leeuw 1957). Plato represents quite a different myth, with quite different ritual and praxis implications, in his portrayal of defect as being intrinsic to the very origins of the world. In a different way, the Babylonian *Enuma elish* also presents an alternative mythic logic. Chaos precedes creation; the violent act of overcoming chaos is itself the creative act (Ricoeur 1967, 175–90).

Other peoples held to the same logic as the Christians in their myths of creation (Long 1963). Wherever this logic occurs, it can be a resource for understanding the coinherence of nature and grace. It is true, as process and feminist theologians have pointed out, that there are other reasons for criticizing the creation out of nothing myth, and they chiefly have to do with concepts of power. My suggestions here indicate that we may wish to deal with those power images in ways that leave intact the logic of the myth's understanding of nature rooted in goodness and in the way things really are. Indeed, by denying the creation out of nothing, the process and feminist theologians interrupt the mythic coherence that would ground their own otherwise salutary suggestions in the way things really are.

The Two Natures of Christ

The dogmatic articulation of Christ's Two Natures, divine and human, was laid down in the fifth century in the normative documents of the Tome of Leo (448 c.e.) and the Chalcedonian Decree (451 c.e.) (Hardy 1954, 359–74). Although it has the status of dogma, stated in metaphysical terms, the Two Natures concept has nearly the same status as myth in much of Christian history. Nearly all systematic theologians discuss these documents and the dogma, generally with the intention of noting the heavy influence of Hellenistic metaphysics, the conceptual contradictions involved in attempting to utilize a generic concept of *nature* to speak both of the human and the divine, and the dissonance between this metaphysical imagery and the narratives of the Synoptic Gospels (Tillich 1951, 141–42; Pannenberg 1968, chap. 8; Braaten 1984, 511–14).

As was observed in the discussion of *creatio ex nihilo,* these are important issues, and the critics have pretty much won the day in their attacks upon the dogma. The status of the dogma in the hearts and minds of the laity is relatively untouched by these technical, albeit quite correct, scholarly attacks. The dogma possesses tremendous mythic power in its flat-out declaration that the natural order is a fit vehicle for the divine grace that is incarnate in Jesus Christ.

Granted the complex church-political situation of the fifth century, we recall that the Tome of Leo was written by the pope against Eutyches because of the latter's denial of nature as a fit vessel for Christ's incarnation. If we can hold in abeyance for a moment our critical philosophical judgments and focus upon the mythic images, we can understand the force of the pope's statement. Like most moderns (including the author of this book), Eutyches denied the egregious claim that Mary carried God in her womb when she was pregnant with Jesus.

At the mythic level, however, what appears to be logical and literal nonsense takes on vivid power. Whoever and whatever God is, or if *God* is a way of referring to *what really is,* it could be present in a woman's womb and in a baby's birth. Leo wrote, "That birth in time in no way detracted from, in no way added to, that divine and everlasting birth; but expended itself wholly in the work of restoring humans who had been deceived" (Hardy 1954, 361–62). This statement is defective from a conceptual point of view (how could the birth in time not add something?), but as myth it is wholesome for its assertion that grace can operate in an earthy set of processes to "restore humans," the naturalness and earthiness of the locus "in no way detracting." As influenced by Hellenistic metaphysics as it may be, this is an astounding claim to be made in the dualistically inclined Hellenistic world, and by one of the church's leading personages. Each of the theologians whose critiques of the dogma was cited above agrees that the dogma carries a message over and above its philosophical inadequacies—although they do not identify it with the mythic undergirding that I am emphasizing.

The technical terms used by Leo and Chalcedon, which continue in the Lutheran theology of the exchange of properties (*communicatio idiomatum*), are also philosophically suspect, but nevertheless useful when interpreted in light of the images they project. I cite several sets of terms:

> While the distinctness of both natures and substances is preserved [*proprietate utriusque naturae et substantiae*] and both meet in one Person, lowliness is assumed by majesty, weakness by power, mortality by eternity . . . the inviolable nature has been united to the possible. . . .

> For each of the natures retains its proper character without defect; and as the form of God does not take away the form of a servant, so the form of a servant does not impair the form of God. . . .

> For as "God" is not changed by the compassion [exhibited], so "Man" is not consumed by the dignity [bestowed]. For each "form" does the acts which belong to it, in communion with the other; the Word, that is, performing what belongs to the Word, and the flesh carrying out what belongs to the flesh. . . . It was equally dangerous to believe the Lord Jesus Christ to be merely God and not man or merely man and not God. . . .

> Christ, Son, Lord, unique; acknowledged in two natures without confusion, without change, without division, without separation—*the difference of the natures being by no means taken away because of the union, but rather the distinctive character of each nature being preserved,* and [each] combining in one Person and hypostasis—not divided or separated into two Persons (Hardy 1954, 363–66, 373).

Although the technical philosophical issues surrounding such statements must be analyzed and even though such a philosophical position is untenable today, it is a mistake to read these passages only in the light of the philosophical influences that taint them. They are straightforward mythic statements, and when read in that way, they are powerful. They seem to enforce a Hellenistic dualism when read philosophically—the divinity cannot be too involved with the humanity. However, these same passages, including the famous four "withouts" in the last citation, from Chalcedon (*asunkutos, atreptos, adiairetos, axoristos*) depict a condition in which God can dwell in a person without that person's ceasing to be a fully natural human being and without God momentarily ceasing to be God. (For the Lutheran rendition, which admittedly is more stylized, eleven centuries years later, see *Formula of Concord,* VIII, Tappert 1959, 597ff.; Schmid 1899, 309–37.)

The understanding of Christ through the image of the incarnation has worked throughout Christian history as a hermeneutic for understanding nature as such. The incarnation demonstrates, as the Chalcedonian documents attest, that nature is fit to be a vessel for the presence and power of God. Martin Luther insisted that "the finite is capable of the infinite"—a maxim that undergirded his sacramental theology and derived from reflection on Christ.

Both the image of God motif and the christological paradigm have grounded that classical Christian axiom concerning nature, *"Gratia praesupponit naturam, non destruit, sed conservat et perficit eam."* This can be translated in at least two ways: "Grace *presupposes* nature; it does not destroy it, rather conserves and perfects it," or "Grace *undergirds* nature. . . ." Both senses have been prominent in the Christian tradition. Bernhard Stoeckle analyzes three notions that derive from this axiom: (1) grace preserves nature, it does not destroy it; (2) grace is the foundation of nature; (3) grace leads nature to its fulfillment (1962, 18).

The Trinity

The Christian symbol of the Trinity is a rich complex of materials that functions at several levels. It has been significant in Christian art, going back at least to the fourth century c.e. in sarcophagus paintings and reliefs in Christian cemeteries in Rome (Tavard 1981, chap. 2). It has also been represented in icons and has been the subject of mystical visions and an element of prayer, doxology, and song. It has been the subject of cartoons designed for the instruction of children, but at the same time it is a normative dogma in most Christian churches, including the Confession of Faith of the World Council of Churches. Nearly every worship service begins and ends with some trinitarian statement. Some of the finest minds in the history of the West have written extraordinarily sophisticated philosophical and theological tomes on the Trinity (Gregory of Nyssa, Augustine, Anselm, Thomas). Today there is a renaissance of theological interest in the doctrine among some of our leading theologians (Jenson 1982, Pannenberg 1991, Jüngel 1976, 1983, LaCugna 1991). Even though in this context we can give no more than cursory attention to the Trinity, it is an important source for reflection.

As with the other complexes of theological material, my reflections view the Trinity from the point of view of its relation to first-order mythic material. The contemporary discussions are in many ways unuseful, because they devote so much attention to such questions as whether the Trinity is the proper name of God, and to the relationship between so-called economic and immanent aspects of the Trinity. The latter requires attention to the internal nature of the godhead, which, of course, we can know nothing about except by pure speculation (LaCugna 1991, 211–32). Such speculation stands in nearly diametric contrast to my approach in this book, which puts first emphasis on the message conveyed by myth and ritual.

From this perspective, the Trinity represents an authentic attempt to engage in world-view construction on the basis of Christian faith (Hefner 1976). It presents an all-encompassing picture of *what really is,* and no sector of nature is distanced from God. Each of the three persons of the Trinity represents an archē, a first principle. "God is creator, first principle on which all is dependent (First Person); God is the ground of all living things, present under all the forms of nature (Third Person); God is also the principle of the meaning, in Jesus, of all things, illuminating us, but also offering redemption through participation in his meaning (Second Person)" (Cochrane 1944, 422–23).

Charles Norris Cochrane, in his great work, *Christianity and Classical Culture* (1944), has shown how the great Christian philosophers, building on the mythic images, brought Christian faith into dialogue with the great philosophical options of the Hellenistic cultures, both borrowing from those cultures and providing an alternative to them. In Cochrane's analysis, the burning issue for Hellenistic culture in the period between the accession of Augustus Caesar and the writings of Saint Augustine was the question of how this world, and our earthly life in it, participates in the life of the gods. This is the question of how this world relates to *the way things really are, what really is*. The social philosophy of the Caesars presented an option, as did the mystery religions and other philosophies. In the Trinity, the Christian thinkers presented their alternative, and it focused particularly on the comparative principles set forth to gain accessibility to meaning, to that which renders the world intelligible. In contrast to Caesar's imperial society or to the orgiastic cults of the mysteries, and to other options, the Christians proposed an all-encompassing world view, rooted in their God, with the center of meaning, the *logos*, in Jesus. All of the options spoke of how nature could be in touch with what really is. Perhaps the Caesars and the Christians proposed the most credible and viable choices.

The provocative character of Cochrane's presentation lies in his showing how the Trinity functioned at a cultural level to enable people to put their worlds together and to construct a cultural information system. It functioned in prayer, as well as in philosophical speculation; it comforted persons at the time of death and mourning; it also presented in Jesus a figure who could galvanize the behavior that would bring ordinary men and women into contact with what really is.

I reiterate that I recognize full well that there are grounds for exercising critique of the doctrine of the Trinity, just as there are for challenging the doctrine of the Two Natures of Christ. Those critical issues have to be sorted out. However, in the sorting out, the mythic and ritual dimensions must be given attention.

Sacraments

Sacraments are based on the principle that a natural entity can participate in ultimacy and mediate it to those who share or use the natural element. The Christian Eucharist takes up the common experience of the meal, bread and wine. Baptism incorporates the bath. Lutheran theology, for example, has emphasized in particular that, in their natural state, the things of nature can be means of grace sacramentally. The bread and wine need not be transformed or spiritualized; when properly interpreted with the divine promise attached to them, they suffice in and of themselves to share in the conveying of grace to the world.

Implications for Nature

The situation in which we find ourselves today requires that we thematize our experiences of ourselves as fully natural beings, created by natural processes, fully dependent upon nature, and yet on the verge of destroying nature—in ourselves and around us. It is strange that Christians have attended so little to the implications of their myths and rituals for nature. Paul Santmire (1985) speaks of the ambiguous promise of the Christian theological tradition with respect to nature. This must be subject to rearrangement. Just as humans between 30,000 and 10,000 years ago had to reform their myths and rituals and create new ones in order to construct the cultural information systems that could inculcate new ways of living with strangers and new ways of relating to the animals they needed for food, so we must find new ways to bring into our cultural forms the information that will be consonant with what we know about our relatedness to the rest of nature and our responsibility for it.

Humans as Created Co-creators

No element of the theory of the created co-creator has received more attention than the analysis of the structures and processes that have constituted *Homo sapiens* to be an emergent co-creator. The double system of information at the heart of the species, genetic and cultural, as well as the situation that we call the condition of freedom, are keystones to the theory. These two facets of the theory are expressed in the fifth and sixth auxiliary hypotheses. From one perspective, the evidence supporting such a concept of the human being is so overwhelming that it would seem almost a banality to do more than call attention to it. In actuality, however, there are at least two problematic points with respect to the concept that require further discussion.

The two problems are almost polar opposites of each other. The first objection is that the concept is arrogant, too anthropocentric to be accepted in theological thematizing of our experience. This position argues that we *ought not* interpret our experience of ourselves in the world under the image of the created co-creator, because to do so will encourage precisely those egocentric, self-serving behaviors that threaten us with disaster.

Theological and scientific critics have taken exception to the *co-creator* term. It is the *co* that causes misgivings for the theologians, because it implies that humans are somehow on the same level with God, at least in the significance of their actions (Cole-Turner 1992, chap. 6). For the scientists, who are deeply impressed with the awesomeness of nature, it seems simply absurd to suggest that human beings are more than tiny actors on a stage whose dimensions in time and space are beyond our capacity to comprehend, let alone master. A substantial number of thinkers are now calling for a biocentric approach to replace anthropocentrism.

The second objection takes its cue from the second auxiliary hypothesis, as I presented it in chapter 3, that the meaning and purpose of human beings are conceived in terms of their placement within natural processes and their contribution to those same processes. This position argues that the image of created co-creator, when the directionality of its activity is placed as I have placed it, in service to the natural order, is *too demeaning* of human beings to function as central symbol for the thematizing of our experience of ourselves in the world. This argument, like the first one with which it is otherwise clearly at odds, holds that this would be the wrong interpretation of human being, and therefore it would elicit inadequate rituals, leading to maladaptive praxis.

Both of these positions, critical of the created co-creator imagery, nevertheless recognize one of its most important dimensions—its tremendous dynamism and energy. Those who raise the first objection fear that this energy will get out of hand; the second, that it will be wasted on ends too small. Precisely because of this enormous energy, the created co-creator concept is a dangerous one. However, this risk is unavoidable. History, from the Stone Age to the present, testifies to this fact. *Homo sapiens,* following the lead of its genetic programming and its neurobiological possibilities—that is, taking advantage of its distinctive qualities—has become the dominator of the planet and the destroyer of it. Human beings are the greatest threat that has appeared on this earth—the greatest threat to the planet as such, and also to each other. At the same time, if humans are repressed or stifled, the danger is just as great, because they may lash out in even fiercer fury than otherwise.

Our religious traditions, in contrast, insist that more fundamental to understanding human being is God's intention that humans be a blessing to the creation. These traditions assert that it is more in harmony with the way things really are to view *Homo sapiens* as a blessing. We must keep these facts about our species in mind as we attempt to use the created co-creator or any other concepts of human distinctiveness as means for thematizing our experience of ourselves in the world today. My discussion turns now to the salient traditions of Christian faith and theology that pertain to the issues of thematizing just surveyed.

Created in the Image of God

Jaroslav Pelikan writes:

> The fundamental concept in the biblical understanding of what it means to be human is the doctrine of creation in the image of God. Despite the obvious analogies between human anatomy or physiology and those of other creatures—recognized long before the theory of evolution was proposed—both Judaism and Christianity have affirmed that there is an even more basic and profound analogy between human existence and the very being of the living God. (1988, 134–35)

Although the Bible provides little elaboration of this concept, it has become important for Christian thinkers as a means of understanding what God intends nature to be, regardless of what it actually has become. To be created in the image of God implies that humans can be the vehicle for grace toward the creation, in a way that is somehow reminiscent of God's graciousness. The concept applies to human beings (Gen. 1:26–27), but it serves in actuality as a formal criterion for interpreting the destiny of all nature under God (Stoeckle 1962, 36–52). Ancient theologians, like Irenaeus and Tertullian, used the image of God concept, in tandem with the platonic analogy of being (*analogia entis*) method, to say that nature could be understood as analogous to divine being—nature and supernature. Today we consider that dualism to be inadequate and demeaning of nature, but it was employed early in Christian thought to assert the relatedness of nature and God (Stoeckle 1962, 34–41).

Throughout Christian history, the "image of God" has functioned as a formal category whose material content has been filled by reliance on secular, often humanistic, modes of thought. Claus Westermann has surveyed the history of the exegesis of Genesis 1:17 and finds six basic interpretations, but concludes that careful study discloses little specification of what the Bible means by "created in the image of God" (Westermann 1980, 204–5; also Childs 1976, 253 ff.). The interpretations seem to fall into the categories of those that speak of the image of God in terms of specific human attributes, such as physical strength, moral responsibility, and reason, and those that view it as consisting in the capacity of human beings to know God, to be co-responding creatures to God (Hefner 1984a, 330–33).

Commonly, Christian writers have defined the image of God in terms of Jesus Christ, who, as the Second Adam, defines human nature as God intended it before sin entered. Even though we may question whether humans were in fact ever without sin (see chapter 8), it remains an important statement, that Christ is the paradigm of what it means to be human. This is consistent with the high view of humanity that dominates the Christian traditional viewpoint. Despite a deep sense of sin and fallibility, human being as such has seldom been demeaned in Christian literature. Nor has nature, for that matter.

In his influential article, "The Historical Roots of Our Ecologic Crisis," historian Lynn White places a large share of the responsibility for the current environmental crisis upon Christianity, "the most anthropocentric religion the world has seen" (1967, 347). He builds his case on the concept of the image of God and the linking of this to Christ. Undoubtedly, Christianity bears a large share of the blame for the inadequate views of nature that have developed in the West during the last millennia. However, White's argument is simplistic and even mistaken at points. By using the image of God analogically to understand human beings, and by linking the image of God to Christ, the Christian tradition opened the way for the attributes of love and servanthood to be ascribed to the image of God. In fact, a careful reading of major Christian thinkers throughout history shows them to be thoroughly anthropocentric indeed, but reveals also that they interpreted the image of God in gentle, caring directions.

If the image of God has been misused, it is probably more by those outside the theological tradition who have co-opted it to reinforce exploitative hopes for human destiny (Pelikan 1988, 139). Christians have indeed been exploiters, but the theological tradition does not sanction such a stance, and decidedly not in its interpretation of what it means to be created in the image of God.

It is the anthropocentrism of the concept of the image of God that requires revision today. The train of thinking traced in Part Two establishes that an evolutionary way of understanding nature and *Homo sapiens* must conclude that whatever we say about the status of the human being applies, at least in potentiality, to all of nature. History indicates that the earlier traditions of Christian thought did use the concept as a basic framework for understanding all of nature. Because the human is made up of the basic stuff of the planet, the image of God in that human being indicates that the world itself is capable of that special relationship to which the image of God points. The planetary ecosystem is a support system that stands in so intimate a relationship to humans that we are fully dependent upon it. Furthermore, the evolutionary processes that produced the ecosystem are the same processes that produced humans.

Whatever the human is, as I proposed in chapter 4, it cannot be isolated from the rest of nature and its history (Hefner 1984b, 202). Even the much-criticized terms in Genesis 1:28—"Be fruitful and multiply, and fill the earth and subdue it; and have dominion"—occur in the context of tilling the soil, and are related to Hebrew terms that also resonate with nuances of guarding, serving, and caring for the earth. Some scholars even challenge the ways in which these passages in Genesis 1 have traditionally been translated (Fuerst 1992; Jenni and Westermann 1976, 182ff.; Cassuto 1961, 121–23). We must acknowledge the traditional anthropocentrism, and we must recast it so that the myth can serve the task of thematizing our experience adequately.

The image of God should be interpreted, consequently, in terms of what is the quintessence of human nature, from the perspective of how that nature may be said to be analogous to God. I suggest that what is at the core of this analogy today is the character of *Homo sapiens* as free creator of meanings, one who takes action based on those meanings and is also responsible for those meanings and actions (Hefner 1984a, 330–33). As the discussion in chapter 7 indicates, human freedom did not spring full blown from Zeus's head, but emerged in a process that extends far back into prehuman physical nature. That same nature can be said to share in the image of God.

I am speaking in terms of myth, remember, not philosophy. Unlike the earlier theologians of the tradition, I am not employing a philosophical method of analogy (and certainly the Bible was not!), but rather my reflections are cast in terms of mythic vision. As such, the point is to render what it is about humans that reflects *what really is*—both with respect to humans and to the dimension of ultimacy connoted by the term *God*. The status of created co-creator is not a matter of either arrogance or subservience. Rather, it is a matter of depicting what it is about *Homo sapiens* that has to do with *what really is*. Created co-creator as I have portrayed it in these pages bears this weight.

Sin, Original Sin, and the Fall

In chapter 8, I concluded that original sin accurately describes the character of the human being when interpreted in a manner that builds upon Eastern views of human vulnerability to the risks entailed in freedom, coupled with the traditional concept of sin of origin (*vitium originis*). I rejected the "first sin" interpretation of the story of Adam and Eve and the serpent, with its etiological approach. Consequently, I reject also a concept of original sinlessness and the fall. The symbol of primeval blessedness in the garden need not connote sinlessness, but rather that human being is grounded in the *way things really are,* that which is conveyed by being created by God, out of nothing.

The impact of the sin of origin, without the fall, is that human being is a marvelous creation, rooted in *what really is* (God), but whose distinctive character, the ground of its being marvelous, is by its very constitution vulnerable, fallible, often predisposed to feeling guilty because of the broad range of evolutionarily originated information that it carries within it, whose expectations it cannot or will not fulfill. One consequence of the vulnerability is sin. The ground of human freedom is also the source of human vulnerability. This fallibility and vulnerability are not subject to transformation to the point of eradication, they are intrinsic to *Homo sapiens*.

Furthermore, this character can and does engender real evil, what the tradition calls *actual sin*. Lust, greed, and destructiveness emerge from the vulnerable freedom, and more seriously, the tendency to fall into deception with respect to *what really is* and what it requires. What the tradition calls "curved in upon itself" (*incurvatus in se*), or following false gods, what Tillich called the demonic, is conveyed by this notion that human freedom and culture-forming capability can be deceived as to *what really is,* and furthermore can be devoted to the deception. There is no greater obstacle to fulfilling the destiny or function for which our teleonomy prepares us than to be committed to that which is genuinely disharmonious with the way things really are.

Bearing the Image, Living in Sin

The creature who bears the image of God is the same creature who lives in original sin. There is no contradiction in holding these two mythic positions together, side-by-side and interpenetrating each other. That which constitutes the image of God in humans—their freedom, their meaning-forming identity, their decisional constitution, which entails commensurate action and assuming responsibility for that action—this image of God is by its intrinsic character marked by the vulnerability and fallibility that are also the occasions for evil, perversion, and death. Original sin, as sin of origin, is not something added to the image of God, it is intrinsic to it. These considerations move us into the issues known as theodicy, trying to explain how God's world can involve evil—issues I shall not explore at this point. The creature who lives in original sin is the one creature about whom it can be said, "That is the image of *what really is.*"

Humility is at the heart of human being, not arrogance. To suppose that the purpose of this creature is something other than to be working in the service of the natural processes for the purposes of *what really is,* is to misunderstand the world and ourselves in it. This is not self-evident to us; we require myth to unveil it.

The Purpose of Being Human

Crafting a viable and compelling image of the purpose of human being has been the highest priority for this study. Confusion as to what humans *are for* lies at the core of the current crisis that threatens the life of humans and also of the planetary ecosystem. I am deeply persuaded that the God who created this world of nature out of nothing has purposes; to say, as Christian tradition does, that God created freely, entails the notion that this created world has purposes, and that they are somehow the purposes of God. Or, put another way, *the way things really are* includes function, and the functions that really matter are consistent with the way things really are. This functionality is the structure of both nonmoral and moral behavior.

Works and Grace

For some readers, this emphasis upon function will seem to be tantamount to ethicizing the Christian faith, a strategy that has been much criticized. It might seem to put sanctification ahead of justification, doing ahead of being, acting upon grace ahead of receiving grace. To others, because it brings behavior integrally into the relationship between God and humans, my position will seem to have violated the center of the gospel, interpreted as forensic justification. That is, the Christian gospel is about our being accepted as we are by God, by God's initiative; to speak of purposes and function implies that receiving God's acceptance somehow requires that we *do* something. As a consequence, our justification is not forensic, the declaration by God, but is completed by the adequacy of our performing our function, that is, by works-righteousness. Or, alternatively, it is shipwrecked by our failure to function well.

In the first place, I reject a dualism between doing and being. Function and being are not two nouns alongside each other. Function is adverbial, it is what constitutes being. If we are made with purposes and functions, then to be caught up in those functions is to be what we were created to be. Further, there is no question here of works-righteousness, faulting the declaration of forensic justification or making grace contingent upon our performance. Rather, God's acceptance comes to us in, with, and under our being what we were created to be. As I will set forth at the end of this chapter, we are accepted by God for what we are, and that includes our being creatures with functions. Forensic justification is the message that our functions are acceptable.

In certain respects my position might appear to be close to the Roman Catholic position at the Council of Trent (Sixth Session, Chap. VII; Schroeder 1960, 33). I do appreciate the emphasis at Trent that behavior is taken up into the reception of grace and transformed by it. The dualisms between being and doing seem nevertheless to be present at Trent also. The *Augsburg Confession* states the matter in a way that conforms to my view here:

> For this is Christian perfection: honestly to fear God and at the same time to have great faith and to trust that for Christ's sake we have a gracious God; to ask of God, and assuredly to expect from him, help in all things which are to be borne in connection with our callings; meanwhile to be diligent in the performance of good works for others and to attend to our calling. (Tappert 1959, 78–79)

The issue here is the theological location of behavior and morality, particularly with respect to grace. The citation above from Article 27 of the *Augsburg Confession* depicts moral behavior as the ambience within which grace occurs and wherein the benefits of grace are made actual.

The reception of grace and righteousness is inseparable from function here, the function of performing one's vocation and serving others. God's grace comes in the form of strengthening trust in God and in this function, heightening our expectation of receiving help in our function, and bearing all that must be borne in connection with our callings or functions. To "have great faith and to trust" in a gracious God in the context of our function or calling is nothing else but to be wholly dedicated to *what really is,* and to permit no distraction from that dedication.

Praxis-oriented Theology

This way of conceiving function, inherent within the being and character of God and the creation, serves also as a way to root behavior, praxis, intrinsically within the theological system. There is no way to separate the content of the faith, the myth, from symbolic action in ritual and ordinary action in praxis; as was noted in chapter 13 (pp. 224–25), the governing purpose of the theological effort is to provide resources from the Christian tradition for revitalizing the myth-ritual-praxis constellation. This is not a politicizing or ideologizing of theology, but rather a way of understanding how theology relates to the myth-ritual-praxis constellation.

Such a perspective flows rather naturally from the interpretation of myth as providing the picture of what really is that engenders ritual and praxis as part of the dialectic by which humans move from *is* to *ought*. Such intimate relationships between theology and praxis are illuminated by the understanding of morality as described in chapter 11, relying on the statement by Nowell-Smith that beliefs about the world and ourselves in it are part of any moral perspective (above, page 177).

Ronald Green deepens this insight in his admittedly controversial work, *Religion and Moral Reason* (1988). In his attempt to retrieve a "deep structure" of moral reasoning in all of the religions of the world, he provides supporting argument for the concept of the myth-ritual-praxis complex. Myth is more than ritual and praxis, and ritual is more than praxis, just as religion is more than morality. However, myth without ritual and praxis consonant with it is incomplete, just as ritual without correlated praxis is incomplete, and religion without morality is rather empty. Myth is not primarily belletristic literature, just as the cave paintings are not primarily art. The process of myth-forming is the core of world-building and culture-forming, and none of these is intended to be abstracted or separated from the actual behavior by which we conduct our lives.

Christ as Paradigm of Being Human

To be created in the image of God, I asserted above, is the central Christian interpretation of human being. The symbol's message is that we are in a special relationship to God. This interpretation of ourselves is also a message about the way things really are with respect to human beings, and consequently it is a statement that we are significant, precisely because we do exist in that relationship. When we are concentrated on *what really is,* what we are and do is very important. We further recognize that Jesus Christ is the paradigm, the model of what it means to be humans in the image of God, of what it means to be the human beings that God intended. The question is, then, what does Jesus Christ tell us about what it means to fulfill our *function* as humans?

This question of how we fulfill our function as humans forms perhaps the most substantial part of the myth-ritual-praxis complex. It may also be the most significant part of the religious community's testimony, as well as the heart of the theological system. This is not an anthropocentric move, nor is it an ethicizing of theology. On the contrary, it is a segment of the theocentric perspective.

For example, in some ancient traditions within the Eucharist, we find prayers during that part of the Great Thanksgiving known as the epiclesis, when God's Spirit is invoked upon the community assembled, that plead, "Send now your

Holy Spirit . . . that we may live to the praise of your glory" (Inter-Lutheran Commission on Worship 1978, 70). Those who have received God's presence want to live, but the principle of their living is to be thoroughly theocentric, that is, completely centered on *what really is*. Another ancient tradition closes the service with these words: "Almighty God, you gave your Son both as a sacrifice for sin and a model of the godly life. Enable us to receive him always with thanksgiving, and to conform our lives to his" (Inter Lutheran Commission on Worship 1978, 74).

The significance of these prayers lies in their position at the nucleus of the central ritual of the Christian community. The Eucharist is a celebration of the action of God that is determinative, in the Christian world picture, for the natural world, specifically for humans. Immediately after receiving the bread and wine that symbolize ritually both God's gift and human reception of the gift, the concern is that this gift and its reception succeed in conforming the behavior of the worshipers to *the way things really are*. It is precisely the way things really are that has been the subject and the object of the Eucharist.

The Model as Sacrifice

What is this "model of the godly life" that has been celebrated in the ritual? It is the Jesus who has given his life for the benefit of others. His body and blood, sacramentally represented by the bread and wine, are the centerpiece of the ritual, the body and blood he gave up for others. In bland interpretations this is termed Jesus' self-giving love. In chapters 11 and 12 this love was identified with the New Testament love command and, further, with altruism. I will up the ante by suggesting that self-giving love and altruism are caught up in the biblical image of sacrifice. I have dealt with this matter at substantial length, but I cannot here go into great detail. In an earlier article, I survey the scholarly literature that may support the train of thinking that follows (1980a).

Sacrifice is the most common and most widely shared hermeneutical category employed by the New Testament writers to interpret the death of Jesus. The image is also relevant to Jesus' life, since the giving of oneself, even if it result in one's death, is an act of living. The image of sacrifice may be unusable today, because the biblical meaning has been very nearly lost altogether. The common usage speaks of sacrifice as a relinquishing, an abandonment, usually under duress and oppression. Nothing could be further from the biblical intention. I summarize the biblical concept of sacrifice as follows (see Hefner 1980a, 421–22):

Sacrifice functions for the Christian as a symbol that gathers to itself a large amount of the data of experience and provides shape and therefore meaning to that experience. The New Testament witness itself reveals how sacrifice functioned as a meaning-giving symbol for the first Christians, who were wrestling with their experience of Jesus and attempting to make sense out of his life of teaching and ministering and his death. They extended the power of the symbol to include their own lives.

Four affirmations guide the New Testament understanding of sacrifice. First, an *affirmation of identity* is present in the act of sacrifice. A declaration of allegiance is implicit in the act, because it points to that to which one believes oneself to belong or to be rooted. The allegiance may be to a nation or to the solitary self. The affirmation may be to all of humankind, or it may be to God, as Saint Paul insists in 2 Corinthians 4:

> . . . always carrying in the body the death of Jesus, so that the life of Jesus may also be made visible in our bodies. For while we live, we are always being given up to death for Jesus' sake, so that the life of Jesus may be made visible in our mortal flesh. So death is at work in us, but life in you. (2 Cor. 4:10–12)

Second, the sacrifice is a *statement of intention*. It is affirmation of one's willingness to let oneself be a part of the reconciliation process in the act of self-giving. To use a popular phrase, in the sacrificial action the actor announces the desire to be part of the solution of evil, rather than part of the problem.

Third, the sacrifice includes an *expression of confidence* that, in the act of self-giving, the power to transmute evil into reconciliation and redemption is indeed available and efficacious, even though one makes no claim to have that power automatically at one's disposal.

Finally, the sacrifice is an *ontological statement,* that is, an affirmation that the very nature of reality supports the identity, the intention, and the confidence that are embedded in the act of sacrifice. The person engaging in sacrifice believes that he or she is acting in harmony with the way things really are. In cultic terminology, this is expressed in the belief that God accepts the sacrifice as pleasing and uses it as the occasion for the work of *shalom.*

The chief point of the sacrifice motif is that Jesus lived his life and died his death in behalf of the world. His life and death were not instrumental, in the sense that they were not carried out in order to obtain something Jesus did not already possess, nor to achieve some extrinsic goal. His life and death for others were intrinsically valuable; giving himself for the world was an end in itself, because that was God's intention all along.

Sacrifice is an image describing how we live. We should not permit the emphasis on Jesus' death to cloud this fact. Jesus' death, like that of each of us, is a statement about what he thought was worth living for—of such great worth that he put himself in harm's way in order to live for it. Consequently, as paradigm for harmony with what really is, Jesus stands as a symbol of one whose identity was drawn from the process of nature and history in which he emerged. He was defined by God's gracious will for the process, and his purpose was to be plowed back into the process, because it was the reconciliation of that world with God that he was to accomplish (John 3:16).

If this is the paradigmatic portrayal of life in harmony with what really is, then the created co-creator is likewise to plow his or her efforts and energies back into the processes of God's creation, for their benefit. Such action is its own reward, it seeks no extrinsic reward. This image of human behavior is continually rejected, because we will not accept that living for the benefit of the world is enough for us. Much of our moral confusion is rooted in this unwillingness to conform to the way things really are in the mode of Jesus' self-giving love.

This image of sacrifice is clearly of great significance. It puts the world together, it grounds behavior, it speaks of human purpose, and it can be key for culture-formation. Sacrifice has been severely criticized—by thinkers like Martin Luther, who believe that it is too close to works-righteousness, and by feminist thinkers who believe that it fosters violence, masochism, and self-demeaning behavior. These are serious issues that I can only touch upon, but I believe that these critiques are aimed chiefly at the inadequate and even perverse images of sacrifice that are contrary to the biblical traditions.

By way of response to possible criticisms, I suggest, first of all, that sacrifice, whether that of Jesus or our own, is an event of grace. It is an event of grace in which activity and receptivity are synthesized beyond our ability to analyze, and in a wholesome manner. Sacrifice, contrary to popular parlance, is not a passive matter. It stands more under the spirit of Mark 8:27–9:1, where Jesus' discussion of his own sacrifice (and that of his followers) is far from passive or self-abnegating or that of a victim of "co-dependence"! Sacrifice is an event of grace because the person engaging in it is both receiving grace and also acting as an agent of grace. Grace is received, in that the action is engendered by the sense that our lives and our actions—fallible and vulnerable as they may be—are suitable. The finitude of our lives is capable of being taken up as part of what really is.

The sacrifice is a covenant act, and the consequence promised for the act is *shalom,* the wholesome belonging of self with God, with the people, with the land, and with oneself. The actor and the act are declared suitable. That is grace; it is also justification by grace for those who articulate their faith in such terms. The act is an agency of grace precisely because *shalom* is a possible outcome. This *shalom* is not just for the actor—indeed, there can be no *shalom* for the actor unless the *shalom* is contextual and relational for the people and the world in which the sacrifice is made. This line of thinking should meet the important concerns expressed by thinkers like Judith Plaskow and Valerie Saiving (Plaskow 1980).

At this point the Reformation insight into justification by grace provides a powerful undergirding for our understanding. The act of self-giving, indeed the wholesome orientation of human life and its behavior in general, requires a confidence that the way things really are resonates to life, specifically to human life, that the most authentic sensibilities and discernments that we derive from our created nature are reliable and not deceptions, and that human action can make a constructive contribution. The gracious promise of the Eucharist tells us precisely this: that it makes sense to conform our lives to the sacrifice of Jesus, and that as fallible and unworthy as we may believe ourselves to be, the judgment of God is that our lives are fit vessels for grace and suitable instruments for fulfilling our vocation as human beings, in accord with the way things really are. There is no greater word of promise conceivable for us in our world today.

We may interpret this message as the proposition that the reality system in which we live is itself basically an ambience in which we truly belong, an ambience that has brought us into being and that enables us to fulfill the purposes for which we were brought into being. The central reality that undergirds all of concrete experience and to which we continually seek to adapt is disposed toward us in a way that we can interpret as graciousness and beneficent support. Gerd Theissen has devoted detailed attention to this very insight (1985, 172–173).

Those who wish to emphasize the forensic quality of grace—that is, that we are declared by God to be righteous apart from our actions—find their concerns preserved in my interpretation of justification. The suitability of the human species to fulfill its vocation is rooted in our very creation, which in turn is grounded in the nature of the reality system in which we have emerged. Whatever the direction taken by any single human life, the evolved vocation of the human species cannot be abrogated. This is the import of the doctrine of justification, its melody, when viewed in the contextual counterpoint of the evolutionary history of creation.

Surely, this is the most daring proclamation of the gospel imaginable in our world today—that life is worth living, no matter who or what we are, because the way things really are is an ambience of grace and meaningfulness. It is also a proclamation that is lacking in our culture. The message of forensic justification by grace received through faith stands as one of the most powerful and critical mythic formulations for our current context.

We have devoted much effort over four and one-half centuries to elaborating its significance within the context of the medieval traditions of the angry God in heaven and also in the context of the guilt-ridden human person. In many respects, this has been a continuation of Luther's wrestling with the issues of the hidden and revealed God. That wrestling grew out of his refusal to divide reality into two realms, the God realm and the non-God realm. It emerged from his sense that unless all of reality has meaning, nothing particular can have meaning. He labored under inadequate concepts of nature, and he was tightly bound to the churchly discussions of his day.

We are in a position to acknowledge the sound intentions of the Reformation and carry its discernment in more adequate and promising directions for our time. Now it is time to restate this myth of forensic justification and its doctrinal elaborations in the context of the natural and social world, as they are understood by the contemporary natural and social sciences and as we encounter them in a global society that is faced increasingly with the questions of quality of life on the one hand and of surviving or not surviving on the other hand.

The mythic, ritual image of sacrifice unveils that which is not self-evident, the meaning of what the evolutionary biocultural scientists call altruism in relationship to what really is. In myth and ritual the deepest meaning of sacrifice is presented. That it is not self-evident is the point of the discussion in chapter 12, which noted the vigor with which the scientists approach the phenomenon of trans-kin altruism, and their insistence that it cannot as yet be explained satisfactorily in biocultural evolutionary terms. Their insistence and their vigor together demonstrate that the mythic and ritual programs of information are real and important, and also that their meaning and dynamic are not self-evident.

Following Sullivan, I suggest that the meaning of these packets of information can be understood only in myth. The reason for this state of hermeneutic affairs is clear: Trans-kin altruism is not simply a scientifically puzzling phenomenon, nor a regrettably neglected virtue; it is a central symbol and ritual of what human beings should be doing with their lives, the symbol and ritual which, above all others, govern the behavior of the created co-creator. Ralph Burhoe has written about this altruism as the core of human culture, in the sense that trans-kin altruism is the behavior par excellence that marks the emergence of *human* being, in contrast to *hominid* being. He draws the conclusion that since religion is the bearer of the tradition of altruism, it is the core of human culture (1981, chaps. 6, 7).

The Paradigm as Liberation

Through the action of its culture, therefore, the human being represents a proposal for the further evolution of the created world. Humans have the potential to actualize a radically new phase of evolution. This is the import of the symbolism of First and Second Adam. Jesus is the Second Adam in that he embodies, not the destruction of the First Adam, but rather the image and accomplishment of what that First Adam can become, that for which the First Adam was intended. Whereas the First Adam is a symbol of the essential humanity that belongs to every member of the species, the Second Adam speaks of what that humanity is created to become.

When the christological symbols are placed in the context that forms the basis of this discussion, Jesus Christ becomes the central event for understanding what it means for humans to be God's proposal for the future of the evolutionary process. Now in freedom, the option is opened up for the race to enact what has been set forth by Jesus as God's purposes.

Gerd Theissen has provided a brilliant first step for understanding Jesus in this perspective. In Theissen's view, we encounter "the central reality," God, on all levels of evolution and of our own life as "opportunity and pressure originating from outside, as resonance and absurdity, as success and failure to adapt" (1985, 114, 143ff.). Jesus offers in his life, death, and teaching the possibilities for raising human living to a higher plane, one that will reveal new ways of adapting to the reality system (God) that determines our lives. Jesus' proposal is a new way of life, but it stretches and bends the requirements of adaptation in novel ways. This proposal was scandalous to many of Jesus' contemporaries, because they were not insightful enough; for them his proposal appeared to be a formula for maladaptation and extinction.

Theissen's thesis holds that the innovation and the element of superiority in Jesus' proposal for cultural evolution have to do with his presentation of the love principle: universal love across all kinds of boundaries. Theissen builds this thesis about love on the work of Burhoe, Campbell, and others, which emphasizes trans-kin altruism as the key to understanding what *Homo sapiens'* stage of evolution offers beyond that of the other higher primates. The cross and resurrection are understood as intensifying the real power and desirability of love, as a prime new direction for the future of human cultural evolution.

What constitutes forgiveness, justification, and redemption in this situation? Certainly redemption does not consist of the kind of word of forgiveness that implies that the works of the co-creator are unimportant, unnecessary, or expendable. Such an image of redemption would be a denial of the co-creator's essential nature and destiny, not its fulfillment. Rather, the reality of redemption is the fact that the artifacts of our co-creating are acceptable and are in fact accepted. The God of the evolutionary process is also faithful and loving; nothing is useless or unimportant for the work of God's evolutionary creation. The mutation and adaptation that appear to be failures are essential for the process that creates those few that appear to be highly successful. The failures are no further removed from the heart and soul of the evolutionary process than are the successes (Theissen 1985, 172–73). All are equally a part of the process and its movement across the epistemic distance from present to future.

Only a theological perspective, one that grows out of the conviction that the process transpires within the being and love of God, sees in the maladaptations of evolution anything except carnage, "red in tooth and claw." In language of the cultus, this is expressed in the thought that our sacrifices are acceptable to the Lord, and they are united mystically with the sacrifice of Jesus Christ, whose sacrifice was the action of God for the world.

In the discussion of the conditioning matrix, in relation to the second basic statement of the theological theory, I spoke of how that conditioning matrix may be subjected to critique or the call to new forms of existence. The destiny of the human being consists of the critical future to which the conditioning matrix of evolution can be brought by our culture so as to actualize the will of God. The will of God, when defined in the light of Jesus Christ, is synonymous with the love principle. We experience God's will for us as we wrestle with the task of shaping our culture so as to fulfill the world, and we hold ourselves accountable to God's will as the criterion that governs our cultural efforts.

If we proceed with care, we may speak of the co-creator's activity of "stretching," "criticizing," or "calling forth the new" as "liberation." In this usage, liberating the process of evolution towards God's ends becomes the God-given destiny of human beings. Use of this term accentuates the danger of accepting any criterion for the co-creator's work that is less worthy than God's own will.

The phenomenon of technological civilization, which forms the conditions of human life today, provides a useful illustration for the context of theology and liberation. This civilization represents a phase of development in which the very survival of persons—and indeed of much of global society—depends directly on human decision and action. This civilization cannot "go back to nature" in any simple sense, if by "nature" we mean ecosystems that are largely prehuman and nonhuman. Technological civilization *is* nature for us today. The entire planetary ecosystem is fully implicated in this civilization, both as resource and as victim.

What marks do we give this civilization when we judge it by the criterion of God's will for the future of the creation? Obviously, we can respond only with ambivalence. There is unmistakable grace mediated through the co-creator's technological accomplishments. The demonic is just as vividly present. Evolution itself will be the instrument of God's judgment and grace with respect to this work of the co-creator. If humans survive, they alone will bear the responsibility for the future and they alone will be able to seize the opportunities to actualize the possibilities for grace that are contained within it.

Sacrifice as Militant Nonviolence

One of the most compelling discussions of the behavior associated with sacrifice and trans-kin altruism is found in the psychiatrist Erik Erikson's discussion of Gandhi and his philosophy of satyagraha (Erikson 1969). This term is now translated as "militant nonviolence," in telling contrast (when one reflects upon the misunderstandings of sacrifice) to former translations as "passive resistance." Not insignificantly, the term also means "truth force"—in touch with what really is. Erikson speaks of this behavior in terms much like those associated with the tradition of sacrifice in the Bible.

Erikson considers this style of behavior, despite Gandhi's significant personal pathologies, the most adequate style of behavior for our time that he has encountered. Interestingly, Erikson places this behavior in the continuum provided by ethologist Konrad Lorenz (Erikson 1969, 395–440), and he relates it to myth and ritual. I cite here only a few comments by Erikson on this behavior of altruism-sacrifice-satyagraha:

> The *acceptance of suffering,* and, in fact, of death, which is so basic to his [Gandhi's] "truth force," constitutes an *active choice without submission* to anyone: it includes the

acceptance of punishment which one knew one courted. All of this is at once a declaration of non-intent to harm others, and (here the parallel to Konrad Lorenz's stags is most striking) an expression of a faith in the opponent's inability to persist in harming others beyond a certain point, provided, of course, that the opponent is convinced that he is not only not in mortal danger of losing either identity or rightful power, but may, in fact, acquire a more inclusive identity and a more permanent share of power. . . .

Gandhi's way, as we have seen, is that of a double conversion: the hateful person, by containing his egotistic hate and by learning to love the opponent as human, will confront the opponent with an enveloping technique that will force, or rather permit, him to regain his latent capacity to trust and love. . . .

At the end only a development which transforms both partners in such an encounter is truth in action; and such transformation is possible only where man learns to be nonviolent toward himself as well as toward others. (1969, 434–39)

It is relevant to recall that these comments grow out of Erikson's analysis of Gandhi's work with the mill workers and mill owners at Ahmedabad in 1918. He is not speaking of one-on-one moral behavior (although it would be relevant to include such behaviors), but rather group behavior aimed at social ends. I consider his portrayal of Gandhi's satyagraha to be a rendition of the behavior set forth in the life of Jesus, inculcated by both the Christian myth and the eucharistic ritual, as well as the cornerstone of the nonviolent behavior of Martin Luther King, Jr. The reciprocal transformation that Erikson speaks of, together with the social ends that were at stake (wages, working conditions, productivity), form an example of what is meant at one level by the term *shalom*.

Revising Christological Doctrines

This section is the heart of the actual content of the program for the created co-creator. The paradigm set by Jesus, as mythically, ritually, socially, and psychologically sketched here, is proposed as the Christian vision for the created co-creator, the human purpose. Here the descriptions have dealt only with relationships between humans, but the satyagraha sacrifice would also have to be extended to the rest of nature, with appropriate modulations of meaning and action.

What is the precise relationship between individuals and Jesus? How does one appropriate unto oneself the Jesus paradigm? These are among the many unanswered questions we leave. How does the ritual relate one to the realities *in illo tempore?* Certainly it is rational, aesthetic, moral, affective, and perhaps involves some understanding of mysticism or ecstasy. It would be easy to dismiss "model of the godly life" rhetoric as superficially moralistic, Jesus a figure to be imitated in a wooden fashion. Such a dismissal would be unworthy, since much more was involved for the ancients who prayed about the model of the godly life, and much more is involved for us.

Yet, Jesus Christ takes the role of revealer, an occasion of our coming to the awareness of our own acceptability in the face of *what really is,* as receivers and agents of gracious *shalom,* and as a paradigm of the behavior we must undertake if we are to be in harmony with what really is. From his placement in the myth and the ritual, we have to conclude that, within the cultural system of information that emerges from that myth and ritual, Jesus is the determinative instantiation of what really is; it is in terms of Jesus that we perceive and define what really is. As with all myth–ritual transactions, Jesus is teacher (revealer), example, and the one with whom we have communion, even though it is difficult to articulate what communion means and how it comes into existence. Myth and ritual do not simply represent, they *are* what they represent; they do not only exhibit to us what really is, in them that reality happens and we participate in it (Tillich 1957a, 42–43; Sullivan 1988, 18, 34).

Within this framework, I suggest that certain revisions will be necessary if the proper resources are to be made available for the revitalization of myth and ritual for our time. These revisions are not directed so much at the originating myth-ritual complex, but rather at the second-order doctrinal overlay that bars the way to that complex for many persons.

The issue here is what traditionally has been called atonement theory, and specifically substitutionary theories. These theories address the questions, What benefits does Christ bestow? and What does one derive from Christ? I cannot go into the complicated history and nomenclature associated with atonement (see Pannenberg 1968, 38–49), nor shall I make concrete constructive proposals. Rather, I shall simply adumbrate the issues briefly.

Western Christianity has elaborated many theories of the atonement, corresponding to the varying types of experience by which Christ's benefits were appropriated by believers. The leading images to describe this process of receiving and appropriating those benefits include those drawn from the battlefield (Christ conquers foes and liberates us); the experience of transformation (Christ grows within us like a tender shoot, gradually reforming us); and the law court (Christ pays for our deserved punishment, thus relieving guilt) (Aulen 1931).

To the extent that the kinds of world pictures utilized in this book are dominant for people today, coming from evolutionary modes of thought, emphasizing the relatedness of humans and nature, it is more difficult for us to comprehend and appropriate those atonement images that emphasize an inside-outside movement—that is, God comes from outside to help us who are inside. Images that portray our relationship to God in terms of a being that is so alienated and hostile that satisfaction must be made for our reconciliation—these are increasingly unintelligible. In this sort of world picture, God is conceived as the source of nature's being and therefore our source also. Images of creation out of nothing and of continuing creation support such a picture of God as source.

Alienation from the way things really are can be real and devastating. We are often dangerously confused concerning what really is, and we conduct our lives in ways that are at odds with what really is. However, this alienation and sin do not occur in a framework of our offending someone or some power that is totally outside nature (we do not even know what "outside nature" could mean). Nor, more to the christological point, do our alienation, confusion, and evil behavior accumulate a debt that must be paid if God is to be real and gracious for us.

Frequently in its history, particularly during the medieval and Reformation periods, theology has been structured on the conceptual framework of our alien-ation and sin engendering such wrath from a good God that God could not come close to us unless the wrath were appeased and the debt paid. This concept clearly makes less and less sense to us today. It is not the matter of sin and alienation that is problematic, but the idea that God (or what really is) must be appeased or paid back if we are to know grace. Theologians have been restive with these images for more than two hundred years. Most of them, like Albrecht Ritschl (1822–1889), refused to accept the picture of a God whose wrath has been engendered at such a deep level by human sin that a price has to be paid, and that price is the death of Jesus (Lotz 1974, 96–106).

As paradigmatic instantiation of what really is, central to myth and ritual, Jesus Christ would rather portray, as the Eucharist does, that our essential reality is placed within the nature that God has created. We are never "outside" God and the grace of God. God will use our lives, weak as they are, for the purposes of what really is. Christ's message is not that he came to pay our debt through his death, but rather that despite our sense of guilt and inadequacy, we have never been outside God's gracious ambience. The cross and death, far from paying some imagined debt, are instantiations of how life for us is to proceed, a project we are part of. That project is the creation's moving toward fulfillment according to God's purposes, a fulfillment that requires our self-giving for the creation, even as Jesus gave himself.

I close by citing again Gerd Theissen's attempt to give expression to the revi-sion I have spoken of in his rendering of the doctrine of forensic justification. The heart of his reinterpretation, which he makes consonant with evolutionary modes of thought, is this:

> Harmony with God is achieved in quite another way: God takes the questionable attempts of human beings to adapt as successful. God affirms them independently of their success or failure. That is the content of the doctrine of justification. . . . The justification of the godless offers everyone that harmony with the ultimate reality which is the inner goal of evolution—regardless of how near to this goal they may be—or how far from it. (1985, 172–73)

15

The Created Co-Creator as
Exploratory Proposal

The reader who has come this far has traversed a difficult trail, passing through several different landscapes, entering thickets that were only partially passable, and walking on paths that often were ill-marked. In this final chapter, I attempt to draw the various phases of the journey together, retrospectively, so as to suggest what it all amounts to. In my effort to weave a coherent tapestry, I shall employ the loom of thought provided by Imre Lakatos, whose ideas I described in some detail in chapter 2 (see Lakatos 1978; Murphy 1990b). I will suggest how the foregoing chapters, focusing as they have upon the theory of the created co-creator, might constitute a Lakatosian research program.

This concluding chapter consists of five sections. The first two sections reflect upon certain basic features of theological thinking, with a view toward locating the contribution of this book and thereby clarifying its basic intention. These sections serve as an entree into the Lakatosian character of my effort. The third summarizes the methodological contribution of the book. The fourth and fifth sections focus upon the potential fruitfulness of the proposals that have been set forth in the preceding chapters by noting the ways in which these proposals deal with falsifiability and novel facts.

The Theological Location of the Created Co-creator

Dogmatic and Apologetic Theologies

Christian theological statements may be viewed in their function of articulating the experience of the community of faith in which they originate. Their primary concern is to articulate that experience from the perspective that is central to the community's formation and gives it its identity. This type of theological effort is *dogmatic theology,* and it is of concern chiefly for the inner life of the community of faith itself. Classical dogmas of the Trinity and the Two Natures of Christ, as well as Reformation doctrines of justification, have often been intended to serve this function, helping Christians understand their experience of the holy and Jesus, as well as (in the case of justification) their own relationship to the holy.

Theological statements may also be viewed in their function of relating the articulation of the faith community's experience to that of human beings in general, so as to illuminate both sets of experience and thus provide explanation and interpretation of both. This type of theological statement may be called *apologetic theology*. The labels *dogmatic* and *apologetic* should be used only for heuristic purposes; on the one hand, the interior life of faith is never fully insulated from the wider culture in which it occurs; on the other hand, the most intimate and parochial expressions of a community's faith may take on startling pertinence for the wider culture.

There are many examples of how Christian theology has turned the interior statements of faith to the task of interpreting general human experience. One of the most illuminating case studies is Charles Norris Cochrane's classic interpretation of the dogma of Trinity in *Christianity and Classical Culture* (1944). Sallie McFague's *Models of God* (1987) constitutes the same sort of attempt that Cochrane traces among the early Christian theologians. Those ancient thinkers were extending the interior statements of Christian faith to the task of clarifying how common human historical existence relates to whatever is considered to be ultimate. In doing so, the Christian theologians and philosophers offered to the Hellenistic world an alternative interpretation of human existence compared to those set forth by Stoicism, the mystery religions, and the political philosophy of the Caesars. Similarly, McFague is extending Christian God-talk to interpret experience that is generally felt today to be pertinent to how humans live their lives.

In both the ancient and the contemporary examples, the work of the theologian presents to Christians a reformulation of their traditional faith statements. Reformation Christians have often employed the concepts of law and wrath (as they appear in formulations concerning law and gospel) to interpret general human experience. Law had personal existential significance for Martin Luther, but it was extended to provide an interpretation of secular history. What Christians like Luther experienced as God's wrath driving them to despair or to the arms of a gracious Father explained why it was that society at large was suffering dislocations, wars, and other ills.

What is accomplished by this extension of the Christian concepts? It relates the experience and knowledge of God to wider human experience, outside the community of faith. The community's extended interpretations of its inner experience were most often not intended to be simply esoteric or obscurantist, but rather to be the basis for credible interpretations of common human experience. To the person outside the community of faith, these extensions had the effect of saying: "If you entertain the reality of the ultimate (or of ultimacy), i.e., God, the theological statements in question present a coherent interpretation of your experience."

Revealed and Natural Knowledge

When theological statements attempt to articulate the community's experience internally, for the community's own private understanding, they base themselves on the community's tradition. When, however, they attempt to provide explanation and interpretation of general human experience, they extend themselves to incorporate materials that originate outside the community. Here the interrelationships between what are often called revealed knowledge and natural knowledge come into play.

When theology mines the understandings that are stored in the community's traditions and articulates them in contemporary forms, it is considered to be using revealed sources, because it appears to be doing nothing more than elaborating (or explicitating, to use an older term) the tradition. When the traditional statements are conjoined with general human experience, certain things happen that give the impression to some observers that theology has based itself upon natural knowledge, thus forsaking the realm of the revealed.

What happens is twofold. First, the theological statements thus conjoined purport, not to articulate the tradition as such, but to illuminate experience that seems foreign to the tradition. This means that the theological statements are cast in a form that is elicited by the general human experience that they seek to illumine, and it is this recasting that appears to cross over from revelation to the realm of natural knowledge. Second, precisely in order to function as illumination of the wider experience, theology must come to terms with criteria of meaningfulness that pertain to that experience. These criteria will be discussed in some detail below. To the extent that these criteria are strange to the interior life of the community of faith, that community may judge theological statements conforming to these criteria to be more beholden to natural knowledge than to revelation. For example, classical theologians of the Trinity have been accused of succumbing to the hegemony of Hellenistic philosophy, and it has been said of McFague that she takes her cues from secular concerns.

Such criticisms of theological statements that illumine general human experience miss the mark to the extent that they fail to recognize that the tradition is not so much being diluted by natural knowledge as it is being extended in its relevance and meaningfulness. Furthermore, the criticisms draw sharp distinctions between natural and revealed knowledge that are artificial and unuseful. Such criticisms fail to understand that it is most often sensitivity to revelation that directs the theologian to see how the tradition can be extended to inform general human experience. Nancey Murphy has recently underscored the importance of theological thinking that can make the appropriate moves between revealed and natural knowledge (Murphy 1990b, 18).

Explanatory Efforts at the Nexus of Theology and Science

Scientific formulation becomes particularly relevant to theology in respect to the wider explanatory function of theological statements, because the obligation is laid upon these statements to frame themselves as theory in a manner that is commensurate with (not identical to) scientific theories. In particular, they must observe the canons of dealing with a wide range of data, falsifiability, and fruitfulness. Theology's claim to convey truth and/or genuine knowledge is directly related to its success in accomplishing the wider explanatory function.

It is important to recognize, however, that the obligation for theology to articulate itself as theory is not a matter of being subjugated, much less reduced, to an alien discipline; rather theology is motivated by its innate thrust to interpret reaches of experience that extend outside the formative events of the community of faith. Theology is motivated intrinsically to extend its interpretations beyond its own originating experiences (Murphy 1990b, 87). The created co-creator theory is intended to enable an extension of the explanatory power of Christian faith, so as to provide genuine knowledge of wider human experience. Whether the theory will stand or fall will depend largely on whether it satisfies this basic intention.

The Popperian-Lakatosian Perspective

In chapter 2, I described briefly the proposals that Karl Popper and Imre Lakatos made for understanding the criteria of scientific knowledge. I will elaborate those proposals here, in order to set the stage more clearly for assessing the theory of the created co-creator. Popper spoke suggestively concerning theories: "Scientific theories are universal statements. . . . Theories are nets cast to catch what we call 'the world': to rationalize, to explain, and to master it" (Popper 1972a, 59). I would paraphrase these comments with the suggestion that *theory is a set of concepts that is capable of interpreting a range of phenomena.* This set of concepts must meet satisfactorily two further criteria: first, *it must in principle be falsifiable, and* second, *it must be fruitful for stimulating further thinking and interpreting new data.*

Lakatos refines the Popperian position in the direction of what he calls the "sophisticated falsificationist" position. He holds that a theory is falsified only if a new theory explains that which is improbable or forbidden by its predecessor. That is, falsification happens if the successor theory accounts for novel facts or if it possesses "corroborated excess content" over and above that of the predecessor theory (Lakatos 1978, 31ff.). Successful theories, for Lakatos, produce research programs, series of theories that result in growth of knowledge. Such a program "consists of methodological rules: some tell us what paths of research to avoid (*negative heuristic*), and others what paths to pursue (*positive heuristic*)" (1978, 47).

Falsifiability and Fruitfulness

If theology is to be faithful to its innate thrust to extend the cognitive significance of its originating revelation by playing an explanatory function for general human experience, then insofar as that wider experience leads into the realm of the sciences, theological statements will be used in constructing theory that conforms to the criteria of falsifiability and fruitfulness. Theology, in extending its knowledge claims out from the community of faith, will want to lay the basis for successful research programs in interpreting general human experience in the context of what is of ultimate concern for humanity, which is equivalent to speaking of God's will for humanity.

Obviously, theological statements do not aim at empirical content with the same degree of precision that scientific statements do, nor do they prize prediction in the way that scientific discourse does. Popper himself, however, recognizes that there are "levels of testability." His axiom is: "The *empirical content* of a statement increases with its degree of falsifiability: the more a statement forbids, the more it says about the world of experience" (1972a, 119f.).

I suggest that theological statements, in the circumstances outlined above, must be potentially falsifiable—that is, they must have a class of potential falsifiers that is not empty. How full that class is, is subject to variation, case by case. Theology's success in extending its explanatory field is directly correlated to how full or empty its class of potential falsifiers is. What I mean by this will become clearer in the next section, which summarizes the materials of the preceding chapters.

God and the Hard Core of Theology

The fundamental distinctiveness of theological statements (that emerge from theistic religions) is their reference to God, and therefore, in a Lakatosian program, God is spoken of in the hard core (Murphy 1990b, 194). Obviously, the reference to God cannot be made object of the falsification process. Furthermore, since theological statements lose their entire raison d'être if the reference to God is omitted, it would seem that the Popperian scheme is not applicable to theology at all.

I suggest that Lakatos's elaboration of Popper is pertinent in dealing with this problem. Lakatos, in his discussion of the methodology of scientific research programs, argues that every research program has a hard core, which, by means of what he calls the negative heuristic, is never permitted to feel directly the abrasion of the falsification process. Evolution in the Darwinian program, for example, is not itself susceptible to verification or falsification. The hard core is surrounded by a vigorous protective belt of auxiliary hypotheses, which take the brunt of falsification. Whether or not the auxiliaries are appropriate depends on whether they contribute to the program's success in producing growth in knowledge (through the positive heuristic). Lakatos writes, concerning the Newtonian program, "This hard core is tenaciously protected from refutation by a vast 'protective belt' of auxiliary hypotheses. And, even more importantly, the research program also has a 'heuristic,' that is, a powerful problem-solving machinery, which, with the help of sophisticated mathematical techniques, digests anomalies and even turns them into positive evidence" (1978, 4).

He goes on to assert that even bodies of thought like Marxism and Freudianism "are all research programmes, each with a characteristic hard core stubbornly defended, each with its more flexible protective belt and each with its elaborate problem-solving machinery" (5). Not all of these research programs are equally good. What distinguishes the superior programs is their ability to make "dramatic, unexpected, stunning" interpretations of the world of experience. These interpretations must be empirically credible. Where the program consists mainly of theories without concrete credible interpretations of the world (i.e., what scientists call facts), "we are dealing with miserable degenerating research programmes" (6).

The theory (or research program) set forth here is intended as a theological theory, and therefore God stands at its center, as that to which all terrestrial and cosmic data are related. The question of the reality of God, however, is placed in the hard core of the program, so that it never enters into the realm of possible falsification. Such considerations do figure strongly in the positive heuristic of the program, however. If the program is finally not persuasive on the basis of the falsification process that has been applied to its auxiliary hypotheses, then ipso facto the reality of God will be rejected, even though it cannot be directly disproven.

The Popper-Lakatos discussion of falsifiability and fruitfulness can be summarized in the following terms. Two points in particular are noteworthy. First, the process of falsification is applied to the auxiliary hypotheses of a research program, hypotheses whose function is to protect the hard core of the program. I attempted to relate the proposals of this book to this aspect of the Lakatosian scheme in chapter 2 in my enumeration of the nine auxiliary hypotheses that surround the core of the created co-creator theory, and in my suggestions as to how, in principle, one could consider ways in which they could be falsified.

Second, the success of a research program depends on its fruitfulness (in Lakatos's terms, it must be "progressive"); that is, whether it is productive of new knowledge through its dramatic, stunning, and unexpected interpretations, which qualify as the production of new facts. I did not deal with this aspect of Lakatos's analysis in the earlier chapters, but I will do so in the next section.

These new facts are the fundamental test of a theory's fruitfulness, and their enumeration serves as a way of summarizing what this book is about.

A theory, or hard core, is considered to be falsified by another theory at the point where that new theory provides interpretations that the earlier theory either could not provide or prohibited. One might suggest that the hard core corresponds to the set of insights that form Thomas Kuhn's celebrated concept of paradigm (1970). Similarly, that which enables the stunning, dramatic new interpretation is akin to Michael Polanyi's discussion of the place and role of tacit knowledge (1966).

I suggest that this Lakatosian argument can be transposed into the realm of theological methodology by the assertion that the reference to God is at the hard core of any theological program. What is at stake in the falsification of theological theories is not whether they can prove the existence of God, but rather whether, with the help of auxiliary hypotheses, they lead to interpretations of the world and of our experience in the world that are empirically credible and fruitful— that is, productive of new insights and research (Murphy 1990b, 194–95). If they can do this, they have indeed succeeded in extending the explanatory function of the community's faith into the realm of wider human experience. If theology is in any sense to be called scientific, it is in this sense.

The Methodological Venture

> . . . . even though Christian theology must begin with the Christian tradition (its revelation and the phenomena of the Christian religion), it must proceed to confirmation vis-a-vis reality external to the tradition—that is to contemporary sorts of data—if it is to fulfill its role as a science of God. (Murphy 1990b, 87)

In these terms, Nancey Murphy characterizes a fundamental methodological assumption in the theological work of Wolfhart Pannenberg, one that she shares with him, and one that grounds my own proposals concerning the created co-creator. In the preceding section, the discussion began to clarify what such a stance entails, in its insistence that theology must be accountable to the criteria of meaningfulness that characterize the sciences and whatever other areas theology moves into. This element is complemented, in Pannenberg's thought, by theology's mandate to make its own distinctive contribution to the domains that are the object of the attention of other disciplines of knowing, whether the sciences, the arts, or some other. Pannenberg expounds this complementary element in his approach to anthropology:

> The aim is to lay theological claim to the human phenomena described in the anthropological disciplines. To this end, the secular description is accepted as simply a provisional version of the objective reality, a version that needs to be expanded

and deepened by showing that the anthropological datum itself contains a further and theologically relevant dimension. (1985, 19–20)

Both of these complementary elements are important to the theory of the created co-creator. The discussion of Popper and Lakatos in the preceding section speaks to the extension of the theological reach into territory external to the religious tradition. The arguments concerning the essential functions of myth and ritual in providing certain kinds of information for human beings as cultural creatures represent the effort to show that the data of human evolution themselves contain a theologically relevant dimension.

Throughout the preceding chapters, while I have taken methodological issues seriously and commented on them at some length, I have refused to construct a tight, coherent methodological structure or to hold myself accountable to unflinching methodological consistency. Intentionally, I have invoked the model of Lydia Hof Mittelstadt. The reader will recognize, however, that despite my unwillingness to espouse an airtight methodological rigor, I have made several decisive proposals for theological methodology. Furthermore, these proposals can stand on their own apart from the adequacy or inadequacy with which I have followed them.

These proposals can be summarized under three headings. First, I have emphasized the need for theology to construct theory, so that it can make a contribution to genuine knowledge. My guide to theory-formation has been the philosophy of science, specifically the Popper-Lakatos strand.

Second, I have insisted that Christian faith is a message about the world, and therefore theology cannot do its work unless it integrates within its procedures the disciplines of thought that are necessary in order to gain knowledge of the world. With respect to the domains that are the focus of attention in this book, it is the natural and anthropological sciences that must be integrated within theological method. Medieval theologians were required to earn their first degree in natural philosophy, what we would call natural science, as prerequisite for studying theology (Schmitz-Moormann 1992, 134).

My use of Joseph Sittler's image of melody and counterpoint makes the same point. As the significance of the melody is dependent upon and conditioned by the counterpoint, so the meaning of the faith is related to the world in which it happens, and knowledge of the world is inseparable from science. In the depiction of the created co-creator, the counterpoint is the scientific picture of evolution, genes and culture, and the function of culture. Without that scientific understanding, the concept of the created co-creator would bear no resemblance to what I have sketched in these pages.

A third methodological proposal, which may be more implicit, permeates my proposals. Biologist Timothy Goldsmith, as I cited him in chapter 13, has emphasized the great need for mature science, in which each realm of reality must be studied on its own terms, but "those terms must relate to the rest of science or the exercise will be of no lasting value." He goes on to speak of the sciences working together "for the discovery of principles that unite hierarchies and cut across species" so as to "enrich our knowledge and our lives" (1991, 141).

Jerome Barkow (anthropology), Leda Cosmides (psychology), and John Tooby (anthropology) have recently carried Goldsmith's idea much further and speak of "conceptual integration," leading to what they call an "Integrated Causal Model" for the future of scientific work.

> *Conceptual integration*—also known as *vertical integration*—refers to the principle that the various disciplines within the behavioral and social sciences should make themselves mutually consistent, and consistent with what is known in the natural sciences as well. . . . A conceptually integrated theory is one framed so that it is compatible with data and theory from other relevant fields.
>
> . . . there is emerging a new framework that we will call the Integrated Causal Model. This alternative framework makes progress possible by accepting and exploiting the natural connections that exist among all the branches of science, using them to construct careful analyses of the causal interplay among all the factors that bear on a phenomenon. . . . Advances in recent decades in a number of different disciplines, including evolutionary biology, cognitive science, behavioral ecology, psychology, hunter-gatherer studies, social anthropology, biological anthropology, primatology, and neurobiology have made clear for the first time the nature of the phenomena studied by social scientists and the connections of those phenomena to the principles and findings in the rest of science. This allows a new model to be constructed—the Integrated Causal Model. (1992, 4, 23–24)

If this be the case, and if a consensus exists that the revealed traditions with which theology begins have to do with this world and how it is related to God, then in order to understand the world—and, more to the point, in order to understand the significance of the world's being related to God—theology must relate itself to the conceptual integration that Goldsmith, Barkow, Cosmides, and Tooby are advancing. I see no compelling reasons why theology cannot assume a place within this integrated conceptuality; on the contrary, there is much to be said for it. Such a methodological move also provides a way of taking seriously the suggestions of Samuel Preus (see chapter 13). The work of Arthur Peacocke and Wolfhart Pannenberg demonstrates that theology can indeed proceed in its work with such a self-understanding, and I intend the theory of the created co-creator to make a contribution along the same methodological lines.

These methodological suggestions are closely related to the even wider area of genuinely interdisciplinary approaches that I have sought to fashion in this book. Eugene d'Aquili (1993) speaks of the "interpenetrated manner" of relating materials from various disciplines, as opposed to the method of "simple juxtaposition." He writes about the sense of uneasiness which any real expert in a field feels when confronted with the data from his field of expertise being presented in a deeply interdisciplinary work. By deeply interdisciplinary I mean that the data from various disciplines are presented in an interpenetrated manner rather than simply juxtaposed. The data from one discipline, therefore, are presented more or less filtered through other disciplines. Even when great care has been observed in preserving the integrity of those data, the effect is somewhat unnerving to the expert. It is not that the data are misrepresented or erroneous, but rather that they acquire an unusual tint, tone, or feel which can be quite disconcerting. (1993)

He goes on to underscore that the lack of depth and rigor the expert feels when confronted by the deeply interdisciplinary work is not the real issue, but rather that this "unusual tint, tone, or feel" is the consequence of a genuinely novel interpretation. That this novelty is the result of the interpenetrating of the disciplines accounts for the surprise and even discomfort that the expert feels. It is risky for the practitioner of the interdisciplinary method to court the disfavor of the experts whose work is being thus exploited, but it is necessary if the advance in insight is to be gained.

The Negative Heuristic

Chapter 2 provides a full description of the created co-creator theory, its hard core and the auxiliary hypotheses that surround it like a belt. I elaborated the core in three basic elements, and I related the auxiliary hypotheses to each of the elements. I reiterate the scheme here, to facilitate a synoptic view of the whole. Hard Core:

Human beings are God's created co-creators whose purpose is to be the agency, acting in freedom, to birth the future that is most wholesome for the nature that has birthed us—the nature that is not only our own genetic heritage, but also the entire human community and the evolutionary and ecological reality in which and to which we belong. Exercising this agency is said to be God's will for humans.

Core Elements + Auxiliary Hypotheses

The First Element: The human being is created by God to be a co-creator in the creation which God has brought into being and for which God has purposes.

Hypothesis #1: Integral to *Homo sapiens* and its evolutionary history are certain structures and processes, the requirements for whose functioning may be said to constitute, at least in a tentative way, goals and purposes for human life.

Hypothesis #2: The meaning and purpose of human beings are conceived in terms of their placement within natural processes and their contribution to those same processes.

Hypothesis #3: A concept of wholesomeness is both unavoidable and useful as criterion governing the behavior of human beings within their natural ambience, as they consider what their contribution to nature should be.

Hypothesis #4: Nature is the medium through which the world, including human beings, receives knowledge, as well as grace. If God is brought into the discussion, then nature is the medium of divine knowledge and grace.

The Second Element: The conditioning matrix that has produced the human being—the evolutionary process—is God's process of bringing into being a creature who represents the creation's zone of freedom and who therefore is crucial for the emergence of a free creation.

Hypothesis #5: Freedom characterizes human existence as the condition in which humans have no choice but to act and to construct the narratives and symbols that contextualize that action. Such contextualization provides justification, explanation, and norms for guiding and assessing the action. This condition is intrinsic to the evolutionary processes at the level of *Homo sapiens*.

Hypothesis #6: *Homo sapiens* is a two-natured creature, a symbiosis of genes and culture.

The Third Element: The freedom that marks the created co-creator and its culture is an instrumentality of God for enabling the creation (consisting of the evolutionary past of genetic inheritance and culture, as well as the contemporary ecosystem) to participate in the intentional fulfillment of God's purposes.

Hypothesis #7: The challenge that culture poses to human being can be stated thus: Culture is a system of information that humans must construct so as to adequately serve the three tasks of interpreting the world in which humans live, guiding human behavior, and interfacing with the physico-biogenetic-cultural systems that constitute the environment in which we live.

Hypothesis #8: We now live in a condition that may be termed technological civilization. This condition is characterized by the fact that human decision has conditioned virtually all of the planetary physico-biogenetic systems, so that human decision is the critical factor in the continued functioning of the planet's systems.

Hypothesis #9: Myth and ritual are critical components of the cultural system of information and guidance. They are marked in linguistic form by declarative or imperative discourse, and their concepts are vastly underdetermined by the data of evidence. In light of human evolutionary history, these marks were necessary if culture was to serve its evolutionary function.

In chapter 2, I indicated sketchily how each of the auxiliary hypotheses might be tested. This matter deserves more attention here. Karl Popper spoke of falsification in terms of "the class of all those basic statements with which it is inconsistent (or which it rules out, or prohibits)" (1972a, 86). Imre Lakatos spoke of falsification in the context of a research program's following the methodological rules: "some tell us what paths of research to avoid (*negative heuristic*), and others what paths to pursue (*positive heuristic*)" (1978, 47). This section is devoted to the negative heuristic; the following section, to the positive heuristic. Popper was correct that the meaning of a theory is enhanced if we can grasp just what it would rule out or contradict. We can quickly, if sketchily, observe a sampling of what the auxiliary hypotheses rule out, that is, what would falsify them.

The hypotheses that cluster around the first element of the theory deal with teleonomy (#1), the placement of human beings within nature (#2), the pragmatic criterion of wholesomeness (#3), and nature as a medium of knowledge and grace (#4). Clearly, the first three hypotheses rule out concepts of human purpose that are unrelated to the natural structures and processes of the human creature, as well as statements that isolate humans from the rest of nature by conceiving of this nature as irrelevant to human purpose, or any statement that would authorize humans, in the name of their purpose, to behave toward nature in a manner that could reasonably be classified as destructive or unwholesome. The fourth hypothesis complements the first three in ruling out concepts of knowledge or grace that somehow make contact with human beings apart from the nature that both constitutes humans and also forms the ambience in which they live.

The two hypotheses related to the second element speak of freedom emerging within the deterministic system of nature (#5) and the human being as constituted by genetic and cultural information (#6). The fifth hypothesis rules out concepts of human freedom that stand in a dualistic relationship to the prehuman world. It also contradicts concepts of the human mind and its ways of knowing that picture humans as passive receptors or conduits for knowledge, thus denying that the individual human mind leaves its distinctive mark upon the information it receives. The sixth hypothesis rules out concepts that separate in a dualistic manner the genetic and cultural elements of human being, especially those that set them in opposition or hostility to each other. Both of these hypotheses differ markedly from theories that attempt to avoid interpreting the function of evolution, specifically natural selection, in shaping the human being.

The hypotheses that come into play with the third element make assertions concerning the challenges posed to humans by virtue of their being cultural creatures (#7), the conceptual location of technology (#8), and of myth and ritual (#9). Hypotheses seven, eight, and nine prohibit concepts of culture that fail to speak of its interface with nature's physical and biological systems. They would also reject notions that remove human initiative and impact upon culture. Dualisms between technology and nature, or between technology and human nature, would also be contradictory of these hypotheses. Any attempt to explain myth and ritual as somehow standing outside the evolutionary processes, or to omit myth and ritual as central elements of culture, would likewise be at odds with these hypotheses. Further, the ninth hypothesis rejects the notion that human beings could have survived as long as they have without the information that myth and ritual provide.

Some of these potential falsifiers are current items for debate among scientists—for example, the arguments that pit genes against culture, in contrast to those that link them as one reality. Others are examples of a longstanding resistance of the humanities and religious studies to possible reductionism by the natural sciences—as when scholars of religion polemicize against functional interpretations of religion or against the thought that myth and ritual could play an evolutionary role in survival and adaptation.

The Positive Heuristic

Lakatos believed that the history of science refutes two of the twentieth century's major proposals for designating the hallmark of science: Karl Popper's concept of "quick kill" falsificationism, because it is naive, and Thomas Kuhn's concept of scientific revolutions, because it is no more than an "irrational change in commitment" that cannot distinguish between science and pseudoscience (Lakatos 1978, 4, 5). Both falsificationism and revolution turn out to be myths. What really happens is that progressive research programs replace degenerating ones because they produce "stunning new interpretations" or "novel facts." This is the central category in Lakatos's philosophy of science. It is its success in discovering novel facts that qualifies a research program as fruitful.

The concept of *novel fact* is complex, and Lakatos changed his definition of the term during his lifetime. Hence, it is not surprising that some dispute still lingers about what Lakatos really meant (Murphy 1990b, 65–68). At the root of Lakatos's insight is the conviction that a research program is progressive, or useful, if it leads to insights that were not possible by other theories or programs. He spoke of this as "excess empirical content." He writes: "a theory is 'acceptable' or 'scientific' only if it has corroborated excess empirical content over its predecessor (or rival), that is, only if it leads to the discovery of novel facts" (1978, 31–32; Murphy 1990b, 59).

Not only are we uncertain how Lakatos would define a novel fact; it is also unclear how the definition of a novel fact changes as one moves from the natural sciences to the social sciences and humanities, not to mention theology. Nancey Murphy offers the following as an attempt to clarify matters:

> A fact is novel if it is one not used in the construction of the theory T that it is taken to confirm. A fact not used in the construction of a theory is one whose existence, relevance to T, or interpretability in light of T is first documented after T is proposed. (Murphy 1990b, 68)

I offer the following, more simplistic, rule of thumb when speaking of novel facts in the context of the humanities and theology: A novel fact is an insight or empirically demonstrated fact, not used in the construction of the theory that it is taken to confirm, that (1) was first documented after the theory was proposed; or (2) was known but not integrated within a larger conceptuality that interpreted it incisively; or (3) even if it was previously integrated within such a larger conceptuality, is now integrated within a different conceptuality that not only accounts for its previous interpretation but also adds a hitherto unrecognized interpretation. The significance of a theory is correlated to the significance and depth of the novel facts it discovers.

The positive heuristic of a theory or program sets forth a strong, innovative, striking vision that can deal with data that other programs find difficult to account for. If the theological theory of the created co-creator is to prove genuinely fruitful, it is essential that it meet the novel facts criterion—either in Lakatosian terms or in some other comparable manner. The discussion that follows is, therefore, a key element in the assessment of the theory.

In setting forth the positive heuristic of the theory of the created co-creator, I will discuss the novel facts or interpretations that it leads to in two classes: with respect to general human experience and also with respect to the Christian faith and theology. Research programs that are interdisciplinary—that is, that seek the conceptual integration that I described above—will be defective if they do not lead to novel facts in more than one discipline. This is especially true of theological research programs that aim at conceptual integration, and it is their success in discovering novel facts in both theological and nontheological (general human experience) domains that enables them to contribute genuine knowledge.

I have elsewhere used this criterion of two classes of novel facts to interpret Pannenberg's work (Hefner 1988b), and also an earlier version of the created co-creator theory (Hefner 1988c). In my use of the criterion of two classes of novel facts, I differ somewhat from Nancey Murphy's use of Lakatos for theology, and I derive different implications from his philosophy of science for theology (Murphy 1990b, 174–78). The discussion of novel facts that follows is intended to be suggestive rather than exhaustive. It indicates generally what I mean by novel facts and the sorts of new insights that the created co-creator theory stimulates.

Novel Facts regarding Human Experience

1. *Human meaning and purpose are referred to the processes of nature.* The second auxiliary hypothesis in particular, and the first four taken together, root human being decisively in the natural order, both in terms of its evolutionary history and its contemporary ecological breadth. This in itself is not a novel approach, but the insistence that human meaning and purpose must be referred to nature is an unusual insight. More common are proposals on either side of this assertion—

namely, on the one hand, that humans are called to shape nature to their own ends and thus bestow meaning upon it; or, on the other hand, that some form of biocentrism should be espoused, placing humans within nature, simply as phenomena within its larger continuum.

The former view often speaks of nature in terms of its instrumental value for human ends, while the latter may speak of the intrinsic value of the rest of nature. The auxiliary hypotheses in question make the distinctive point that human life is intended to reflect back upon the welfare and purposes of the rest of nature, and (particularly when linked to the hypotheses concerning culture) has a unique and significant contribution to make to the rest of nature, at least on planet earth. Instrumentalism fails to understand the significance of *Homo sapiens'* placement within the processes of nature's evolution, while biocentrism does not adequately account for the evolved characteristics of the species. Previous thinkers, like Gerard Manley Hopkins, have made this observation, but they have not placed it within a large conceptuality in the way that the created co-creator theory does. This novel fact includes the prediction that adopting this understanding of human meaning and purpose will enhance the future of all the components of the planet.

2. The teleonomy of Homo sapiens is raised in a context of urgency. While teleonomy is itself not a new concept, the first auxiliary hypothesis, when linked with the other hypotheses concerning nature and also those that deal with culture, brings teleonomy together with precisely those characteristics of the human being that mark its most striking function—namely, the creation and maintenance of culture as a system of information, and the function that is at the nub of the life-threatening crises that mark our time. This concatenation of elements moves the discussion of human purpose to a different plane, one that is defined by the simultaneous posing of the two urgent questions, What should we be doing to meet the crises? and What is the function of the human species? The responses to these two simultaneous questions constitute a new way to speak of human purpose, one that focuses both upon the evolutionary past of the species and also upon its future and possible extinction.

When the second element of the theory is underscored in this context, the problematic that I have just described also offers an opportunity to reflect upon the purposes of natural selection, a notoriously difficult issue. My comments below concerning evil and theodicy are relevant here. I have adopted John Hick's discussion of evil as the starting point for reflecting upon the purpose of natural selection (Hick 1981). This novel problematic also leaves open the possibility of introducing a discussion of the existence of God; if we bring ultimacy into our thinking, we have a better grounding for the behaviors that are wholesome for the human species and the planet. This novel state of affairs includes the prediction that were we to take these two questions seriously, in tandem, our chances of resolving the crises that face us would be greater.

3. Genes/culture and the biocultural evolutionary model are introduced to deepen our understanding of human existence today. The course of the discussion of the hypotheses that pertain to nature and culture has led in the direction of the biocultural model of evolution. This model serves as a conceptuality for binding together the several elements that the hypotheses focus upon. Since I did not have the biocultural model in mind in the first versions of the theory, this may count as a prediction that the biocultural model of evolution is a successful research program in its own right for the study of human being. This prediction appears to be in the process of validation at this time.

4. The perennial issues of freedom and determinism are conceptualized in more complex ways. The theory correlates determinism to the evolutionary process that has produced *Homo sapiens,* and it conceptualizes freedom as the condition in which humans must comprehend and interpret the natural process that has created them and act upon their interpretations with intentionality. This conceptuality is made more complex by the recognition that the deterministic process of prehuman nature was itself a subtle interweaving of determinism and indeterminism, just as there is a deterministic dimension to the condition of freedom.

5. Technology is integrated within the evolution of nature and human nature. One of the most perplexing conceptual challenges that has faced us in the last century is that of understanding technology. Again, two extremes have dominated: the view that technology is alien from nature and human beings, on the one hand, and, on the other, the view that humans and the rest of nature should be subordinated to technology and its advances. The theory of the created co-creator, in contrast, conceptualizes technology as fully part of evolution, rooted in the genes/culture symbiosis and representative of human cultural evolution. As such, the theory underscores human responsibility for technology. At the same time, the theory calls attention to the necessity and possibilities of technology, as well as its demonic role in the crises of culture that beset us today. Thus, the theory retains the hopes and fears of the two extremes, but, in contrast to them, is able to give technology a significant conceptual placement for our understanding.

This insight was not included in the earliest versions of the created co-creator theory, a situation that suggests that this insight was documented after the theory. This insight lends itself to a number of predictions concerning the possible outcomes for our societal life, depending on what kind of conceptual location we give to technology and how we act upon those concepts.

6. The crisis of culture and the role of myth and ritual are given conceptual force. The hypotheses that deal with culture relate it to the basic structures and processes of human evolutionary history in such a way that they describe the present human situation in terms of a crisis of the information systems we call culture. This roots the crisis in the very nature of nature and specifically human nature, and acknowledges both the alluring possibilities and the demonic self-destructive capabilities of culture in our time.

The ninth hypothesis relates myth and ritual to this constellation of factors, including the evolutionary history of *Homo sapiens*, notably in the Pleistocene. It brings to bear concepts of myth, ritual, and morality that are consistent with what we know about the evolutionary history of our species. This aspect of the created co-creator theory insists that myth, ritual, and religion are essential to human being. The prediction is implied that as the human sciences progress and become more adequate, they will recognize this essentiality.

7. *Evil and theodicy function as potential falsifiers.* The greatest potential falsifier of the created co-creator theory—and of all other theories that speak of God— is the reality of evil. Evil challenges all that the theory asserts about meaning, purpose, and goodness as the rationale of the created world, and in particular about the meaningfulness and goodness of the evolutionary processes.

The theory can deal with evil only by placing the theodicy problem in the hard core of the program, which is never subjected to the abrasion of falsification. As a result, the program must rely on two basic strategies: demonstration of the cogency of the other aspects of the theory, particularly the auxiliary hypotheses; and emphasis on the philosophical insight that answers to the final ontological questions (e.g., Is there a God? Will evil be overcome and compensated for finally?) are not susceptible to demonstration. At the end of the day, one must simply acquiesce to the fact that it is equally reasonable to believe or to disbelieve in God and the triumph of goodness, and choose for one or the other on the basis of the overall cogency or lack of persuasiveness of the program.

As far as the questions of evil and theodicy are concerned, however, the created co-creator theory will accept as a starting point the theodicy of John Hick, as he revised it in 1981. He interprets evil as the unavoidable accompaniment of the kind of natural system that is required if freedom and personhood are to emerge, an evolutionary system. Hick's hypothesis thus assumes the status of an auxiliary hypothesis.

Linking Experience, Faith, and Theology

We encounter a provocative double-sidedness in the effort to conjoin the originating interpretations of a religious community's experience and common human experience. It is akin to the famous drawing taken from Gestalt psychology textbooks, which from one perspective shows a fashionable young woman and, from another view, reveals an old crone. With practice, the observer can make the Gestalt "switch" from young woman to old at will. The effort to relate distinctly religious interpretations of experience to the common human realm may seem to explain away the religious, reducing it to nonreligious explanations, or it may establish the religious dimension in all experience, eliminating the category of the nonreligious altogether.

This is what I derive from Lawrence Sullivan's insights, which appeared in chapters 9 and 10. On the one hand, ultimacy, or God, is not accessible or rightly understood except within the forms of life that have evolved to the present. These forms include those that shape our understanding. On the other hand, the forms of life and understanding are not rightly interpreted if they are not perceived as configurations of the ultimate.

For the religious or theological reader, the challenge is to perceive that religious faith is significant precisely because it concerns the reality that science has focused upon, to which all persons want to adapt in some way. For readers who do not identify themselves as either religious or theological, the challenge is to consider that the commitment of the scientist to understand human being as fully as possible, as well as the commitment of all persons to advance the survival of the human species and the planet, make no sense except as an effort to take seriously *that which really is*; what really is, is finally grounded in the ultimate, else neither commitment is fully worthwhile.

Novel Facts regarding Faith and Theology

1. Reinterpretations of nature and grace and their interrelationship. The created co-creator rests on the insight that nature and grace coinhere—that is, they exist together, they interpenetrate each other, neither can exist without the other. In chapter 14, I based this view of nature and grace on the classical axiom, *gratia praesupponit naturam*, which carries the meaning that grace undergirds nature and also that grace presupposes nature. This double meaning exemplifies the coinherence that I speak of.

The created co-creator theory opens up the understanding that the classical axiom is undergirded by contemporary scientific insights and also that it is the only completely viable theological understanding of nature and grace. The theory interprets four major blocks of traditional Christian theological material so as to provide the foundation for this understanding of nature and grace: creation out of nothing, asserting that nature originates solely from divine grace; the Trinity, asserting that God is the all-encompassing reality; the Chalcedonian Two Natures of Christ, asserting that natural structures can be the vessels of grace, without thereby undergoing any change themselves; and the classical understanding of sacraments, asserting that God's ordinary mode of acting in the world is through nature. The research program based on the created co-creator presents the concept of the coinherence of nature and grace as a reasonable explicitation of and inference from these classical theological materials. As such, it qualifies as a novel articulation of the Christian tradition.

2. Created co-creator as interpretation of the image of God. The idea of humans as the image of God (Gen. 1:26) has been interpreted in many ways through centuries (see chapter 14). The concept of the created co-creator presents itself as a suitable way of interpreting this biblical notion, thereby suggesting four insights. First, concerning God, the created co-creator asserts that the activity of envisioning the direction and purposes of nature and bringing that direction into actuality is central to the nature of God in relationship to the created world. Second, concerning human nature, the creator co-creator asserts that its distinctive essence is constituted by humans participating in this activity of God's. The concept of freedom developed in chapters 6 and 7 reveals the shape of this essence of human nature.

Third, concerning the human activity of envisioning the purpose of nature and acting upon the vision, the theory asserts that the norm for such activity is nothing else but God's own nature, as we know it. Finally, concerning the rest of nature, the theory asserts that since humans emerged within the processes of nature's evolutionary history, nature itself participates in this image of God; the fact that the co-creator is created through nature's evolutionary processes justifies the inference that nature itself shares in the image of God. This is a novel interpretation.

3. The purpose of being human. The created co-creator theory places the concept of purpose at the center of the theological understanding of human being. Closely related to purpose are the concepts of destiny and vocation. The justification for this central placement of purpose is provided through the interpretation of works and grace, morality, function, and praxis. I have attempted to place works, morality, and praxis at the heart of Christian faith, and I have done so by interpreting function and functionality as intrinsic both to the evolutionary processes of nature as interpreted by the sciences and also to processes of creation endowed with purposes by God, as interpreted by Christian faith. The justification for placing function in such a favored position is rooted in the way God has created the world, namely, with purposes that flow from God's own will.

From one point of view, this placement of works and morality is a response to the insights deriving from feminist and liberation theologies that move us toward understanding that praxis is intrinsic to Christian faith and theology and not an afterthought or a conclusion derived through theological argumentation. The research program of the created co-creator theory grounds the praxis orientation profoundly in the most primordial dynamics of the nature that God has created. From another point of view, my emphasis on function flows from the judgment that theology ought to carry on its thinking so as to be suitable for inclusion in the conceptual integration model that I have advanced as desirable for theological methodology.

I have presented this interpretation of works, morality, and praxis as a motif of Christology, specifically as Christ is viewed through the image of sacrificial living. Inasmuch as the concept of sacrifice is discredited today from many quarters, including feminist approaches, much of psychology, and mainline Protestant theological positions (including Lutheran, Anglican, and Calvinist), my research program exerts a great deal of pressure for recognition of this Christology as a novel fact of Christian interpretation.

The emphases of praxis, sacrifice, and their correlative notions are not novel in the sense that they have never been suggested before. In fact, they have been prominent in theological discussions for some time. What is novel are the grounding of praxis intrinsically in the nature of God's will and in the emergence of Christian faith; the interpretation of the motif of sacrifice as a foundation within the Christian tradition for a praxis orientation as well as a theological rendering of functionality; and the attempt to demonstrate that sacrifice can be a wholesome image, in the face of much opinion to the contrary. Implicit in this argument is the prediction that the concepts of functionality and sacrifice will emerge in the future as significant elements of those theological approaches that are recognized to be most adequate.

4. The doctrines of atonement, justification, and original sin. Theological research receives encouragement from the created co-creator theory to pursue certain directions with respect to these three blocks of Christian doctrinal material. With respect to the atonement, we are encouraged to interpret Christ's work in ways that reject the notion that human beings have incurred through their inadequacies a debt to God that must be paid. Rather the atonement is to be interpreted as God's statement that God has never been alienated from us and that our lives, modeled in the form of Jesus, are suitable for God's work. That is to say, our lives can be commensurate with the way things really are, and Jesus' life is the pattern for us. To understand Jesus in this manner is to understand why Jesus is the Christ and what his atoning work is.

Justification receives the impetus for new interpretations. It has been interpreted in its significance for understanding God's nature and the relation of human beings to God, but it has not been elaborated in ways that show its relevance for understanding nature, God's relation to nature, and the relation of humans to nature. If these directions for interpreting justification are pursued, Gerd Theissen's interpretations will be vindicated. Perhaps this qualifies as a prediction from the theory.

The classical doctrines of the fall and original sin receive complex new interpretations from the created co-creator theory. The fall is rejected except in a decidedly figurative manner, since we cannot accept that humans ever existed in a prior state of perfection. Original sin, on the contrary, is proposed as adequate and necessary for our understanding, particularly if certain Eastern traditions are given attention and if our interpretation of the "sin of origin" is taken seriously. Taken in this direction, the concept of original sin is interwoven with the concepts of freedom and sacrifice.

This constellation of concepts—original sin, freedom, and sacrifice—is important, because it is in them that the program of the created co-creator integrates within itself the element in Christian tradition that variously goes under the terms dialectical, the element of negation, the theology of the cross, and the eschatological proviso. In some traditions, particularly those of the so-called neo-orthodox theologians of the mid-twentieth century, including Karl Barth and Emil Brunner, whose influence is in some respects in resurgence today, God's presence is interpreted as the negation of nature. This position asserts the inadequacy of nature unless it is corrected and purified by the introduction of grace.

The power of the neo-orthodox view lies in its clear sense of evil and the need for transformation. The theory of the created co-creator has been criticized for omitting this element, even for baptizing what is, to the exclusion of dialectic and transformation. These criticisms are misguided. The theory rather insists that nature, as a vessel of grace under the axiom "grace undergirds and presupposes nature," is itself a process of transformation. Evolution, as described by the sciences, itself makes this point. Consequently, there is no contradiction in asserting the "nature-grace, grace-nature" position that appeared in chapter 14 or in interpreting the work of Jesus under the motif of sacrifice and liberation (pp. 241–51).

Comparably, the evolutionary history of nature includes the element of transformation throughout. This is another example of the Gestalt switch: the religious symbols of Christ's sacrifice are correlated to phenomena that are already present in nature, or, under the creative presence of grace, nature shares in the transformation that the Christ symbol announces. In any case, the emphasis upon nature in no way minimizes the presence of evil, the elements of suffering and pain, or the transformation, even though the languages in which we ordinarily talk about nature and those we customarily associate with religious discipleship may on occasion employ quite different vocabularies.

This final chapter poses the criteria by which the theological theory of the created co-creator is measured against the goals that I set for it in the opening chapters. Here again, a kind of double-judgment is called for: Does the theory meet the expectations set for it as a progressive research program? and, Is the process of determining the answer to this questions itself a process of discovery and fruitfulness? Both of these questions are central to the assessing of the theory. It can be said that the theory is itself an invitation to probe the dimensions of life that it points to. The theory is an exploratory one, and its function is as an instrument for those who would undertake the exploring.

Epilogue

Taking Leave of a Theme

I will take leave of this theme simply by recounting where we have come on our journey—or where I think we have come.

First, I raised Steven Weinberg's concern: Because there seems to be little evidence written into the natural world ascertainable by science concerning the meaning and purpose of human life, we have to write our own stories about what it means and what its purpose is (chapter 1).

Second, I announced that I would propose a theory, á la Imre Lakatos, that speaks of human purpose, while at the same time suggesting auxiliary hypotheses about the world and our place in it (chapter 2). My claim is that the theory and all its parts will provoke challenging questions, the exploration of which will be useful. The theory, in other words, will prove to be fruitful. This theory goes by the title, The Theological Theory of the Created Co-Creator. My proposal is that, properly understood, the concept of the created co-creator tells us what the meaning and purpose of our lives is. This theory and its auxiliary hypotheses are summarized on pages 264–65. The theory is theological because I believe that it is rooted in ultimacy, in the way things really are.

Third, I went to great lengths (chapters 3 through 12) to show that this theory is grounded deeply within the natural order. This created co-creator has emerged from within the natural evolutionary processes as a creature who can and must (if it is to survive) scan its world, collect data, and construct complex interpretations of the world and its experience of the world. This creature not only creates its meanings, grounded in its experience of the natural world, of course, but it has adapted so successfully to its global ecosystem that it has been able to impose an overlay upon the pre- and nonhuman systems of nature, such that those systems are thoroughly conditioned by human cultural inputs. All of this is rooted in the evolved human creature, who is within itself a symbiosis of genes and culture, and who through its culture continually seeks to bring its genes and the rest of its environment into conditions of existence that only the culture-forming co-creator would ever dream of. The point is that nature should function, in large part, as *Homo sapiens* desires it to function, so as to become in fact the world that the created co-creator believes is most desirable for its existence.

Fourth, throughout the book I have argued that in the situation to which biocultural evolution has brought us (the created co-creator), the life not only of the human species, but of the entire planetary ecosystem is made to depend on a great wager going well. This wager is that the cultural systems of information that the co-creator fashions will interface with the natural systems and with the global human culture so as to promote survival and a wholesome future.

Fifth, up to this point, I have attempted to demonstrate that the created co-creator is a product of biocultural evolution. I have also described the wager that creature has made normative for the entire planet, as well as the challenge it poses to the planetary community.

Sixth, I called attention to the fact that the wager is not going well. The cultural systems of information are not meshing adequately enough with the other systems, and calamity is the prospect.

Seventh, I looked to our evolutionary past, and discovered that in the Upper Paleolithic period, between 100,000 and 20,000 years ago, a comparable situation faced humans. I presented an audacious conjecture that these humans met the challenge and surmounted it through the formation of myths, rituals, and appropriate praxis deriving from the myths and rituals. I proposed that myth and ritual organized the information that was necessary for survival, resulting in viable cultural systems.

Eighth, I suggested that the times call for revitalization of our mythic and ritual systems, in tandem with scientific understandings, so as to reorganize the necessary information. This may help us to put our world together, to discern *how things really are*, so that we can test which actual everyday praxis is most adequate for us.

Ninth, I insisted that this entire enterprise is a religious one. We need resources to meet this challenge from as many places as we can find them. Christians will want to contribute what they can to the enterprise, and I devoted the last pages of the book to reflection on what Christians can contribute.

So, one might say that I have described a crisis, put it in biocultural historical perspective, suggested that the image of the created co-creator best describes how we got this way and what is required of us to live wholesome lives. And then I have reflected upon how Christian traditions may be of help in the crisis.

Many important questions remain for exploration:

- Where did myth and its information packets come from?
- What is the status of this information? What accounts for its adaptive value over the millennia?
- Is this information comparable to genetic information?

- Why do humans turn all information into hypothetical statements that need to be tested and stretched?

What I offer in this book is a set of recipes for understanding our lives and their meaning. I leave it to the reader to decide which of Lydia Mittelstadt's verdicts about her recipes fits mine: "These recipes are a joke; realize that." Or, "This may work out."

Glossary

This glossary should be used in conjunction with the Index, where definitions are marked with an asterisk (★). The following reference books are recommended: Donald W. Musser and Joseph L. Price, eds., *A New Handbook of Christian Theology* (Nashville: Abingdon Press, 1992); F. L. Cross and E. A. Livingstone, eds., *The Oxford Dictionary of the Christian Church* (2nd ed.,: Oxford: Oxford University Press, 1974); Ian Barbour, *Religion in an Age of Science* (San Francisco: Harper and Row, 1990); G. Ledyard Stebbins, *Darwin to DNA, Molecules to Humanity* (San Francisco: W. H. Freeman and Co., 1982). Evelyn Fox Keller and Elisabeth A. Lloyd, eds., *Keywords in Evolutionary Biology* (Cambridge: Harvard University Press, 1992); Ernst Mayr, *Toward a New Philosophy of Biology* (Cambridge: Harvard University Press, 1988).

agape   A Greek term for love, appearing in the New Testament. Theologically, it refers to God's unmerited love of human beings or the love that humans have for one another, which is created and motivated by God's love.

altruism   Behavior that increases the fitness of recipient, at the risk of reducing the fitness of the doer.

atonement   Etymologically, "at-one-ment"; refers to the benefit that we derive from Jesus Christ's life, death, and resurrection. Many theories have developed over the centuries to explain these benefits.

biocultural evolution   The study of evolution that includes both biological and cultural dimensions; see diagram, p. 198.

bricolage   French term employed to describe the processes of evolution in which new developments are made possible by putting together elements that are available from existing circumstances, rather than by fabricating altogether new elements. Also used to refer to "junk art," e.g., sculpture that is created out of already existing objects.

caritas   A Latin term for love, used in the Vulgate version of the Bible to translate agape (q.v.).

Chalcedonian decree   The statement of faith issued by the Council of Chalcedon (a city in Asia Minor) in 451 B.C.E. It is noteworthy as the official statement of the Dogma of the Two Natures of Christ, his humanity and divinity.

281

CNS, central nervous system   The brain and spinal cord, in vertebrate animals.

continuing creation   Latin, *creatio continua:* classic Christian doctrine that asserts God's ongoing creative and sustaining activity in the world.

creation out of nothing   Latin, *creatio ex nihilo;* classic Christian doctrine that asserts that God created the world, in terms of its beginning and thus is the originating source of the created order. The temporal implications are less significant than the assertion of God as ultimate source. The doctrines of continuing creation and creation out of nothing form one unified statement concerning the relation of God and the natural world.

critical realism   The philosophical position that our minds can be in touch with an objective reality and therefore can gain understanding of reality, even though our concepts do not stand in a one-to-one relationship with reality and consequently must be subjected to rigorous critique. This position differentiates itself from *naive realism,* which does not exercise critique and does affirm a one-to-one relationship between mind and reality.

culture   The system of learned patterns of human behavior, together with the symbols that contextualize and interpret the behavior.

economic trinity   The concept of the trinity as referred to the external, salvatory action of God in the world. See *immanent trinity.*

epiclesis   The invocation of the Holy Spirit in the eucharistic prayers that accompany the blessing of the bread and wine.

epigenetic   In biology, to refer to a succession of events, each of which is dependent upon the completion of the preceding phase in the sequence. Thus, epigenesis accounts for directionality in evolution, even though it is a random process.

epistemological   From the term *epistemology,* that branch of philosophy dealing with theories of knowing.

eschatology   Classically, the "doctrine of last things"; some interpretations emphasize the actualization of the power of final fulfillment in the present, chiefly in Jesus (*realized eschatology*); others underscore that every moment of history is part of a continuum moving toward its final destiny, and that an awareness of this fact defines each moment.

etiology   Theory of the origins of a phenomenon. An etiological approach to the story of Adam and Eve and the apple, for example, interprets the story as an explanation of the origins of human sinfulness. This approach to biblical myth is contested by current scholarship.

Eucharist   A central Christian worship service, also called Holy Communion or the Lord's Supper, centering in the sacramental eating and drinking of the bread and wine that correspond to Jesus' body and blood from his crucifixion.

evolution   Scientific theories of the processes by which nature changes over time. The term is now employed by scientists to speak of the evolution of the physical universe, of chemical and geological processes, as well as of biological and cultural processes. Evolution is most often associated with Charles Darwin's theories of biological change. In most general terms, evolution consists of the production of variations, selection from this pool of variants, and survival of the selected variants.

forensic justification   The doctrine that sinful human beings are set right with God, or considered to be righteous, not through any merit or attractiveness on their part, but by God's gracious declaration (hence, *forensic*).

freedom   There are many interpretations of this term. In this book, the emphasis is on freedom as a condition of human existence, in which humans can and must deliberate on courses of action, carry them out, and take responsibility for their consequences. Furthermore, humans must interpret the significance of these actions and justify them. Freedom refers to this entire complex of ideas.

function, functionalism   The sciences that are most relevant to biocultural evolution employ methods that use the concepts of function and adaptation. Such methods apply the analogy of the engineer or designer to biocultural processes. They assume that adaptations have served the survival of the organism, and that natural selection favors structures and processes that serve the functions that make adaptation possible. When the function of a thing is understood, advance in knowledge has been made. These methods assert a kind of teleology, speaking of biological systems as goal-directed. There has been much controversy over functional/adaptationist assumptions. These assumptions persist because they have been so fruitful for research.

genotype   The total amount of inherited or genetic information contained in an organism. See *phenotype*.

grace   Chief Christian theological term referring to the beneficent action of God, primarily in Jesus Christ.

hermeneutics   The science of interpretation; usually, but not exclusively, applied to the study of texts. Generically, it refers to the analysis of the human capacity for interpreting and understanding the world. In this book, it can generally be considered as a synonym for *interpretation*.

heuristic   A method that facilitates understanding by means of speculations, the usefulness of whose resulting interpretations is not dependent upon the truth or falsity of the initial speculation.

immanent trinity   The concept of the trinity as referred to the interior being of God. It is asserted that the trustworthiness of God's character as revealed in history (*economic trinity*) is grounded in the confidence that what is revealed is intrinsic to the inner nature of God.

information   Messages that represent states of the environment so as to be a resource for behavior that is appropriate to those states.

in illo tempore   Literally, "in times of yore," the reference is to primordial times, associated with the fundamental character of the world. The term is associated with the claims of myth and ritual that they are means for bringing persons into relationship with the primordial times and realities.

justification   Theological doctrine concerning the process by which sinful persons are made right with God, or righteous, and its consequences.

liberation   Actual transformation. In theology, originally associated with Latin American theology emerging in the 1960s. It refers to the actual transformation of persons and situations that are marked concretely by circumstances of oppression.

myth   Stories that deal with fundamental or primordial realities, and thus are sacred. They deal with beginnings and serve to place the persons and groups that are spoken of in the stories, as well as providing grounds for rituals and ethical action.

naturalistic fallacy   A philosophical doctrine that it is not possible to move from descriptive to prescriptive statements, that is, from *is* to *ought*. David Hume and G. F. Moore are associated with the origins of this doctrine. The doctrine has been hotly debated and significantly contested in the last half century.

ontological   From the term *ontology,* that branch of philosophy dealing with theories of being, that which is grounded in the fundamental character of reality.

otiose   Applied to theories or conceptual proposals that are ineffective, of no usefulness or fruitfulness.

paradigm   In philosophy of science, a network of presuppositions, conceptual and methodological, that are determinative for a body of scientific work, such as Darwin's evolutionary theory. Thomas Kuhn gave coinage the term, suggesting that important shifts in a scientific field result from the displacement of one paradigm by another. In religion, a pattern or model that is of fundamental significance. In this book, Jesus Christ is spoken of as the paradigm of what it means to be human.

phenotype   The totality of the physical, observable qualities of an organism; the actual forms that have developed from the genotype, in the organism's interaction with the environment. See *genotype*.

praxis   Action that grows out of theoretical reflection and in turn leads to further reflection. In liberation theology (q.v.), it is a term that underscores the close interrelationship between theory and practice; theory's goal is action, and action is a source for reflection. In this book, praxis is spoken of as the behavior that flows from myth and the reflection upon myth that is embodied in ritual. Thus, the term, "myth–ritual–praxis complex."

process theology   The school of theological thought that is based on the philosophy of Alfred North Whitehead and Charles Hartshorne. The term "process" comes the insistence that fundamental reality is comprised of events, called "actual entities," that in turn are constituted by an internal process of becoming.

realism   A classical philosophical term that refers to the theory that there are "real" objects that the mind can know; therefore, human thought can grasp reality.

research program   A term coined by the philosopher Imre Lakatos to account for progress in scientific knowledge. He held that scientific inquiry is organized in such programs, which center in a hard core of concepts that cannot be falsified, but which prove to stimulate fresh insights, producing novel facts, through the functioning of auxiliary hypotheses that surround the core like a belt of satellites. These hypotheses rule out certain paths of research (the negative heuristic) and show others to be fruitful (the positive heuristic). A program that fails to produce novel facts is said to be degenerating and will give way to a competing program that does unveil such facts. This book is one of several attempts to show the relevance of this concept to theology.

ritual   A set of actions that portray how human beings should behave in order to be in harmony with the fundamental nature of reality. It is central to religion (although not confined to religion), and it acts out the behavior that is thought to be mandated by the basic myths to which the community holds.

selection, natural selection   A concept that describes the demise of the least adaptive individuals and the flourishing of adaptive ones within biological processes. "Natural" selection asserts that the processes of nature exercise this selection without teleological guidance.

shalom   Hebrew term for peace. Its context in the covenant that God made with Israel and others (e.g., with the earth and all living things after the Flood) emphasizes belonging as a central element of shalom—belonging to God, to the community, to the earth. At the Last Supper, Jesus spoke of his death as a new covenant that would bring shalom.

symbiosis   A relationship between two organisms of differing species, in which benefits often (but not always) accrue to both. Biological processes are replete with symbioses, one of the most famous of which is the termite, which is host to organisms that inhabit its belly, enabling termites to feed on wood, a substance that is otherwise indigestible.

technological civilization   Used to characterize the present conditions of life on planet earth, in which human culture conditions all of the natural systems of the planet. This produces conditions in which the planet and its systems are decisively dependent upon human decisions and the actions that carry them out. The most relevant aspect of human culture in this situation is human technology and the global civilization that depends upon it.

teleology   Theory that explains natural phenomena in terms of a guiding purpose or design.

teleonomy   Goal-directedness that is based on the functioning of programmed information. In this book, it is argued that such goal-directedness, when considered together with the behavior that is required to satisfy the programmed information, provides a basis for speculating about the purpose of human beings.

theodicy   Etymologically, "vindicating God." The theological reflection upon evil that seeks to reconcile three premises: that God is all-powerful, that God is all-good, and that evil exists. Historically, there have been many different solutions to the theodicy problem.

Tome of Leo   Letter written by Pope Leo I in 449 C.E., insisting upon both the humanity and divinity of Jesus Christ. It was acknowledged as possessing formal authority by the Council of Chalcedon. See *Chalcedonian decree*.

transkin altruism   Altruistic behavior that is extended to individuals who are not related by close kinship. This behavior is made possible by culture, and it complements genetic theories that altruistic behavior is limited to close kinship groups. See *altruism* in index.

underdetermined Concepts, theories, hypotheses, and other information whose claims are not adequately demonstrated by evidence are said by philosophers to be underdetermined by the data. The argument in this book asserts that such information is required by the human central nervous system, if action is to be possible, and that myth and ritual are instances of such information.

way things really are This term, along with the phrases, "how things really are" and "what really is" is employed to denote the most fundamental reality or nature of things. In this book, these terms are attempts to clarify what is meant by the terms *God* and *ultimacy,* particularly in speaking of the function of myth and ritual.

Bibliography

Alexander, Richard D. 1987. *The Biology of Moral Systems.* New York: Aldine de Gruyter.

Allison, Paul D. 1991. "A Neo-Darwinian Theory of Beneficent Norms." Paper delivered at the Annual Meeting of the American Sociological Association.

Aquinas, Saint Thomas. 1945. *Summa Theologica.* New York: Random House.

Ashbrook, James. 1984. *The Human Mind and the Mind of God: Theological Promise in Brain Research.* Lanham, MD: University Press of America.

————. 1992. "Making Sense of Soul and Sabbath: Brain Processes and the Making of Meaning." *Zygon: Journal of Religion and Science* 27 (March): 31–49.

Augustine. 1955. *Augustine: Confessions and Enchiridion.* Trans. and ed. Albert C. Outler. Philadelphia: Westminster Press.

Aulen, Gustaf. 1931. *Christus Victor.* Trans. A. G. Hebert. New York: Macmillan Co.

Barbour, Ian. 1974. *Myths, Models, and Paradigms: The Nature of Scientific and Religious Language.* London: SCM Press.

————. 1990. *Religion in an Age of Science: The Gifford Lectures 1989–1991,* vol. 1. San Francisco: Harper & Row.

Barkow, Jerome H., Leda Cosmides, and John Tooby. 1992. *The Adapted Mind: Evolutionary Psychology and the Generation of Culture.* New York: Oxford Univ. Press.

Bell, Catherine. 1992. *Ritual Theory, Ritual Practice.* New York: Oxford Univ. Press.

Berger, Peter, and Thomas Luckmann. 1966. *The Social Construction of Reality.* New York: Doubleday Anchor Book.

Birtel, Frank T. 1990. "Theology and Post-Modern Ethics." Lectures given in spring 1990 at the Chicago Center for Religion and Science.

Bertram, B. C. R. 1982. "Problems with Altruism." In *Current Problems in Sociobiology,* ed. King's College Sociobiology Group, 251–68. Cambridge: Univ. Press.

Betz, Hans Dieter. 1985. *Essays on the Sermon on the Mount.* Philadelphia: Fortress.

Bischoff, N. 1980. "On the Phylogeny of Human Morality." In *Morality as a Biological Phenomenon,* rev. ed., ed. Gunther Stent, 48–66. Berkeley: Univ. of California Press.

Bolle, Kees. 1967. "History of Religions with a Hermeneutic Oriented toward Christian Theology?" In *The History of Religions. Essays on the Problem of Understanding,* ed. Joseph Kitagawa, 89–118. Chicago: Univ. of Chicago Press.

Bowker, John. 1976. "Information Process, Systems Behavior, and the Study of Religion." *Zygon: Journal of Religion and Science* 11 (December): 361–79.

———. 1983. "Editorial." *Zygon: Journal of Religion and Science* 15 (December): 353–58.

Boyd, Robert, and Peter J. Richerson. 1985. *Culture and the Evolutionary Process.* Chicago: Univ. of Chicago Press.

Braaten, Carl E. 1984. "The Person of Jesus Christ." In *Christian Dogmatics,* ed. Carl Braaten and Robert Jenson, vol. 1, Philadelphia: Fortress Press, 469–569.

Braaten, Carl E., and Philip Clayton. 1988. *The Theology of Wolfhart Pannenberg.* Minneapolis: Augsburg Publishing House.

Bronowski, Jacob. 1970. "New Concepts in the Evolution of Complexity: Stratified Stability and Unbounded Plans." *Zygon: Journal of Religion and Science* 5 (March): 18–35.

Brown, Donald E. 1991. *Human Universals.* New York: McGraw-Hill.

Brown, Peter. 1969. *Augustine of Hippo: A Biography.* Berkeley: Univ. of California Press.

Browning, Don S. 1991. *A Fundamental Practical Theology: Descriptive and Strategic Proposals.* Minneapolis: Fortress Press.

Browning, Don S., and Francis Schüssler Fiorenza. 1991. *Habermas, Modernity, and Public Theology.* New York: Crossroad.

Burhoe, Ralph. 1966. "Determinism and Freedom." Unpublished article.

———. 1972. "Natural Selection and God." *Zygon: Journal of Religion and Science* 7 (March): 30–63.

———. 1976a "Religion's Role in the Context of Genetic and Cultural Evolution—Campbell's Hypotheses and Some Evaluative Responses: Introduction." *Zygon: Journal of Religion and Science* 11 (September): 156–62.

———. 1976b. "The Source of Civilization in the Natural Selection of Coadapted Information in Genes and Culture." *Zygon: Journal of Religion and Science* 11 (June): 263–303.

———. 1979. "Religion's Role in Human Evolution: The Missing Link between Ape-Man's Selfish Genes and Civilized Altruism." *Zygon: Journal of Religion and Science* 14 (March): 135–62.

———. 1981. *Toward A Scientific Theology.* Belfast: Christian Journals Limited.

———. 1982. "Pleasure and Reason as Adaptation to Nature's Requirements." *Zygon: Journal of Religion and Science* 17 (March): 135–62.

———. 1988. "On 'Huxley's Evolution and Ethics in Sociobiological Perspective,' by George C. Williams." *Zygon: Journal of Religion and Science* 23 (December): 417–30.

Burhoe, Ralph Wendell, and Solomon H. Katz. 1986. "War, Peace and Religion's Biocultural Evolution." *Zygon: Journal of Religion and Science* 21 (December): 439–72.

Calvin, William H. 1989. *The Cerebral Symphony: Seashore Reflections on the Structure of Consciousness.* New York: Bantam Books.

———. 1991a. *The Ascent of Mind. Ice Age Climates and the Evolution of Intelligence.* New York: Bantam Books.

————. 1991b. "Islands in the Mind: Dynamic Subdivisions of Association Cortex and the Emergence of a Darwin Machine." *Seminars in the Neurosciences* 3 (November).

Campbell, Donald T. 1965. "Variation and Selective Retention in Sociocultural Evolution." In *Social Change in Developing Areas: A Reinterpretation of Evolutionary Theory,* ed. H. R. Barringer, G. I. Blanksten, and R. W. Mack, 19–49. Cambridge, MA: Schenkman.

————. 1975. "The Conflict between Social and Biological Evolution and the Concept of Original Sin." *Zygon: Journal of Religion and Science* 10: 234–49.

————. 1976. "On the Conflicts between Biological and Social Evolution and between Psychology and Moral Tradition." *Zygon: Journal of Religion and Science* 11 (September): 167–208.

————. 1991. "A Naturalistic Theory of Archaic Moral Orders." *Zygon: Journal of Religion and* Science 26 (March): 91–114.

Campbell, Joseph, with Bill Moyers. 1988. *The Power of Myth.* New York: Doubleday.

Cassuto, Umberto. 1961. *From Adam to Noah: A Commentary on the Book of Genesis.* Trans. from the Hebrew from Israel Abrahams. Jerusalem: Magnes Press, Hebrew Univ.

Cavalli-Sforza, L. L., and M. W. Feldmann. 1981. *Cultural Transmission and Evolution: A Quantitative Approach.* Princeton, NJ: Princeton Univ. Press.

Chagnon, N. A., and W. Irons, eds. 1979. *Evolutionary Biology and Human Social Behavior: An Anthropological Perspective.* North Scituate, MA: Duxbury.

Chaisson, Eric. 1979. "Cosmic Evolution: A Synthesis of Matter and Life." *Zygon: Journal of Religion and Science* 14 (March): 23–29.

————. 1981. *Cosmic Dawn: The Origins of Matter and Life.* Boston and Toronto: Little, Brown, and Co.

————. 1987. *The Life Era: Cosmic Selection and Conscious Evolution.* New York: Atlantic Monthly Press.

Childs, James. 1976. *The Imago Dei and Eschatology.* Philadelphia: Fortress Press.

Clayton, Philip. 1989. *Explanation from Physics to Theology: An Essay in Rationality and Religion.* New Haven, CT: Yale Univ. Press.

————. 1992. "Clayton Response to Robbins: Religion/Science without God?" *Zygon: Journal of Religion and Science* 27 (December): 457–59.

Cloak, F. T., Jr. 1976. "The Evolutionary Success of Altruism and Urban Social Order." *Zygon: Journal of Religion and Science* 11 (September): 219–40.

Cobb, John B., Jr. 1965. *A Christian Natural Theology: Based on the Thought of Alfred North Whitehead.* Philadelphia: Westminster Press.

Cobb, John B., Jr., and David Ray Griffin. 1976. *Process Theology: An Introductory Exposition.* Philadelphia: Westminster Press.

Cochrane, Charles N. 1944. *Christianity and Classical Culture.* London: Oxford.

Cole-Turner, Ronald. 1992. *The New Genesis: Theology and the Genetic Revolution.* Louisville, KY: Westminster/John Knox Press.

Collingwood, R. G. 1945. *The Idea of Nature*. Oxford: The Clarendon Press.

Collins, H. M. 1982. *Sociology of Scientific Knowledge: A Source Book*. Bath, England: Bath Univ. Press.

Cone, James H. 1972. *The Spirituals and the Blues: An Interpretation*. New York: Seabury Press.

———. 1975. *God of the Oppressed*. New York: Seabury Press.

Cragg, Kenneth. 1968. *The Privilege of Man*. London: The Athlone Press, University of London.

Cronk, Lee. 1991. "Communications as Manipulation: Implications for Biosociological Research." Paper delivered at the annual meetings of the American Sociological Association.

Csikszentmihalyi, Mihaly. 1987. "On the Relationship between Cultural Evolution and Human Welfare." Paper delivered before the American Association for the Advancement of Science, February 1987, Chicago.

———. 1991. "Consciousness for the Twenty-First Century." *Zygon: Journal of Religion and Science* 26 (March): 7–26.

———. 1993. *Tomorrow's Mind*. San Francisco: Harper Collins.

Csikszentmihalyi, Mihaly, and Fausto Massimini. 1985. "On the Psychological Selection of Bio-Cultural Information." *New Ideas in Psychology* 3: 115–38.

d'Aquili, Eugene. 1978. "The Neurobiological Bases of Myth and Concepts of Deity." *Zygon: Journal of Religion and Science* 13 (December): 257–75.

———. 1983. "The Myth-Ritual Complex: A Biogenetic Structural Analysis." *Zygon: Journal of Religion and Science* 18 (September): 247–69.

———. 1993. "Apologia pro Scriptura Sua: Or, Maybe We Got It Right after All." *Zygon: Journal of Religion and Science* 28 (June).

d'Aquili, Eugene, and C. Laughlin. 1975. "The Biopsychological Determinants of Religious Ritual Behavior." *Zygon: Journal of Religion and Science* 10 (March): 32–58.

Dawkins, Richard. 1978. *The Selfish Gene*. London: Granada.

———. 1986. *The Blind Watchmaker: Why the Evidence of Evolution Reveals a Universe without Design*. New York: W. W. Norton & Co.

Deacon, Terrence. W. 1990a. "Brain-Language Coevolution." In *The Evolution of Human Languages,* ed. J. A. Hawkins and M. Gell-Mann. SFI Studies in the Sciences of Complexity, Proc. Vol. X.

———. 1990b. "Rethinking Mammalian Brain Evolution." *American Zoologist* 30: 629–705.

Dobzhansky, Theodosius. 1956. *The Biological Basis of Human Freedom*. New York: Columbia Univ. Press.

Doty, William G. 1986. *Mythography: The Study of Myths and Rituals*. University, AL: Univ. of Alabama Press.

Dunbar, R. I. M. 1982. "Adaptation, Fitness, and the Evolutionary Tautology." In *Current Problems in Sociobiology,* ed. King's College Sociobiology Group, 9–28. Cambridge: Univ. Press.

Eaves, Lindon. 1989. "Spirit, Method, and Content in Science and Religion:

The Theological Perspective of a Geneticist." *Zygon: Journal of Religion and Science* 24 (June): 185–215.

———. 1991. "Adequacy or Orthodoxy? Choosing Sides at the Frontier." *Zygon: Journal of Religion and Science* 26 (December): 495–503.

Eaves, Lindon, and Lora Gross. 1992. "Exploring the Concept of Spirit as a Model for the God-World Relationship in the Age of Genetics." *Zygon: Journal of Religion and Science* 27 (September): 261–87.

Eigen, Manfred, and Ruthild Winkler. 1981. *Laws of the Game*. New York: Harper and Row.

Eliade, Mircea. 1959. *Cosmos and History: The Myth of the Eternal Return*. New York: Harper and Bros.

———. 1963. *Patterns in Comparative Religion*. Cleveland: Meridian Books, World Publishing Co.

———. 1967. "Cultural Fashions and the History of Religions." In *The History of Religions. Essays on the Problem of Understanding,* ed. Joseph Kitagawa, 21–38. Chicago: Univ. of Chicago Press.

Emerson, Alfred E. 1943. "Ecology, Evolution, and Society." *American Naturalist* 77: 117–18.

Engel, J. Ronald, and Joan Gibb Engel. 1990. *Ethics of Environment: Global Challenge and International Response*. London: Belhaven Press.

Erikson, Erik H. 1969. *Gandhi's Truth: On the Origins of Militant Nonviolence*. New York: W. W. Norton & Co.

Fine, Arthur. 1986. "Unnatural Attitudes: Realist and Instrumental Attachments to Science." *Mind* 95: 149–79.

Flam, Faye. 1992. "COBE Sows Cosmological Confusion." *Science* 257 (3 July): 28–30.

Fletcher, Joseph. 1966. *Situation Ethics*. Philadelphia: Westminster Press.

Freeman, L. G. 1987. "Meanders on the Byways of Paleolithic Art." In *Altamira Revisited and Other Essays on Early Art,* ed. L. G. Freeman, et al., 15–66. Chicago: Institute for Prehistoric Investigations.

Freeman, L. G., F. Bernaldo de Quiros, and J. Ogden. 1987. "Animals, Faces and Space at Altamira: A Restudy of the Final Gallery ('Cola de Caballo')." In *Altamira Revisited and Other Essays on Early Art,* ed. L. G. Freeman, et al., 179–247. Chicago: Institute for Prehistoric Investigations.

Freeman, L. G., and J. Gonzalez Echegaray. 1987. "Spatial Organization in Religious Symbolism: Searching for Models in the Northern Spanish Romanesque." In *Altamira Revisited and Other Essays on Early Art,* ed. L. G. Freeman, et al., 129–77. Chicago: Institute for Prehistoric Investigations.

Fuerst, Wesley. 1992. "Creation Themes from the Old Testament." Unpublished paper delivered at the Created-Co-Creator Conference, 24 April 1992, St. Luke's Lutheran Church, Chicago.

Gates, Henry Louis, Jr. 1988. *The Signifying Monkey: A Theory of Afro-American Literary Criticism*. New York: Oxford Univ. Press.

Geertz, Clifford. 1973. *The Interpretation of Cultures*. New York: Basic Books.

Ghiselin, Michael. 1974. *The Economy of Nature and the Evolution of Sex*. Berkeley: Univ. of California Press.

Gilkey, Langdon. 1970. *Religion and the Scientific Future: Reflections on Myth, Science and Technology*. New York: Harper & Row.

———. 1981. *Society and the Sacred: Toward a Theology of Culture in Decline*. New York: Crossroad.

———. 1985. *Creationism on Trial: Evolution and God at Little Rock*. Minneapolis: Winston Press.

Gigerenzer, G., et al. 1989. *The Empire of Chance: How Probability Changed Science and Everyday Life*. Cambridge: Cambridge Univ. Press.

Goldsmith, Timothy H. 1991. *The Biological Roots of Human Nature. Forging Links between Evolution and Behavior*. New York: Oxford Univ. Press.

Goodenough, Ursula, and Loyal Rue. 1992. "The End of Theology, the Beginning of Religion." Paper delivered at a session of the Chicago Advanced Seminar in Religion and Science, 18 May 1992.

Goodenough, Ward. 1988. "Self-Maintenance as a Religious Concern." *Zygon: Journal of Religion and Science* 23 (June): 117–28.

———. 1992. "Belief, Practice and Religion." *Zygon: Journal of Religion and Science* 27 (September): 287–95.

Gould, S. J., and R. Lewontin. 1979. "The Spandrels of San Marco and the Panglossian Paradigm: A Critique of the Adaptationist Programme." *Proceedings of the Royal Society of London* B205: 581–98.

Graham, Jorie. 1980. *Hybrids of Plants and of Ghosts*. Princeton, NJ: Princeton Univ. Press.

———. 1983. *Erosion*. Princeton, NJ: Princeton Univ. Press.

Greeley, Andrew. 1988. "Imagination as a Rag Picker." In *Andrew Greeley's World: An Anthology of Critical Essays 1986–1988,* ed. Ingrid Shafer. New York: Warner Books.

———. 1989. *Myths of Religion*. New York: Warner Books.

———. 1991. "The Pragmatics of Prayer." Paper delivered at the annual meeting of the Inter-University Consortium for Political and Social Research, 26 October 1991, Ann Arbor, MI.

Gregorios, Paulos Mar. 1988. *Cosmic Man the Divine Presence: The Theology of St. Gregory of Nyssa*. New York: Paragon House.

Green, Ronald. 1988. *Religion and Moral Reason*. New York: Oxford Univ. Press.

Griffin, David Ray. 1976. *God, Power, and Evil: A Process Theodicy*. Philadelphia: Westminster Press.

Grimes, Ronald. 1990. *Ritual Criticism*. Tuscaloosa: Univ. of Alabama Press.

Gustafson, James M. 1978. "Theology Confronts Technology and the Life Sciences." *Commonweal* (16 June): 386–92.

———. 1981, 1984. *Ethics from a Theocentric Perspective*. 2 vols. Chicago: Univ. of Chicago Press.

———. 1990. "Explaining and Valuing: An Exchange between Theology and the Human Sciences." Tempe: Department of Religious Studies, Arizona State Univ.

————. 1991. "Theological Anthropology and the Human Sciences." In *Theology at the End of Modernity,* ed. Sheila Greeve Davaney. Philadelphia: Trinity Press International.

Habermas, Jürgen. 1971. *Knowledge and Human Interests.* Boston: Beacon Press.

Harding, Sandra, ed. 1987. *Feminism and Methodology: Social Science Issues.* Bloomington: Indiana Univ. Press.

Hardy, Edward Rochie. 1954. *Christology of the Later Fathers.* Philadelphia: Westminster Press.

Harlow, H. F., and M. K. Harlow. 1969. "Effects of Various Mother-Infant Relationships on Rhesus Monkey Behaviors." In *Determinants of Infant Behavior,* vol. 4, ed. B. M. Foss. London: Methuen.

Hefner, Philip. 1970. "The Relocation of the God Question." *Zygon: Journal of Religion and Science* 5 (March): 5–17.

————. 1973. "The Self-Definition of Life and Human Purpose: Reflections upon the Divine Spirit and Human Spirit." *Zygon: Journal of Religion and Science* 8 (September): 395–411.

————. 1975. "Dogmatic Statements and the Identity of the Christian Community." In *The Gospel as History,* ed. Vilmos Vajta, 202–46. Philadelphia: Fortress.

————. 1976. "The Foundations of Belonging in a Christian Worldview." In *Belonging and Alienation: Religious Foundations for the Human Future,* eds. Philip Hefner and Widick Schroeder, 161–80. Chicago: Center for the Scientific Study of Religion.

————. 1979. "Is Theodicy a Question of Power?" *Journal of Religion* 59: 87–95.

————. 1980a. "The Cultural Significance of Jesus' Death and Sacrifice." *Journal of Religion* 60 (October): 411–39.

————. 1980b. "Survival as a Human Value." *Zygon: Journal of Religion and Science* 15 (June): 411–39.

————. 1981. "Is/Ought: A Risky Relationship between Theology and Science." In *The Sciences and Theology in the Twentieth Century,* ed. A. R. Peacocke, 58–78. Notre Dame, IN: Univ. of Notre Dame Press.

————. 1984a. "The Creation." In *Christian Dogmatics,* vol. 1, ed. Carl E. Braaten and Robert W. Jenson, 269–357. Philadelphia: Fortress.

————. 1984b. "Creation: Viewed by Science, Affirmed by Faith." In *Cry of the Environment: Rebuilding the Christian Creation Tradition,* ed. Philip N. Joranson and Ken Butigan, 198–217. Santa Fe, NM: Bear and Co.

————. 1984c. "God and Chaos: The Demi-Urge vs. the Ungrund." *Zygon: Journal of Religion and Science* 19 (December): 469–86.

————. 1984d. "Sociobiology, Ethics, and Theology." *Zygon: Journal of Religion and Science* 19 (June): 85–207.

————. 1985. "Just How Much May We Intimate about Reality? A Response to Arthur Peacocke." *Religion & Intellectual Life* 2 (Summer) 4: 32–38.

————. 1987a. "Can a Theology of Nature be Coherent with Scientific Cosmology?" In *Evolution and Creation: A European Perspective,* ed. Svend Andersen and Arthur Peacocke, 141–51. Aarhus: Aarhus Univ. Press.

————. 1987b. "Theology in the Context of Science, Liberation, and Christian Tradition." In *Worldviews and Warrants,* ed. William Schweiker and Per Anderson, 33–49. Lanham, MD: Univ. Press of America.

————. 1988a. "The Evolution of the Created Co-Creator." In *Cosmos as Creation,* ed. Ted Peters, 211–34. Nashville: Abingdon Press.

————. 1988b. "The Role of Science in Pannenberg's Theological Thinking." In *The Theology of Wolfhart Pannenberg,* ed. Carl Braaten and Philip Clayton, 266–86. Minneapolis: Augsburg Publishing House.

————. 1988c. "Theology's Truth and Scientific Formulation." *Zygon: Journal of Religion and Science* 23 (September): 263–80.

————. 1991. "Myth and Morality: The Love Command." *Zygon: Journal of Religion and Science* 26 (March): 115–36.

————. 1992. "Nature's History as Our History: A Proposal for Spirituality." In *After Nature's Revolt: Eco-Justice and Theology,* ed. Dieter T. Hessel. Philadelphia: Fortress Press: 171–83.

Hegel, G. F. W. 1969. *Hegel's Science of Logic.* Trans. A. V. Miller. London: George Allen and Unwin.

————. 1977. *Phenomenology of Spirit.* Trans. A. V. Miller. Oxford: Clarendon Press.

Heidegger, Martin. 1977. *The Question concerning Technology and Other Essays.* Trans. W. Lovitt. New York: Harper and Row.

Hertz, Joseph H. 1975. *The Authorized Daily Prayer Book.* New York: Bloch Publishing Co.

Hesse, Mary. 1981. "Retrospect." In A. R. Peacocke, ed. *The Sciences and Theology in the Twentieth Century.* Notre Dame, IN: Univ. of Notre Dame Press, 281–95.

Hick, John. 1981. "An Irenaean Theodicy." In *Encountering Evil,* ed. Stephen Davis, 39–68. Atlanta: John Knox.

Hlasko, Marek. 1958. *The Eighth Day of the Week.* New York: E. P. Dutton and Co.

Hofstadter, Douglas R. 1980. *Gödel, Escher, and Bach: An Eternal Golden Braid.* New York: Vintage Books.

Holmes, Rodney. 1991. "Did *Homo Religiosus* Emerge from the Evolution of the Brain?" *Insights: The Magazine of the Chicago Center for Religion and Science* 3 (June): 10–14.

Hopkins, Gerard Manley. 1953. *Poems and Prose of Gerard Manley Hopkins.* Selected and with an introduction by W. H. Gardner. Baltimore: Penguin Books.

Hrdy, Sarah Blaffer. 1988. "Comments on George Williams's Essay on Morality and Nature." *Zygon: Journal of Religion and Science* 23 (December): 409–11.

Inter-Lutheran Commission on Worship. 1978. *Lutheran Book of Worship*. Philadelphia: Board of Publication, Lutheran Church in America.

Irons, William. 1991. "Where Did Morality Come From?" *Zygon: Journal of Religion and Science* 26 (March): 49–90.

———. 1992a. "Comments on Hefner's 'Altruism and Christian Love.'" Personal communication, 25 May 1992.

———. 1992b. "Theories to Explain Altruism from Sociobiology." Lecture delivered at the symposium on altruism, 4 April 1992, at the Evangelical Academy, Loccum, Germany.

———. 1993. "Are There Any Moral Absolutes?" Paper delivered at the annual meeting of the American Association for the Advancement of Science, 15 February 1993, Boston.

Jay, Martin. 1973. *The Dialectical Imagination: A History of the Frankfurt School and the Institute of Social Research 1923–1950*. Boston: Little Brown and Co.

Jaynes, Julian. 1977. *The Origin of Consciousness in the Breakdown of the Bicameral Mind*. Boston: Houghton Mifflin.

Jelinek, Arthur J. 1988. "Technology, Typology, and Culture in the Middle Paleolithic." In *Upper Pleiostocene Prehistory of Western Eurasia*, ed. Harold L. Dibbler and Anta Montet-White, 199–212. Philadelphia: Univ. Museum, Univ. of Pennsylvania.

Jenni, Ernst, and Claus Westermann, eds. 1976. *Theologisches Handwörterbuch zum Alten Testament*, vol. 2. Munich: Chr. Kaiser Verlag.

Jenson, Robert W. 1982. *The Triune Identity*. Philadelphia: Fortress Press.

Jerrison, Harry J. 1976. "Paleoneurology and the Evolution of Mind." *Scientific American* (January): 3–16.

Jowett, B. 1937. *The Dialogues of Plato*, 2 vols. Trans. Benjamin Jowett. New York: Random House.

Jüngel, Eberhard. 1976. *The Doctrine of the Trinity*. Trans. Horton Harris. Edinburgh: Scottish Academic Press.

———. 1983. *God as the Mystery of the World*. Trans. Darrell Guder. Grand Rapids, MI: Wm. B. Eerdmans Publishing Co.

Katz, Solomon H. 1980. "Biocultural Evolution and the Is/Ought Relationship." *Zygon: Journal of Religion and Science* 15 (June): 155–68.

———. 1989. "Toward a New Concept of Global Morality." Paper delivered at the Year 2000 and Beyond Conference of the Evangelical Lutheran Church in America, 31 March 1989, St. Charles, IL.

———. 1991. "The Emerging Shape of Our Agenda: A Model of Secular Morality." Paper delivered at the symposium, "Human Viability and a World Theology," sponsored by *Zygon* and the Chicago Center for Religion and Science, 16 November 1991, Chicago.

———. 1992. "An Evolutionary Theory of Cuisine." *Human Nature* 1, no. 3: 233–39.

———. 1993. "Exploring the Model of Biocultural Evolution." Paper delivered at the 159th National Meeting of the American Association for the Advancement of Science, Boston, 15 February 1993.

Katz, S. H., and J. Schall. 1979. "Fava Bean Consumption and Biocultural Evolution." *Medical Anthropology* 3: 459–76.

Kaufman, Gordon. 1985. *Theology for a Nuclear Age.* Philadelphia: Westminster Press.

———. 1991. "Foreword." In *Theology at the End of Modernity: Essays in Honor of Gordon Kaufman,* ed. Sheila Greeve Davaney, ix–xii. Philadelphia: Trinity International Press.

———. 1992. "Nature, History, and God: Toward an Integrated Conceptualization." *Zygon: Journal of Religion and Science* 27 (December): 379–401.

———. 1993. *In Face of Mystery: A Constructive Theology.* Cambridge, MA: Harvard Univ. Press.

Klein, Richard. 1989. *The Human Career: Human Biological and Cultural Origins.* Chicago: Univ. of Chicago Press.

Knorr-Cetina, Karin. 1981. *The Manufacture of Knowledge: An Essay on the Constructivist and Contextual Nature of Science.* New York: Pergamon Press.

———. 1983. "The Ethnographic Study of Scientific Work: Towards a Constructivist Interpretation of Science." In *Science Observed: Perspectives on the Social Study of Science,* ed. Karin D. Knorr-Cetina and Michael Mulkay, 115–40. London: Sage Publications.

Kohlberg, Lawrence. 1969. "Strategy and Sequence: The Cognitive Developmental Approach to Socialization." In *Handbook of Socialization Theory and Research,* ed. D. Goslin, 347–480. Chicago: Rand McNally.

Kolakowski, Leszek. 1989. *The Presence of Myth.* Chicago: Univ. of Chicago Press.

Kroeber, A. L. 1952. "Sign and Symbol in Bee Communities." *Proceedings of the National Academy of Science* 38: 753–57.

Kroeber, A. L., and C. Kluckhohn. 1952. "Culture, a Critical Review of the Concepts and Definitions." Papers of the Peabody Museum of American Archaeology and Ethnology 47 (1): 1–223.

Kuhn, Thomas. 1970. *The Structure of Scientific Revolutions,* 2d ed. Chicago: Univ. of Chicago Press.

La Barre, Weston. 1954. *The Human Animal.* Chicago: Univ. of Chicago Press.

LaCugna, Catherine Mowry. 1991. *God for Us: The Trinity and Christian Life.* San Francisco: Harper.

Lakatos, Imre. 1978. *The Methodology of Scientific Research Programmes.* Cambridge: Cambridge Univ. Press.

Laming-Emperaire, Annette. 1962. *La Signification de l'Art Rupestre Paleolithique.* Paris: A. et J. Picard.

Laughlin, Charles D., John McManus, and Eugene d'Aquili. 1990. *Brain, Symbol & Experience: Toward a Neurophenomenology of Human Consciousness.* New York: Columbia Univ. Press.

Lerner, Gerda. 1986. *The Creation of Patriarchy.* New York: Oxford Univ. Press.

Leroi-Gourhan, Andre. 1967. *Treasures of Prehistoric Art.* New York: Harry N. Abrams, Inc.

———. 1982. "La grotte du renne a Arcy-sur-Cure." In *Les habitats du Paleolithique superieur,* vol. 1, ed. J. Combier, 235–40. Paris: CNRS.

———. 1984. *Arte y grafismo en la Europa prehistorica.* Madrid: Istmo.

Leroi-Gourhan, Arlette, Allain, et al. 1979. *Lascaux Inconnu.* Paris: Presses Universitaires de France.

Levin, Michael. 1989. "Ethics Courses: Useless." *New York Times* (25 November): 15.

Lewin, Roger. 1989. *Human Evolution.* Boston: Blackwell Scientific Publications.

Lindbeck, George. 1984. *The Nature of Doctrine: Religion and Theology in a Postliberal Age.* Philadelphia: Westminster Press.

Long, Charles. 1963. *Alpha, the Myths of Creation.* New York: George Braziller.

———. 1967. "Archaism and Hermeneutics." In *The History of Religions. Essays on the Problem of Understanding,* ed. Joseph Kitagawa, 67–88. Chicago: Univ. of Chicago Press.

Lotz, David. 1974. *Ritschl and Luther.* Nashville: Abingdon Press.

MacIntyre, Alasdair. 1967. "Egoism and Altruism." In *Encyclopedia of Philosophy,* vol. 1, 462–66. New York: Macmillan and the Free Press.

———. 1984. *After Virtue: A Study in Moral Theory,* 2d ed. Notre Dame, IN: Univ. of Notre Dame Press.

MacLean, Paul. 1973. "The Brain's Generation Gap: Some Human Implications." *Zygon: Journal of Religion and Science* 8 (March): 113–27.

McFague, Sallie. 1985. *Metaphorical Theology: Models of God in Religious Language,* 2d printing with new preface. Philadelphia: Fortress Press.

———. 1987. *Models of God.* Philadelphia: Fortress Press.

McMullin, Ernan. 1991. "Plantinga's Defense of Special Creation." *Christian Scholar's Review* 21 (September): 55–79. Reprinted in *Zygon: Journal of Religion and Science* 28 (September 1993): 3.

Martin, Calvin Luther. 1992. *In the Spirit of the Earth: Rethinking History and Time.* Baltimore: Johns Hopkins Univ. Press.

Mayr, Ernst. 1988. *Toward a New Philosophy of Biology: Observations of an Evolutionist.* Cambridge, MA: Belknap Press.

Midgley, Mary. 1980. *Beast and Man.* Ithaca, NY: Cornell Univ. Press.

Mulkay, Michael. 1979. *Science and the Sociology of Knowledge.* London: George Allen and Unwin.

Murphy, Nancey. 1988. "From Critical Realism to a Methodological Approach: Response to Robbins, Van Huyssteen, and Hefner." *Zygon: Journal of Religion and Science* 23 (September): 287–90.

———. 1990a. "Scientific Realism and Postmodern Philosophy." *British Journal of the Philosophy of Science* 41: 291–303.

———. 1990b. *Theology in the Age of Scientific Reasoning.* Ithaca, NY: Cornell Univ. Press.

————. 1993. "The Limits of Pragmatism and the Limits of Realism." *Zygon: Journal of Religion and Science* 28 (September).

Nasr, Seyyed Hossein. 1968. *The Encounter of Man and Nature.* London: George Allen and Unwin.

Niebuhr, Reinhold. 1949. *The Nature and Destiny of Man.* New York: Charles Scribner's Sons.

Norris, Richard A. 1965. *God and World in Early Christian Theology.* New York: Seabury Press.

Nowell-Smith, Patrick H. 1967. "Religion and Morality." In *Encyclopedia of Philosophy,* vol. 7, 150. New York: Macmillan and the Free Press.

Nygren, Anders. 1953. *Agape and Eros.* London: SPCK.

Ode, Philip E. 1994. "Past and Present Views on the Unity of All Life on Planet Earth." *Zygon: Journal of Religion and Science,* in press.

Ogden, Schubert. M. 1966. *The Reality of God and Other Essays.* New York: Harper & Row.

Pagels, Elaine. 1988. *Adam, Eve, and the Serpent.* New York: Vintage Books.

Pannenberg, Wolfhart. 1968. *Jesus—God and Man.* Trans. Lewis L. Wilkins and Duane A. Priebe. Philadelphia: Westminster Press.

————. 1976. *Theology and the Philosophy of Science.* Trans. Francis McDonagh. Philadelphia: Westminster Press.

————. 1985. *Anthropology in Theological Perspective.* Trans. Matthew J. O'Connell. Philadelphia: Westminster Press.

————. 1991. *Systematic Theology,* vol. 1. Trans. Geoffrey W. Bromily. Grand Rapids, MI: W. B. Eerdmans Publishing Co.

Peacocke, Arthur. 1971. *Science and the Christian Experiment.* London: Oxford Univ. Press.

————. 1976. "Reductionism: A Review of the Epistemological Issues and Their Relevance to Biology and the Problem of Consciousness." *Zygon: Journal of Religion and Science* 11 (September): 306–34.

————. 1979. *Creation and the World of Science.* Oxford: Clarendon Press.

————. 1984. *Intimations of Reality: Critical Realism in Science and Religion.* Notre Dame, IN: Univ. of Notre Dame Press.

————. 1986. *God and the New Biology.* London: Dent.

————. 1990. *Theology for a Scientific Age: Being and Becoming—Natural and Divine.* Oxford: Basil Blackwell.

Pelikan, Jaroslav. 1960. "Creation and Causality in the History of Christian Thought." In *Issues in Evolution,* ed. Sol Tax and Charles Callender, 29–40. Chicago: Univ. of Chicago Press.

————. 1971. *The Christian Tradition: Volume 1—The Emergence of the Catholic Tradition (100–600).* Chicago: Univ. of Chicago Press.

————. 1988. *The Melody of Theology: A Philosophical Dictionary.* Cambridge, MA: Harvard Univ. Press.

Peters, Karl. 1982. "Religion and an Evolutionary Theory of Knowledge." *Zygon: Journal of Religion and Science* 17 (December): 285–415.

———. 1989. "Humanity in Nature: Conserving Yet Creating." *Zygon: Journal of Religion and Science* 24 (December): 469–85.

———. 1992. "Story Tellers and Scenario Spinners: Some Reflections on Religion and Science in Light of an Evolutionary Theory of Knowledge." Paper delivered 13 April 1992 at a session of the Chicago Advanced Seminar in Religion and Science.

Peters, Ted. 1991. "Review of Viggo Mortensen and Robert C. Sorensen (eds.), *Free Will and Determinism.*" *Zygon: Journal of Religion and Science* 26 (March): 178–80.

Pfeiffer, John. 1982. *The Creative Explosion: An Inquiry into the Origins of Art and Religion.* Ithaca, NY: Cornell Univ. Press.

Piaget, Jean. 1932. *The Moral Judgment of the Child.* Glencoe, IL: Free Press.

Placher, William. 1989. *Unapologetic Theology: A Christian Voice in a Pluralistic Conversation.* Louisville, KY: Westminster/John Knox Press.

Plaskow, Judith. 1980. *Sex, Sin, and Grace: Women's Experience and the Theologies of Reinhold Niebuhr and Paul Tillich.* Lanham, MD: University Press of America.

Polanyi, Michael. 1966. *The Tacit Dimension.* Garden City, NY: Doubleday.

Polkinghorne, John. 1988. *Science and Creation: The Search for Understanding.* London: SPCK.

———. 1989. *Science and Providence: God's Interaction with the World.* Boston: Shambhala.

Popper, Karl. 1972a. *The Logic of Scientific Discovery.* London: Hutchinson.

———. 1972b. *Objective Knowledge; An Evolutionary Approach.* Oxford: Clarendon Press.

Potter, Van Rensselaer. 1988. *Global Bioethics: Building on the Leopold Legacy.* East Lansing: Michigan State Univ. Press.

———. 1992. "Global Bioethics as a Secular Source of Moral Authority for Long-Term Human Survival." *Global Bioethics* 1 (1): 5–11.

Preus, J. Samuel. 1987. *Explaining Religion: Criticism and Theory from Bodin to Freud.* New Haven: Yale Univ. Press.

Prigogine, Ilya. 1980. *Order out of Chaos.* New York: Bantam.

Pugh, George Edgin. 1977. *The Biological Origin of Human Values.* New York: Basic Books.

Rahman, Fazlur. 1980. *Major Themes of the Qur'an.* Minneapolis: Bibliotheca Islamica.

Ravetz, Jerome R. 1971. *Scientific Knowledge and Its Social Problems.* New York: Oxford Univ. Press.

Richards, Robert J. 1987. *Darwin and the Emergence of Evolutionary Theories of Mind and Behavior.* Chicago: Univ. of Chicago Press.

Richerson, Peter J. 1992. "Evolution of Social Organization." Paper delivered at the symposium on altruism, 2–5 April 1992, at the Evangelical Academy, Loccum, Germany.

Ricoeur, Paul. 1967. *The Symbolism of Evil.* New York: Beacon Press.

———. 1974. *The Conflict of Interpretations*. Evanston, IL: Northwestern Univ. Press.

———. 1981. *Hermeneutics and the Human Sciences*. Cambridge: Cambridge Univ. Press.

Rolston III, Holmes. 1987. *Science and Religion: A Critical Survey*. New York: Random House.

Rouse, Joseph. 1991. "The Politics of Postmodern Philosophy of Science." *Philosophy of Science* 58: 607–27.

Rue, Loyal. 1989. *Amythia: Crisis in the Natural History of Western Culture*. Tuscaloosa: Univ. of Alabama Press.

Ruether, Rosemary Radford. 1983. *Sexism and God-Talk: Toward a Feminist Theology*. Boston: Beacon Press.

Ruse, Michael. 1979a. *The Darwinian Revolution: Science Red in Tooth and Claw*. Chicago: Univ. of Chicago Press.

———. 1979b. *Sociobiology: Sense or Nonsense?* Boston: D. Reidel.

———. 1986a. "Evolutionary Ethics: A Phoenix Arisen." *Zygon: Journal of Religion and Science* 21 (March): 95–112.

———. 1986b. *Taking Darwin Seriously: A Naturalistic Approach to Philosophy*. Oxford: Basil Blackwell.

———. 1988. "Response to Williams: Selfishness is not Enough," *Zygon: Journal of Religion and Science* 23 (December): 413–16.

Russell, Robert John, William Stoeger, and George Coyne, eds. 1988. *Physics, Philosophy, and Theology: A Common Quest for Understanding*. Vatican City State: Vatican Observatory.

Santmire, Paul. 1985. *The Travail of Nature: The Ambiguous Ecological Promise of Christian Theology*. Philadelphia: Fortress Press.

Schleiermacher, Friedrich. 1928. *The Christian Faith*. Edinburgh: T. & T. Clark.

Schmid, Heinrich, 1899. *The Doctrinal Theology of the Evangelical Lutheran Church*. Minneapolis: Augsburg Publishing House.

Schmitz-Moormann, Karl. 1987. "On the Evolution of Human Freedom." *Zygon: Journal of Religion and Science* 22 (December): 443–58.

———. 1992. "Theology in an Evolutionary Mode." *Zygon: Journal of Religion and Science* 27 (June): 133–51.

Schreiter, Robert. 1985. *Constructing Local Theologies*. Maryknoll, NY: Orbis Books.

Schroeder, H. J., trans. 1960. *Canons and Decrees of the Council of Trent*. St. Louis: B. Herder Book Co.

Schüssler-Fiorenza, Elisabeth. 1983. *In Memory of Her: A Feminist Theological Reconstruction of Christian Origins*. New York: Crossroad.

Segal, Robert A. 1990. "Misconceptions of the Social Sciences." *Zygon: Journal of Religion and Science* 25 (September): 263–78.

Shafer, Ingrid, ed. 1988. *Andrew Greeley's World: An Anthology of Critical Essays 1986–1988*. New York: Warner Books.

———. 1989. "Non-Adversarial Criticism, Cross-Cultural Conversation and Popular Literature." *Proteus* 6 (1): 6–15.

———. 1991. "The Catholic Imagination in Popular Film and Television." *Journal of Popular Film and Television* 19 (Summer) 2: 50–57.

Shweder, Richard A. 1991. *Thinking through Cultures: Expeditions in Cultural Psychology.* Cambridge, MA: Harvard Univ. Press.

Shweder, Richard A., and Robert A. LeVine. 1984. *Culture Theory: Essays on Mind, Self, and Emotion.* Cambridge: Cambridge Univ. Press.

Singer, Peter. 1981. *The Expanding Circle: Ethics and Sociobiology.* New York: New American Library.

Sittler, Joseph. 1961. *The Ecology of Faith.* Philadelphia: Muhlenberg press.

———. 1962. "Called to Unity." *Ecumenical Review* 14: 177–187. References are to its reprinted form, *Currents in Theology and Mission* 16 (February 1989) 1: 5–13.

———. 1972. *Essays on Nature and Grace.* Philadelphia: Fortress Press.

———. 1978. "The Sittler Speeches." In *Center for the Study of Campus Ministry Yearbook, 1977–78.*

Smith, John Maynard. 1982. "Introduction" and "The Evolution of Social Behavior—A Classification of Models." In *Current Problems in Sociobiology,* ed. King's College Sociobiology Group. Cambridge: Cambridge Univ. Press.

Smith, Norman Kemp, trans. 1958. *Immanuel Kant's Critique of Pure Reason.* New York: St. Martin's Press.

Sperry, Roger. 1983. *Science and Moral Priority.* New York: Columbia Univ. Press.

———. 1987. "The Science-Values Relation: Impact of the Consciousness Revolution." In *Religion, Science and the Search for Wisdom,* ed. David M. Byers, 110–18. Washington, DC: United States Catholic Conference, Inc.

———. 1990. "Search for Beliefs to Live by Consistent with Science." *Zygon: Journal of Religion and Science* 26 (June) 2: 237–58.

Stent, Gunther, ed. 1980. *Morality as a Biological Phenomenon.* Berkeley: Univ. of California Press.

Stevens, Anthony. 1983. *Archetypes: A Natural History of the Self.* New York: Morrow.

Stevens, Wallace. 1954. *The Collected Poems of Wallace Stevens.* New York: Vintage Books.

Stoeckle, Bernhard. 1962. *Gratia Supponit Naturam: Geschichte und Analyse eines Theologischen Axioms.* Rome: Pontifical Institute of St. Anselm.

Sullivan, Lawrence E. 1988. *Icanchu's Drum: An Orientation to Meaning in South American Religions.* New York: Macmillan Publishing Co.

Swinburne, Richard. 1977. *The Coherence of Theism.* Oxford: Clarendon Press.

Tappert, Theodore G., ed. 1959. *The Book of Concord: The Confessions of the Evangelical Lutheran Church.* Philadelphia: Fortress Press.

Tavard, George H. 1981. *The Vision of the Trinity.* Lanham, MD: University Press of America.

Teilhard de Chardin, Pierre. 1964. *The Future of Man.* New York: Harper & Row.

Theissen, Gerd. 1985. *Biblical Faith: An Evolutionary Approach.* Philadelphia: Fortress Press.

Tillich, Paul. 1936. "The Demonic." In *The Interpretation of History*, 77–122. New York: Charles Scribner's Sons.

———. 1948. "You Are Accepted." In *The Shaking of the Foundations*, 153–63. New York: Charles Scribner's Sons.

———. 1951. *Systematic Theology*, vol. 1. Chicago: Univ. of Chicago Press.

———. 1957a. *Dynamics of Faith*. New York: Harper & Bros.

———. 1957b. *Systematic Theology*, vol. 2. Chicago: Univ. of Chicago.

———. 1958. "The Religious Symbol," *Daedalus:* (Summer) 3–21.

———. 1959. *Theology of Culture*. Ed. Robert C. Kimball. New York: Oxford Univ. Press.

———. 1963. *Systematic Theology*, vol. 3. Chicago: Univ. of Chicago.

Tipler, Frank J. 1989. "The Omega Point as *Eschaton:* Answers to Pannenberg's Questions for Scientists." *Zygon: Journal of Religion and Science* 24: (June) 217–53.

Toulmin, Stephen. 1977. "Back to Nature." *New York Review of Books* 9 (June): 3–4.

Tracy David, and John B. Cobb, Jr. 1983. *Talking About God: Doing Theology in the Context of Modern Pluralism*. New York: Seabury Press.

Trivers, R. L. 1971. "The Evolution of Reciprocal Altruism." *Quarterly Review of Biology* 46 (4): 35–37.

Turner, Victor. 1983. "Body, Brain and Culture." *Zygon: Journal of Religion and Science* 18: (June) 221–45.

van der Leeuw, Gerardus. 1957. "Primordial Time and Final Time." In *Man and Time,* ed. J. Campbell, vol. 3 of *Papers from the Eranos Yearbooks*. New York: Pantheon Books.

———. 1963. *Religion in Essence and Manifestation*, 2 vols. Trans. J. E. Turner, with appendices by Hans H. Penner. New York: Harper Torchbooks.

van Huyssteen, Wentzel. 1989. *Theology and the Justification of Faith: Constructing Theories in Systematic Theology*. Grand Rapids, MI: Wm. B. Eerdmanns.

———. 1992. "Van Huyssteen Response to Robbins: Does the Postfoundationalist Have to Be a Pragmatist?" *Zygon: Journal of Religion and Science* 27 (December): 455–56.

Vööbus, Arthur. 1964. "Theological Reflections on Human Nature in Ancient Syrian Tradition." In *The Scope of Grace,* ed. Philip Hefner, 99–119. Philadelphia: Fortress Press.

Wald, George. 1965. "Determinacy, Individuality, and the Problem of Free Will." In *New Views of the Nature of Man,* ed. John R. Platt, 16–46. Chicago: Univ. of Chicago Press.

Weinberg, Steven. 1977. *The First Three Minutes*. New York: Basic Books.

Westermann, Claus. 1974. *Creation*. Philadelphia: Fortress Press.

———. 1980. *Genesis,* vol. 1, *Biblischer Kommentar, Altes Testament*. Neukirchen: Neukirchener Verlag.

White, Jr., Lynn. 1967. "The Historical Roots of Our Ecologic Crisis." *Science* 155: 1203–1297. I quote from the reprinted version in *The Subversive Science:*

Essays toward an Ecology of Man, 341–50, ed. Paul Shepard and Daniel McKinley, Boston: Houghton Mifflin Co., 1967.

Whitehead, Alfred North. 1933. *Adventures of Ideas.* New York: Macmillan Publishing Co.

———. 1978. *Process and Reality: An Essay in Cosmology.* Corrected ed. New York: Free Press.

Wicken, Jeffrey. 1987. *Evolution, Thermodynamics, and Information: Extending the Darwinian Program.* New York: Oxford Univ. Press.

———. 1989. "Toward an Evolutionary Ecology of Meaning." *Zygon: Journal of Religion and Science* 24 (June): 153–84.

Wieman, Henry Nelson. 1946. *The Source of Human Good.* Chicago: Univ. of Chicago Press.

Wilbur, Richard. 1988. *New and Collected Poems.* New York: Harcourt Brace Jovanovich.

Wildiers, Max. 1982. *The Theologian and His Universe.* New York: Seabury Press.

Wilken, Robert. 1971. *The Myth of Christian Beginnings.* Garden City, NY: Doubleday & Co.

Williams, G. C. 1966. *Adaptation and Natural Selection.* Princeton: Princeton Univ. Press.

———. 1988. "Huxley's Evolution and Ethics in Sociobiological Perspective," *Zygon: Journal of Religion and Science* 23 (December): 383–407.

Williams, Robert R. 1982. "Sin and Evil." In *Christian Theology,* ed. Peter Hodgson and Robert King, 194–221. Philadelphia: Fortress Press.

Wilson, E. O. 1975. *Sociobiology: The New Synthesis.* Cambridge, MA: Harvard Univ. Press.

———. 1978. *On Human Nature.* Cambridge, MA: Harvard Univ. Press.

———. 1987. "Religion and Evolutionary Theory." In *Religion, Science and the Search for Wisdom,* ed. David M. Byers, 82–90. Washington, DC: United States Catholic Conference, Inc.

Wilson, E. O., and Charles J. Lumsden. 1981. *Genes, Mind, and Culture.* Cambridge, MA: Harvard Univ. Press.

Wright, Robert. 1988. *Three Scientists and Their Gods: Looking for Meaning in an Age of Information.* New York: Times Books.

Index

Definitions of terms are marked with an asterisk (*)